Land Use Controls

Land Use Controls: Present Problems and Future Reform

Edited by David Listokin

CENTER FOR URBAN POLICY RESEARCH
Rutgers University—The State University of New Jersey
New Brunswick, New Jersey

THE CUPR SURVEY SERIES

Series Editors George Sternlieb and Virginia Paulus

CONTENTS

LAND USE CONTROLS: PRESENT AND
FUTURE REFORMS

I

Introduction

INTRODUCTION

Land use controls, born in controversy, but eventually accepted and expanded, are now the center of renewed social debate and intensive scrutiny. This cyclical evolution is exemplified by changing attitudes towards zoning, perhaps the predominant land use regulation. Zoning has passed through four evolutionary stages: controls established, controls affirmed, controls expanded and controls challenged. An evaluation of these transitional periods will set the stage for our own analysis.

THE HISTORICAL CONTEXT OF LAND USE CONTROLS

Control Established

American local municipalities, up until the late 19th century, enacted practically no formal land use controls. A survey of planning during this period concluded that "apart from building regulations designed to prevent conflagrations in the densely-settled areas of the city, governments had almost no inclination or capacity to regulate the use of land or to take steps to correct abuses."[1]

The rapid expansion of cities following the Civil War brought to the fore two differing approaches. The first contended that the historical laissez-faire approach to land use should be continued. This position was supported by many court decisions which held that zoning and comparable regulations violated due process and other constitutional guarantees. The second argued that with the growth of cities the traditional "hands-off" policy had become increasingly unrealistic and intolerable.

Demographic and business forces tended to strengthen the position of the zoning advocates.[2] The late 19th century and early 20th centuries saw a rapid increase in urban density and population. Such

3

growth posed fire and health hazards that called for public control. Responding to this need, Boston and Washington, D.C., among other cities enacted statutes regulating such conditions as the maximum tenement lot coverage and the maximum heights of buildings.

These statutes, although welcomed by many city officials and planners, were viewed by some as not going far enough; these dissidents sought the implementation of a system that would rationally segregate the city's land area into residential, industrial and commercial sectors. Additionally, influential municipal merchants felt that the uncontrolled mixing of land uses threatened the success of their retail establishments and consequently, devalued their parcels' worth. To prevent such downgrading, businessmen lobbied for the passage of zoning ordinances. Their efforts met with considerable success, most notably in New York City, where the Fifth Avenue Association spearheaded a compaign that resulted in the passage in 1916 of the nation's first comprehensive zoning provisions.[3]

In the 1920s, many states passed statutes authorizing municipalities and other local units of government to enact zoning ordinances. Most of these enabling statutes were modeled after the Standard State Zoning Act, which had been published in the mid 1920s by the U.S. Department of Commerce. This model enabling act, often adopted verbatim as state law, broadly granted municipalities the right to zone so long as such zoning promoted the health, safety, morals or the general welfare of the community. But while zoning received practical acceptance, its legality was in doubt until clarified by the Supreme Court.

Control Affirmed

In the decade following New York's adoption of zoning, a number of state courts began reviewing the many ordinances that had been adopted. Their reaction was mixed;[4] some regarded zoning as a needed constitutional regulation, while others held that it violated the Constitution's protection of property rights. Zoning's legal future continued in doubt until the 1926 *Euclid v. Ambler*[5] decision.

This case involved a challenge of Euclid's (Ohio) zoning ordinance which divided the municipality into districts and imposed land use classifications on the basis of these subdivisions. The district court ruled that Euclid's zoning statute was unconstitutional because it had the effect of taking property without due process. The Supreme Court, however, overruled this decision; it declared Euclid's zoning ordinance constitutional, stating that it was justifiable under the state's police power as a necessary measure for the public's general welfare.

Euclid had a significant impact on the zoning process. In the words of Robert Anderson, a leading zoning authority:

The Euclid Case firmly established the constitutionality of comprehensive zoning. It determined that the main features of the orthodox type of zoning ordinance—the division of the community into districts, the restriction of the use of private land in such districts, and the exclusion of certain industrial, commercial and residential uses from certain residential districts—were within the reach of the police power. In addition, the Euclid decision tipped the judicial scales so heavily in favor of approval of this kind of land use control that the courts of all the states finally approved it.[6]

Control Expanded

The Euclid decision opened the floodgates on land use controls. From 1925 to 1930, the number of municipalities adopting zoning ordinances more than doubled. By the late 1960s zoning had become almost a universal municipal regulation—especially in the nation's larger municipalities and townships.[7]

But there was more than just a quantitative increase; zoning scope and range was also expanded. To illustrate, one-two-three-acre and larger lot zoning was instituted by numerous municipalities and upheld by many courts. Zoning's coverage was expanded to include often quite large minimum floor area regulations. Outright restrictions against multiple dwelling and mobile homes units were often upheld as were extensive setback requirements, height regulations and other controls.[8]

Such actions were not universally aclaimed; there were some vigorous judicial dissents as well as criticism from planners, attorneys and public officials. But such opposition was the exception rather than the rule; from the 1920s to the early 1960s zoning's expanded adoption and scope were largely accepted and acclaimed.

Control Challenged

This receptive atmosphere has been shattered in recent years. There have been increasing legal challenges as well as a proliferation of critical planning and economic studies directed at zoning.[9] Among the diverse critics, though often on diverging grounds, are: environmentalists, civil rights and related groups, and private developers. And alternatives to existing controls have also been proposed by the American Law Institute as well as state and federal governments.

The evolution of other land use regulations, has been roughly comparable. Initially opposed as intrusions on property rights they gradually received both greater judicial and practical acceptance. Subdivision regulations, for example, were not accepted until approximately the 1920's when extensive land frauds alerted the public to the many dangers of unrestricted development and established "a sympathetic climate for land subdivision controls."[10] Recently however subdivision regulations and other land use controls have increasingly been criticized of causing adverse environmental and social byproducts.

OVERVIEW OF THE READER

This cyclical, thesis-antithesis development of land use controls in general and of zoning in particular raises a number of questions. What are the causes of current hostility to existing land use regulations? Why the call for change in an established body of law and tradition? What changes and reforms in land use devices have already been effected? What reforms are being proposed for the future? Will the reforms correct current deficiencies? And, if so, how?

The answers to such questions are critical to anyone currently involved in existing land use regulations as well as to the general public. Past zoning regulations and similar devices have been instrumental in shaping our physical landscape and in directing the intensity and scope of our housing efforts. Future controls may have an even greater impact because the social, economic and environmental problems influenced by land use regulations have increased both in magnitude and frequency. Future change should therefore be made only after intense scrutiny of past land use devices and an evaluation of a broad range of possible alternatives.

This reader is directed at facilitating such analysis, at answering the questions we have posed concerning land use controls—past and future. It is divided into two parts: the first focuses on land use controls—the existing state of the art, the second concentrates on both present and future reforms of such regulations. To guide the reader through our analysis we shall briefly describe our selections.

PART I: LAND USE CONTROLS—STATE OF THE ART

This part, containing seven articles, is divided into two subsections: "Overviews and Deficiencies" and "Empirical Analysis."

OVERVIEW AND DEFICIENCIES

The first subsection sets the stage for the analysis, adding perspective to the examination. A selection from the National Commission on Urban Problems traces the development of land use regulations; expanding our zoning historical overview and tracing the evolution of nonzoning land use controls. John Reps discusses the shortcoming of zoning from a planning perspective. The American Society of Planning Officials summarize some of the administrative and other problems of land use controls. And Daniel Mandelker first discusses the historical and philosophical bases of zoning and then analyzes how current zoning often impedes efficient and equitable metropolitan development.

EMPIRICAL ANALYSIS

This subsection provides an interface between the alleged origins and impact of land use controls and their "actual" genesis and effect as demonstrated by empirical examinations.

Eric Branfman, Benjamin Cohen and David Trubek analyze how zoning affects the extent of income segregation as well as the motivation for implementing such controls. Their conclusions, especially those questioning the alleged strong relationship between property taxation and land use controls, are of special interest.[11]

John Crecine, Otto Davis and John Jackson focus upon one of zoning's alleged justifications—reducing external diseconomies, i.e., an uneconomic mixture of uses in the urban housing market. The reservations they raise as to whether such uniform diseconomies exist, pose serious doubts about zoning's desirability.

The last two articles in the "Empirical Analysis" subsection focus on a variety of exclusionary zoning devices. Norman Williams and Thomas Norman evaluate these regulations and describe the extent of such devices in Northeast New Jersey. George Sternlieb and Lynne Sagalyn examine the impact of various exclusionary land use controls upon housing cost. They then discuss the policy implications of their findings, focusing upon whether eliminating or reducing exclusionary zoning would enable low- and moderate-income families to afford housing.

PART II: LAND USE CONTROLS: PRESENT AND FUTURE REFORMS

The second section evaluates both already-implemented reforms in existing land use regulations as well as proposals for future revision. It contains the following four subsections:

1. The Courts and Exclusionary Zoning
2. More Flexible Controls
3. Greater Regional Control and Intervention
4. A Private Market Alternative to Public Land Use Regulations

THE COURTS AND EXCLUSIONARY ZONING

Here we attempt to summarize and place in perspective the sweeping changes already effected by the courts with reference to exclusionary zoning controls.

Erwin Elias discusses some of the issues involved in the exclusionary zoning cases and reviews some of the major decisions. Daniel Lauber's has effected a similar analysis and we include two exhibits in which he summarizes the legal issues involved in the more significant state and federal anti-exclusionary zoning cases.

But what impact will these decisions have? John Levy suggests that eliminating exclusionary controls may or may not "open" up the suburbs to low- and moderate-income families, depending on which public and private housing policies are pursued. (The Sternlieb and Sagalyn selection, already described, also casts some doubt about the practical impact of revising some present restrictive controls. And other articles[12] not reprinted here have also questioned whether court action striking down exclusionary devices will actually result in the construction of low-and moderate-income housing in the suburbs).

MORE FLEXIBLE CONTROLS

Critics of existing land use controls usually cite the rigidity of these regulations. This subsection discusses reforms directed at correcting this deficiency—reforms that are either in the process of adoption or that are proposed for the future. Jan Krasnowiecki discusses Planned Unit Development (PUD), an increasingly popular strategy for both facilitating a mixture of land use and for controlling the sequence and tempo of such development. He compares PUD's land use theory (as formulated in the early 1960s) with its actual application.[13]

Daniel Mandelker, long a leader in the land regulation reform movement, discusses two zoning philosophies: restraint versus incentive. The former, the prevailing philosophy, has contributed to zoning's negative character. Mandelker discusses some of the benefits of incentive zoning and describes some of the legal and planning issues involved in this approach to land use control.

Robert Freilich discusses the need for interim development controls,* suggesting that they will provide the necessary interface between flexible planning and zoning. He illuminates the theory behind interim controls and the legal problems attendant upon their implementation. (Ramapo, New York utilized interim development controls as well as longer term timing and sequential controls described below.)

*Freilich defines such controls as being "used to prevent land development, during the formulation of planning policies, which would conflict in any way with permanent legal controls implementing the basic planning policies."

The next article[14] by Fred Bosselman discusses the New York *Golden v. Planning Board* decision, which upheld the right of Ramapo, New York to institute a long range controlled or phased growth approach to land use controls. Bosselman discusses the Ramapo ordinance and criticizes[15] the impact that large scale adoption of such controls may have. He suggests, however, that time controls may be beneficial if implemented in conjunction with other strategies, i.e., greater regional planning and land banking. (These two approaches are elaborated in the next section.)

The last article by Jerome Rose briefly describes one proposed innovative land use technique—the transfer of development right. As described by Rose "Development rights legislation seeks to utilize the separability and transferability of development rights as a basis of a technique to induce owners of undeveloped land to preserve their land in open space." This article briefly explores why this technique is being considered and possible problems attendant on its implementation.

GREATER REGIONAL CONTROL AND INTERVENTION

This subsection focuses on regional alternatives to the present locally oriented land use control structure. This approach has gained many adherents who believe that only regional bodies or levels of government have the insight and foresight to formulate rational, equitable land use regulations. (The Reps article already described also advocated a regional orientation.)

Daniel Mandelker, for example, has concluded that

From all that I have said, the conclusion can most certainly be drawn that the locally-based and autonomous character of our present zoning system often produces planning and zoning results which inhibit the proper division of housing for all income groups within our metropolitan areas. For this reason, and in spite of all the difficulties that this change in the system creates, some method will have to be found to remove zoning and planning decisions to higher governmental levels if we are to avoid the often very serious impediments to the construction of housing which the exercise of local zoning power creates. The question to decide is how the higher governmental presence should make itself felt.[16]

The first section is by Paul Davidoff and Neil Gold, co-founders of Suburban Action Institute, one of the most active organizations attempting to reform existing land use regulations. Davidoff and Gold argue for greater regional control and then propose specific regional strategies. Their proposals, presented in 1968, at the time seemed radical but today there is a growing trend towards regional land use control and review.

The second selection, from the *Quiet Revolution in Land Use Controls* by Fred Bosselman and Edward Callies documents this trend. They discuss and analyze a number of innovative zoning and environmental laws enacted by some states (e.g., Hawaii, Vermont and Massachusetts) and other regional bodies. The innovations reviewed by Bosselman and Callies may very well become commonplace in the near future.

The next article, by the author, analyzes fair share housing plans as an alternative to piecemeal local housing-zoning decisions. As formulated by regional levels of government, fair share plans attempt to distribute housing, especially low- and moderate-income units, according to sound social, economic and environmental criteria. This article analyzes the scope of fair share as well as its impact to date and its future potential. It draws heavily from a prior study by Mary Brooks entitled *Lower Income Housing: The Planners' Response.*[17]

Regional approaches to land use decisions are also currently being considered by the American Law Institute (ALI) and the federal government. Richard Babcock, who has been involved in helping developing the ALI proposals, describes and analyzes the reforms that are being considered.[18] William Reilly traces the evolution of the federal government's involvement in land use control and discusses pending legislation that will greatly augment this involvement.[19]

How do the proposed federal land use bills compare to the regional innovations already adopted by numerous states? This question is addressed by the Library of Congress Environmental Policy Division and we present a summary of their findings.

But greater regional involvement in land use controls may not in itself be adequate, especially to facilitiate housing construction where it is most needed.* For example, regional zoning may not solve the problems of land assembly nor will it provide the capital needed for additional housing production. Rounding out the regional control discussion is Charles Haar's article on federal interventionary policies directed at alleviating these problems. He focuses upon two strategies—metropolitan land and federal urban development banks—discussing the need for such approaches and the impediments to their implementation. (We present only his discussion of land use banks.) If the federal government is to become an effective force in land use matters and is to ultimately facilitate adequate, well-placed housing construction, then the policies discussed by Haar may very well be indispensible.[20]

---

*Additional regional environmental controls may also cause significant housing price increases to the detriment of low and moderate income families. See Ira Heyman, "Legal Asaults on Municipal Land Use Regulation," *The Urban Lawyer,* Winter 1972, pp. 1-24.

A PRIVATE MARKET ALTERNATIVE TO
PUBLIC LAND USE CONTROL

Many of the land use reforms described above have called for greater public intervention and control. This thesis is contested by Bernard Siegan, who after extensively examining Houston's no-public-zoning policy, concluded that such a private regulation approach is far preferable to the public zoning norm. Siegan's advocacy of a private approach to land use control provides a counterbalance to the preponderance of proposals calling for increased governmental intervention in the land use process.

* * *

The purpose of this reader is to present the major issues involved in the current effort to reform existing land use controls. It attempts to synthesize some of the legal and social science methodologies for evaluating such regulations and to provide some interface between the land use controls of today and regulations of tomorrow.[22] Along with the other Center for Urban Policy Research publications it aims to provide the basic building blocks of data and thought essential to careful, thorough policy analysis and decisions.

FOOTNOTES

1. William Goodman and Eric Freund, *Principles and Practice of Urban Planning* (Washington, D.C.: International City Managers Association, 1968), p. 15.

2. For an excellent history of zoning's origins see Seymour Toll, *Zoned America* (New York: Grossman Publishers, 1969) and John Delafons, *Land Use Controls in the United States* (Cambridge, M.I.T.—Harvard Joint Center for Urban Studies, 1962).

3. See Toll and Stanislaw Makielski, *The Politics of Zoning* (New York: Columbia University Press, 1966).

4. Robert Anderson, *American Law of Zoning* (Rochester: Lawyers Co-operative Publishing Company, 1968) Volume I, pp. 46-49.

5. Euclid v. Ambler Realty Co. 272 US 365.

6. Anderson, *American Law of Zoning*, p. 53.

7. Allen Manvel, *Local Land and Building Regulations,* prepared for the National Commission on Urban Problems (Research Report No. 6) (Washington, D.C.: U.S. Government Printing Office, 1968).

8. Scores of law reviews have discussed these developments includ-

ing Charles Haar, "Zoning for Minimum Standards: The Wayne Township Case," *Harvard Law Review* Vol. 66. (1953); Richard Babcock and Frederick Bosselman, "Suburban Zoning and the Apartment Boom," *University of Pennsylvania Law Review.* Vol. 105 (1963) pp. 1040-1091; Norman Williams, Jr. and Edward Wacks, "Segregation of Residential Areas Along Economic Lines: Lionshead Lake Revisited" *Wisconsin Law Review* Vol. 1969 pp. 827-847; Lawrence Sager, "Tight Little Islands: Exclusionary Zoning; Equal Protection, and the Indigent," *Stanford Law Review* Vol. 21 (1969), pp. 767-800.

9. See Geoffrey Shields and L. Sanford Spector, "Opening Up the Suburbs: Notes on a Movement for Social Change," *Yale Review of Law and Social Action,* Vol. 6 (1972), pp. 300-333.

10. Richard Yearwood, "Land Subdivision and Development: American Attitudes on Land Subdivision and its Control," *American Journal of Economics and Sociology,* Vol. 29 (1970), p. 120. See also Richard Yearwood *Land Subdivision Regulations Policy and Legal Considerations for Urban Planning* (New York: Praeger Publishers, 1971).

11. Some of their findings have been contested by Bruce Hamilton. See Hamilton "Property Taxation Incentive to Fiscal Zoning," in George Peterson (editor) *Property Tax Reform* (Washington, D.C.: The Urban Institute, 1973).

12. Leonard Rubinowitz, "Exclusionary Zoning: A Wrong in Search of a Remedy," *Journal of Law Reform* Vol. 6 (1972), pp. 625-669 and "Towards Improved Housing Opportunities: A New Direction for Zoning Law," *University of Pennsylvania Law Review,* Vol. 121 (1972), pp. 330-350.

13. See also Robert Burchell (editor) *Frontiers in Planned Unit Development: A Synthesis of Expert Opinion* (New Brunswick, N.J.; Rutgers University Center for Urban Policy Research, 1974).

14. See also "A Zoning Program for Phased Growth: Ramapo Township's Time Controls on Residential Development," *New York University Law Review* Vol. 47 (1972), pp. 723-760.

15. The Ramapo timed growth plan has evoked both positive and negative reactions. For an example of the former, see Robert Freilich, "Golden v. Town of Ramapo: Establishing a New Dimension in American Planning Law," *The Urban Lawyer* Vol. 4 (1972). For an example of the latter, see Herbert Franklin and Arthur Levin, *Controlling Urban Growth—But for Whom?* (Washington, D.C.: The Potomac Institute 1973).

16. Daniel Mandelker, "The Role of Zoning in Housing and Metropolitan Development" in Committee on Banking and Currency, House of Representatives, *Papers submitted to Subcommittee on Housing Panels on Housing Production, Housing Demand and Developing a Suitable Living Environment* (Washington, D.C.: Government Printing Office, 1971), p. 799.

17. ASPO Report No. 282 (July-August 1972).

18. See also Allison Dunham, "The ALI Land Development Code" *Real Property Probate and Trust Journal* Vol. 8 (1973), pp. 510-522.

19. See also Vance Hartke, "Toward a National Growth Policy," *Catholic University of American Law Review,* Vol. 22 (1973), p. 279.

20. For another discussion of the public acquisition of land see Donald Hagman, "Public Acquisition and Disposal of Lands," *Land Use Policies* (Chicago: American Society of Planning Officials, 1970).

21. Siegan's arguments are elaborately developed in his *Land Use Without Zoning* (Lexington, Mass.: D.C. Heath and Co., 1972).

22. There are currently a number of studies projecting future land use controls and considering their impact such as the UCLA project, "Windfalls for Wipeouts" headed by Professor Donald Hagman.

ACKNOWLEDGMENTS

American Society of Planning Officials. *Problems of Zoning and Land-Use Regulation* (excerpts). Washington, D.C.: Government Printing Office, 1968, pp. 1-3.

Babcock, Richard, "Comments on Model Land Development Code," in *Urban Law Annual 1972,* pp. 59-67.

Bosselman, Fred, Can The Town of Ramapo Pass a Law to Bind The Rights of The Whole World?

Bosselman, Fred and David Callies, *The Quiet Revolution in Land Use Controls* (excerpts). Washington, D.C.: Government Printing Office, 1971.

Branfman, Eric J., Benjamin I. Cohen and David M. Trubek, "Measuring the Invisible Wall: Land Use Controls and the Residential Patterns of the Poor," *Yale Law Journal,* January 1973. Reprinted by permission of the Yale Law Journal Company and Fred B. Rothman and Company from *The Yale Law Journal,* Vol. 82, pp. 483-508.

Crecine, John, Otto Davis and John Jackson, "Urban Property Markets: Some Empirical Results and Their Implications for Municipal Zoning," *The Journal of Law and Economics,* October 1967, pp. 79-99.

Davidoff, Paul and Neil Gold, "The Supply and Availability of Land for Housing for Low- and Moderate-Income Families," (excerpts) in U.S. President's Committee on Urban Housing, *Technical Studies, Volume II.* Washington, D.C.: Government Printing Office, 1969, pp. 392-396.

Elias, Erwin, "Significant Developments and Trends in Zoning Litigation," (excerpts). Copyright © 1973, by Matthew Bender & Co., Inc., and reprinted with permission from the 1973 *Proceedings of the Institute on Planning, Zoning and Eminent Domain, the Southwestern Legal Foundation.*

Freilich, Robert, "Interim Development Controls: Essential Tools for Implementing Flexible Planning and Zoning," *Journal of Urban Law,* August 1971.

Haar, Charles M. "Wanted: Two Federal Levers for Urban Land Use—Land Banks and Urbank." In U.S. House. Committee on Banking and Currency. *Papers Submitted to Subcommittee on Housing Panels . . . Part 2.* Washington, D.C.: Government Printing Office, 1971.

Krasnowiecki, Jan, "Legal Aspects of Planned Unit Development in Theory and Practice." In *Frontiers in Planned Unit Development,* edited by Robert W. Burchell. New Brunswick, N.J.: Center for Urban Policy Research, Rutgers University, 1973.

Lauber, Daniel, *Recent Cases in Exclusionary Zoning* (excerpts). ASPO Planning Advisory Service Report No. 292, June 1973. Chicago, Illinois: American Society of Planning Officials, 1973.

Levy, John, "Exclusionary Zoning: After the Walls Come Down," *ASPO Planning,* August 1972, pp. 158-160. Chicago, Illinois: American Society of Planning Officials, 1972.

Library of Congress, Congressional Research Service, Environmental Policy Division, "Comparative Analyses of State Land Use Laws, Legislative Proposals and Model Codes," in *National Land Use Policy Legislation, 93d Congress, An Analysis of Legislative Proposals and State Laws.* Washington, D.C.: Government Printing Office, 1973, pp. 95-97.

Listokin, David, "Fair Share Housing Distribution: Will It Open up the Suburbs to Apartment Development," *Real Estate Law Journal,* Spring 1974.

Mandelker, Daniel, "The Basic Philosophy of Zoning: Incentive or Restraint?" From *The New Zoning: Legal, Administrative and Economic Aspects,* edited by Norman Marcus and Marilyn W. Groves. © 1970 by The Center for New York City Affairs, New School for Social Research. Excerpted and reprinted by permission of Praeger Publishers, Inc., New York.

Mandelker, Daniel, "The Role of Zoning in Housing and Metropolitan Development." In U.S. House. Committee on Banking and Currency. *Papers Submitted to Subcommittee on Housing Panels . . . Part 2.* Washington, D.C.: Government Printing Office, 1971.

National Commission on Urban Problems, "Land Use Controls: Zoning and Subdivision Regulations," in *Building the American City*. Washington, D.C.: Government Printing Office, 1969.

Reilly, William, "New Directions in Federal Land Use Legislation," in *Urban Law Annual 1973*, pp. 29-57.

Reps, John, "Requiem for Zoning," in *Planning 1964*. Chicago, Illinois: American Society of Planning Officials.

Rose, Jerome, "From the Legislatures: Proposed Development Rights Legislation Can Change the Name of the Land Investment Game," *Real Estate Law Journal*, Winter 1973.

Siegan, Bernard, "Non-Zoning in Houston," *Journal of Law & Economics*, April 1970, pp. 129-144.

Sternlieb, George and Lynne Sagalyn, *Zoning and Housing Costs* (excerpts). New Brunswick, N.J.: Center for Urban Policy Research, Rutgers University, 1972.

Williams, Norman, Jr., and Thomas Norman, "Exclusionary Land-Use Controls: The Case of Northeastern New Jersey," *Land-Use Controls Quarterly*, No. 4, p. 1 (Fall 1970). Copyright © Land-Use Controls Quarterly, No. 4 (Fall 1970). Reprinted with permission of the American Society of Planning Officials, Chicago, Illinois.

II

Overview and Deficiencies

1

National Commission on Urban Problems

LAND-USE CONTROLS: ZONING AND SUBDIVISION REGULATIONS (excerpts)

Land-use regulations—zoning and subdivision controls—are the chief regulatory tools used by local governments to guide development within their borders.[1] All 50 States authorize these local regulations, and more than 10,000 local governments have adopted them. One of the tasks assigned to this Commission was to study these regulations and the purposes they were designed to serve, and to recommend how they could be made to serve those purposes better.

Regulations, of course, do not build cities. Among the many public and private decisions that produce urban growth and decay, regulatory decisions play a relatively minor part. When governments at all levels build and spend and tax, they shape cities directly, and they set in motion market forces that regulations cannot fundamentally alter.

Yet, though regulations are not the most important of public actions that guide development, they do significantly, influence the complex process of city building. And that influence extends beyond the physical relationships that are their primary concern, affecting such diverse matters as employment opportunity, housing opportunity, and local tax rates. Critics today are attacking land-use regulations, particularly zoning, both for what they are doing and for what they fail to do. There are charges that regulations act to reinforce racial and economic segregation, raise the costs of housing and stifle interesting and innovative design. And there are charges that regulations are failing to protect established neighborhoods, to prevent sprawl on the outskirts of cities and decay within them. Finally, there are charges that the administration of regulations is too often riddled with favoritism and corruption. The next two chapters explore these criticisms, evaluate the present state of land use controls and suggest how such controls may better carry out the social, political, economic, and physical objectives of American urban life.

ORIGINS AND CONVENTIONAL PATTERNS

Beginnings

Today's zoning and subdivision regulations are but the current stage of a long-established process. From the earliest days of Colonial America, governments and private interests have continually sought better ways to build good cities. The public and private responsibilities have been very different at different times. Sometimes government has been the planner and builder, the chief architect of the urban environment. At other times, government has tried to withdraw almost entirely from the field. Today, the mix is somewhere between the extremes of earlier times. The process of evaluation and change continues, stimulated by growing complaints that the results of past efforts are inadequate.

Prezoning

In Colonial America it was common practice for government to take the initiative in urban development. As early as 1573, Philip II of Spain issued the laws of the Indies that governed the establishment of towns from St. Augustine to Los Angeles. In the latter half of the 17th century and the early years of the 18th, colonial legislatures in Virginia and Maryland designated sites for towns, established the method of land acquisition and valuation and provided for their layout and for the disposition of town lots. Public land acquisition for urban development was common in these two colonies in the 17th century. A total of 77 sites were designated for settlement, including such elaborately planned towns as Annapolis and Williamsburg.[2]

[1] A third form of regulation, much less widely used, is the "official map," which designates areas in advance for later public acquisition for use as streets, parks or other public facilities.

[2] The source for much of this material is John W. Reps, "The Future of American Planning—Requiem or Renascence?" *Land Use Controls*, Vol. 1, No. 2, 1967, pp. 1–16.

The tradition of public land acquisition for new cities continued after the Revolution. A persistent George Washington persuaded even the most stubborn land owners to sell the land needed for the Nation's new Capital. The new city of Washington was planned on 5,000 acres of land, all publicly acquired from private owners. Among many other examples of cities initially laid out on public land (either already in the public domain or acquired for the purpose) are Raleigh, Tallahassee, Detroit, Chicago, Columbus, and Indianapolis.

Another, stronger current also runs through the Nation's urban history. This is the tradition of individual land ownership largely unfettered by public control of its use. It was the lure of virgin land that brought many settlers to America, and the prospect of getting land cheap—or free—led many of them to the West. Only a few years after the Revolution, the Continental Congress provided for the division and sale of the vast territories belonging to the new nation. The free market in land, including speculation and "boom and bust," was to be a dominant force in 19th century America.

The "invisible hand" of the market dominated the growth of most 19th century cities. In 1811, the commissioners' plan for New York City established a grid of "paper streets" many miles north into the then undeveloped territory of Manhattan. Unlike the plans for Washington or Williamsburg, which proposed or recognized urban centers and focal points, this plan consisted essentially of a uniform grid of streets and avenues. The role of government was limited to drawing up a giant chessboard on which the forces of the market would build the future city. This *laissez faire* city planning was to be repeated endlessly in new and growing communities across the land.

It was soon apparent, however, that the invisible hand could not alone provide a good life for the growing numbers of people crowding into the cities. Two broad kinds of public response resulted:

An emphasis on minimum standards to which everyone is entitled. Early tenement house laws responded to this emphasis, as do today's housing codes and programs for subsidized housing.

A broad concern with amenity and efficiency in urban life. The 19th century "park planners" operated in this tradition, and much of today's planning movement is its outgrowth.

In 1867 the first New York tenement legislation was enacted, a year after the city health department had been established. The 1867 law slightly restricted the tenement's lot coverage, and further legislation in 1879 and 1901 reduced coverage to 65 percent. Within a few years, New Jersey, Pennsylvania and Connecticut passed comparable laws, and between 1905 and 1908, Chicago, Boston, and Cleveland adopted similar ordinances.[3]

Other cities were restricting building heights and land use in the interests of public health and safety. San Francisco and Los Angeles passed ordinances in the 1880's limiting the location of laundries.[4] In 1889 height restrictions were placed on buildings in Washington, D.C. In Boston, height regulations were enacted in 1903 and upheld by the U.S. Supreme Court in 1909 as a valid exercise of the police power.[5] Fire district ordinances, prohibiting the building of wooden structures in designated areas, were also becoming increasingly common.

The park planners, meanwhile, were pressing for other public action to improve the quality of urban environment. The crusade for parks took hold after 1860. The Columbian Exposition of 1893 stimulated the "city beautiful" movement that was to produce such influential plans as the Senate Park Commission's replanning of Washington in 1901 and Burnham's Chicago plan of 1909.

Zoning grew up against the background of these developments—and out of the efforts of property owners to prevent unwanted change of their neighborhoods. In 1907, a group of Fifth Avenue merchants banded together to try to protect the fashionable shopping district from encroachment by the new factories of garment manufacturers. The Fifth Avenue Association joined forces with city planning advocates to bring about the establishment of the Advisory Commission on Height and Arrangement of Buildings, which in turn laid the foundation for the drafting and adoption of the New York zoning resolution. That resolution, adopted in July 1916, set the basic pattern for zoning ordinances to the present day.[6]

The spread of zoning

Zoning spread quickly during the 1920's. By 1925, 368 municipalities had passed ordinances; and by the end of 1930, more than 1,000.

[3] *Principles and Practices of Urban Planning*, edited by William I. Goodman and Eric C. Freund, published by International City Managers' Association, 1968, p. 17.
[4] At first such ordinances were struck down by the courts as discriminatory against the Chinese, but they were later upheld as valid measures designed to protect public health and safety.
[5] *Welch* v. *Swasey*, 214 U.S. 91 (1909). An earlier effort to control height in Boston through use of the eminent domain power was upheld in *Attorney General* v. *Williams*, 55 N.E. 77 (1899), *aff'd* 188 U.S. 491 (1908). The Massachusetts court indicated by way of dicta that the police power could be used to limit building heights.
[6] Los Angeles had in fact "zoned" its entire area in one way or another by 1915. The city was divided into one large residence district in which only the very lightest manufacturing was permitted; 27 industrial districts, permitting all uses; and about 100 residence exception districts permitting all but heavy and objectionable uses.

State enabling legislation, giving municipalities specific authority to zone, became common during the 1920's. This State action was substantially aided by the Federal Government. In 1921, Herbert Hoover, then Secretary of Commerce, appointed an Advisory Committee on Zoning in the Department of Commerce. In 1924, the Committee issued the Standard State Zoning Enabling Act, a model upon which a great deal of State zoning legislation is still based.[7] By 1925, 19 States had adopted statutes substantially similar to the model. By the end of 1930, some or all localities in every State were legally empowered to adopt zoning ordinances.

The reaction of the courts was a central preoccupation of zoning's founders, and early judicial response in the State courts was mixed. Constitutional doubt about the concept of zoning was settled in 1926, however, when the Supreme Court of the United States decided the landmark case of *Village of Euclid* v. *Ambler Realty Co.*[8]

Subdivision regulations

The regulation of land subdivision existed in this country from its earliest days and survived in some form even during the 19th century. Much of the 19th century regulation, however, was mainly designed to assure the adequacy of engineering data and the accurate recording of plats. Gradually, however, the objectives were broadened. Some States required that new streets be designed to tie into existing ones and that streets be dedicated to the public. Enforcement was achieved by requiring governmental approval of street layouts before plats could be officially recorded and lots sold.[9]

The present form of subdivision regulation, like that of zoning, bears the stamp of the 1920's. At that time, subdivision regulation began to be widely considered as a means of guiding urban growth. In 1928, the Department of Commerce issued the Standard City Planning Enabling Act, a model act that made subdivision regulation one of the tools of comprehensive planning and placed major responsibility for administering subdivision regulations in local planning boards. While the Standard City Planning Enabling Act did not take State legislatures by storm in quite the fashion of its zoning predecessor, many States did enact planning statutes that bore some resemblance to the Standard Act.

Local subdivision regulations were becoming widespread by the time the depression halted most subdivision activity. A 1934 survey found 269 municipal planning commissions in 29

States with power to regulate land subdivision, and an additional 156 commissions empowered to act in an advisory capacity on such regulations.[10]

Conventional patterns

Despite increasingly important changes, the form of today's land use regulations, and often their substances as well, still commonly fall within the conventional patterns established in the 1920's. Of course, no one local regulation is typical of these patterns: Objectives, techniques, and administrative practices reflect the varying desires of thousands of local governments. A rudimentary zoning regulation in a rural village may do little more than exclude a few noxious uses from residential areas, while a regulation for a large city or a prosperous suburb may establish an array of districts and a complex administrative process. There are, however, some elements that are common to most of the current regulations that fall within the conventional pattern.

(1) The zoning ordinance

a. *Regulated subjects.*—A zoning ordinance typically prescribes how each parcel of land in a community may be used. Most regulations cover at least these subjects—

Use: First, zoning ordinances designate permitted "uses" (activities). Many divide uses into three basic categories: Dwellings, businesses, and industry. These basic categories are usually divided into subcategories. It is common practice, for example, to distinguish between one-family detached houses and apartment buildings, between "light" and "heavy" industry. Over the years ordinances have tended to establish more and more use categories. Ordinances with more than 20 different use categories are now common, and many ordinances now make specific provision for hundreds of listed uses.

Population density: A limitation on population density is also part of today's accepted zoning pattern. Most ordinances establish this limitation by setting a minimum required size for each lot. Alternatively, they may limit the number of families per acre or set a minimum required lot area for each dwelling unit on a lot. Some, particularly in large cities, establish more refined density controls that try to take account of the likelihood that more people will live in larger apartment units than in smaller ones.

Building bulk: Zoning regulations also limit building bulk. Usually, they do this by requiring yards along lot boundaries, by limiting building height, and by limiting the proportion

[7] A revised version was issued in 1926.
[8] 272 U.S. 365 (1926).
[9] *Principles and Practices of Urban Planning*, op. cit., p. 444.

[10] Reps, "Control of Land Subdivision by Municipal Planning Boards," 40 Cornell L.Rev. 258 (1955).

of lot area that may be covered by buildings. Refinements of these devices have become common, in recent years, as communities have recognized that rigid yard and height requirements often deter imaginative design. "Floor area ratio" and "usable open space" requirements are among the increasingly common refinements.

Offstreet parking: As an addition to the original pattern, most zoning ordinances now contain offstreet parking requirements. These are intended to assure that new development provides for at least some of its own parking needs rather than adding to the number of parked cars on already crowded streets.

Other subjects: Many other requirements also appear in zoning regulations. Minimum house size, landscaping, signs, appearance of buildings, offstreet loading, view protection, and grading are just a few of the other subjects sometimes regulated.

b. *The zoning map.*—In recognition of differing conditions and planning policies in different parts of each community, zoning regulations establish "zones" or "districts." Within each of these districts a uniform set of regulations dealing with uses, bulk, and the like apply. Thus, for example, stores may be permitted in one district but not in another. To show the location and boundaries of these districts, the ordinance includes a zoning map.

The number of districts and the nature of the differences between them vary greatly from town to town. Most ordinances contain at least one district in which single-family detached dwellings are the only permitted residential use. Often there are several such "single family" districts, distinguished from each other primarily by differences in the required minimum lot size; one district may require each lot to contain at least 2 acres, another at least 1 acre, and so on. Many ordinances also contain general residence districts, in which other types of dwellings are also permitted; these, too, are often differentiated by density requirements. Ordinances also commonly contain a variety of commercial districts bearing such names as neighborhood retail, central business, heavy commercial, and commercial recreation. They are commonly distinguished from one another by variations in permitted activity, bulk, and parking requirements. And industrial districts may differ from each other with respect to permitted activities, bulk regulations, and "performance" regulations limiting the amount of smoke, noise, or odor that industries may produce.

In addition to the basic districts—those based on the traditional triad of dwellings, business and industry—scores of other kinds of districts have been devised since the early days of zoning and are now commonly used to fit local conditions and policies. Agricultural districts, industrial-park districts, and special districts for public land are examples. Some of the newer districts allow a mixture of traditionally separated uses, such as residential-office and residential-commercial districts. Others are intended to meet unique conditions of a particular area, such as flood plain districts.[11]

c. *Administration.*—To apply substantive requirements, every regulation needs an administrative apparatus. The originators of zoning anticipated a fairly simple administrative process. They thought of the zoning regulation as being largely "self-executing." After the formulation of the ordinance text and map by a local zoning commission and its adoption by the local governing body, most administrations would require only the services of a building official who would determine whether proposed construction complied with the requirements. This official was not expected to exercise discretion or sophisticated judgment. Rather, he was to apply the requirements to the letter. In the case of new construction, he was to compare the builder's plans with the requirements governing the particular land and either grant or deny a permit. Even today, this nondiscretionary permit process is at the heart of zoning administration.

Nevertheless, it was recognized from the outset that the permit process was not enough. Zoning statutes and regulations commonly provide for these additional kinds of administrative action:

Appeals: First is the appeal from a decision of the building official. The applicant may allege, for example, that the official has misinterpreted the ordinance or applied it arbitrarily. In most States, such appeals are taken to a local board of zoning appeals (or adjustment).

Variances: Because of special conditions, strict application of ordinance requirements sometimes causes hardship that is unnecessary to achievement of the public purposes of the ordinance. A lot may be oddly shaped, for example, or topography may be unusual. To alleviate these hardships, and also to safeguard the constitutionality of regulation where strict application of requirements would amount to a "taking" of land, zoning regulations have traditionally provided for "variances." The variance power, too, most often belongs to the board of appeals. To qualify for a lawful variance, the applicant is normally required to show that strict application of the rules would cause "un-

---

[11] Some of the special conditions are quite exotic. One ordinance, for example, established a "laboratory rodent" district, permitting the raising of mice for laboratory use.

necessary hardship" due to "unique circumstances."

Special exceptions: The third type of administrative decision is the "special exception" which has now grown to include many types of discretionary decisions bearing such names as "conditional uses" and "special-use permits." The zoning ordinance will list particular uses (e.g., airports or cemeteries or gas stations) and permit them only with some sort of discretionary review in each case. The review may be by the board of appeals or governing body (or sometimes by a planning commission or a zoning administrator). The ordinance may set up specific standards to guide the discretionary review. Often, however, standards are very general.

Amendments: Finally, the administrative apparatus of zoning includes a provision for changing the rules. It was foreseen from the outset that both the text and the map would occasionally become out of date, and provision was made for revision of both by the local governing body. Although statutes normally require notice and hearing, the amendment process is otherwise much the same as that used to amend other local laws. The vast majority of amendments are changes in the zoning map, commonly called "rezonings."

To assure that regulatory actions stay within the limits set by constitutions, statutes, and ordinances, zoning statutes further provide for review by the courts.

(2) The subdivision regulation

While conventional zoning normally applies to individual lots, subdivision regulations govern the process by which those lots are created out of larger tracts.

a. Regulated subjects.—

Site design and relationships: Subdivision regulations typically seek to assure that subdivisions are appropriately related to their surroundings. Commonly, they require that the subdivision be consistent with a comprehensive plan for the area (e.g., by reserving land for proposed highways or parks). Requirements normally assure that utilities (local streets, sewers) tie into those located or planned for adjoining property. Other requirements are intended to assure that the subdivision itself is related to its own site and that it will work effectively. The widths of streets, the length of blocks, the size of lots, and the handling of frontage along major streets, are among commonly regulated subjects.

Allocation of facilities cost—dedications and fees: Second, subdivision regulations may contain provisions that effectively allocate costs of public facilities between the subdivider and local taxpayers. Commonly, regulations require subdividers to dedicate land for streets and to install, at their own expense, a variety of public facilities to serve the development. These often include streets, sidewalks, storm and sanitary sewers, and street lights. In recent years, more and more subdivision regulations have also been requiring subdividers to dedicate parkland, and sometimes school sites, or to make cash payments in lieu of such dedication. Some regulations go further still, requiring payment of fees to apply toward such major public costs as the construction of sewage disposal plants.

b. Administration.—Subdivision regulations contemplate a more sophisticated administrative process than do conventional zoning regulations. Instead of prescribing the precise location of future lot lines, for example, subdivision regulations provide more general design standards (based in part on local plans). The local planning commission or governing body then applies these standards, at the time of subdivision, to preliminary and final plats submitted by property owners.

THE NATURE AND EVOLUTION OF CONVENTIONAL REGULATIONS

Considering the era of its birth, the pattern of land-use regulations devised in the 1920's was a heroic if hesitant reassertion of public responsibility to guide development. The nature of the regulatory pattern, of course, responded to the needs of that time, to the objectives then determined, and to the techniques then available for achieving them.

(1) Characteristics

From today's standpoint, the following characteristics of that pattern seem especially noteworthy:

a. Responsibility: Local.—Regulatory power was given to local governments. Although State enabling legislation prescribed the general nature of the regulations and established the administrative process, regulatory initiative and discretion were local. Regulations responded to local policies and were administered by local officials.

b. Technique: Self-executing, noncompensative, negative.—Like the building and other codes whose form they resembled, these regulations were self-executing, noncompensative, negative.

Self-executing: The detailed zoning requirements—down to the last zone boundary and side-yard width—were to be determined in advance. (Subdivision regulations, as already noted, established both specific requirements and more general standards to be applied to the facts of each individual case.) Once adopted, the zoning ordinance was to be basically self-enforcing. Provisions for administrative relief and rezoning were thought of more as occasional adjustments than as parts of the day-to-day regulatory process.

Noncompensative: The regulations did not provide for compensation to property owners. Affected property remained in private ownership, and regulatory limitations on its use were authorized under the State's police power to protect the public health, safety, and welfare. This approach had the advantage of resembling established codes. It also saved public funds and avoided the administrative complexity of purchasing or condemning interests in affected property.

Negative: The role of the regulating government was essentially negative. Similar in concept to the law of nuisance, regulations were normally intended to prohibit inappropriate development—to keep out the bad rather than to achieve the good. Development initiative was left with private builders.

c. *Policy: Limited control.*—Finally, most early regulations were remarkably lax by today's standards. Even in the most restrictive residential district, some early regulations prohibited only a handful of specified commercial and industrial uses, and many district regulations provided neighborhoods only minimal protection against incompatible intrusions. Permissiveness was revealed even more clearly by zoning maps. Substantial areas in some communities were placed in unrestricted districts, in which all uses were allowed. "Overzoning"—particularly for business and industry—was the rule rather than the exception. Out of local optimism, an absence of planning, and a concern not to depress speculative property values, came zoning maps in many towns that provided for development beyond the dreams of land promoters.

(2) *Causes of the conventional pattern*

Why did the pattern take this form? In large part because it was based on the building codes and tenement house laws for which there was both political and legal precedent. At the time, regulations were considered by many to be a radical encroachment on the rights of owners to exploit their property. Precedent was important.

From today's perspective, however, three additional influences seem to have been particularly important in shaping the zoning response: (1) the generally limited objective of preventing change within established neighborhoods, rather than achieving broader planning objec-

tives; (2) the small scale of land developments; and (3) the inherent problem of achieving varied development with "uniform" regulations.

a. *Preventing change in established residential neighborhoods.*—The primary demand behind zoning in thousands of communities was to protect established neighborhoods—especially residential ones—from the intrusion of incompatible uses. Zoning in these situations was intended more to prevent change than to guide it. The location of residential districts on zoning maps could largely reflect established development patterns. And the lists of permitted uses and bulk standard could largely be derived from what was already on the ground and from what was traditionally considered compatible with what was on the ground. In effect, regulations for this purpose could follow the broad directions already established by the market.

b. *The small scale of land development.*—A second influential factor was the small scale of landownership and land development at the time. This small scale meant that regulation of relationships among land *uses* required regulation of relationships among land *users* as well.

Conventional zoning regulations apply to each individual lot, not to a block or a neighborhood or a town as a whole. Lots are normally in separate ownership after development. When zoning was devised, they were also normally in separate ownership *before* development.

In the 1920's, when zoning became prevalent, the small scale of ownership and development had to be accepted. Builders were unable to build 1,000 houses at a time or a whole "new town"; they often built one house at a time or three or four. And the owner of a single small lot was almost wholly dependent on his neighbors for his environment—a dependence which was increased by the American tradition of using yards rather than walls as dividers between residential properties. The buyers and sellers of lots needed some device to stabilize property values, keep out unwanted intrusions, encourage investment in land and construction—in sum to assure neighborhood "character." The fee simple land tenure, which gives owners a freedom of use that modern homeowners are frightened to have their neighbors possess, did not provide the needed protection. Zoning did.

c. *Achieving variety with uniform regulations.*—A third influential factor, accentuated by the small scale of ownership and development, was the inherent regulatory problem of permitting varied development with "uniform" regulations. Cities, neighborhoods, even blocks, are mixtures of disparate activities and buildings, each normally on a separately owned lot.

Any attempt to control the mixture requires regulations that differ from lot to lot. Yet our traditions and laws called for public action to be uniform, equitable, "fair." In practice, this meant that regulations should *not* differ from lot to lot, should treat all owners alike if their properties were physically alike. This demand for uniformity of regulation was strongly reinforced by demands of administrative convenience.

Without reconciling the conflict between demands for unique treatment and demands for uniformity, zoning attempted a practical compromise. The regulations established a number of different zones and then mixed the zones on the map. The demands of uniformity were partially satisfied by the uniformity of regulation within each zone. The price of this uniformity was a significant oversimplification of the complex potential relationships among buildings and activities within small areas. Some areas were overprotected, many others not protected enough; demands for more refined regulation—and particularly for variances and amendments to permit "harmless" prohibited development—naturally emerged. Moreover, zoning still required gross differences in treatment of land in different zones. Although these differences were relatively inoffensive when based primarily on established development patterns, the very existence of the regulatory differences added to the special pressures on zoning administration. When regulations caused vast differences in land values, these pressures detracted both from the effectiveness and the fairness of regulations.

(3) Evolution of the regulatory pattern

Although today's regulations still normally resemble those of the 1920's in some respects, many also show marked differences from the early pattern. Regulatory techniques have been substantially refined, and standards have been generally raised. Objectives have become more ambitious, particularly where the old negativism has given way to the view that regulations should be part of a process to guide development affirmatively toward desired public objectives. And both techniques and objectives have been adapted to changes in the process of city building itself, particularly to the increased scale and pace of change since World War II.

a. *Refinement of regulatory techniques.*—One direction of change has been toward refinement of regulatory techniques. Among the many common examples of such refinement are these:

Specification of permitted uses: Instead of listing prohibited uses in each district, as the oldest ordinances did, regulations now normally list uses permitted in each district and prohibit all others. This plugs loopholes and establishes more clearly the intent of the regulations to guide development affirmatively in desired directions.

Noncumulative regulations: Old zoning ordinances set up a kind of use pyramid. Residences were "highest," businesses next, and industry was at the bottom. Each district permitted all the "higher" uses but excluded the "lower" ones. Thus, while industry was prohibited in residence zones, residences were permitted in industrial zones. Recent ordinances, however, attempting to assure that land is put to its planned use are much more likely to prohibit residences in industrialized zones as well as *vice versa.*[12]

More districts: Another sign of increasing refinement of control is the ever-increasing number of districts. A small suburban community that may have had half a dozen districts 30 years ago may have several times that many today.

More subjects regulated: There is a tendency to regulate more characteristics of development. Landscaping and screening provisions, for example, are now common. Many community regulations reflect public concern about such diverse matters as the appearance of buildings, the economic compatibility of the uses permitted in business areas, or the unwelcome glare from lights in parking lots.

Performance standards: Finally, a number of regulations contain performance standards. Performance standards fashion regulations more precisely to public objectives than do traditional or conventional regulations. Industrial performance standards, for example, may establish odor limits instead of prohibiting all paint plants. Performance standards hold great promise wherever the regulatory purpose is clear, where a standard can be precisely determined, and where compliance with it can be objectively and easily measured. Nevertheless, standards of this type are not even potentially available to govern many of the most important land-use relationships; there are simply too many purposes to be weighed in each situation and too many that defy objective measurement.

b. *More restrictive requirements.*—Another widespread tendency of recent regulations has been toward increased restrictiveness. In part, this has stemmed from greater public acceptance of land use regulations. Particularly in

[12] A Commission survey of local governments shows that in 1967, some 70 percent of local zoning ordinances contained at least one exclusively commercial or exclusively industrial zone. Larger governments and governments within metropolitan areas are more likely to have such zones than are smaller nonmetropolitan jurisdictions. See Manvel, Commission Research Report No. 6.

well-to-do suburban communities, newer regulations are likely to remove some of the undeveloped "strip commercial" zoning that characterizes so many regulations. Sign regulations may be tightened up. Much higher standards may be established to achieve quality development in commercial and industrial areas.

The most dramatic increase in restrictiveness has been a widespread reduction of permitted residential densities. In recent years, communities across the Nation have amended their ordinances to require larger and larger lots. "Acreage" zoning, the extreme situation, is now common, and lot sizes in community after community are being raised across the board.

The objectives of these density restrictions vary from place to place and time to time. Because real objectives are sometimes unspoken, it is often difficult to know which ones predominate in any particular situation. All of the following are important:

First, is a disturbing group of exclusionary objectives, discussed in detail later in this chapter. For a variety of reasons, citizens of some communities want to prevent as much development as possible for as long as possible, or to increase development cost to provide locations for people who choose low-density living, or to prevent people of low or moderate income from being able to afford homes in the community.

Second, density restrictions often represent a simple desire to raise development quality or carry out conventional local plans. When detached houses are built on the narrow lots permitted by many regulations, there is little space for adequate side yards. As houses increase in size, space for yards is smaller still. The intent of many regulations is, in effect, to assure adequate space between detached dwellings in the interest of privacy, amenity, and compatibility. Even the 1- and 2-acre zones that fill so many zoning maps may simply express a municipal intention that the land be developed for 1- and 2-acre lots (perhaps coupled with a hope that no building will occur). Such requirements may be intended to carry out a community plan that designates locations for various development intensities. Essentially they may carry out community policy relating to development timing—channeling development pressures of today into higher density areas elsewhere in the community with the intent of changing the zoning later, after those areas are developed. In each case, density regulations can be an essential adjunct of plans for the location and timing of public facilities.

Third, large-lot zones may be symptomatic of the "wait and see" regulatory approach, serving to assure that any future development receives discretionary review by the municipality. (Indeed, large-lot zoning may achieve this result whether or not this was its original intent.) Large-lot zoning can effectively prevent economically attractive development until the municipality grants rezoning. When the owner applies for that rezoning, the municipality has an opportunity to look over the proposal and give it the broadest of discretionary review. Such a "wait and see" approach to regulation is now gaining acceptance very rapidly.

c. *Changes in administration: "Wait and see."*—The "wait and see" approach to regulations represents a change in the administrative procedure applied to proposed development. In place of the older "self-executing" regulations, the approach contemplates discretionary public review of development proposals shortly before development occurs. In essence, the traditional administrative process in zoning is giving way to the more general standards and administrative discretion traditional in subdivision regulations. The developer proposes, and the municipality disposes. Sometimes the process is guided by useful plans and standards, but often not. Increasing reliance on discretionary review may well represent a more fundamental change in land-use regulations than any changes in substantive requirements.

Many techniques are being used today to achieve a "wait and see" result:

The variance has always been available as a "wait and see" tool and has long been used as such. Another device is the *"conditional use"* or *"special permit use,"* a use tentatively approved by the regulation but only if each applicant satisfies stated (but often meaninglessly vague) standards. Use of this technique has grown enormously during the past decade. In granting conditional use permits, as in the case of variances, the community may try to assure compatibility by imposing detailed conditions limiting bulk, prescribing location of curb cuts, limiting hours of operation, requiring erection of boundary fences, and the like.

The *"floating zone"* is another device, usually affecting a larger area than variances or special permit uses. The "floating zone" is described in the text of the regulations but is not put on the map until a developer applies for rezoning.

As noted above, *low density zoning* is an increasingly common "wait and see" device. The community obtains *de facto* control over land development by zoning undeveloped areas for very low densities and then waiting for landowners to seek a map change. The real decisions—perhaps in accordance with an approved plan or prestated policies but more often not—

are then taken by the local governing body when each application for rezoning is filed.

Conditional rezoning is a related technique, through which the municipality grants rezoning but imposes specific conditions on future use of the rezoned land, either directly or by causing the owner to impose deed restrictions on his land. Like other discretionary decisions, conditional rezoning can provide the more particularized control of development that many communities now want, but it is easily abused if public objectives are unclear or unstated. Moreover, the practice is not always effective: present zoning statutes do not normally contemplate conditions on rezoning, and the community may later find them unlawful or otherwise impossible to enforce. Too often, applicants mislead local governing bodies by obtaining rezoning on the basis of commitments to use the rezoned property in a particular way—and then break the commitments. If conditions on rezoning are effective, they can stop this practice; if not, they can play into the hands of unscrupulous applicants.

"Planned unit development" is the name most frequently given to a group of "wait and see" techniques that have come into widespread use only during the last 5 years. These provisions are intended to permit greater flexibility of site design and greater freedom to combine building types and uses in ways that would be prohibited by the detailed predeterminations of traditional zoning. At a minimum, the provisions do two things. First, instead of the lot-by-lot requirements traditional in zoning, they apply some requirements to entire projects. Second, to assure that developers use their greater resulting freedom consistently with public objectives, the provisions require discretionary public review of proposed site plans or designs.

Under conventional zoning, for example, a builder of 1,000 dwelling units in a 250-acre residential development might be required to put every unit roughly in the middle of a quarter-acre lot. Under planned unit development, he might (or might not) still be limited to 1,000 dwelling units, but he would have greater freedom to vary lot sizes and building types in ways aimed at satisfying people with different tastes and needs. Under some provisions, he would be permitted to introduce limited commercial or other development as well.

The provisions are usually applicable only at the option of the developer, who is free to adhere to conventional zoning if he prefers. Properly applied, the provisions can combine zoning and subdivision control into a single administrative process.

Local provisions vary widely in form, content, even in name. Some provisions establish few, if any, substantive requirements even for the entire project, leaving great discretion to municipal authorities; others establish specific requirements (permitted uses, maximum density, and so on) for entire projects. Some provide for great flexibility in choosing building types, building locations and uses within projects; others provide for much less.

Why the growing reliance on "wait and see" provisions? Again, answers vary from place to place, but these are often important:

First, these provisions enable communities to relate their regulatory process more closely to the process of development. Especially in undeveloped areas, detailed decisionmaking can be postponed until the pertinent facts become available. Depending on how carefully general policies and requirements are determined in advance, this approach may carry out a plan or mark the absence of one.

Second, municipal discretion provides great opportunities to overcome some imperfections in the usual process used to achieve development that is compatible with its immediate surroundings. Most regulations rely essentially on probabilities to achieve such compatibility: regulations thus permit uses, buildings, densities and public facilities that will probably fit together properly. From the standpoint of development quality, such reliance on probabilities is a weakness of current regulations. Because the focus is on what will probably happen, regulation must often prohibit the good as well as the bad—or permit some bad as well as the good. (For example, such arbitrary standards as a limit of eight row houses in a row or a requirement for twenty-foot side yards may be salutary when dealing with usual low-quality design; but they also prohibit innovation—and would even prohibit some of the great urban designs of the past.) "Wait and see" provisions permit local reviewing agencies to exercise more refined, particularized control. Instead of having to be content with probabilities, they may consider all the special circumstances of the individual case—lot shape, traffic consequences, landscaping, sometimes even style of architecture, and many more.

Third, "wait and see" permits localities to obtain concessions that may be—or are feared to be—beyond local legal powers to demand directly. The concessions may have exclusionary objectives; these are discussed in the next section. They may be aimed at achieving particularized design control. Or they may involve land dedications—especially for parks and school sites, but also for street widening or other public uses: the developer "voluntarily" provides these in return for development permission.

In summary, land-use regulations in many communities have evolved in three directions, all aimed at achieving higher standards and more ambitious objectives. One direction is toward more detailed and refined text provisions. The second is toward more restrictive requirements, especially toward lower density. And the third, increasingly important, is toward more sophisticated administrative techniques, resembling those of traditional subdivision control more than traditional zoning. Where the evolution serves sound and carefully thought out public objectives, it is clearly desirable; indeed, it is to be encouraged in the many communities where it has not yet taken place. Nevertheless, the evolving regulations make increasing demands on the wisdom and integrity of local legislators and administrators. The central problem of land-use regulation today is how to achieve the ambitious objectives of these regulations without, in the process, sacrificing other essential public objectives. Of greatest concern to the Commission is how to achieve the legitimate objectives without misuse of the rules to raise housing costs and exclude the poor.

2

John Reps

REQUIEM FOR ZONING (excerpts)

The year 1966 will be a significant one for American Planning. It marks two anniversaries: the beginning of the fifth century of the oldest city in the United States and the ending of the fifth decade of comprehensive zoning. It is a nice question which is less obsolete—the St. Augustine plan of 1565 or the comprehensive zoning ordinances of this country based on the New York City Zoning Resolution of 1916. The quaint, narrow streets of the old Spanish town serve at least to attract the tourist dollar; the quaint, narrow provisions of our zoning ordinances, judging from current comments, attract only the lawyers.

Zoning is seriously ill and its physicians—the planners—are mainly to blame. We have unnecessarily prolonged the existence of a land use control device conceived in another era when the true and frightening complexity of urban life was barely appreciated. We have, through heroic efforts and with massive doses of legislative remedies, managed to preserve what was once a lusty infant not only past the retirement age but well into senility. What is called for is legal euthanasia, a respectful requiem, and a search for a new legislative substitute sturdy enough to survive in the modern urban world.

The powers of zoning and all of our other techniques for controlling urban development appear grossly inadequate when measured against the often radically different development patterns which modern metropolitan plans propose. I am not here judging the desirability of such alternative urban configurations as advocated by the Dutch in their Rim City plan, the Danes in their finger plan for Copenhagen, the British in their satellite city and greenbelt design for Greater London, or the radial corridor scheme for Washington, D. C. I am contending only that our existing system of development guidance permits us to hope for nothing better than partially controlled sprawl and that such bold plans now have little chance of success.

My concern today is with only one of the means of planning implementation, but it is necessary first to view its position in the matrix of urban shaping devices. In another context I have suggested, as have others, that the mechanisms for directing the urban pattern might be regarded as a guidance system.[1] Like the components of the machinery that places a satellite into a planned orbit, this urban guidance system comprises a number of subsystems that can be used to steer a metropolis through time to a predetermined goal.

Also, like the guidance system of missiles or satellites, mine takes its name from the acronym formed by the initial letters of its four groups of components. The word thus formed—ACID—is unfortunately not very inspiring, but it does tend to burn itself in one's memory.

What do those letters stand for? What are these methods by which the patterns of urban growth and change can be shaped? I suggest that all of our activities in this direction can be classified under one of the following: advice, controls, inducements, and development. The order in which I have listed them is roughly the order in which they have been employed in our attempts to assert greater public leverage in constructing urban patterns.

When the first public planning agencies were created, their sole power was that of advice: advice to governmental departments and officials, to other levels of government, to civic organizations, to individuals. Advice, and the closely related techniques of persuasion and inspiration, still play important roles in guiding development. Indeed, at the metropolitan scale this is the chief technique on which we rely. But the power of advice necessarily has its limits, especially where advice runs even faintly counter to the dictates of the marketplace.

Next in point of time came our inventions of various kinds of control devices—zoning, subdivision regulations, official map techniques, and building, housing, and sanitary codes. But controls are negative instruments—they can prevent but they cannot compel, and their usefulness proved limited.

We then turned to various types of inducements or incentives as a method of attracting private building of types and in locations and under conditions that contributed to the public good. Through low-interest loans, tax exemptions, aids in land acquisition, direct subsidy payments, guarantees against financial loss, and other techniques, public bodies began to influence the urban pattern by combining the carrot of inducements with the lash of controls. Early redevelopment projects resulted from programs extending such financial incentives. The cluster subdivision concept provides another example.

Finally, direct public development has now taken its place as an urban forming force. In one sense, of course, this is nothing new. Vast public construction of streets and utilities in advance of need during the 1920's made possible the land boom of those wild years and certainly influenced

[1]John W. Reps, "Mechanisms for Directing and Controlling Future Development Patterns," Barclay Jones and Burnham Kelly (eds.), *Long-Range Needs and Opportunities in New York State* (Ithaca: Cornell University Center for Housing and Environmental Studies, 1962), pp. 306-337.

the form of cities. But acquiring, planning, and selling land in central redevelopment areas to reshape the city's core is employing public development powers in a new way. Expressways, rapid transit routes, trunk utility lines, and major public buildings have powerful influences on the growth patterns of cities, and coordinated planning of these and other city-shaping elements offers great promise as an effective guidance mechanism.

I would go much farther in the direction of public development and use some modification of redevelopment techniques at the urban fringe. To be specific, some public agency with metropolitan jurisdiction might acquire raw land, plan it, provide street, utility, park, and other needed improvements, and then convey lots, blocks, or neighborhoods to private builders for development as planned and as controlled by deed restrictions. This would accomplish three things: it would provide a public yardstick operation against which purely private land development activities could be measured, it would establish a more precise tool of environmental control and guidance, and it would, paradoxically enough, aid private enterprise and the competitive market by making it possible for small builders who cannot afford the uncertainties and costs of the modern scale of land development to stay in business.

I hope my position is clear that the incentives and public development components of the urban guidance system need much further examination and expansion. I am convinced that in the long run these are the areas in which much of our intellectual resources should be invested. It should also be clear that what I shall now have to say about zoning and its future deals with a minor, although far from unimportant, aspect of urban planning implementation.

Having narrowed the subject for discussion while at the same time placing it in its larger context, let me now attempt a working definition of zoning for purposes of analysis. I suggest the following: zoning is a police power measure enacted by units of local government under permissive state legislation. Zoning regulations establish, in advance of applications for development, groups of permitted uses that vary from district to district. These regulations are not necessarily related to other regulatory devices or to any community plan. They are administered by officials having only limited discretionary powers. Ultimate review of the regulations and the actions of administrative officials under them is by appeal only and is a judicial function.

Now let me challenge the wisdom of zoning as so defined. This is, frankly, an effort to free your minds of whatever convictions you may have that our present system of zoning is somehow the only or the best method for controlling the bulk, use, intensity, location, and density of development. The sanctity of half a century of tradition stands between me and this goal, but let me make the attempt. A number of propositions will elaborate on the elements of my definition, against each one of which I will pose a question for your consideration.

One: Zoning is a police power measure. It follows that the impact of zoning regulations must be reasonable and that their effect must not be so burdensome that they amount to a taking of property instead of a mere restriction in the interests of protecting or promoting the public health, safety, morals, or general welfare. Regulations found to be unreasonably burdensome are invalidated by court action. Constitutional rights are protected, but the community is stripped of this power to guide land development, and the public at large may suffer unfortunate consequences from the assertion of private rights in land. *Question:* Would it not be desirable to introduce a system of compensation to supplement the police power where severe limitations on land use are deemed essential or desirable to shape and guide community development?

Two: Zoning is permissive. While much state legislation requires municipalities to carry out specified services or to provide certain facilities, the choice of regulating or not regulating land use is optional under American enabling statutes. *Question:* Would it not be desirable for state legislation to require all communities or those having certain characteristics to enact such regulations?

Three: Zoning is enacted by units of local government. Zoning regulations are intensely parochial. Standards required in any single metropolitan area may vary enormously depending on the whims of local legislators. We make much of the principle that land similarly located must be similarly zoned within a given municipality, but this concept is cruelly violated when a homogeneous area is zoned for industry on one side of a municipal boundary line and for high-class, low-density residential uses on the other side. Standards of enforcement vary equally widely. The possibility of achieving coordinated and balanced metropolitan development under such a situation, insofar as land use regulation is effective at all, can be written off as a mere fiction. *Question:* Would it not be desirable to deny zoning powers to the smaller units of government and place this responsibility at the county level, or as a duty of some metropolitan government or agency, or as a function of the state government?

Four: Zoning establishes regulations in advance of applications for development permission. As Daniel Mandelker has so well put it, "One difficulty with American legal techniques is that they borrow constitutional trouble by making land-use decisions with constitutional impact before the fact. Thus, exclusive agricultural zoning is restrictive immediately upon its enactment. It immediately raises a constitutional issue throughout its area of application regardless of the fact that many affected landowners would be quite happy with an exclusive agricultural restriction. But under the present system, an attack by a few will affect the entire ordinance."[2] *Question:* Would it not be desirable to have a method of control which avoided this difficulty and left the issue of legal validity to be raised when dealing with each application to develop land or to change its use?

[2]Daniel L. Mandelker, "What Open Space Where? How?," *American Society of Planning Officials, Planning 1963* (Chicago: ASPO, 1964), p. 25.

Five: Zoning establishes groups of permitted uses that vary from district to district. In our understandable attempt to simplify in a complex and bewildering world we have done three things. We have attempted to prepare detailed standards for development which are supposed to cover all conceivable situations. We have Balkanized our cities into districts with precise and rigid zone boundary lines. We have established categories of uses that have segregated rather than integrated functional portions of cities and which have often disregarded the interrelationships between rather widely separated categories of uses. *Question:* Would it not be desirable to do away entirely with, or at least place far less emphasis on, the creation of districts and lists of supposedly compatible uses?

Six: Zoning is not necessarily related to other regulatory devices. Forget the theory here, and look at the facts. There is a multitude of regulatory measures—zoning, subdivision regulations, building codes, sanitary retrictions, housing ordinances, official map regulations, and others—enacted at different times, often by different bodies, enforced by different sets of officials, and reviewable by different administrative tribunals or courts. It is a rare zoning ordinance that does not in several ways conflict with the community subdivision regulations. It is a rare community that has not omitted some vital provision from both. It is a common necessity for the developers of all but the most routine and standardized projects to deal with several boards or officials and to secure amendments, approvals, waivers, or variances from the provisions of a number of ordinances and codes in order to proceed. *Question:* Would it not be desirable to consolidate all or most regulations dealing with control of urban growth into a single development ordinance that provided a sensible and efficient system of administration and enforcement, and which was purged of ambiguities, conflicting provisions, and redundancies?

Seven: Zoning is not necessarily related to any community plan. Again, forget the theory and look at the facts, including the depressing but understandable record of judicial review on this point. There are few communities that can claim with much justification that their regulations stem directly from any comprehensive, long-range plan. Charles Haar has demonstrated, in perhaps the most frequently court-cited law review article on zoning ever written, that whatever we think state legislation says about the necessity to ground zoning in a well-considered or comprehensive plan, the courts by and large have interpreted such a plan to be the zoning map itself.[3] This circular reasoning will prevail until new legislation changes the rules of the judicial game. *Question:* Would it not be desirable for statutes to require any local development regulations or discretionary administrative decisions reached on development proposals to be clearly based on a community plan, expressed graphically and/or as meaningful statements of development policy?

Eight: Zoning is administered by officials with limited discretionary powers. I am not here concerned with the scandal of unwarranted dis-

[3]Charles Haar, "In Accordance with a Comprehensive Plan," 68 *Harvard Law Review* 1154 (1955).

cretionary decisions by boards of appeals or such comparative novelties as floating zones or site plan approval procedure, but with the amount of discretion normally exercised by administrative officials in reviewing applications for zoning or building permits. It is in the nature of controls by districts, use lists, and bulk and density standards that present administrative review is essentially mechanical and requires only a check-list mentally. *Question:* Would it not be desirable to construct a system of development controls in which, as is the case of subdivision review, informed discretionary judgment plays the dominant or at least a much larger role in the process of reviewing applications to build or develop?

Nine: Ultimate review of the regulations and the actions of administrative officials under them is by appeal only. Only a person who feels aggrieved and who has the ambition, time, and money to appeal can obtain some kind of review of the wisdom or legality of a zoning enactment or administrative decision. State governments, which have conferred regulatory powers on localities, have failed to provide any form of central review of the regulations as originally established or as amended or of administrative actions taken under them. There is no county or metropolitan review of local regulatory activities except the most peripheral. *Question:* Would it not be desirable to establish a system of state or metropolitan review of zoning-type regulations that could insure conformity with state or metropolitan development objectives and, in the case of local appeals situations, conformity with standardized fair procedures that would insure adequate attention to due process requirements and would curb both excessive restrictiveness and undue liberality on the part of administrative officials exercising wide discretionary powers?

Ten: Ultimate review of zoning regulations and administrative action is a judicial function. Courts are more and more being called on to decide issues which are increasingly technical and complex. Most courts have taken refuge in the doctrine of the presumption of legislative validity, but as the thrust of regulations becomes more vigorous it is unlikely that courts can refuse to decide issues on their merits. Yet, courts are ill-equipped to make decisions on technical matters, and it is far from clear that the adversary system provides the best approach to decision-making. *Question:* Would it not be desirable to create state administrative tribunals, assisted by an expert staff, authorized to obtain evidence in a variety of ways, and empowered to decide appeals or claims arising from the application of land use controls?

•   •   •

3

American Society of Planning Officials

PROBLEMS OF ZONING AND LAND USE REGULATION

URBAN GROWTH DURING the remainder of the 20th century will require the development of 18 million acres of new land--land now devoted to such non-intensive uses as agriculture and forests. If the present pattern of urban growth continues, 75 percent or more of the growth will take place in the present metropolitan areas, and almost entirely in the suburbs rather than in the central cities.

City and metropolitan planning attempt to guide urban expansion into an efficient pattern that will produce a rational balance among residential, commercial, industrial and public land uses. The actual development of new areas is regulated by zoning and subdivision control ordinances, although development is also greatly affected by many other governmental ordinances and actions, such as building and housing codes, licensing ordinances, tax and assessment policy, etc.

Prior to the end of World War II, both zoning and subdivision control had been generally regarded as successful and adequate to the task of protecting existing development and regulating growth. After the War, the rate of development increased rapidly, new methods of mass building production were devised, and the weaknesses of traditional zoning and subdivision control became apparent.

It is now being charged that:

* Excessive zoning restrictions and subdivision standards interfere with construction of low- and moderate-cost housing.

* Land-use regulations have failed to halt wasteful urban sprawl.

* Zoning for large lots is used to prevent Negroes from living in the suburbs.

* Zoning favors are for sale by public officials in many communities.

* Land-use regulation has become so complex that it cannot properly be administered by laymen--city councils, planning commissions, boards of zoning appeals.

* Archaic and rigid zoning ordinances prevent the use of design innovations such as cluster subdivisions, which could provide higher standards of amenity and bring housing within the reach of families that cannot now afford it.

* Zoning is not adequate to guide or regulate urban development.

* Local government actions in land-use regulation are often against the public interests of the metropolitan region.

* Zoning has never been able to carry out a comprehensive plan.

* Zoning and subdivision regulations are used primarily to correct the fiscal problems of local government and not to guide urban expansion in an efficient pattern. (This is called fiscal zoning.)

There are many misconceptions about the purpose, practice and authority of land-use regulations. Nevertheless, there is enough truth in the statements listed above to make it worthwhile for the benefit of (1) the public, and (2) the building industry, to document exactly how much truth, and to suggest corrective action.

Analysis of land-use regulations and the objectives which they are supposed to achieve reveals a number of goal conflicts. That is, by drafting and administering the ordinances to achieve one desirable purpose, the community may be taking action contrary to the achievement of another desirable purpose. The most obvious goal conflicts are:

Regional versus Local. Action in its own best interest by a local govern-ment is sometimes against the best interests of its neighbors or of the metropolitan region as a whole; action by senior government, such as the county or state, sometimes creates unusual hardship in a particular community.

Public Interest versus Private Rights. All land-use regulations infringe on private property rights by taking away a landowner's freedom to do with his property as he pleases. There is a constant debate as to where the line should be drawn between public interest and private freedom.

Conservation versus Change. In all developed areas, and especially in suburban areas, most of the citizens are satisfied with the situation as it is. But technological change and population pressures are creating a demand for change, which is resisted by the citizens who desire to, and have a right to, preserve and protect their own property.

Quality versus Quantity. This conflict relates primarily to the construc-tion of housing. There is a national need to increase the quantity of low- and moderate-cost housing. Developers are anxious to supply this need because the market for higher-cost housing is getting thin. Local governing bodies are suspicious, with considerable justification, of anything that cheapens the cost of housing by reducing the quality. For this reason, many local communities resist any lowering or change of standards.

Identity versus Diffusion. At its worst, this conflict includes the

improper, but nonetheless real, desire of a community to maintain its
white identity by excluding Negroes, contrary to the national goal of
protecting the Constitutional rights of minority groups. But it also
includes the struggle of a minority group to maintain its own identity
against urban redevelopment projects that require mass relocation.

Major problem areas to which Federal efforts should be directed are four:

Regional Problems in Land-Use Regulation. Zoning and subdivision control
problems are only part of the larger metropolitan problem, but some
improvements in land-use regulation are possible.

Local Financial Problems. Fiscal zoning can be eliminated only by eliminating the maladjustments in tax and assessment policies that create
local financial problems, and not by any changes in land-use regulatory
ordinances.

Technical and Procedural Problems. These are the result of insufficient
knowledge, funds, manpower, and legal authority. (It should be noted
that the legal problem is now under expert examination by the American
Law Institute.)

New Techniques. This might be included as a sub-class of the foregoing
group. But it is so important to the enormous urban expansion expected
in the next 30 years that it deserves special treatment.

The improvement of land-use regulations will be a complex task. This task
will be further complicated by the fact that land-use regulation is carried
out under authority delegated from 50 state legislatures to several thousand
or more local governing bodies. The fact that there is by no means unanimous belief in state or local legislatures that there are weaknesses in
present land-use regulations presents further difficulty.

The Federal Government will not, of course, be adopting or administering
local land-use ordinances. But there is a clear national interest in the
subject, and the Federal Government is justified in doing what it can to
solve the problems.

●   ●   ●

Daniel Mandelker

THE ROLE OF ZONING IN HOUSING AND METROPOLITAN DEVELOPMENT (excerpts)

Accelerating urbanization, increasing housing pressures, and constantly growing demands for urban land require constant attention to the institutional and legal devices that our society has available to shape and direct the development of our metropolitan regions. Zoning is almost certainly no exception. Originally conceived with the rather modest objective of allocating land uses to prevent friction between incompatible demands on urban space, it has in recent years been put to the much more ambitions and at the same time more difficult task of implementing regional plans for urban development. In the process, the original purpose of zoning has been much changed, and tensions have appeared in the legal structure which supports the zoning system.

In this paper I intend to examine the present state of zoning controls in this country, especially as they relate to the implementation of housing objectives. An introductory section presents a brief review of the origins and changes in the zoning idea. Following this, I outline the relationship of zoning to metropolitan development problems, and especially to the problem of meeting housing production objectives in a metropolitan setting. Finally, I make a series of recommendations, some requiring legislative action, which should help shape the zoning technique to make it a more effective legal method of achieving the social objectives, especially in the housing field, which our society considers increasingly important.

I INTRODUCTION: RULE AND PURPOSE IN THE ZONING FUNCTION

An initial point to make is that zoning was never conceived as a legal technique which was expected to have significant impact on the urban development process. Careful historical inquiry has now made clear what we have always known, that zoning was born as the result of intensive and competing land use pressures on Manhattan Island in New York City, and was adopted as a means of preventing seemingly bad land uses from driving out the good in an important commercial area of the island. An important footnote to this history is that zoning, having been born in New York City, was "sold" to the rest of the country partly as a defensive measure. Astute New York lawyers were afraid that the absence of zoning regulations in other communities would leave New York City in an exposed legal position once the New York ordinance was challenged in court. This lesson is worth remembering as we move on to the construction of even more sophisticated legal measures, to be applied in an ever more varied context of urban settings.

This early history of the zoning idea is important, for it explains what the early pioneers had in mind when they urged the adoption of the zoning mechanism. As originally conceived, zoning was not intended as a means of directing and shaping market forces as they affected the development of cities and of urban regions. In New York, the physical limitations of the area made much debate on growth directions foregone, and the intensive market demand for land helped to blind the early draftsmen to the problem of market-zoning relationships in areas where market demand was neither so strong nor as concentrated. From this perspective, it is fair to say that the early zoning was defensive, a better word than the usual characterization of the early zoning ordinances as negative. That is, zoning ordinances as they were first conceived were aimed at preventing the worst in conflicting mixtures of land uses which were considered harmful to the urban environment.

It is certainly true that this legal approach to zoning regulation was legally well contrived. At the time zoning was initially adopted, legal restrictions on the free use of land in the name of a larger public interest were suspect. Perplexing and difficult constitutional problems were avoided by fastening the zoning technique on ancient and well-accepted legal notions which arose out of the law of nuisance. Long before the first zoning ordinances were passed, courts had been willing to issue prohibitory decrees at the request of private landowners either prohibiting or restricting offending land uses in areas in which they were considered incompatible. For example, courts had long issued decrees which had the effect of keeping nonresidential land uses out of residential areas. In doing so, they necessarily had to adopt a judicial position toward the neighborhood, and even the city, which they sought to protect. Judicial zoning was the result. Courts would inquire into the character of neighborhoods which were under review, and would or would not issue court orders prohibiting intruding and offending uses depending on how they characterized the area into which the use sought entry.

Zoning merely codified this long-established judicial function. It did this by means of a local ordinance which set, in advance and by preregulation, the various destricts in which uses of different kinds were or were not to be allowed. Two important aspects of the zoning fuction emerge from this early history: 1) zoning was based on pre-regulation, avoiding legal objections of unfairness and illegality in the distribution of land uses by allocating areas of competing land uses comprehensively and in advance of development; 2) possible legal objections to restrictions on the private right of land development were avoided by fastening zoning on well-established legal notions of frictional land use incompatibilities. Zoning thus did not pretend to make more ambitious land use decisions with the larger objectives of community and regional development in mind.

It is obvious to most observers of the urban scene that, on both counts, the original nature of the zoning process has been completely turned around. Preregulation of land uses has not worked in developing and urbanizing areas, and the original and limited objectives of separating frictional land uses has been displaced by more ambitious objectives related to larger and more comprehensive planning purposes. Some comment on both of these points is in order. Preregulation of land use simply did not work on the fast-growing urban fringe. Not only were there legal objections to the prezoning of undeveloped land in which land use patterns had not been fixed, but the pace of development in urbanizing areas often outstripped and outdated earlier planning and zoning determinations. Other factors probably played a part. Zoning was (and is) a gross tool at best. Fairly crude legal distinctions could be made among types of land uses, but zoning administrators were interested in more control. Often *who* the developer was turned out to be more important than *what* he actually proposed to do with his land. As a result, zoning was gradually converted from a system which preregulated land uses to a system of administrative control in which individual applications for development were considered *ad hoc* as applications for zoning changes of various kinds came before zoning administrators. This change in the basic decision-making function inherent in the zoning process came about through the adaptation of existing legal powers rather than through their formal legal reconstruction. Tensions in the use of the zoning power have therefore resulted which continue to remain both troublesome and unresolved.

These changes in thepurpose of zoning largely came about with changes in methods of land development. While development in the early decades of the century took place piecemeal, on small lots, changes in building methods stimulated by the greater accessibility induced by the automobile led to answer development techniques in which urban development came to occur on large aggregates of land especially assembled for development purposes. The large subdivision or apartment complex replaced the single home on the individual lot. Extensive regional shopping centers replaced the corner store. Where these massive developments would go would have important effects on the shape and character of urban areas. Moreover, the coming of the automobile and the high-speed expressway significantly widened the area in which new development could occur. Control over the location of major developments in largely open territory came to be an important zoning problem. No longer could the exercise of zoning controls be justified in the name of preventing narrower land use incompatibilities. Zoning was increasingly used as a method of implementing larger objectives based on a comprehensive plan.

We can summarize these trends by imagining the position of a large-scale developer who seeks sites on the fringers of a growing metropolitan community on which to build large-scale multiple housing. Let us assume that most of this area, for zoning purposes, is in the hands of a county zoning authority. If he consults the zoning map the chances are that our would-be developer finds little or no land prezoned for multiple housing purposes. What land has been zoned is in the course of development or has been optioned. If he is to buiild his project, our developer will have to go to the zoning authority to get a zoning change. What form that change will take will depend on the variety of legal options which the zoning authority has chosen to exercise. Should he buy or option a likely piece of land, our developer will find himself making arguments to the zoning authority which are a far cry from the purposes of the original zoning ordinance. While questions of incompatibility, no doubt with adjacent single family residential homes, will not no doubt be rasied, our developer will be asked to justify the increase in density which his development will bring in terms of the planning objectives of the county—relationship to schools, public services, highway networks, and places of employment. Whether he succeeds or not will depend on how the local zoning authority views his request, and in view of the present state of zoning law and planning theory, the decision which is finally taken may often be justly characterized as largely *ad hoc*.

II THE RELATIONSHIP OF ZONING TO PROBLEMS OF METROPOLITAN GROWTH AND HOUSING PRODUCTION

With this background in mind, we can turn next to the impact of present-day zoning controls and their exercise on problems of facilitating metropolitan development, and of assuring an adequate flow of housing production at income and cost levels where it is most needed. Let it be said initially that these issues have received very little in the way of rigorous attention. Those comments that follow are primarily intended to highlight problem areas in which remedial and corrective and public action may be required. But I would strongly urge that while the line of possible public intervention is clear in some cases, additional investigation is clearly warranted before we become too committed to any particular course of action. What may seem intuitively to be a proper remedial step may turn out on further analysis to produce other results which cancel out the intended good effects of what was attempted in the first place. Past experience with programs gone awry demands that we proceed with caution.

1. *The Exclusionary Zoning Issue.* Much has been made of late of the so-called exclusionary zoning issue. Zoning ordinances, through the substance of their regulation or in their administration, are said to exclude low-income and minority racial groups, especially from suburban areas. How this exclusion is accomplished depends on the exclusionary technique employed. Some zoning ordinances exclude certain kinds of dwellings outright, such as mobile homes or apartments. Other zoning jurisdictions are more sophiscated. For example, a

zoning ordinance may provide a procedure through which administrative changes for apartments may be granted, but no such administrative changes are ever made. Other aspects of zoning controls pointed out for criticism are density requirements. Often large areas in developing suburban sections will be zoned at very low densities, much too low for moderately priced not to speak of low cost housing. Indeed, recent studies indicate low density zoning of this type to be widespread in many metropolitan areas along the eastern seaboard and elsewhere. In other cases, unreasonable minimums are placed on house sizes, or apartment areas are limited to projects with only one-bedroom units, so that large families can be kept out.

Quite clearly, exclusionary zoning practices are a block to the effective implementation of a housing program for lower income families in suburban areas. Just how the impediment of exclusionary zoning should be handled is another matter. The present trend is in the direction of extensive litigation in state and federal courts, challenging the constitutionality of exclusionary zoning practices. While such litigation, if successfully prosecuted, can have salutary effects on the conduct of the zoning system, I would submit that victories in court litigation of this kind will only have a symbolic impact of the zoning structure as it affects lower cost housing. The trouble is that only the worst excesses of exclusionary practices can be reached through judicial attack. While a municiplaity restrictive enough to exclude all apartments from its jurisdiction may be successfully confronted in court, more subtle attempts at evasion will be more difficult to reach. Some municipalities, for example, merely zone clearly undesirable sections of their community for mobile home parks and other allegedly undesirable developments, well knowing that development at these locations probably will never take place. Nonetheless, even presumably arbitrary zoning designations of this kind are difficult to reach through the judicial review process. While exclusionary zoning practices are clearly an obstacle to the implementation of housing production programs, more than successful judicial challenge is needed to remedy this problem.

2. *Zoning inefficiencies.* Other zoning practices, while not rising to the level of outright exclusion and discrimination, nevertheless produce inefficiencies in land use which hinder the effective implementation of housing policies. To a large extent, this issue is tied in with the problem of local autonomy in the enactment of zoning regulations, which deeply affects the land use allocation pattern which is a product of the zoning process. As is well known, but not sufficiently emphasized, the exercise of local powers of planning and zoning is the one local government function which, in almost all states, remains entirely at the local level with no opportunity for higher governmental review. It is this absence of institutional legal machinery to provide a check on the local zoning process which makes judicial action to challenge allegedly improper zoning practices the only available outside recourse in most jurisdictions. Just how and whether zoning reviews at higher govern-

mental levels could or should provide a check on local government decision-making in this area is another problem. At this point we can only isolate some of the difficulties which local autonomy in decision-making produce in this area of public control.

The simple point to make here is that a zoning allocation which may appear optimal from the standpoint of the zoning municipality may not be optimal when viewed from the perspective of an entire urban or metropolitan region. What is at issue is not simply the patently arbitrary decisions of many suburban municipalities to legislate zoning patterns which are aimed, openly or not, at excluding undesirable population groups. Even apparently well-motivated zoning efforts by some local governments may be seen as undesirable from a larger regional viewpoint. For example, heavy governmental fragmentation in most metropolitan areas, and the lack of any central control over local zoning decisions, makes it no secret that many large developers simply "shop" for a municipality which will give them a favorable zoning answer. Especially is this true in the case of developers of such important land users as large regional shopping centers. The municipality, attracted by the opportunity to enhance its tax base, and which makes land available to a developer of a large shopping center, may be doing a disservice from a regional perspective if the result is to distort local and regional development patterns.

Other, more subtle, problems arise. Developers of such uses as mobile home courts, finding themselves frustrated by comparatively sophisticated zoning authorities in the inner and middle sections of metropolitan areas, often seek more distant locations, in governmental areas in which zoning is weakly exercised, if at all. The result, again, may be a distortion in housing patterns, with such uses as mobile homes locating in distant areas, far from employment and jobs. Correction of inter-municipal zoning inefficiencies is difficult under the present system. For example, some courts have been asked to intervene in zoning decisions when the land involved, though it lies in one municipality, is located near or on the borders of other communities. Judicial correction is difficult in these cases because the court has before it only the zoning allocation of the municipality under review. It cannot, by judicial decree, force more appropriate zoning actions, either by the challenged municipality or by its neighbors.

Closely related to the problem of inefficiences in zoning allocations is the impact on the zoning process of the tax structure. It is still true that American municipalities in most states rely heavily on the property tax as a source of local revenues. Since this is so, zoning administrators quite obviously exercise their zoning powers with one eye on tax receipts. Zoning policies are often explicitly designed to attract major tax-producing uses and to exclude uses which make heavy demands on revenue. This issue is especially important in the housing area, since it can be expected that housing built at greater densities for lower income groups will make heavier demands on public facilities than will housing built at lower densities for higher income groups. The problem is not only one of providing more extensive public education facilities to meet greater school demands. When housing is built at very low densities and supporting public facilities are not provided, the added cost of supplying substitute private facilities is usually borne by the housing occupier. For example, in the absence of public transportation in low density suburban areas, the average American householder owns two cars. He may also provide his own water and sanitation system. Since families in lower income groups cannot afford to make these expenditures, they will have to be met out of the public pocket. It is not surprising, then, that suburban communities resist the intrusion into their areas of higher density housing serving lower income groups.

3. *Zoning and its effect on land values.* While the zoning system clearly has important effects on the land market and on the level of land prices, much of the formal doctrine of zoning controls reads as if no such relationship exists. The impact of zoning on land values is especially important to consider in relation to housing programs. Not only does the cost of land make up an important proportion of housing costs, but the ratio of site to housing value has been constantly on the increase. By some measures, as much as thirty percent of housing unit costs is represented in the land price. For this reason, any public policy which has important effects on the land price structure must be considered in any evaluation of the implementation of a housing program, all the more so because other elements of housing costs are more difficult to manipulate. For example, building and labor costs are clearly affected by the movement of general price levels. Interest costs are fixed by the money market. Reduction of these costs can only be accomplished through direct subsidy or, in the case of labor and materials, by cutting quality or by cost savings, the present impetus of Operation Breakthrough.

Land costs, on the other hand, are very much affected by the way in which the zoning process is operated. Not only is this important fact often overlooked, but an argument can be made that, given the present assumptions of our planning process, *the more effective the planning and zoning system becomes, the higher land prices will tend to be.* This additional cost must either be absorbed by the housing consumer, taxed away from the housing supplier, or absorbed by a public subsidy. Otherwise, given the present ingredients of the housing cost package, housing that is made available on the market will simply be priced out of the income range of those groups that need it most.

Let us examine this problem more closely. Many factors affect land values for housing, among them accessibility and density. As a rough rule of thumb, land values decline with a decrease in accessibility and in density. For example, low density zoning, such as zoning which requires three acres for each dwelling unit, is troublesome primarily because the land required for each dwelling is excessive. The effect of low density zoning on land prices is not yet altogether clear. But it appears that prices per acre of land are lower at very low densities than they are at very high densities, but that the cost of land for each housing unit is higher because so much more land is required. Accessibility also affects land prices because dwellings built with good accessibility enjoy reduced trip costs, and these savings are reflected in the capital price of land in the land market in short, land with good accessibility is more desirable, and thus more expensive. With these quick observations in mind, let us look at the way in which American planning and zoning is practiced with reference to density and accessibility problems, and then let us look at the way in which most planners would have it practiced. This analysis should give us some interesting clues concerning the impact of the zoning process on the land market and on land values.

The key to present zoning practices lies in assumptions made about regional accessibility, and about the distribution of land use densities in metropolitan areas. Probably it is fair to say that the assumption behind the construction of Interstat and expressway highway networks in and around most metropolitan areas is to provide equal and relatively comparable accessibility from any one point of the area to another. True, accessibility will vary with distance from interchanges and highway entry points. But highway systems blanket and encircle most metropolitan regions, largely cancelling out intra-regional differences, especially as highway systems by federal design are intended to be built to standards which are congestion free throughout the areas they serve. To put it another way, accessibility to the highway network is more or less equal throughout metroplitan areas. No attempt is usually made to strengthen or weaken highway access and capacity at strategic points to shape and affect the growth of regional development.

As a result of this highway configuration, any attempt to differentiate among parts of a metropolitan area for purposes of growth and development must come from the planning and zoning system, and runs counter to the development tendencies which the highway encourages. That is, any attempt to suppress growth at one point in a metropolitan region and to encourage it at another must come from the zoning system, and the land allocation decisions it makes. For a variety of reasons, policies of this type cannot be expected in the American zoning system as it is presently operated. Some of these have already been noted. Local autonomy in the exercise of zoning powers prevents coordinated regional action to implement regional objectives which may differentiate various parts of the region for strategy purposes. Tendencies toward protectionism in local zoning practices lead to exclusionary and inefficient zoning decisions which tend to result in very low density zoning patterns. This system has its advantages. When zoning spreads residential land uses at comparatively low densities, land is comparatively cheap at its cost for each unit of land, though it may be comparatively expensive at its cost for each unit of housing. Relatively equal highway accessibility and low density patterns also help to even out the differences between higher and lower land prices. No one landowner suffers too much from zoning restrictions, and no one landowner has that much to gain. Under these conditions, operation of the planning and zoning system is politically that much easier.

As it happens, housing for lower income groups requires much higher desnities than the densities now prevailing in many suburban areas. This fact, together with the need for providing more in the way of public facilities for lower income housing, drives up the cost of land for each unit of land that is needed for housing at lower income levels. In part, these higher prices reflect the need to provide through public funds the very services which in higher income housing is provided privately, and this shift of services to the public sector is simply reflected in the higher cost of land.

Higher land prices at higher densities also reflect the greater accessibility of these developments. Not only do lower income groups often require access to public transportation or at least greater accessibility to jobs, but the higher concentrations of housing at these income levels necessarily mean an improvement in land accessibility patterns. They simply need more and better roads. As a result, while land costs per housing unit may decline, land costs for each unit of land will increase, often substantially. To put it another way, increases in land densities will result in substantial increases in per unit land values. Just how great these increases have to be to make provision of housing for lower income groups economically impossible has not been fully explored. But it is certainly no secret that, given the present way in which the zoning system is administered, the local zoning decision has a major role to play in the level of land values which follow density increases. We had pointed out earlier, for example, that most zoning authorities zone land at densities for too low for most residential development, and allow higher density development only after an application for a zoning change has been approved. It is the zoning decision to allow higher densities which has a direct effect on land values and thus, indirectly, on housing prices.

We must now observe that to follow the planning proposals put forward by planning agencies would simply aggravate rather than help the problem of land value increases that are associated with higher density patterns. Let us return to our comment that present American highway-building and zoning practices tend to favor a land use allocation system in which zoning densities are spread rather evenly over most metropolitan areas. Planners, or at least most of them, would not have it that way. For a variety of reasons, many of which are not always clearly articulated, planners tend to favor a land allocation system in which the distance between the highest and the lowest densities are much greater than they are at present, a result of planning policies which favor greater urban compaction at the expense of what is commonly called urban spread, or sprawl. As planners would have it, urban development would largely occur at selected urban growth points, at densities much higher than are now typical of most metropolitan areas. At the same time, large areas of most urban regions would be totally restricted from any development at all. We can see policies of this kind in evidence in the well-known *Year 2000 Plan* for the Washington, D.C., metropolitan area, and in the many other regional plans that have followed its lead.

Compaction approaches to regional planning also tend to increase land accessibility, because they often relate higher densities to the availability of transportation networks. This tendency is also evident in the *Year 2000 Plan*, which relates its radial development corridors to the metropolitan transportation network. Greater compaction and greater densities also facilitate the provision of linear public services, such as sewer and water lines, to new development, and it is assumed in most plans that high-density development will not (indeed it often cannot) be left to be serviced by privately-provided on-lot facilities.

We should be sensitive at once to the impact that planning policies of this kind will have on the distribution of land values. Assuming that demand is constant under either the present system or the more compacted development patterns projected by most regional planning proposals, the result of following the more compacted planning policies of regional plans will be to force more development into less space. Land values in the areas selected for development will escalate. Land values in the areas restricted from development will fall considerably. Planning systems of this kind require the making of decisions which heavily favor the lucky ones and heavily disfavor the unlucky ones and are hard to operate politically in a locally-based governmental system such as ours. Moreover, by concentrating more development on less land, unless policies will raise land prices for each unit of land used, and improved accessibility and availability of public services will also mean price increases. It is no answer that costs to the public in the long run may well be less than they are under present systems, which favor dispersion of development and which defer the provision of most public facilities. We have no present method of absorbing the short-run cost of land for development, and if it is higher it is simply passed on to the housing consumer unless it is absorbed into a public subsidy.

One answer to these problems is to raise zoning densities high enough so that, for each unit, they cancel out the increases in land prices. Apart from the fact that higher densities may be undesirable in their own right, there seems to be some evidence that even with higher densities land costs for lower income housing are simply so high that cost limitations in government programs are often exceeded, given the fixed nature of other housing costs. What all of this means is that land costs are often so high at the higher zoning densities that the housing that is built is out of the reach of lower income families, even under the present subsidy system. And we are suggesting here, given the present assumptions about regional planning patterns, that the more successful the regional planning effort tends to be the more the effect on land values will be inflationary. From another perspective, should we break some of the exclusionary zoning practices of some of the worst suburbs, and open up suburban areas to lower income housing at higher densities, we may find land prices rising so fast that lower cost housing is priced out of the market. Suburbs might be better off if they tried high densities rather than low densities as a zoning strategy.

Unfortunately, there are few ready answers to this problem. One approach is simply to increase the public subsidy to absorb added land costs, assuming that the regional development patterns that lead to these costs are both acceptable and desirable. However, subsidy increases of this magnitude may not only be politically difficult, but may be unacceptable to the extent that they subsidize windfall gains to fortunate landowners. An equity problem is presented. One possibility, of course, is to tax this gain away from the favored landowner, perhaps applying the tax in the form of a subsidy to reduce housing costs. We already tax away some of this gain through the capital gains feature of the federal income tax, but the proceeds of this tax go into general revenues. Steps to impose a land value or betterment tax are probably beyond the capacity of our political system. Two attempts at such a tax in England, with its very difficult political climate, have failed, an experience which does not speak well for the chances of any such effort in the American context. Perhaps, on balance, subsidies will appear to be the most desirable remedy. Advance land acquisitons of land needed for housing may also hold down land costs for government agencies, although they may at the same time make land on the open market more expensive.

4. *The issue of zoning standards and levels of housing production.* Much of what we have been saying so far relates very closely to the issue of housing standards as they affect the production of lower income housing. We might now make some additional points which arise because of the rather special character of that housing. Remember that, for the most part, a large proportion of lower income housing will be provided as multiple housing, in apartment developments. Housing provided by way of apartment projects presents some special problems that are not presented by single family developments. In particular, areas of the apartment development site must be set aside for accessory uses related to dwelling occupancy, especially for parking and open space. We might focus on on-site parking problems because land reserved for parking areas makes up a large part of the development site, and thus affects dwelling unit densities and indirectly the amount of land to be made available for housing purposes and thus land costs.

What with increasing use of the automobile, private and unsubsidized multiple dwelling developments have increasingly been required to set aside ever larger amounts of on-site land for parking purposes. These land reservations push up development costs, especially with concurrent increasing demands for adequate aesthetic treatment of parking areas, as through landscaping, which can be very expensive. Now the fact is that if housing is built specifically with lower income housing use in mind, a case can be made for setting aside less land than is usual for parking purposes. Doing so will, accordingly, reduce land costs. Especially in the case of public housing, whose tenants often do not have automobiles, land reservations for on-site parking can be substantially less. The same point can be made about housing for the aged.

On-site parking is only one of several problem areas in which the problem of adequate zoning standards for housing, especially for lower income housing, can be raised. The problem is whether standards ought to be the same for lower income housing as they are for all housing. A second question, assuming that standards for lower income housing can be reduced, is how and whether this distinction can be carried out legally. There are several dimensions to this problem. One is that it may be difficult legally to justify different treatment for lower income housing than for other housing solely on the basis that occupants of lower income housing will be lower income groups with less, for example, in the way of automobile demand. A few courts have of late dealt with this problem, with varying results, although the suggestion can be made that the courts will probably find a way around this dilemma, if only for reasons that are more pragmatic than sound. Even if judicial acceptance is secured, however, obvious political problems face the jurisdiction which seeks to provide favored treatment for housing solely on the basis of occupancy patterns.

In addition, some serious problems of housing strategy are presented by outright deviations from housing standards to take care of the special case of housing units designed for lower income groups. Strong arguments are likely to be made that housing quality standards in the community are being dropped for questionable reasons related to fulfilling regional and national goals, with no concern for the quality standards which have been imposed by the community. The point can also be made that to build housing for lower income groups is self-defeating if from the beginning it is substandard from the community's point of view. Even under present housing programs, which usually tie housing subsidies to particular units and developments, the expectation is that with improvement in the income levels of occupants, housing subsidies can be removed and those occupying the dwellings can pay market rents which will support the carrying and other charges on the units. In other words, the hope is that subsidies can often be removed over time on subsidized units as the economic standard of the occupants improves. However, if these units are substandard as compared to other units which were built at the start for an unsubsidized market, the units initially subsidized will not be attractive for occupants who find that with increased purchasing power they can buy better accomodation. This kind of problem becomes increasingly worrisome as we shift to subsidy programs based on the housing consumer rather than the housing unit. Under such a system, it will be increasingly difficult, if not undesirable, to contemplate the construction of developments which from the start are at a competitive disadvantage. To do so would relegate them for their useful life to a weak position in the market, and probably doom them to continued occupancy by groups who cannot afford better housing constructed to conventional quality standards.

Once again, finding solutions to this problem is not easy. Apart from other considerations, cost limits on subsidized housing units often force public agencies and subsidized private developers to seek concessions from zoning agencies which otherwise they would not demand. While the problem can be handled by simply requiring all new housing construction, subsidized or not, to conform to all community quality standards, to do so would not only raise housing costs, in some cases substantially, but in the beginning would produce housing not adapted to the needs of its occupants. To put it in terms of our parking problem, developments would be produced with available but unused parking areas that could present troublesome maintenance and supervision problems. While some quality standards are excessive and no doubt could be lowered, the push of public policy in this area is almost entirely in the other direction, especially in connection with amenity features such as landscaping and open space. In other words, the push is in the direction of demanding more and not less from developers in the way of environmental quality. But to do so will only mean an increase in housing costs.

5. *The passive character of zoning regulation as it affects housing location.* It is typical of our zoning system, as it is of the zoning and land use control systems in most democracies, that it functions primarily to create a benevolent environmental setting in which appropriate land use and housing allocations can occur. No institutionalized legal means is provided outside the public housing program by which public agencies can act positively to secure the location of housing units in locations that are considered desirable by public policy-makers. And even public housing agencies, under most legislation, must follow and abide by the zoning decisions of the zoning authorities. There are some court decisions to the contrary, and the problem of zoning override to implement housing goals will receive more explicit attention below. But once more, to move in the other direction and provide by law that all public housing agencies and subsidized housing developers can disregard local zoning allocations, simply creates problems of departure from acceptable zoning standards of the kind considered in the last section. For example, we would want to think carefully whether we would want housing producers to be able to move without restraint to place new housing in areas in which public facilities are inadequate, or in which municipalities would face heavy burdens to provide those facilities which the housing requires.

At the same time, continuing with the present system simply means that housing location decisions are often made on the basis of land availability patterns that may or may not accord with housing policies. For example, land for public and subsidized housing can be obtained at comparatively cheap prices under present law in urban renewal project areas. Availability of cheap land in these locations may lead to the construction of new housing at these points even though ideally it might be constructed elsewhere. From another perspective, community resistance in suburban areas may discourage developers who seek to build housing for lower income groups in suburban locations. Without overriding powers of land acquisition, these developers are left to duel on their own with local zoning authorities, and the legal system is ill-equipped at present to adjudicate the conflicting interests that arise in these cases. Inevitably, the issues are posed as arising between individual developers and the municipality in which the new housing seeks to locate, with little attention to more encompassing regional and even national strategies. To some extent, this problem is also a result of the fact that the autonomous character of local zoning decisions leaves us without a higher governmental level which can or could be equipped to deal with these problems. We are not making choices at this point, incidentally, between housing programs that do or do not aid in the dispersal of racial and economic ghettos. The point to make is that whatever our policy on this issue, its implementation will be difficult indeed unless we have legal instrumentalities which can intervene more psoitively in the land use environment.

Possible solutions for these difficulties are easier to suggest, since quite clearly we need to create authorities at regional if not at state and national levels which have the power not only to plan for effective housing production programs but to carry them out, through land acquisition and development if necessary. But some difficult political problems present themselves, for the choice and creation of such an agency poses some hard problems. Apart from other issues, the creation of yet another independent authority, legally isolated from other agencies with an important role to play in the environment, should give us pause. Problems of balance are also presented. How can we be sure that all interests in the solution of housing problems will be fairly represented in the decisions of so powerful an agency? How can we prevent excessive provision of housing in suburban locations, on the one hand, and an overly restrictive policy limited to inner city locations on the other? For example, it is no secret that public housing authorities utilizing the leased public housing program and private developers taking advantage of housing subsidies have tended to avoid frictional problems by seeing to it that much of their housing intended for racial minorities is either in the ghetto, on its edge, or in transitional areas. Is there any guarantee that our regional or state or even national housing authority will take a bolder stance?

The problem, in the last analysis, is one of control, and finding mechanisms of control is difficult in the Americal legal context, as we have indicated. We can even imagine, at a later day, that outraged civil libertarians might bring a series of court challenges to the practices of a metropolitan housing agency accused of using its substantial powers to locate much of its new housing in unattractive ghetto areas, assuming, that is, that such a policy is really undesirable.

Nevertheless, given the passive nature of the zoning system, we clearly need to fashion public agencies with the legal powers to both assemble needed land for housing construction sites, and either to build the housing that is needed or see that it gets built by the private sector. What is needed is to find some way to accomodate the clash of interest that will necessarily arise in so bold and so innovative a program, and it is here that the problem of zoning override, or of external review of the autonomous zoning decision, becomes critical.

6. *The zoning override problem.* We can now begin to put the zoning override problem in a clearer perspective. Given the importance of zoning density and location decisions and zoning quality standards on housing costs and housing strategies, and given the accepted autonomy of American local governments in the exercise of zoning powers, it would seem clear that some form of overriding governmental review of local zoning decisions is essential if we are to avoid the worst excesses of exclusionary local practices, and if we are to utilize the zoning system more positively in the implementation of housing goals. To some extent, of course, zoning override powers provide a technique which is complementary to and perhaps a substitution for the creation of regional housing agencies with the power actually to build housing at locations where it is considered desirable. In the absence of housing authorities with actual power to build housing, that is, we can substitute some form of outside review of the zoning system to correct what are seen as abuses, and then rely on the private market actually to provide new housing at those sites which the override power makes available.

Unfortunately, some of the characteristics of the zoning system, which we have already noted, make the creation of an appropriate override authority somewhat difficult. Two problems seem paramount. One is that the zoning system in any one community processes vast numbers of cases. Unless we want to take the zoning power completely away from local units of government, we will find that we will have to divide it between the local unit of government initially responsible for the zoning decision and the governmental level which possesses the power to review and to override the decision that is made at the local level. Just how to create a workable division of authority presents some very perplexing problems. Second, the fact that the zoning system has largely evolved into an administrative process in many jurisdictions complicates the override function. Zoning decisions tend to be made on a case-by-case basis, as applications for development are presented. Since it is the content of these decisions as they are applied to actual developments which creates the real issues, any system of override to be effective must be able to deal with individual decisions in individual cases. The trouble here is that the override function, like the zoning system itself, will tend to find itself in a passive developmental role. That is, for the override to be effective, we must be able to find a developer who (1) has been able to acquire land in the locality, and (2) has presented an application for development, and (3) is willing and financially able to carry his case up to the override authority should he be defeated by the local government unit below. An override system of this kind with an appeals feature has recently been adopted in the state of Massachusetts, and has received widespread national attention. The reviewing function has been lodged with an appeals board located in the state's community affairs agency. That state's experience with this system will have to be closely watched.

One another possibility for an override system is to link directly with specific subsidized housing projects, and to locate the override power in the agency which provides the subsidy. A proposal of this kind was put forth by the Kaiser Committee, and would have given the federal Secretary of Housing and Urban Development the power to override contrary local zoning decisions in cases in which they block federally subsidized housing projects. This system depends once more on finding a housing initiative outside the overriding agency, and again carries the danger of *ad hoc* decision making which can possibly be destructive of local zoning and planning policies. Moreover, the very fact that the override power is located at a high federal level which carries considerable political and weight will probably argue for limiting its use to extreme cases. The chances that a federal override alone can provide a routine and easily used method of introducing housing for lower income groups into urban areas would appear remote.

These possibilities do not exhaust all of the variants which are available for the development of override techniques within our present legal system, but one more alternative does deserve discussion. As is well known, the State of Hawaii has experimented with a state land use plan with legal implementation and which, at the state level, blocks out the major areas of urban development. Local powers to administer zoning remain, but must be exercised in a manner consistent with the state zoning scheme. For example, developments at the urban scale may only be authorized within those areas which the state plan has set aside for urban growth.

The problem with this kind of system is that it simply cannot be fine-grained enough to deal with the kinds of zoning issues which are presented by housing developments for lower income families. As we have indicated, zoning issues at these income levels often turn on density questions. At best, a generalized state plan of this type can only indicate the range of densities that are permitted within each of the areas selected by the state plan. For example, it would be possible under this system to indicate generally what areas of an urban region should be developed at the higher urban densities. But the plan cannot indicate at what specific points within this area the local communities should allow housing developments at densities high enough to meet the needs of lower income groups. Decisions on this kind of issue will have to be left to the zoning process as individual applications for development are presented, suggesting once more the need for some attention in an overhaul of the legal framework for the zoning process which will make that process more amenable to external correction.

●   ●   ●

III

Empirical Analysis

5

Eric Branfman, Banjamin Cohen and David Trubek

MEASURING THE INVISIBLE WALL: LAND USE CONTROLS AND RESIDENTIAL PATTERNS OF THE POOR

The poor are not randomly distributed throughout the American metropolis. Within any metropolitan area, some political subdivisions —usually but not always the "central city"—contain a greater than average concentration of residences of the poor, while other political subdivisions—usually but not always the "suburbs"—contain a lower than average concentration. This phenomenon, which we shall call income group clustering, is thought by many observers to be highly undesirable for many reasons. It is seen as a symptom of social disorder, as an indication that constitutional norms are being violated, and as an obstacle to the realization of widely held public policy goals.[1] Consequently, litigation and legislative efforts have been mounted to reduce the degree of income group clustering.[2] A major target of the effort has been suburban land use controls, alleged to be a cause of clustering. The attack has led to judicial consideration of the equal protection issues involved,[3] and has inspired several policy proposals currently under debate.[4]

1. *See, e.g.,* NATIONAL COMMISSION ON URBAN PROBLEMS, BUILDING THE AMERICAN CITY, H.R. DOC. No. 91-34, 91st Cong., 1st Sess. (1968) [hereinafter referred to as DOUGLAS COMM. REPORT]; PRESIDENT'S COMM. ON URBAN HOUSING, A DECENT HOME (1968); Gold & Davidoff, *The Supply and Availability of Land for Housing for Low- and Moderate-Income Families,* in 2 TECHNICAL STUDIES 287 (President's Committee on Urban Housing 1968); HEARING BEFORE THE UNITED STATES COMMISSION ON CIVIL RIGHTS, JUNE 14-17, 1971.

2. For a general discussion of this subject see Shields & Spector, *Opening Up the Suburbs: Notes on a Movement for Social Change,* 2 YALE REV. L. & SOC. ACTION 300 (1972).

3. *See, e.g.,* James v. Valtierra, 402 U.S. 137 (1971), *rev'g,* Valtierra v. Housing Authority, 313 F. Supp. 1 (N.D. Cal. 1970); Dailey v. City of Lawton, 425 F.2d 1037 (10th Cir. 1970); Southern Alameda Spanish Speaking Organization v. City of Union City, 424 F.2d 291 (9th Cir. 1970); Kennedy Park Homes Ass'n v. City of Lackawanna, 318 F. Supp. 669 (W.D.N.Y. 1970), *aff'd,* 436 F.2d 108 (2d Cir. 1970), *cert. denied,* 401 U.S. 1010 (1971). In most of these cases—as is typical of cases attacking "exclusionary zoning" in its many forms—claims both of racial discrimination and of wealth discrimination are raised.

4. For a discussion of some proposals see CIVIL RIGHTS HEARINGS, *supra* note 1, at 828 (Testimony of David M. Trubek).

Until we know more about income group clustering, it is doubtful that the legal issues will be resolved or effective policies shaped. Because much more effort has been devoted to attacking and defending clustering than to understanding it, constitutional debate has been murky, and the potential effects of proposed legislative measures are unclear. This article attempts to fill the gap, by reporting and explaining a statistical study of clustering which we recently conducted.

By surveying American metropolitan areas, the study produces significant evidence that clustering is aggravated by the imposition of public land use controls—such as zoning—in the suburbs. It also suggests that such controls are not typically imposed for fiscal reasons, *i.e.*, to increase the taxable value of real property in the jurisdiction and to exclude low income residents who would heavily burden the jurisdiction's public services. Finally, the study finds that income group clustering is greater the more heavily non-white are the low income groups involved. These findings thus raise but do not resolve the question whether clustering results to a degree from racially motivated public controls. We stress that our conclusions are very tentative, and subject to many qualifications. They are presented not to close inquiry but to suggest the potential fruitfulness—and the limits—of ordinary statistical methods in investigating the etiology of income group clustering.

The First Section of the article identifies various factors which might conceivably explain clustering, and notes briefly how the resolution of several legal issues will depend in part on which factors are in fact operative. The Second Section selects from among the possible explanatory factors several which have especial relevance to constitutional law and social policy and describes our attempt to *quantify* these factors —*i.e.*, to fashion operational "variables" which plausibly represent the factors—so that the relative impact of each factor on clustering could be measured by statistical analysis. In the Third Section, we present and explain the results of our statistical analysis, and in the Fourth Section, we draw conclusions from these results.

I.   Clustering: The Two Questions

A.   *What Causes Clustering?*

Public land use controls may increase the degree of income group clustering in a straightforward manner. Controls—zoning, subdivision regulations, building codes, and the like—raise the cost to a family of living in the controlled jurisdiction: the controls require a family to buy or rent more or better land or dwelling space than it might need,[5] and they simultaneously reduce the total supply of residences in the community, thus creating an artificial shortage of residences, with a resultant rise in rents or sales prices. The poor are excluded because they cannot afford to move in.[6]

But income group clustering might occur even if suburbs were not surrounded by an "invisible wall" of public controls. Private restrictive covenants, running with the land, can control land uses almost as effectively as public controls and may thus constitute an invisible wall of their own. Further, some suburban land owners may individually sell or rent on a racially discriminatory basis, even at a sacrifice to their pecuniary profits: racial discrimination will result in income clustering because non-whites have on the average lower personal income than whites. Finally, some clustering—perhaps a great deal—might occur even if the real estate market were unconstrained by public controls and restrictive covenants and untainted by racial discrimination. The poor may be unable to afford to live in portions of the metropolis which—even in the absence of zoning and covenants—are universally thought desirable and in which, as a consequence of high buyer and renter demand, rents and sales prices are very high. (It is also possible, of course, that the poor *wish* to live among other poor.)

No social or legal policy can eliminate or substantially reduce clustering without addressing its causes. For policy formation, it is thus crucial to discover to what extent the observed degree of clustering in the United States results from, respectively, public land use controls, private covenants, racial discrimination by individual lessors and sellers, and the workings of an unconstrained market in which real properties are of various qualities and buyers have varying tastes and incomes.

---

5. A recent example of the cost-increasing type of requirements through which towns attempt to exclude poorer potential residents is found in Molino v. Mayor of Glassboro, 116 N.J. Super. 195, 281 A.2d 401 (1972). The zoning ordinance required, among other things, that each apartment have central air conditioning and an automatic garbage disposal, that each building have a master TV antenna, that there be an automatic laundry washer and dryer provided for every eight bedrooms, that there be eight square feet of swimming pool or tennis court area for every 100 square feet of living space, and that there be two off-street parking places for each unit, despite the fact that there could be an average of only 1.35 bedrooms per unit.

6. *See* DOUGLAS COMM. REPORT, *supra* note 1, at 214; Aloi, Goldberg & White, *Racial and Economic Segregation by Zoning: Death Knell for Home Rule?*, 1 U. TOLEDO L. REV. 65, 74-80 (1969); Bowe, *Regional Planning Versus Decentralized Land-Use Controls—Zoning for the Megalopolis*, 18 DEPAUL L. REV. 144, 155 (1968); Davidoff & Gold, *Exclusionary Zoning*, 1 YALE REV. L. & SOC. ACTION 56, 60 (1971); Davidoff & Davidoff, *Opening the Suburbs: Toward Inclusionary Land Use Controls*, 22 SYRACUSE L. REV. 509 (1971).

B. *What Motivates Imposition of Public Controls?*

Suppose one had identified and measured the relative weight of the several possible causes of clustering and discovered that public controls were prominent among them. There would remain a second empirical question relevant to the legal and social policy issues raised by income group clustering: What motivated public officials to impose *these controls?* An answer is important because the constitutionality of public controls may depend on the reasons animating their imposition; and because legal and social policies addressed to issues other than clustering may incidentally affect clustering if they strike at the factors which lead local authorities to impose land use controls.

Exclusionary zoning—constitutional attacks: A number of constitutional challenges have been mounted to the use of public land use controls by suburban and other jurisdictions,[7] alleging that these controls prevent minority groups and the poor from residing in suburbs and thus discriminate against them in violation of the Equal Protection Clause. These challenges present difficult doctrinal issues on which the law is both unclear and in substantial flux.[8] Here we aim only to indicate how the empirical issue of causation may affect the doctrinal debate.

The Equal Protection challenge rests on the assumption that state action is denying a constitutionally-protected right. The Equal Protection challengers assert that some lower income and minority groups would reside in jurisdictions imposing controls if the controls were lifted—contending that controls are at least one effective cause of clustering.

The challengers also allege, however, that controls are imposed for constitutionally proscribed motives. The suits thus move beyond the causes of clustering to delve into the causes of controls. To discover or measure what considerations animate the actions of public officials is, of course, a staggeringly complex task. "Motive" is important, however, because the constitutional defect of public controls must be demonstrated, if at all, through an indirect analysis. Public controls which expressly exclude racial groups or raise the cost of housing services beyond the means of expressly identified racial minorities are undoubtedly unconstitutional.[9] Moreover, it is at least arguable that

---

7. *See* cases cited note 3 *supra.*
8. For a discussion of doctrinal problems, see Note, *The Equal Protection Clause and Exclusionary Zoning After* Valtierra *and* Dandridge, 81 YALE L.J. 61 (1971).
9. Zoning lines drawn on racial grounds were outlawed by Buchanan v. Warley, 245 U.S. 60 (1917). *See also* Gomillion v. Lightfoot, 364 U.S. 339 (1960); Dailey v. City of Lawton, 425 F.2d 1037 (10th Cir. 1970). Although no court has considered the issue

explicit exclusion of low income groups is constitutionally suspect.[10] But public ordinances do not admit their purposes so baldly, and public officials typically justify the imposition of controls by reference to constitutionally neutral goals; *e.g.*, protection of health; preservation of property values; maintenance of an attractive physical environment; reduction of pressure on local services, and attraction of land uses which provide a favorable ratio of property tax generated to public services required.[11]

To prevail, challengers of current controls probably must demonstrate that constitutionally permissible motives did not in fact animate imposition of the controls in question. This is a difficult burden: Whether the challenge is mounted on Due Process or Equal Protection grounds, the courts tend to presume the legitimacy of the legislation or ordinance creating the controls and to accept at face value the neutral motives asserted by challenged officials.[12] Further, challengers must probably do more than throw the asserted motives into serious question. They may also have to show at least that among the *actual* motives of the enacting jurisdiction were ones that are constitutionally impermissible.[13]

squarely, it would seem to follow that economic barriers explicitly and specifically created to exclude racial groups would be found to create an invidious classification. Of course, the "fit" between the group excluded and a racial minority would have to be close. *Cf.* Note, *The Equal Protection Clause and Exclusionary Zoning, supra* note 8.

10. *See* Southern Alameda Spanish Speaking Organization v. City of Union City, 424 F.2d 291 (9th Cir. 1970); *But cf.* James v. Valtierra, 402 U.S. 137 (1971).

11. For a discussion of this "fiscal motive," see Josephs v. Town Bd. of Clarkstown, 24 Misc. 2d 366, 368-69, 198 N.Y.S.2d 695, 699 (Sup. Ct. 1960); Becker, *The Police Power and Minimum Lot Zoning,* 1969. WASH. U.L.Q. 263, 282-86, Stuart & Teska, *Who Pays for What: A Cost-Revenue Analysis of Suburban Land Use Alternatives,* URBAN LAND, March, 1971, at 3-16.

12. *See, e.g.,* James v. Valtierra, 402 U.S. 137 (1971).

13. The doctrinal issues are complex. There are some indications that the courts will invalidate a law neutral on its face if it can be shown to be motivated by racial animus. Gomillion v. Lightfoot, 364 U.S. 339 (1960). But there are contrary indications in recent cases. *See* Jefferson v. Hackney, 406 U.S. 535 (1972); Palmer v. Thompson, 403 U.S. 217 (1971). The confusion and difficulty may stem more from the problem of proving motive than from any feeling that racially-motivated but formally neutral laws should stand. In most cases "motive" is difficult to identify: The truly biased legislator or administrator rarely makes his views public. Some cases have suggested that a neutral law placing a heavier burden on racial minority groups than on the populace generally should be presumed to have been motivated by racial animus and thus should fall before the Fourteenth Amendment. *See* Hunter v. Erickson, 393 U.S. 385 (1969), Reitman v. Mulkey, 387 U.S. 369 (1967); Kennedy Park Homes Ass'n v. City of Lackawanna, 436 F.2d 108 (2d Cir. 1970), *cert. denied,* 401 U.S. 1010 (1971); Southern Alameda Spanish Speaking Organization v. City of Union City, 424 F.2d 291 (9th Cir. 1970); Norwalk CORE v. Norwalk Redevelopment Agency, 395 (2d 920 (2d Cir. 1968); Hobson v. Hansen, 269 F. Supp. 401 (D.D.C. 1967). But recent Supreme Court opinions have cast considerable doubt on this principle. *See* Jefferson v. Hackney, *supra;* James v. Valtierra 402 U.S. 137 (1971); Dandridge v. Williams, 397 U.S. 471 (1969). For discussion of doctrinal issues, *see* Brest, *Palmer v. Thompson: An Approach to the Problem of Unconstitutional Legislative Motive,* 1971 THE SUPREME COURT REVIEW 95; Ely, *Legislative and Administrative Motivation in Constitutional Law,* 79 YALE L.J. 1205 (1970).

While the doctrine on *racial* motive and effect is unclear, the law in the area of

The list of impermissible motives is not long. It almost surely includes racial motivation. Whether a motive to exclude low income groups generally is constitutionally impermissible is less certain. We suggested above that an ordinance might well fall if it expressly prohibited or expressly made especially costly the inmigration of low income groups. But it is an open question whether an ordinance which, on its face, merely requires large lot sizes or which prohibits multi-family structures becomes invalid if the motive for its passage is shown to be the exclusion of low income groups.

The question is important because many observers believe that such ordinances are typically enacted for fiscal reasons: to exclude both new low income housing, which adds relatively little to the jurisdiction's property tax base, and the low income inhabitants of such housing, who impose high demands on local public services, especially education.[14] This "fiscal motive" looms large, at least as a hypothesis, because local governments in the United States finance themselves heavily through the local property tax and because these governments are frequently charged with providing services, such as welfare and education, of which the poor make relatively heavy use.[15]

economic exclusion is even more murky. Opponents of exclusionary zoning have reposed great hopes in the development of a doctrine of "substantive equal protection" and in the expansion of this doctrine to cover land-use controls whose intent or effects were to disadvantage the *poor. See, e.g.,* Sager, *Tight Little Islands: Exclusionary Zoning, Equal Protection and the Indigent,* 21 STAN. L. REV. 767 (1969); Note, *Exclusionary Zoning and Equal Protection,* 84 HARV. L. REV. 1645 (1971). These efforts received some encouragement in the lower federal courts; *see, e.g.,* Southern Alameda Spanish Speaking Organization v. City of Union City, 424 F.2d 291 (9th Cir. 1970). But to date the Supreme Court has refused to take this doctrinal step. *See* James v. Valtierra, 402 U.S. 137, 143 (1971) (dissent of Marshall, J.). Since the court has not yet specifically defined any substantive "right to housing" or "access to housing" under the Fourteenth Amendment, judges have given little attention to the constitutional significance, if any, of the existence of an economically segregating motive or effect behind land-use controls and other public measures. Commentators, however, have argued that race and class motives underlie these measures. For critical discussion of the "fiscal motive" theory and suggestions that racial and class motives lie behind land-use controls, see Babcock & Bosselman, *Suburban Zoning and the Apartment Boom,* 111 U. PA. L. REV. 1040, 1068-72 (1963); Davidoff & Davidoff, *supra* note 6.

14. On fiscal motive *see* D. NETZER, ECONOMICS AND URBAN PROBLEMS: DIAGNOSES AND PRESCRIPTIONS 192 (1970); W. ISARD & R. COUGHLIN, MUNICIPAL COSTS AND REVENUES (1957); Margolis, *On Municipal Land Policy for Fiscal Gains,* 9 NAT. TAX J. 247 (1956). *See also* the many studies by which towns determine whether to disallow various types of land use based on cost-benefit analyses, *e.g.,* Stuart & Teska, *supra* note 11; BOARD OF EDUC., SCHOOL DIST. 68, SKOKIE, ILLINOIS, A STUDY OF THE EFFECT OF ZONING ON PUPIL ENROLLMENT AND FINANCIAL SUPPORT OF AN ELEMENTARY SCHOOL; Del Guidice, *Cost-Revenue Implications of High-Rise Apartments,* URBAN LAND, February, 1963, at 3; and the many studies cited in R. MACE, MUNICIPAL COST-REVENUE RESEARCH IN THE UNITED STATES (1961).

15. On "exclusionary" practices, *see* DOUGLAS COMM. REPORT, *supra* note 1, at 199, 212, 214; PRESIDENT'S COMM. ON URBAN HOUSING, A DECENT HOME 14243 (1968); Gold & Davidoff, *supra* note 1, at 59. In 1966-67, forty-three percent of local government revenues were derived from the property tax. By comparison, all other local taxes contributed only 6.8% of local revenues. U.S. BUREAU OF THE CENSUS, 4 CENSUS OF GOVERNMENTS, 1967, No. 5: COMENDIUM OF GOVERNMENT FINANCES, Table 4 (1969).

Both municipal revenues and municipal costs are substantially affected by the type

If a bare motive to exclude low income groups is constitutionally impermissible, the "fiscal motive" is at least suspect. Those who profess it are admitting that they *intend* to exclude the poor and are merely suggesting that their intent is excusable because their ultimate goal, *i.e.*, fiscal benefits for themselves, is "neutral." This is somewhat different from the reasoning which validates public controls imposed for motives such as public health, safety and aesthetics. In these cases, the defendant *disavows* any intention to exclude the poor, and claims that the de facto exclusion of the poor is merely an unfortunate incident of pursuing an unrelated and permissible goal.

At any rate, the constitutional issues surrounding "exclusionary" zoning clearly depend in large part on two distinct factual questions: (1) Do such public controls appreciably contribute to income group clustering (and thus inevitably to racial clustering)? (2) Is the imposition of such controls animated by racial motives, fiscal motives, a non-fiscal motive to exclude the poor, or by clearly permissible "neutral" motives? The answers to these questions will obviously vary both between metropolitan areas and within each area over time. Statistical studies like ours, which attempt to illuminate the issues of causation and motivation for the nation as a whole at a particular point in time, cannot themselves settle the empirical questions that arise in specific law suits concerned with specific controls in specific suburbs.

By showing national tendencies, however, such general statistical studies, if sufficiently refined, can indicate what sorts of rebuttable presumptions the courts ought to entertain. If, for instance, it were shown that public controls and clustering were strongly correlated across the nation, a court might be well advised to impose on the defending local government the burden of proving that, in the specific case at hand, public controls were not in fact the crucial barrier to an inmigration of poor families. Similarly, if a particular motive were shown to animate (or not to animate) controls in many instances nationally, the burden of proof should, arguably, be imposed on the

of land use allowed in the town. Certain uses, such as industry, generate high revenues and require small increases in municipal budgets. Such uses are considered to be good "tax-ratables." Other uses generate low amounts of taxes in relationship to the demands they create for additional services. *See* Schmandt, *Municipal Control of Urban Expansion*, 29 FORD. L. REV. 637, 651 (1961); Barnes & Raymond, *The Fiscal Approach to Land Use Planning*, 21 J. AM. INST. PLANNERS 71 (1955); G. ESSER, ARE NEW RESIDENTIAL AREAS A TAX LIABILITY? (1956); Williams & Wacks, *Segregation of Residential Areas Along Economic Lines: Lionshead Lake Revisited*, 1969 WIS. L. REV. 827, 828-29; Stuart & Teska, *supra* note 11; Williams, *The Three Systems of Land Use Control*, 25 RUTGERS L. REV. 80, 82-85 (1970). According to one study, the effect of lot size on minimum housing cost has been greatly overemphasized. URBAN LAND INSTITUTE, THE EFFECTS OF LARGE LOT SIZE ON RESIDENTIAL DEVELOPMENT (Technical Bull. 32 1958).

party claiming that that motive was absent (present) in the particular case at bar.

Other Attacks on Clustering and Related Measures: Recent court decisions such as *Serrano*[16] and *Rodriguez*[17] have challenged the system of financing education through the real property tax.[18] If the fiscal motive theory is correct, these decisions may eliminate exclusionary land use controls by eliminating the animating reasons for their enactment. If, however, the fiscal motive theory is not a valid explanation for exclusionary practices, it would be rash to expect that educational finance reform will, like Joshua's trumpet, bring down the invisible wall.

Similarly, data on the causes of clustering and the motives for controls are needed to assess proposed statutory remedies for clustering. Any efforts, for example, to structure statutes that might curb the effects of exclusionary zoning must take into account the underlying forces that have led to them.[19] Also, the role of fair housing legislation and other civil rights measures in limiting clustering cannot be predicted until we know whether minority racial groups are frozen out of white suburbs by private discrimination or by "neutral" land use controls, imposed by restrictive covenants or by local governments.

II.   Definitions of Variables and Methods of Study

A.   *The Approach*

Our study, based primarily on census data, measures variations in the degree of income group clustering among America's major metropolitan areas and examines whether these variations are correlated with inter-area variations in factors which we associate, respectively, with the racial motive and the fiscal motive for imposing public land use controls. About this approach, three preliminary comments are necessary.

First, our study presents only a "snapshot" of the United States at a particular point in time. That is, we have been concerned only with differences in clustering between different metropolitan areas, rather

---

16.   Serrano v. Priest, 5 Cal. 3d 584, 487 P.2d 1241, 96 Cal. Rptr. 601 (1971).

17.   Rodriguez v. San Antonio Independent School Dist. (W.D. Tex. 1972), *prob. juris. noted*, 406 U.S. 966 (1972).

18.   *See also* Robinson v. Cahill, 118 N.J. Super. 223, 287 A.2d 187 (1972); Van Dusartz v. Hatfield, 334 F. Supp. 870 (D. Minn. 1971). *Contra* Spano v. Bd. of Educ. of Lakeland Central School Dist. No. 1, 68 Misc. 2d 804, 328 N.Y.S.2d 229 (Sup. Ct. 1972).

19.   *See* CIVIL RIGHTS HEARINGS, *supra* note 1, at 828 (testimony of David M. Trubek).

than with variations in the degree of clustering which occur within each area over time. Trends over time are obviously important for policy analysis, but reliable census data for metropolitan areas are available only decennially, and only the two most recent censuses presented data in a sufficiently detailed manner for our purposes.

Second, our study—like any statistical study—deals only with correlations, *i.e.*, associations, between variables. The fact that changes in variable A are highly correlated with changes in variable B does not itself prove that the changes in B are causing the changes in A. The reverse might equally be the case, or it might be that changes in some undetected variable, C, are causing the observed changes in *both* A and B. Suppose, for instance, that in comparing one city with another we find that, in the latter, people both work longer hours and have shorter life-spans. This bare correlation between work hours and life-span is consistent with three divergent hypotheses: that long hours shorten life, that people who know their lives will be short choose to work long hours, and that some third factor, *e.g.*, poverty, causes both long work hours and a short life-span. Further statistical study might permit us to narrow the possibilities, but at some point we would probably have to invoke experience and common sense to interpret the raw correlations. The correlations we establish in our study often permit of several hypotheses. At times a rough standard of plausibility must be invoked to decide between hypotheses; at other times, we simply leave the question open for further investigation.

Third, our study unfortunately mixes together the two distinct questions which, in the previous section, we noted as being important for purposes of policy: (1) To what extent is clustering caused by public land use controls, rather than other factors—such as restrictive covenants, the racial attitudes of individual sellers and renters, or free market bidding for locations made desirable by factors other than land-use controls? (2) What motivates local officials to impose public land-use controls? An ideal statistical study would proceed in two steps. First, it would measure the correlation between inter-area variations in income group clustering, on the one hand, and inter-area variations in public controls on the other hand. Next, it would measure the correlation between inter-area variations in controls and inter-area variations in factors associated with the possible motives for imposing controls. But such an approach would require, at both stages, quantification and measurement of the extent to which "controls" are imposed in metropolitan areas. We found this an impossible task: controls take myriad forms, from lot size zoning to building codes, and there is no objective method by which all these devices can be compared, measured, and ranked along a single quantitative scale. Even if such an objective method were found—which we think unlikely—the costs in data gathering would be enormous.

Therefore, our approach represents a compromise. Rather than proceeding in two steps, our study probes directly the relationship between various "motives" and clustering. Findings about this relationship require cautious interpretation: some of the factors which we associate with the fiscal and racial motives may themselves operate through the *private* real estate market to aggravate clustering. Thus, if we find that a particular "motive"-factor correlates with clustering, it need not follow that that "motive" in fact animated public officials to impose controls which then caused the observed degree of clustering. Rather, we may merely have isolated a factor which influenced the preferences of buyers toward clustering or which encouraged sellers and renters to discriminate individually or to execute restrictive covenants regarding land use. Despite all these qualifications, however, our study does provide *some* indication that public controls influence the degree of clustering and *some* information about the motives which influence imposition of public controls. Further discussion of our results, however, must await a fuller description of the study itself.

B.   *The Variables*

Clustering (Y): The Dependent Variable

Our first task was to develop a way to measure income group clustering. We decided to look at the patterns of where poor people actually live and to contrast these patterns with a hypothesized "norm" of dispersion. The norm we selected was that the poor people as a percent of municipal population be the same for every town in a metropolitan region. We define the deviation between this arbitrary norm and actual patterns as the degree of "clustering" present.

It was, of course, necessary to define a standard of poverty. Food, housing, and clothing are the major items purchased by the poor. Due to differences in climate and geography, the costs of these items differ in various urban areas. Rather than use the same absolute monetary definition for all metropolitan areas, we defined poverty in relative terms for each metropolitan area. Consider the analysis for 1960. For each metropolitan area, we defined as poor any family which had less than the median family income in 1959, rounded to the nearest one thousand dollars. Thus our "poverty" standard is considerably higher than the $3,000 usually used in government publications.[20] For example, in 1959 the median family income in the New York metropolitan area was $6,696; we round this to $7,000 and consider as poor all families with a 1959 income below $7,000. By this definition, in the New York metropolitan area 54 percent of the families were poor in 1959. We then computed the proportion of poor families in each town in the New York metropolitan area; this ranged, in 1959, from 6.7 percent in East Hills to 79.5 percent in Mastic Shirley.

We next sought to summarize the information about residential patterns in each metropolitan area into a single number, *i.e.*, a clustering index, so that we could compare clustering between metropolitan areas.

To appreciate the complexity of this task, consider two hypothetical metropolitan areas, A and B, each having 100,000 persons:

	metropolitan area A			metropolitan area B		
	total population	poor	poor as percent of total	total population	poor	poor as percent of total
town 1	40,000	10,000	25	38,500	8,500	22.1
town 2	10,000	0	0	11,500	1,500	13.0
town 3	50,000	40,000	80	50,000	40,000	80
	100,000	50,000	50	100,000	50,000	50

In each area town 3, the central city, has half the metropolitan population and has 80 percent of the poor, and each area has two suburbs, towns 1 and 2. Which metropolitan area deviates more from our norm of an equal proportion of poor in each town? From the point of view of the mayor of the central city (town 3), both areas represent an equal degree of clustering, since in both hypothetical cases the central city has 80 percent of the poor. A poor person might consider area B to be less "clustered," since the poor there can live in either of two suburbs, as compared to only one suburb in area A. On the other hand, town 1 in area A is nearer the norm of fifty percent poor than town 1 in area B (and town 2 is further away from the norm in area A than in area B). In constructing an index, what weights should be used to "average" the clustering of town 1 and the clustering of town 2?[21]

20. We chose median income to define the "poor" so as to capture exclusionary effects aimed at buyers and renters of *unsubsidized* "cheap" housing. We did not wish to investigate only the exclusion of low income subsidized housing projects.

21. We could have weighted the clustering of each town by its residential land area, so that towns with a large amount of residential land count for more than small towns. We rejected this scheme because (1) we could not obtain data on the amount of land considered by local observers to be residential in each town in each metropolitan area and (2) the amount of residential land in a town depends on the amount of money available for converting land to residential uses; one could consider a body of water as "residential land," since homes can be built over water.

We also rejected weighting each town by the number of its poor inhabitants, since a town with very exclusionary zoning would have no poor and so receive a weight of

Any set of weights is somewhat arbitrary. We decided to weight the deviation of the poor in each town from the percentage of the poor in the entire metropolitan population by the relative population of the town, *i.e.*, its share of the total metropolitan population. If all the towns in an area met our norm, the index for the area would be zero.

We call the resulting index for each area the clustering index[22] and

TABLE I

Metropolitan Area	1970 Population (thousands)	Median Family Income 1959 $	Median Family Income 1969 $	Clustering Index of Poor Families 1960 Census	Clustering Index of Poor Families 1970 Census
(1)	(2)	(3)	(4)	(5)	(6)
Birmingham, Ala.	739	5,103	8,499	144	206
Los Angeles, Cal.	7,030	7,066	11,286	71	112
Sacramento, Cal.	801	7,100	10,362	107	70
San Diego, Cal.	1,358	6,545	10,133	45	41
San Francisco-Oakland, Cal.	3,116	7,092	11,762	71	129
San Jose, Cal.	1,065	7,417	12,456	78	83
Denver, Col.	1,228	6,551	10,777	39	118
Miami, Fla.	1,268	5,348	9,245	192	227
Atlanta, Ga.	1,390	5,758	10,695	71	171
Baltimore, Md.	2,070	6,199	10,566	111	176
Boston, Mass.	2,754	6,687	11,449	131	179
Detroit, Mich.	4,200	6,825	12,117	130	184
Minneapolis-St. Paul, Minn.	1,814	6,840	11,682	86	169
Buffalo, N.Y.	1,349	6,455	10,430	103	119
Akron, Ohio	679	6,735	11,047	50	98
Cleveland, Ohio	2,064	6,962	11,417	219	236
Columbus, Ohio	916	6,425	10,460	121	122
Dayton, Ohio	850	6,687	11,234	144	198
Pittsburgh, Pa.	2,401	5,954	9,737	142	130
Providence, R.I.	911	5,666	9,929	70	95
Dallas, Texas	1,556	5,925	10,405	59	82
Fort Worth, Texas	762	5,617	10,101	62	98
Seattle, Wash.	1,822	6,896	11,033	40	102
Milwaukee, Wis.	1,404	6,995	11,291	96	156
Chicago, Ill.-Ind.	7,612	7,268	11,841	134	191
Kansas City, Mo.-Kan.	1,254	6,317	10,623	136	142
St. Louis, Mo.-Ill.	2,363	6,275	10,546	228	293
New York, N.Y.-N.J.	16,179	6,696	11,169	129	174
Cincinnati, Ohio-Ky.	1,385	6,318	10,257	118	192
Philadelphia, Pa.-N.J.	4,817	6,433	10,783	135	101
Total of Above	77,157				
Total of U.S.	203,200				
Total of U.S. Metro.	139,400				
Percent of Metro.	55.3				
Percent of U.S.	38.0				

zero. Nor did we want to give each town in a metropolitan area an equal weight since the number of towns in a metropolitan area depends heavily on state annexation laws and historical factors and ranges, in our sample, in 1960 from nine in Akron to 300 in New York.

22. Let p_i be the proportion of the population in town i that is poor and let w_i be the proportion of the metropolitan population living in town i. Let p be the proportion of poor families in the entire metropolitan population. Then the clustering index for a metropolitan area with n towns is

$$\sum_{i=1}^{n} w_i (p - p_i)^2$$

show in columns 5 and 6 of Table I[23] its value for each metropolitan area in our sample for 1960 and 1970.[24]

A comparison of columns 5 and 6 in Table I reveals that the ranking of areas by the clustering of their poor families is similar in both 1959 and 1969.[25] In only four of the thirty metropolitan areas—Sacramento, San Diego, Pittsburgh, and Philadelphia—were the poor less concentrated in 1970 than in 1960.[26]

Our sample consists of the two Standard Consolidated Areas—New York[27] and Chicago—and twenty-eight Standard Metropolitan Statistical Areas (SMSA's).[28] The twenty-eight SMSA's were chosen from among 327 SMSA's other than New York and Chicago on criteria set out in the note.[29] Our sample area contains fifty-five percent of the metropolitan population of the United States in 1970.

For the two hypothetical metropolitan areas in the text, the clustering indices are:
area: A: $.4(.50 - .25)^2 + .1(.5 - 0)^2 + .5(.5 - .8)^2 = .095$
area B: $.385(.50 - .221)^2 + .115(.50 - .13)^2 + .5(.5 - .8)^2 = .0907$

23. In Table I we multiply each actual clustering index by 10,000 to avoid decimals.

24. The 1970 index uses 1969 income.

25. The correlation between 1959 rankings and the 1969 rankings is .71.

26. It is interesting to note that two out of the four SMSA's which showed a decline in concentration of the poor during the decade were in Pennsylvania. This state has consistently restricted local zoning powers more stringently than most other states. Moreover, during the 1960's Pennsylvania courts struck down a number of exclusionary land-use practices, including bans on multi-family dwellings and large lot zoning. See, e.g., Concord Twp. Appeal, 439 Pa. 466, 268 A.2d 765 (1970); Girsch Appeal, 437 Pa. 237, 273 A.2d 395 (1970); National Land & Inv. Co. v. Easttown Twp. Bd. of Adjustment, 419 Pa. 237, 273 A.2d 395 (1970).

27. One might note that New York, which is the origin of much of the publicity on "exclusionary zoning," and is one of the few areas where detailed data on actual zoning policies have been collected, ranked twelfth in the amount of clustering in 1959 and eleventh in 1969.

28. The federal government defines a standard metropolitan statistical area as an integrated economic and social unit with a large population nucleus. More specifically, "each standard metropolitan statistical area must contain at least one city of at least 50,000 inhabitants . . . . The standard metropolitan statistical area will then include the county of such a central city, and adjacent counties that are found to be metropolitan in character and economically and socially integrated with the county of the central city. In New England the requirement with regard to a central city as a nucleus still holds, but the units comprising the area are the towns rather than counties." U.S. Bureau of the Census, Standard Metropolitan Statistical Areas 1967, at vii-viii (1967). The New York Standard Consolidated Area consists of the New York SMSA, Newark SMSA, Jersey City SMSA, Paterson-Clifton-Passaic SMSA, Middlesex County and Somerset County. The Chicago Standard Consolidated Area consists of the Chicago SMSA and the Gary-Hammond-East Chicago SMSA. We use 1960 definitions of each SMSA.

29. (1) The SMSA was among the fifty largest SMSA's as of July 1, 1968;

(2) the SMSA has one city of at least 150,000 population in both 1960 and 1970; this excluded San Bernardino-Riverside-Ontario and Albany-Schenectady-Troy;

(3) the Washington, D.C. SMSA is omitted because the District of Columbia does not receive funds from a state government;

(4) Newark and Paterson-Clifton-Passaic are omitted because they are part of the New York Standard Consolidated Area;

(5) Anaheim-Santa Ana-Garden Grove is not counted separately but is included in the Los Angeles SMSA;

(6) the SMSA (a) has at least fifteen "places" of over 2,500 population (Census data for our variables do not exist for smaller "places") or (b) had nine or more "places" in 1960, with the suburban "places" having at least half

Explanatory Variable—Fiscal Incentives (X_1, X_2, X_3, X_4)

We surmise that individuals and local governments are concerned with the fiscal implications of having poor families to the extent that (1) the local property tax absorbs a large proportion of the local citizens' income, (2) the local property tax is an important source of local revenues, (3) the local government finances a large fraction of local expenditures, and (4) the allocation of state funds among communities ignores the number of poor families in the community. These four factors taken together measure the "strength" of the fiscal incentive for imposing land use controls. We label them X_1, X_2, X_3, X_4 and define them more precisely as follows:

X_1—*property tax burden:* As an index of the importance of the local property tax, for each of the thirty metropolitan areas, we measure the local property tax as a proportion of personal income in the 1950's and in the 1960's;[30] in the 1950's this ranged from 1.7 percent in Birmingham to 5.4 percent in Boston, and in the 1960's from 1.8 percent in Birmingham to 6.1 percent in Boston.[31]

X_2—*municipal property tax dependence:* This measures the percentage of total local government revenues in the entire metropolitan area that accrue from the local property tax. This ranged in the 1950's from 30.5 percent in Birmingham to 69.8 percent in Providence, and in the 1960's from 26.6 percent in Birmingham to 65.8 percent in Providence.

X_3—*local school burden:* On the expenditure side, we examined only education, because it represents the largest single item in the budget of local governments and because it responds more to changes in local population than many other items in the local budget. As a measure of the relative burden on local taxpayers, we used the proportion of expenditures on local schools that is financed by the local property tax. In 1957 this ranged from 18.8 percent in Birmingham to 87.7 percent

the suburban population. (We denote as "suburbs" all places within a SMSA which are not considered by the Census Bureau to be "central cities.") We wish to exclude SMSA's with only a few suburbs unless these few suburbs contain a majority of the population living outside the central city. Thus Akron, Columbus, and Sacramento were included although they contain less than fifteen suburban "places," but the following were excluded: Houston, Phoenix, New Orleans, Indianapolis, Portland (Oregon), Tampa, St. Petersburg, Rochester, San Antonio, Hartford, Louisville, Bridgeport, Memphis, New Haven, and Toledo.

30. The proportion for the 1950's was that found in 1957. The proportion for the 1960's was the average of that in 1962 and 1967. The source of this data is the *Census of Governments*, which was published, during these decades, only in the above years.

31. We do not use the ratio of the property tax to property values because we consider income a superior measure of people's ability to pay.

in Boston, and in 1967 this ranged from 16.1 percent in Birmingham to 81.6 percent in Boston.

X_4—*educational equalization formula:* States allocate educational funds by formulas which, at one extreme, ignore differences in the wealth of local communities and, at the other extreme, enable poor school districts to spend as much as wealthy ones. Because of the absence of an effective objective indicator of educational equalization, we examined the educational aid formulas contained in past and present state statutes and the commentary on many of them contained in the works in this field,[32] and from this information we created a series of ratings of effectiveness of equalization for each state for each year, from 1950 to 1959, and from 1960 to 1969. Ratings from one to ten were assigned, one for a strict flat grant system or the equivalent, ten for a plan in which all aid was equalizing. Theoretically, a rating below one could be achieved, since some aid has been given out in direct proportion to wealth, but no state achieved either this dubious distinction or a rating above nine. For those seven metropolitan areas covering two states,[33] we computed an equalization rating as the rating for each state weighted by the proportion of metropolitan population in each state.

We considered that a state aid formula was more equalizing to the extent that:

(1) A larger proportion of the aid was equalizing aid, rather than flat grant aid, in actual effect.

(2) There were no (or low) floors and no (or high) ceilings on equalizing aid.

(3) There was "negative" aid for especially wealthy districts (found only in Utah).

(4) The local share was a large proportion of total local costs. (Where the local share was particularly low, as in Washington, Georgia, Florida, and Alabama, even though all aid may have been nominally equalizing, some was effectively flat grant, since all districts received *some* aid.)

(5) The state provided no increase in aid to those districts employing better qualified teachers.

(6) The foundation level approached the level of actual costs.

32. J. Burkhead, Public School Finance, Economics and Politics (1964); J. Coons, W. Clune & S. Sugarman, Private Wealth and Public Education (1970); R. Garvue, Modern Public School Finance (1969).

33. Chicago, Cincinnati, Kansas City, New York, Philadelphia, Providence, and St. Louis.

(7) The state matched local effort above the foundation level on an equalizing basis.

(8) The state did not match local effort above the foundation level on a strictly matching basis.

(9) There was special aid for districts with high proportions of children from low income or AFDC families.

(10) Local taxes were levied or redistributed by a larger unit of government, such as the county.

(11) There was special aid for high tax districts.

(12) Actual rather than theoretical costs were used to determine the foundation level.

(13) Aid was not increased for consolidated school districts.

In the 1950's the most equalizing state was Pennsylvania and the least equalizing was Washington; in the 1960's the most equalizing state was Wisconsin and the least equalizing was Ohio.

Note that, if the fiscal motive is important, one would expect this variable to vary inversely with clustering. The other fiscal variables, by contrast, would be expected to vary directly with clustering.

Explanatory Variable—"race" (X_5)

We conjectured that racial discrimination motivates government policy and also affects covenanting and other behavior on the private real estate market. Thus, we calculated the proportion of the metropolitan population in 1960 or 1970 that was either Black or "Spanish Heritage"[34] and predicted that the greater the proportion of these two minority groups in the population, the greater would be income group clustering. In 1960 this proportion ranged from 1.95 percent in the Minneapolis SMSA to 34.6 percent in the Birmingham SMSA, and in 1970 it ranged from 2.7 percent in the Minneapolis SMSA to 38.6 percent in the Miami SMSA.

Explanatory Variable—housing availability (X_6)

We include a low-cost housing "availability" variable, lagged by nine years. We do this for two reasons. First, it helps us measure (and hold constant) the spatial distribution of poor people one decade before

34. We followed the Census Bureau definition as to Spanish Heritage. In 1970 this meant "persons of Spanish language or Spanish surname" in New Mexico, Colorado, Arizona, California, and Texas; "persons of Puerto Rican birth or parentage" in New York, New Jersey, and Connecticut; and "persons of Spanish language" in all other states. In 1960, this meant "persons of Spanish surname" in New Mexico, Colorado, Arizona, California, and Texas and "persons of Puerto Rican birth or parentage" in all other states.

the year in question, and thus to account for the multitude of historical factors peculiar to each metropolitan area. Second, to the extent that, for one reason or another, a community had low-cost housing occupied by families of above median income a decade before our clustering observations, this variable measures the "built-in" ability of the community to increase its proportion of poor families through remodelling, the filtering process, or other forms of "down-grading."

This variable is computed in a fashion closely related to that used to compute clustering. Consider the analysis of housing availability before 1960. We deflate each 1959 SMSA median income by the change in the consumer price index for housing in the metropolitan area during the 1950's.[35] For each locality in the metropolitan area, we then compute the percentage of units which in 1950 could be afforded by poor families living in the SMSA in 1959. We assume that these dwellings include (a) rental units renting for twenty percent or less of the deflated 1959 SMSA median income and (b) owner-occupied units for sale at no more than two times the deflated 1959 SMSA median annual income. The weighted variance in the percentage among the different localities within the SMSA is then computed and serves as our housing availability variable in the 1960 analysis. An analogous procedure is followed for the 1970 analysis.

Explanatory variable—zoning fragmentation (X_7)

There is substantial variation in the "balkanization" of land-use control powers in metropolitan regions. The number of zoning authorities per million persons ranged in 1957 from 3.7 in the Baltimore metropolitan area to 132.1 in the Pittsburgh metropolitan area; in 1967 the number ranged from eight in the Sacramento area to 128.2 in the Pittsburgh area. Under prevailing law each separate authority can act autonomously. We conjecture that the degree of fragmentation of land-use control power should affect the nature of the decisions that are made. The existence of large numbers of small districts may encourage each district to look after its own interests without considering regional impact. The smaller the unit, the more likely that voters will reflect relatively uniform values and interests. All other things being equal, the greater the number of zoning authorities in a metropolitan area, the more clustering should occur.

35. For those eleven SMSA's for which the consumer price index for housing is not published, we use the average housing price index for other SMSA's in the state or, in the 4 cases for which there is no index for any SMSA in the state, we use the national housing price index. Price indices are from U.S. BUREAU OF LABOR STATISTICS, HANDBOOK OF LABOR STATISTICS 1971 Table 118 (1972).

The values for our seven explanatory variables are set out in the Appendix.[36]

III.   Results

The extent of correlation between one variable and a set of "explanatory variables" may range between zero and one hundred percent. In the social sciences correlations are rarely as high as in the natural sciences. For example, the "Coleman Report" on factors influencing student achievement was able to "explain" only about twenty percent of the variation of scores on a verbal test in a sample of 570,000 school pupils in the U.S.[37]

The seven variables in our study together "explain" fifty-five percent of the variation in the dispersion of poor families in our thirty metropolitan areas.[38]

The most significant explanatory variables are the "availability" of housing (X_6), the racial composition of the metropolitan population (X_5), and the number of zoning authorities per million persons (X_7). These three variables all influence clustering in the direction indicated by our conjectures. Our results indicate that the clustering index is larger, all other things equal, (1) the greater the number of zoning authorities, (2) the greater the proportion of racial minorities, and (3) the more concentrated was the housing stock a decade earlier. The proportion of the local school budgets that is financed locally (X_3) is only weakly related to the degree of clustering.

By contrast, the other three fiscal variables—local property tax as percentage of personal income (X_1), local property tax as a percentage of local revenues (X_2) and state educational equalization formula (X_4) —have no statistically significant impact on clustering after the impact of the other variables has been taken into account. (In addition to being statistically insignificant, the coefficient of X_4 is positive rather

---

36. We did not include a variable for the dispersion of jobs for two reasons, one practical and one theoretical. We did not have good data on the physical dispersion of jobs that a poor person might reasonably be expected to fill. As for theory: if all jobs were located in one area and if poor people had equal access to all residential land within the metropolitan area, then we would expect poor people to live in a circle whose center would be the place of employment; if there are several concentrations of jobs for the poor, we would expect each to have poor people living in a circle about it, and our clustering index cannot distinguish these two alternative patterns.

37. OFFICE OF EDUCATION, U.S. DEPARTMENT OF HEALTH, EDUCATION AND WELFARE, EQUALITY OF EDUCATIONAL OPPORTUNITY (COLEMAN REPORT) (1966).

38. The "F ratio" is 9.16, which indicates that the probability that our results could occur by chance is less than one percent.

than, as conjectured, negative and the coefficient of X_2 is negative rather than, as conjectured, positive.)

These results are derived through the technique of least squares regression and are well summarized in a regression equation:[39]

$$Y = .27X_1 - .54X_2 + .82X_3 + 2.83X_4 + 2.93X_5 + .14X_6 + .72X_7$$
$$\quad (.35) \quad (-.61) \quad (1.80) \quad (.62) \quad (3.76) \quad (4.01) \quad (3.09)$$

The coefficient for each explanatory variable indicates its impact on the dependent variable—the clustering index—when all other explanatory variables are held constant. Below each coefficient we indicate in parentheses the ratio of the coefficient to its standard error; the larger the absolute value of this ratio (the T-ratio) the more confidence one has that the coefficient is significant, *i.e.*, that the variable in question has an influence on clustering.[40]

IV.   Legal and Policy Implications: Preliminary Speculations

A—*The Fiscal Motive*

The first, and perhaps clearest, implication of the study for policymaking is negative; we find no substantial relationship between residential patterns and fiscal incentives for imposition of controls. There is some evidence that a reduction in the locally funded share of school expenditures might have some slight impact on residential patterns,

---

39.   Least squares regression is a standard statistical technique for finding the equation which best predicts the dependent variable—in our case, the clustering index of poor families—from the observed values of a group of explanatory variables. The best predictive equation is the one that minimizes the sum of the squared deviations between the predicted values of the dependent variable and the observed values of the dependent variable. Since we are interested in the coefficients of the explanatory variables, we do not report the constant term in our regression equations.

The regression in the text uses the data for both 1960 and 1970. The separate regressions for 1960 and 1970 are consistent with this regression and are available upon request. Some readers of an earlier draft thought that peculiarities of southern states might have led to misleading results on a national basis. However, we get similar results when we omit the five southern metropolitan areas (Miami, Birmingham, Atlanta, Dallas, and Fort Worth). For the twenty-five non-southern metropolitan areas the combined regression is:

$$Y = .36X_1 + .15X_2 + .76X_3 - .95X_4 + 3.08X_5 + .14X_6 + .77X_7$$
$$\quad (.43) \quad (.16) \quad (1.60) \quad (-.21) \quad (3.20) \quad (3.97) \quad (3.39)$$
$$R^2 = .63$$

40.   We judge significance by the size of the T-ratio. Economists tend to consider a variable as insignificant if its T-ratio is less than 2.0. Jencks, in his critique of the Coleman Report data on public Schools, considered a variable as insignificant if its T-ratio was less than 1.0. Jencks, *The Coleman Report and the Conventional Wisdom*, in ON EQUALITY OF EDUCATIONAL OPPORTUNITY 112 (F. Mosteller & D. Moynihan eds. 1972). The size of the coefficient on each explanatory variable depends on the scale on which it is measured; for example, the coefficient for variable X_7 would be ten times larger if it were measured as the number of zoning authorities per 100,000 persons.

but the statistical relationship is quite weak. And the data suggest that changes in the formulas governing state aid to education would have a negligible effect on clustering.

This may mean either that public controls and restrictive covenants are not in fact motivated by fiscal considerations or that, however motivated, controls and covenants have little effect on clustering. In either event, however, our results raise tentative doubts that decisions like *Serrano* and *Rodriguez,* if upheld, would significantly affect clustering. It is premature to say what remedies will be framed in the school financing cases. One remedy would be complete state financing of education. Our sample does not include any system of pure state finance of education.[41] Therefore, it can offer no prediction of what might happen under a radical change of this type.

It is more likely, however, that the school financing cases will precipitate less drastic changes. State aid formulas might be altered so that only a small change is made in the share of school expenditures coming from the local property tax. Our statistical evidence suggests that this approach would not have much impact on clustering.[42] Thus even if every state adopted a system of local finance approximating that of Alabama, whose system seems to present the weakest fiscal motive, we would anticipate no significant change in residential patterns.

B—*Metropolitan Fragmentation*

The strong relationship between clustering and the number of independent zoning bodies in a metropolitan region indicates that the less the public power to control land use is fragmented in a metropolitan region, the less clustering one finds. This finding is quite important. Not only does it lend credence to several theories about local exclusionary behavior; it also provides the clearest evidence we could secure that public controls do, in fact, materially influence the degree of clustering.

41. Hawaii would fit this criterion, but it also has state-wide zoning, so that it does not offer an opportunity to study the effect of educational finance on decentralized land-use decision-making.

42. An extensive series of interviews with planning officials in the New Haven SMSA indicates that finances have little impact on their zoning decisions. Fear of change in the style of the town (sometimes related to fears of change in the racial composition of the population) is the dominant factor for these officials. R. Colloff, Serrano and the Suburbs: The Impact of Education Finance Return on Suburban Zoning Practices (Senior Studies Paper, Yale Law School, May 1972). A recent study of two Boston suburbs concludes that racial and class discrimination, not the fiscal burden, led to the refusal to allow small public housing projects. ENGLER, SUBSIDIZED HOUSING IN THE SUBURBS: LEGISLATION OR LITIGATION? (Joint Center for Urban Studies of M.I.T. and Harvard U., Abstract No. 4, 1971.)

On this latter point, it might be argued that "balkanization" makes residents more aware of the fiscal advantages of excluding the poor and makes it easier for substantial *private* covenant schemes to preserve the fiscal character of political subdivisions. Thus, conceivably, balkanization increases clustering not through its effect on the decisions of public officials but through encouraging private covenants. But this thesis assumes that fiscal incentives are an important motivation for private covenanting behavior, and—as noted above—our results show at most a marginal role for the fiscal motive.

Heavy reliance on the fiscal motive, by contrast, is unnecessary to explain how a more fragmented system of land-use control administration would lead to more exclusionary *public* policies. In any community, there may be interest groups concerned to preserve the status quo—whether this be fiscal, racial, economic class, or environmental. The larger and more inclusive the jurisdiction, the less likely it is that these interest groups will be able to dominate decision-making. Further, communities may exclude the poor not to attain some *absolute* quality of life in the community but only to give the community a *relative* advantage, compared with neighboring communities, as to fiscal structure, aesthetic environment, snob appeal, and the like. That is, exclusion may be a competitive phenomenon, and competition is more likely where there is a multiplicity of competing jurisdictions than where only a few large political subdivisions compose the metropolitan area. In the latter case, a subdivision will know clearly that its practices will be detected by its few "rivals" and that retaliation by them will be virtually certain and usually effective. Moreover, the larger the jurisdiction, the more likely it is that policies must actually be made through public and formal procedures, and the less likely that ethically or legally questionable motives and arguments would affect decision-making. Finally, it is possible that land-use control decision-making is more professionalized in larger entities, reducing the impact on actual decisions of political passions and popular prejudices.

The findings on fragmentation suggest that efforts to dismantle controls, and thereby "perfect" the market, and efforts to impose greater regional and state control over local decision-making, may both reduce income group clustering.

C—Race

When we turn to the racial data, the task of evaluating our findings becomes more complex. The data show that there is significantly more clustering in metropolitan areas with large minority group populations, and thus that clustering is in some sense a racial as well as a class phenomena. What our data cannot determine, however, is whether racial considerations alter the locational preferences of buyers, the selling and leasing decisions of landowners, the incidence of covenants restricting land use, the incidence of public controls or some mix of all of these.

Because the incidence of poverty is greater among minority families,[43] the high-minority SMSA's are areas where a relatively larger percentage of the *poor* are from minority groups. The greater degree of clustering in these areas could, then, be explained by at least four distinct hypotheses:

    (i)   Poor Blacks and "Spanish Heritage" groups have a higher propensity to cluster voluntarily than do the poor of other origins.

    (ii) Racial discrimination by individual sellers and lessors inevitably increases income group clustering in high-minority SMSA's.

    (iii) Covenants restricting land use, while operating to keep out all lower income groups, are *motivated* by fears and dislike of the minority group poor.

    (iv) Public land-use controls, while operating to keep out all lower income groups, are motivated by fears and dislike of the minority group poor.

The first hypothesis is not wholly implausible. Blacks, Chicanos, and Puerto Ricans are generally among the most recent immigrants to urban areas. They may, accordingly, have greater cultural and economic needs for association with others like themselves than those who are further from rural or foreign origins. Or, there may be historical and ethnic factors which cause them to value center city neighborhoods and communities more highly than the white poor.[44]

While the "voluntary clustering" hypothesis is speculative, there *is* evidence that the private real estate market does discriminate against racial minority groups.[45] To the extent that private discrimination keeps the minorities—and thus a large percentage of the total poor in

---

43. Using the Social Security Administration's poverty level of about $770 per person per year, one finds, for example, that in 1964 one-tenth of the whites in metropolitan areas were poor, as compared to about one-third of the non-whites. Non-whites comprised one-third of the metropolitan poor in 1964. Orshansky, *The Poor in City and Suburb, 1964*, 29 Social Security Bull. 25 (1966).

44. We know little of the residential preferences of different racial groups. A recent study indicates that a significantly larger fraction of Blacks than whites moved within a metropolitan area between 1966 and 1969, but many of the Blacks were forced to move. McAllister, Kaiser & Butler, *Residential Mobility of Blacks and Whites: A National Longitudinal Survey*, 77 Am. J. Sociology 445-56 (1971).

45. Douglas Comm. Report, *supra* note 1, at 78-80.

the high minority SMSA—out of the suburbs, it would lead to the higher degree of clustering observed there.

Finally, our findings may mean that clustering is caused by racially motivated public controls or restrictive covenants which erect barriers to the poor generally: that is, suburbanites may perceive that economic integration means racial integration. No town can lawfully adopt general policies that explicitly exclude racial minorities, and covenants phrased in racial terms are unenforceable in the courts. Moreover, it is extremely difficult to operate public land-use controls on a selective case-by-case basis in a way that will effectively keep out minority group members but not other persons of lower income: it would be difficult to identify in advance which units, areas, or developments would be occupied by Blacks. Thus a *class* policy may be the only effective way to achieve *racial* goals.

Since our data are consistent with all four rival hypotheses, further research will be needed to clarify the policy and legal significance of our preliminary findings. A further study we contemplate, when the necessary data are available, will compare the clustering of poor whites with the clustering of poor non-whites. If we find that poor whites are not significantly less clustered than poor non-whites, we will have strong evidence to dispute the first two hypotheses and to support a conclusion that it is racially motivated governmental policies or restrictive covenants which prevent poor minority families from moving to the suburbs. This is so because if the overall clustering of the poor resulted from racial differences in locational preferences, or from racial discrimination by sellers and lessors acting individually, there would be no reason to find a correlation between the proportion of minority group members in the population and the degree of clustering among *whites.*

Even if the first two hypotheses were refuted, however, it would still be necessary to fashion tests to distinguish between the last two. Earlier we noted that our data suggest that public controls do have an impact on income group clustering and that these controls are not motivated significantly by fiscal considerations. It is possible that the racial factor discussed in this subsection affects the incidence only of *private* covenants restricting land use, and that public controls are motivated by *neither* fiscal nor racial considerations but are rather motivated by such "neutral" concerns as health, safety, aesthetics, and the like. But this seems to us unlikely: public controls and private covenants have nearly identical effects and are commonly viewed as interchangeable; that the two devices are animated by totally distinct motives is implausible. Thus, if the presence of racial minorities were correlated with clustering among whites, we would be inclined to conclude that *both* public controls and private covenants are racially motivated to a substantial degree in the United States.

V.   Conclusion

Challenges to suburban land-use controls have made a number of factual assumptions. We found some qualified support for two of those made by the Equal Protection challenges: that public controls do affect the degree of income group clustering, and that these controls may, to an extent, be racially motivated.

While we stress the importance of further empirical research in this area, such research cannot itself resolve the complex questions raised by the challenges. Indeed, the interpretation of empirical findings will often depend on the resolution of normative issues. For instance, further research may show that public controls aggravate clustering but that residential patterns are largely established by differential buyer preferences and purchasing power. To determine *how much* impact on clustering public controls must have before those controls become "troublesome" or "undesirable" is a normative question. Similarly, further research may show that racial considerations and permissible considerations (of health, aesthetics, and safety) *both* animate the imposition of controls in most cases. The question of when a contributing factor becomes a "primary" or an "important" motive is again normative.

The debate on "exclusion" of the poor and of minorities is now too often a matter of flat empirical assertion and of colorful, but imprecise, rhetoric. We need rather a careful dialogue between empirical researchers and those prepared to sort out the subtle, and often conflicting, normative issues at stake.

APPENDIX

Sources for Table II:

X_1: 1957 CENSUS OF GOVERNMENTS, Vol. 3, No. 6, Table 3; 1962 CENSUS OF GOVERNMENTS, Vol. 5, Table 12; 1967 CENSUS OF GOVERNMENTS, Vol. 5, Table 12; SURVEY OF CURRENT BUSINESS INCOME DATA (May 1970); HISTORICAL STATISTICS OF THE UNITED STATES, Table 1; STATISTICAL ABSTRACT OF THE UNITED STATES (1963) Table 433.

X_2: 1957 CENSUS OF GOVERNMENTS, Vol. 3, No. 6, Table 3; 1962 CENSUS OF GOVERNMENTS, Vol. 5, Table 12; 1967 CENSUS OF GOVERNMENTS, Vol. 5, Table 12.

X_3: 1957 CENSUS OF GOVERNMENTS, Vol. 3, No. 1, Table 7; 1967 CENSUS OF GOVERNMENTS, Vol. 4, No. 1, Table 8; various state sources for those states with "dependent" school districts.

X_4: Estimated from evaluation of state statutes and J. COONS, W. CLUNE & S. SUGARMAN, PRIVATE WEALTH AND PUBLIC EDUCATION (1970); R. GARVUE, MODERN PUBLIC SCHOOL FINANCE (1969); J. BURKHEAD, PUBLIC SCHOOL FINANCE, ECONOMICS AND POLITICS (1964).

X_5: U.S. CENSUS OF POPULATION AND HOUSING (1960) Table p-1; U.S. CENSUS OF POPULATION (1970) Table PC(1)-C1, Tables 81, 91, & 96 for pertinent states.

X_6: Computed from U.S. CENSUS OF HOUSING (1950) Tables 21 & 24 for pertinent states; U.S. CENSUS OF HOUSING (1960) Tables 16, 17, 21, 24, & 26 for pertinent states.

X_7: 1957 CENSUS OF GOVERNMENTS, Vol. 1, No. 2, Table 3; 1960 CENSUS OF POPULATION, Vol. 1, Table 5; 1962 CENSUS OF GOVERNMENTS, Vol. 1, Table 15; 1967 CENSUS OF GOVERNMENTS, Vol. 1, Table 19; 1970 CENSUS OF POPULATION, Table PC(1)-C1, Table 13.

TABLE II

(1960 Data)

	X_1	X_2	X_3	X_4	X_5	X_6	X_7
Birmingham, Ala.	16.9	30.5	18.8	5.0	34.63	197.7	44.3
Los Angeles, Cal.	39.0	45.2	52.6	4.0	18.15	98.8	11.4
Sacramento, Cal.	37.2	39.4	35.4	4.0	13.53	150.6	11.7
San Diego, Cal.	33.5	38.6	38.4	4.0	11.84	36.5	11.4
San Francisco-Oakland, Cal.	40.4	48.5	52.2	4.0	18.82	251.7	18.5
San Jose, Cal.	42.8	48.0	49.0	4.0	15.33	95.7	28.6
Denver, Col.	36.3	51.7	70.6	3.2	10.70	6.2	24.3
Miami, Fla.	39.8	49.5	53.6	5.0	16.13	134.4	31.7
Atlanta, Ga.	25.4	49.8	34.0	5.0	22.86	78.2	33.7
Baltimore, Md.	33.4	47.4	72.3	4.0	22.25	17.4	3.7
Boston, Mass.	53.5	63.3	87.7	5.0	3.44	243.6	25.7
Detroit, Mich.	44.6	55.3	53.5	3.3	15.13	141.4	35.9
Minneapolis-St. Paul, Minn.	36.8	56.9	54.6	2.4	1.95	121.7	84.7
Buffalo, N.Y.	43.1	53.7	46.9	5.0	7.26	430.8	51.2
Akron, Ohio	34.5	53.1	78.2	2.2	8.15	66.8	64.7
Cleveland, Ohio	39.5	60.6	80.2	2.2	14.77	642.9	51.2
Columbus, Ohio	26.7	42.5	74.2	2.2	12.01	224.4	70.6
Dayton, Ohio	28.4	49.2	66.6	2.2	10.20	498.8	86.2
Pittsburgh, Pa.	29.3	53.9	44.1	6.0	6.83	156.7	132.1
Providence, R.I.	37.8	69.8	80.0	2.3	1.99	125.8	35.1
Dallas, Tex.	29.1	56.9	54.6	2.5	17.99	242.2	28.9
Fort Worth, Tex.	26.2	49.5	42.3	2.5	14.20	15.2	54.6
Seattle, Wash.	17.9	33.9	34.1	1.8	4.80	22.0	23.5
Milwaukee, Wis.	44.9	54.8	57.2	4.5	8.36	269.9	46.2
Chicago, Ill.-Ind.	37.1	62.4	79.5	5.1	15.35	265.7	46.1
Kansas City, Mo.-Kan.	31.3	54.4	57.8	3.8	11.40	25.2	48.8
St. Louis, Mo.-Ill.	27.8	54.6	65.8	2.8	14.48	333.5	102.1
New York, N.Y.-N.J.	43.7	51.8	69.8	4.8	15.62	197.7	27.9
Cincinnati, Ohio-Ky.	33.4	45.9	76.5	2.5	12.09	192.5	51.2
Philadelphia, Pa.-N.J.	27.8	47.0	66.2	5.7	16.20	97.8	82.1

continued on next page

TABLE II—continued

(1970 Data)

	X_1	X_2	X_3	X_4	X_5	X_6	X_7
Birmingham, Ala.	18.08	26.6	16.1	5.0	29.77	316.9	48.5
Los Angeles, Cal.	51.65	48.8	56.5	4.3	26.76	200.1	13.0
Sacramento, Cal.	52.32	41.4	45.9	4.3	14.78	346.4	8.0
San Diego, Cal.	48.15	41.2	44.7	4.3	17.38	95.4	10.6
San Francisco-Oakland, Cal.	51.53	47.8	53.3	4.3	22.23	325.9	20.1
San Jose, Cal.	60.52	46.1	52.3	4.3	19.20	159.4	19.2
Denver, Col.	46.55	50.5	61.9	4.5	14.35	201.8	29.6
Miami, Fla.	46.51	47.8	40.9	5.0	38.56	351.1	24.9
Atlanta, Ga.	33.18	44.1	36.7	5.0	23.34	15.3	37.1
Baltimore, Md.	40.76	40.4	63.4	5.1	24.56	165.3	9.6
Boston, Mass.	61.30	58.2	81.6	5.9	5.90	502.2	28.9
Detroit, Mich.	44.31	50.6	46.0	5.3	19.36	252.2	35.0
Minneapolis-St. Paul, Minn.	45.79	52.9	53.5	3.5	2.69	262.1	95.6
Buffalo, N.Y.	50.52	46.4	35.8	5.2	8.46	614.0	47.5
Akron, Ohio	41.91	49.8	54.8	2.8	8.60	266.7	60.2
Cleveland, Ohio	47.90	59.4	74.7	2.8	17.14	854.2	46.2
Columbus, Ohio	34.58	43.4	68.0	2.8	12.22	345.5	57.3
Dayton, Ohio	37.52	48.0	64.9	2.8	11.56	296.6	101.4
Pittsburgh, Pa.	32.68	45.6	53.7	6.6	7.11	380.9	128.2
Providence, R.I.	44.66	65.8	70.5	3.0	3.24	86.6	37.7
Dallas, Tex.	36.47	55.0	49.2	3.5	30.28	176.1	57.5
Fort Worth, Tex.	33.52	46.2	39.3	3.5	16.61	78.7	63.8
Seattle, Wash.	27.02	33.4	36.3	3.5	4.61	238.8	37.2
Milwaukee, Wis.	53.17	49.0	65.2	7.5	9.15	400.7	35.2
Chicago, Ill.-Ind.	43.19	57.2	62.9	5.1	22.40	417.6	54.1
Kansas City, Mo.-Kan.	37.24	50.0	53.8	3.8	14.06	362.9	51.2
St. Louis, Mo.-Ill.	36.54	51.0	58.7	3.6	16.93	445.0	97.6
New York, N.Y.-N.J.	49.18	45.0	74.7	5.8	20.72	359.5	25.7
Cincinnati, Ohio-Ky.	38.72	42.2	68.9	3.0	11.49	275.1	73.0
Philadelphia, Pa.-N.J.	33.34	53.2	54.1	6.6	18.39	403.2	74.4

6

John Crecine, Otto Davis and John Jackson

URBAN PROPERTY MARKETS: SOME EMPIRICAL RESULTS AND THEIR IMPLICATIONS FOR MUNICIPAL ZONING

I. INTRODUCTION

GIVEN the growing urbanization of our society, it appears likely that the urban property market will command increased scholarly attention. Aside from the fact of the mere importance of this market in our modern economy, it deserves such increased attention because it seems to be so poorly understood. Of course, it is true that many of the statements defining perfect markets are applicable to this one. There are many small independent buyers and sellers, none of whom usually control the market. Participants can easily obtain good information about prices from real estate agents and classified advertising. On the other hand, the product is far from homogeneous. More important for the present purpose, this market is supposedly characterized by interdependence. Externalities are said to abound. Introspective evidence as well as informal discussions with those persons in the act of selecting housing lend support to the view that "neighborhood effects" indeed exert important influences in this market. The existence of zoning ordinances tends to indicate that society has accepted this view. Consider the following statement of Haig:

It so happens that unless social control is exercised, unless zoning is fully and skillfully applied, it is entirely possible for an individual to make for himself a dollar of profit but at the same time cause a loss of many dollars to his neighbors and to the community as a whole, so that the social result is a net loss. A glue factory on the corner of Park Avenue and 50th Street might show a net profit, considered by itself and ignoring the losses of its neighbors. The truth is that an individual simply by buying title to a single lot should not be given the right to use it as he chooses, whenever by merely buying a lot he does not meet his full site costs. Zoning finds its economic justification in that it is a useful device for ensuring an approximately just distribution of costs, forcing each individual to bear his own expenses.[1]

Others too seem to think that zoning is needed because of the external diseconomies which are supposed to exist in the urban property market. Consider the following statement of Dunham:

Much of the enabling legislation for zoning recognized this distinction between an external cost and an external benefit. Such legislation speaks of "securing" or "preserving," "avoiding" or "preventing" certain enumerated evils as the purpose for which zoning is permitted.[2]

Zoning is based upon the acceptance of the notion that external diseconomies exert important influences in the urban property market.

Despite the widespread acceptance of zoning and the practice of land planning, despite the importance of the urban property market, little if any systematic and scholarly attention has been devoted to the study of available data in an effort to determine the nature and the extent of these externalities or neighborhood effects. This paper aims at exploring this issue. After a brief characterization of zoning and a discussion of the nature of externalities in the urban property market, a model which should be capable of determining the effects of certain kinds of externalities is formulated. The nature of the data is discussed and parameters are estimated. The implications of the empirical results for the phenomenon of municipal zoning are pointed out. A final section contains a summary and proposals for future work.

II. THE METHOD OF MUNICIPAL ZONING

A municipal zoning ordinance, which partly consists of a map, divides a municipality into mutually exclusive "zones" or districts. These areas can be categorized according to use, height, and area restrictions as well as to the allowable exceptions to these restrictions which may be granted by administrative authority. In addition, such an ordinance usually makes provision for variances and other adjustments and spells out certain rules applicable to nonconforming structures and uses.

A typical categorization of zones is shown in Table 1 where only residential categories are stated. Any exhaustive listing would show commercial, institutional, special, and industrial categories also. It should be noted that in the residential categories the higher numbers indicate less restrictiveness on uses. In addition, uses such as churches and schools are generally freely

[1] Haig, Toward an Understanding of the Metropolis: The Assignment of Activities to Areas in Urban Regions (pts. 1-2), 40 Q.J. Econ. 179, 402, 433-434 (1926).

[2] Dunham, City Planning: An Analysis of the Content of the Master Plan, 1 J. Law & Econ. 170, 182 (1958).

allowed as special exceptions. Sometimes an ordinance will further refine these categories or "zones" by attaching additional letters to the indicated names. Thus there might be an R1-A category which would be the same as R1 as far as use and height restrictions were concerned but would require larger lots and yards.

TABLE 1
ZONING CATEGORIES AND RESTRICTIONS

Category	Use Restrictions	Area Restrictions	Height Restrictions
R1	single family dwellings	lot size (5000 sq. ft.) front yard (30 ft.) side yards (10 ft.) back yard (20 ft.)	2½ stories or 45 feet
R2	single family dwellings two family dwellings	same as R1 for single family dwellings and somewhat reduced otherwise.	same as in R1
R3	single family dwellings two family dwellings row houses	dependent upon the use	some as in R1
R4	single family dwellings two family dwellings row houses apartment houses	dependent upon the use	dependent upon the use

To allow for such situations as odd shaped lots, zoning ordinances usually make a provision for the administrative granting of variances and other specified exceptions to the formal rules of the ordinance. In addition, since structures and uses existing at the time of passage or amendment of the ordinance cannot be declared illegal, those not conforming to the provisions of the ordinance are termed "nonconforming" and are governed by specified rules which generally prohibit such things as the expansion of the structure. Thus an area which is zoned R1, for example, might have an existing apartment house in it. This apartment house is simply nonconforming and could continue to exist as such.

III. EXTERNALITIES AND THE URBAN PROPERTY MARKET

If the views of Haig and Dunham are taken as correct, then the economic function of zoning is to remove or at least mitigate the influence of external diseconomies in the urban property market.[3] Supposedly, then, the zoning

[3] See Haig, *supra* note 1 at 433-434 and Dunham, *op. cit. supra* note 2. See also Davis, Economic Elements in Municipal Zoning Decisions, 39 Land Econ. 375 (1963), and Davis and Whinston, The Economics of Complex Systems: The Case of Municipal Zoning, 17 Kyklos 419 (1964), where this view is accepted and some of its implications worked out.

ordinances reflect the external diseconomies. It appears appropriate to explore the nature of these externalities on the basis of the assumption that they are so reflected in the ordinances.

One fact is clear. The ordinances incorporate the notion that the neighborhood or environment around a given piece of property is important. Concentrating this discussion on the single family dwelling, one should anticipate from the ordinances that the external diseconomies operated in the direction of the greater restriction. Thus two family dwellings, row houses, and apartment houses should exert diseconomies upon single family dwellings. Row and apartment houses should negatively influence two family dwellings. Similarly, buildings with relatively small lots and yards should exert external diseconomies upon those residences with larger lots and yards. Tall buildings should negatively influence the relatively shorter ones.

Note that aside from manufacturing uses where noise and smoke might have negative influences and aside from commercial and office uses where congestion might create something of a problem, the externalities under discussion are a matter of taste. There is no physical or technological reason why, say, apartment houses and single family dwellings should not exist side by side. Taste must be the reason why apartment houses are prohibited in an area zoned for only single family dwellings. The possible existence of external diseconomies must depend upon individual valuations of any given property being in terms of the characteristics of the neighborhood.

It should be noted that if the characteristics of a neighborhood affect the value of some given property, then it is possible that some characteristics which are not covered by the zoning ordinances could also have an influence. Examples easily come to mind. One might think that the condition of the other structures in the neighborhood should have an effect. Similarly, whether the neighborhood is "over-crowded" and whether the population is white or non-white might exert an influence.

Finally, it should be observed that for tastes concerning the neighborhood to be sufficiently strong to affect or be relevant to the market, there must be a significant number of prospective buyers with similar taste or with implicit agreements concerning those aspects of a neighborhood which are not desirable. Since urban property markets are rather competitive, it takes more than a few buyers to affect prices. Hence, to assert that external diseconomies exist in the urban property market is to assert that there are significant similarities in taste among prospective buyers concerning undesirable aspects of neighborhoods.

IV. MODEL FORMULATION

It is obvious that the sale of a piece of property means that at least two people have agreed upon the value of that property after all relevant considerations have been taken into account. It has been maintained by Brigham and others that the value of land in an urban area can be expressed as a function of a relatively few factors.[4] Consider the following definitions:

V_i: The value of the ith site.
P_i: The ith site's accessibility to economic activities.
A_i: The "amenities" (including the nieghborhood effects) of the ith site.
T_i: The topography of the ith site.
U_i: The present (and future) use of the ith site.
H_i: Historical factors affecting the utilization of the ith site.

Given these definitions, Brigham asserts that the value of a site is given by

$$(4.1) \quad V_i = f(P_i, A_i, T_i, U_i, H_i)$$

and, using the appraised value per square foot as well as an assumption of linearity, presents empirical results which support his claim. It will be seen that the methodological approach used here is at least partly related to that used by Brigham.

The purpose here is to attempt to ascertain the effects of certain externalities (a part of the "amenities") upon the value of single family dwellings as this value is reflected in market prices. The research strategy is to hold all independent terms in (4.1) roughly constant except for those constituting the A_i. By restricting each of the set of estimates to a relatively small geographic area (a census tract), one roughly holds constant accessibility to the central business district or other economic activities. Further, topography does not vary greatly within a census tract and only a negligible portion of the data referred to units which were classified other than level. Present land use is controlled by considering only the sales of single family dwellings. Future possible use of land is at least partially controlled by holding constant the present zoning in each estimate. Historical factors, at least as this term is used by Brigham, refers to the fact that land was developed in a way which is no longer suitable. For the areas under consideration here, this factor can safely be ignored or at least assumed randomly distributed among the sets of observations.

The relationship between the value specified in an agreement on price between buyer and seller and (at least some of) the externalities influencing that price will be approximated by a single regression equation. Since in any reasonably sized urban area the stock of housing is so large in relation to additions and deletions to it, it probably is appropriate to view the stock as being fixed, even over a period of several years, so that price is a demand

[4] See, e.g., Brigham, The Determinants of Residential Land Values, 41 Land Econ. 325 (1965), and Czamanski, Effects of Public Investments on Urban Land Values, 32 J. Am. Institute of Planners 204 (1966) where value per unit area is used.

phenomenon. It is also worthwhile pointing out that the geographical areas constituting the samples are largely developed. In addition, during the period under consideration (1956-1963), the population of the city (Pittsburgh) from which the samples are taken remained relatively stable. Thus, as a first approximation, one might consider both aggregate demand and supply to be fixed during the period. Under this consideration, the values of various properties differ only because of characteristics associated with the properties and their neighborhoods. It is precisely this relationship which is of interest here. Ideally, if complete data were available, one might specify this relationship exactly. Full data is not available here so that one must be content with a "partial" relationship and assume that the additional factors are taken into account in the error term. Consider the following definitions:

W_i: The market price of the ith property (single family dwelling) divided by the number of square feet in the site.

X_{ij}: The percentage of the total area occupied by the jth land use in the neighborhood (land use block) of the ith property. These uses might be termed "zoning externalities."

Y_{ik}: A measure (percentage) of the kth phenomenon in the neighborhood (census block) which might impose an externality but which is not related (directly) to zoning.

T_i: An index (monthly) indicating the time of sale of the ith property.

β_o: A constant term.

α_j, β_k, δ: Regression coefficients.

ε_i: A stochastic disturbance.

The relationship which is to be estimated can be stated as follows:

$$W_i = \beta_o + \sum_{j=1}^{n} \alpha_j X_{ij} + \sum_{k=1}^{m} \beta_k Y_{ik} + \delta T_i + \varepsilon_i. \qquad (4.2)$$

Note that (4.2) expresses the indicated value of a single family dwelling as a constant term plus influences attributable to zoning type externalities, non-zoning externalities, a time trend, and a stochastic disturbance.

V. On the Observations

The data used to estimate the parameters of (4.2) relate to selected census tracts of the city of Pittsburgh during the period 1956 to 1963. Pittsburgh's Department of City Planning maintains records concerning all transactions of urban property.[5] Since the address (as well as the date) of each parcel

---

[5] The authors are indebted to Pittsburgh's Department of City Planning for supplying the data which made this study possible.

which is sold is recorded, it is possible to relate market prices to land use and census data as is indicated in (4.2).

It should be noted that only transactions where the sales price should reflect considerations relevant to the market were included in the estimations. Since the interest here is in determining the extent to which externalities relevant to the market are present, sales between relatives, for example, should be excluded since the bequest motive might be a dominant motive in the transaction. (Some obvious cases of such a motive were apparent in the data.)[6] Similarly, it was desirable to avoid possible political and other such motives which are not related to the intent of this study.

Other problems (or at least those that could be tackled) with this formulation were handled by careful stratification of the data. Separate regression estimates of (4.2) were made for each of the categories indicated in Table 2.

TABLE 2
BASIC SAMPLES

Census Tract	Zoning Category	Number of Observations
3G and 3H	R4	41
14A	R1-A	74
14A	R1	100
14A	R2	29
17C	R3	66
17C	SO	86
24A	R2	21
24A	R3	49
24A	SO	79
32C	R1	195

It is important to note the reasons for this stratification. The most obvious reason for stratifying by census tract is to control (roughly) the influence of location on price. The fact that the accessibility to the central business district and other economic activities has an influence upon assessed values has been documented several times.[7] One certainly would expect such an influence to obtain in terms of market values. A census tract should be small enough to hold this factor relatively constant.

The reasons for stratifying by zoning category are not nearly so obvious. However, it is clear that the possible use of a site, which might not be limited to single family dwellings alone, could exert an influence upon price. For example, the purchaser might have in mind the possible conversion of

[6] The following types of sales were excluded from the estimations: (1) Sales by the City of Pittsburgh; (2) Sales classified as "other" or "unique"; (3) Sales either to or from Authorities or governmental agencies; (4) Sale of part interest in a property; (5) Sales between apparent relatives; (6) Transactions involving tax exempt property, (either before or after the sale).

[7] See, e.g., Brigham, *supra* note 4 and Czamanski, *id.*

the property to a use different from a single family dwelling, whether or not the seller considered this possibility, and thus be willing to pay a higher price than otherwise would have been acceptable. Stratification by zoning category at least introduces some known control in this factor if the purchaser does not anticipate an alteration in the zoning ordinance.[8]

A second reason for stratification by zoning category is to institute at least a partial control over the amenities associated with a given house. It is well known, or at least well suspected, that zoning categories reflect what property is rather than what it "should be." Even a casual look quickly convinces one that an area zoned R1-A, for example, is likely to contain "nicer" (and more expensive!) houses than an area zoned R1 (not to mention R2, etc.). Stratification by zoning category helps to lessen the possibility of obtaining spurious results from this kind of amenity.

It is obvious, of course, that stratification does not control for all of the amenities associated with particular properties. Even (or especially) single family dwellings are not built in standard sizes and shapes. Although the larger dwellings are more likely to be built in areas zoned as R1 rather than R2, for example, it appeared wise to follow the practice of others and institute the additional control of dividing the sales price by the number of square feet in the site.[9] Thus the dependent variable in (4.2) is stated in terms of dollars per square foot. Aside from this (admittedly crude) control upon the amenities associated with particular properties, no further efforts were practical as closer checks. For example, data on the age of single family dwellings is not available and could not be taken into account. These additional amenities are subsumed into the stochastic disturbance where, if there are no obvious biases, they should merely act to increase the unexplained variance.

There is one additional objection which might be brought against the proposed dependent variable. It might be claimed that market prices are not the relevant consideration. Indeed, this objection might take two forms. First, one might claim that in the urban property market, and especially the market for single family dwellings, sellers might have "reservation prices" which are lower bounds for exchange so that a concentration upon actual transactions might understate the external diseconomies. This objection, however, seems to be of little relevance in view of the time period covered (1956-1963) and of the fact that the externalities under consideration here have no dramatic changes. Second, one might argue that the emphasis upon market transactions results in an understatement of the external diseconomies since owners who are affected might still choose not to sell. Two answers

---

[8] The zoning category of each observation is the one in effect at the time of the transaction.

[9] Both Brigham, *supra* note 4, and Czamanski, *id.*, for example, have followed the practice of dividing by square feet.

are appropriate to this objection. One is that this line of argument must logically imply also that external economies are also understated which, in light of the empirical results, reduces the importance of the argument. The other answer is that interest here is centered only upon external effects which are relevant in the market.

It is obviously true, of course, that available data do not permit an assessment of whether or not all things which might exert external diseconomies actually do exert them. In particular, data on the height of buildings, lot and yard size, etc., are simply not available. According to the zoning ordinances, these features should create externalities; but they have to be ignored here. All that can be considered, from the point of view of the ordinances, are externalities related to uses. In addition, certain other possibilities are included as was previously indicated.

The "zoning externalities," or externalities which should be related to land uses, are operationally defined for the purpose of estimation as the percentage of the total land area devoted to the jth use in the "neighborhood" of the sale of a single family dwelling. "Neighborhood" is operationally (and arbitrarily) defined to be the "land use block" in which the sale took place. Note that when a sale is on the boundary of such a block, this definition does not include the properties across the street. Unfortunately, the data are in such a form as to force this arbitrary definition of a neighborhood.

The other possible externalities are operationally defined from census data to be the percentage of the total dwellings units falling in the kth classification in the "neighborhood" of the sale of a single family dwelling. Here "neighborhood" means the "census block" in which the sale took place. Here too, it is impossible to avoid the problem of the boundary line.

Finally, it should be noted that the time index (in months beginning in January, 1956) is merely a device to pick up the trend in housing prices if there happens to be one in the data.

VI. Interpretations, Expectations, and Trouble Spots

Essentially, expression (4.2) states the price per square foot of single family dwellings as a linear function of time and things supposed to produce externalities. Since, ceteris paribus, relatively lower prices should be associated with increased values of those things imposing external diseconomies and relatively higher prices with increased values of those causing external economies, the estimated coefficients of the independent variables (except for the time index)—that is, the estimated α_j and the β_k—should indicate both the extent and the direction of the influence of those things postulated to cause externalities. In other words, the sign of an estimated coefficient should indicate whether the associated independent variable caused an external economy (positive) or a diseconomy (negative). Similarly, the magnitude of an estimated coefficient gives an indication (subject to statistical error) of the relative strength of the externality since all independent variables (except the time index) are measured in terms of percentages.

It is obvious that if the ordinances are to be taken at face value under this interpretation of the purpose of zoning, then at the very minimum those structures or uses which are not allowed in a particular zoning district (R1, R2, etc.) by implication should be considered to impose external diseconomies upon uses or structures explicitly allowed in the district. Table 3 presents a list of the independent variables along with an indication of whether the zoning code (under this interpretation) implies that particular use should impose an external diseconomy. Predictions for those independent variables

TABLE 3
IMPLICATIONS FOR INDEPENDENT VARIABLES

Variable	Description	Prediction					
	Per Cent of Land Use Block Devoted to:	R1A	R1	R2	R3	R4	S0
X_1	Two Family Residences	—	—	?	?	?	—
X_2	Row Type Housing	—	—	—	?	?	—
X_3	Multiple Family Dwellings	—	—	—	—	?	—
X_4	Special Residences	—	—	—	—	—	—
X_5	Retail Stores	—	—	—	—	—	—
X_6	Commercial Services	—	—	—	—	—	—
X_7	Commercial Auto Parking	—	—	—	—	—	—
X_8	Commercial Wholesaling	—	—	—	—	—	—
X_9	Light Industry	—	—	—	—	—	—
X_{10}	Transportation other than rail	?	?	?	?	?	?
X_{11}	Railroads	—	—	—	—	—	?
X_{12}	Warehousing	—	—	—	—	—	—
X_{13}	Local Government	—	—	—	—	—	—
X_{14}	Public Schools	?	?	?	?	?	?
X_{15}	Cemeteries	?	?	?	?	?	?
X_{16}	Vacant Buildings	?	?	?	?	?	?
X_{17}	Vacant Land	?	?	?	?	?	?
	Per Cent of Dwelling Units in Census Block Classified as:						
Y_1	Group Quarters	—	—	—	—	—	—
Y_2	Deteriorating	—	—	—	—	—	—
Y_3	Dilapidated	—	—	—	—	—	—
Y_4	Non-White	—	—	—	—	—	—
Y_5	Crowded (more than 1.01 persons per room)	—	—	—	—	—	—
	An Index:						
T	Time index (in months) of sale	?	?	?	?	?	?

taken from census data are obvious and are implicitly implied in many publications.[10]

Minus signs in the table indicate that an external diseconomy is expected. A question mark indicates that it is not clear from the zoning ordinance whether or not an external diseconomy is implied. Part of the difficulty is the fact that the land use code does not always classify uses in the same manner as the classifications in the zoning ordinance. A second difficulty stems from the fact that the zoning ordinance allows some uses in almost all districts or categories as a "special exception" so that the use is permitted if and only if the administrative authorities agree. A third difficulty stems from an inherent ambiguity in the zoning ordinances themselves. Does the fact that, say, apartment houses are allowed to co-exist with single family dwellings in R4 districts but not in R1 districts imply that they impose an external diseconomy (upon the single family dwellings) in the latter but not in the former? On the other hand, could it be that apartments always impose external diseconomies upon single family dwellings (as might be implied from R1-A and R1) but that it simply is not "practical" to extend protection in all areas of a city? Finally, note that no presumption is made for the time index since its only purpose is to pick up any possible trend.

Table 3 should make clear that (4.2) expresses the per unit value of single family residences as a linear function of time and things which are supposed to produce externalities. Note especially that it is possible to interpret β_o, the constant term in (4.2), as the "natural" price per unit of "average" single family dwellings in any stratified area where (4.2) is estimated. In other words, β_o represents (excepting statistical error) the price per unit of a single family dwelling in a specified area if there were no external effects or influence of time.

The very list of variables in Table 3, as well as the entries in that table, also reveal two additional problems. First, not all of the signs of the coefficients of the independent variables in the table are predicted. This fact merely reflects the notion that the zoning ordinance does not make "strict implications" in these cases since it allows the uses under the heading of "exceptions" if the administrative authorities decide to issue such a ruling. One can argue, of course, that since such special provision has to be made for these uses, there must be a danger of their imposing external diseconomies since otherwise there would be no reason for the special treatment. Also, little is indicated under the classification SO since in this "special" district almost all uses, including single family residences, are allowed only through the administrative authority of the "special exceptions" clause of

10 See, Davis, *supra* note 3, and Davis and Whinston, *supra* note 3, and Davis & Whinston, Economics of Urban Renewal, 26 L. & Contemp. Prob. 105 (1961).

the ordinance. Thus, it is difficult to say what the ordinance implies in this instance unless one interprets it to mean that every use is likely to impose external diseconomies upon the other ones.

The second problem indicated by Table 3 is that not all the things which might impose externalities are included. Indeed, it has been noted that even those additional features which the zoning ordinances indicate as creators of external diseconomies—namely, the height, lot size, and yard area of buildings in the neighborhood—are not included. Data concerning these features simply does not exist in a form which is feasible for use. Thus those externalities caused by these features must be included in the error term or the stochastic disturbance ε_i. If the proper conditions are satisfied, these omissions should only increase the unexplained variance.

One difficulty which is not indicated by Table 3 is that the dependent variable covers the time span 1956-1963 while the independent variables (with the exception of the time index) refer to a point in time. The land use data (the X's) refer to 1958 and the data from the census (the Y's) refer to 1960. This potentially serious problem was ameliorated first by the selection of only relatively stable census tracts for consideration so that these data will be at least approximately correct. Second, only existing single family dwellings are considered so that the little development which did take place in one of the tracts would not prove to be a factor. Third, sales to public authorities (as well as specified other sales) were eliminated in order to account for the possible influence of redevelopment which infringed upon one of the tracts. Finally, if any remaining changes are randomly distributed among the observations, the result should be only an addition to the unexplained variance.

Finally, observe again that the "individual amenities" of the single family dwellings such as age, improvements, details of construction, etc., are omitted from the data. Thus the stochastic disturbance ε_i also has to account for these influences. Again, if the proper conditions are satisfied, these omissions should only increase the unexplained variance.

The above paragraphs should make clear that one should not expect to obtain exceptionally good fits in the empirical estimations of (4.2). Nevertheless, despite all difficulties, if the externalities implied by the zoning ordinances and other sources do exist in the urban property market, and if these forces are strong and of the nature implied by this formulation, then empirical estimations should reveal these forces for the variables included here.

VII. The Empirical Results

Six census tracts were selected for the empirical testing. Two of the tracts, 3G and 3H, were combined since they are adjoining and together make up a distinct "section" of the City of Pittsburgh. These two tracts constitute a Negro ghetto area commonly called "The Hill." On the other hand, tract 14A covers a part of a very high-class neighborhood where a majority of the residents are of a Jewish cultural background. Many of the residents of tract 17C are of Polish or German origin and can be characterized as blue collar workers. Tract 24A, although located in a different area of the city than 17C, has many similar demographic characteristics. Tract 32C comprises an area with a large Italian population. These people have an income somewhat above the city median and many own their homes. Table 4 gives some data related to the characteristics of the housing and the population of these areas. These data should make clear the diversity of the samples.

TABLE 4
SOME CHARACTERISTICS OF SAMPLE TRACTS

Tract	3G+H	14A	17C	24A	32C
Percentage owner-occupied	15.0	60.0	58.0	54.0	84.0
Average number of rooms of owner-occupied units	5.15	8.20	5.10	5.20	5.60
Average number of rooms of renter occupied units	2.75	4.40	3.60	3.70	4.40
Percentage non-white units	90.3	00.2	01.5	01.5	01.5
Percentage crowded units	18.9	02.7	17.0	13.2	05.3
Percentage deteriorating units	50.5	02.6	24.9	40.2	04.9
Percentage dilapidated units	25.6	00.0	06.9	04.4	00.1
Population of tract	8535	5137	4506	5168	3634
Number of census blocks in tract	63	31	35	81	58

Of course, several difficulties are to be expected in making the empirical estimations of (4.2). Observe that the dependent variable in (4.2) is the result of a sale of a single family dwelling while the independent variables (except for the time index) refer to the block in which the sale took place. Thus if several sales take place in one block, differing values of the dependent variable correspond to the same values of those independent variables which refer to the given block. While this fact causes no difficulty from the point of view of the theoretical characteristics of the estimating procedure, it is (or was) a matter of practical concern. If, for example, several sales take place in the only block of a given tract which has a cemetery and an apartment house; then these two uses (cemeteries and multiple family dwellings) are perfectly correlated so that the problem of collinearity appears. The procedure followed when such an instance was encountered (as well as in instances where there was high but less than perfect correlation between independent variables) consisted of an arbitrary choice of one of the variables for inclusion and the deletion of the other. Since it is impossible to determine whether it was the included or excluded variable which exerted a possible influence in such instances, the empirical results relating to specific independent variables should be interpreted with caution in such instances and reference should be made to the notes for Table A which is presented at the end of the text. It should be mentioned, however, that after the indicated variables were deleted very little correlation between the independent variables remained so that, at least on this score, the estimates given in Table A should be highly reliable.

An inspection of Table A reveals several interesting facts. First, the magnitudes of the estimated coefficients vary across both zoning districts and census tracts. Second, and of even greater importance, the signs of the estimated coefficients also vary. The very method of zoning, with its categories of zones or districts with specified restrictions, would seem to imply a certain "uniformity" of taste so that whatever constitutes an external diseconomy in one R1 district, for example, also constitutes an external diseconomy in any other R1 district. The results reported in Table A cast serious doubt upon this uniformity assumption. The fact that the signs of estimated coefficients of a given independent variable differ across district and tract suggests that the use which causes an external diseconomy in one district might cause an external economy in another.

Since the method of restriction inherent in zoning indicates external diseconomies, the appearance of positive signs (indicating external economies) in Table A is not to be taken lightly. This result casts serious doubt upon the major assumption (the presence of uniform external diseconomies) of one of the basic economic arguments supporting the imposition of restrictive zoning upon the use of urban land. Excluding the time index, 49 of the estimated coefficients are negative (generally agreeing with the predictions) and 49 are positive (not agreeing). If those variables which are based upon census data are excluded so that only land use variables remain, then 32 of the estimated coefficients are negative and 33 are positive. Certainly, this evidence cannot be interpreted as supporting the notion that external diseconomies exist uniformly across uses in the urban property market.

The fact that there is such an even split between the positive and negative signs of the estimated coefficients suggests an alternate hypothesis concerning the results. It may be that the results are "random." In other words, suppose that the independent variables under consideration here impose neither external economies or diseconomies upon single family dwellings. In such an instance one might view the set of observations as being random in the sense that the dependent variable is "truly independent" of the explanatory variables. If one considers drawing a random sample of such a set of observations from, say, a multivariate normal distribution in which all covariances are zero and then running a regression on these observations, one would expect to find that some of the coefficients were significantly different from zero. In fact, one should expect that 10 per cent of the coefficients would be significantly different from zero at the 10 per cent level of significance. Similarly, 20 per cent should be significantly different from zero at the 20 per cent level. In fact, if the distribution is centered at zero so that one expects 50 per cent of the coefficients to be negative and 50 per cent positive and if one measures in units of 10 percentage points from the level of none to absolute significance, then 10 per cent of the estimated coefficients are "expected" to fall in each category. Table 5 presents these categories with the expected and actual numbers of coefficients falling into each. The coefficients for the time index are omitted here since they are of no interest.

TABLE 5
NUMBERS OF EXPECTED AND ACTUAL COEFFICIENTS IN TERMS OF SIGNIFICANCE LEVEL

Significance	0 to	10 to	20 to	30 to	40 to	50 to	60 to	70 to	80 to	90 to 100
Expected	9.8	9.8	9.8	9.8	9.8	9.8	9.8	9.8	9.8	9.8
Actual	17	6	6	8	12	10	8	8	7	16

Although there is some concentration at the two ends of the distribution, the actual results do not differ greatly from what is expected under the hypothesis of randomness. A Chi square goodness of fit test performed upon the data of Table 5 gives a statistic with the value 14.44 which, with 9 degrees of freedom, is not significant at the 10 per cent level. Therefore, it appears that the results reported in Table A do not support the notion that external diseconomies (or external economies) abound in the urban property market. Instead, these results suggest that there is a great deal of independence in that market.

VIII. APOLOGIES, RATIONALIZATIONS, AND IMPLICATIONS

The fact that the empirical results suggest independence rather than interdependence as a characteristic of the urban property market should not be interpreted as meaning that there are no externalities in that market. Indeed, the empirical results only indicate that there was no evidence in support of the existence of externalities of the kind with which the model was concerned. In other words, it may be that the measure, or the implied distance over which influences extend, is simply incorrect.

Recall that the independent variables related to zoning were defined as the percentages of the land use block devoted to the existing uses. There would seem to be two possibilities. Suppose the external effects extend beyond a block. In this instance these neighborhood effects should "increase" the unexplained variance. However, the influence certainly should extend within the block in this case so that if the effects were at all important, then they should have been reflected in the estimated results.

Another possibility is that the neighborhood effects are so local that they are essentially a "next door" phenomenon. This case could certainly be compatible with the results obtained here. However, if the externalities are so local, then the entire method of modern zoning would seem to be in need of reconsideration.

A final possibility worthy of consideration here is that the urban property market is not characterized by great interdependence and that externalities do not abound in that market. In fact, the economic literature on zoning often seems to cite only extreme cases where interdependence is obvious. Consider, for example, the quotation from Haig which was cited in the introduction of this paper. Haig mentions a glue factory on the corner of Park Avenue and 50th Street. Presumably, few persons would deny that there might be an externality associated with the glue factory in the suggested location. However, one might ask why a glue factory would find it desirable to locate on the corner of Park Avenue and 50th Street when cheaper and seemingly just as desirable alternative locations are available. The point to be considered is the suggestion that a natural process of self selection in location decisions helps to remove what otherwise might be extreme interdependence from the urban property market.

In the market for single family dwellings one must admit to a process of self selection which helps to remove the externalities relevant to the market. The fact that persons consider the neighborhood around a dwelling as important in the decision concerning the purchase of a house does not automatically mean that externalities exist in the market. Similarity of taste among prospective purchasers in regard to uses and features which are undesirable (considering only diseconomies) in the neighborhood is the necessary and sufficient condition. If there is differing taste among prospective purchasers, then the mere fact that the seller and the buyer are both seeking the best possible individual deal acts to minimize the negative neighborhood effects in the market. Buyers finding certain uses or features undesirable in a neighborhood simply search for alternative dwellings; and those finding the same uses and features desirable (or at least less undesirable) tend to be better prospects for location in the given neighborhood. Thus in a situation without pervasive similarity of taste a natural process of self selection tends to reduce the interdependence in the market.

The possibilities which are discussed above do have certain implications for the phenomenon of municipal zoning. If there is true independence in the market, at least with respect to a great many of the uses normally associated with residential areas, the present methods of zoning appear to be far too detailed. It should be possible to place far greater reliance upon the market mechanism and yet achieve desirable allocations. True independence or the lack of externalities taken together with the other characteristics of this particular market suggest that it should function rather efficiently so that the greater part of the regulations are not necessary if zoning is designed to protect properties from suffering from external diseconomies.

On the other hand, suppose that the neighborhood effects are so local that they are essentially a "next door" phenomenon. In this instance too the methodology of modern zoning would appear to be somewhat less than fully appropriate. Emphasis should not be upon the neighborhood. There would seem to be little reason to attempt to create homogeneous districts with the aid of the modern restrictions of municipal zoning. Instead, zoning should be aimed at aiding the market to function efficiently. With such local external diseconomies it should be possible to create independence in the market through the use of other kinds of restrictions which do not require elaborate planning. One might think, for example, of requiring fences, hedges, or other kinds of obstructions to be built around those types of uses or structures which impose the local external diseconomies so that the neighborhood effects will be stoped at the boundary of the offending property. Given this artifically created independence, there would be no reason to designate certain areas for specified types of uses as is the present practice since the market could be trusted to achieve the appropriate allocation.

IX. CONCLUDING COMMENTS

The evidence which was examined in this paper casts doubt upon the notion that neighborhood effects abound in the urban property market. The evidence suggests independence rather than interdependence. Of course, one cannot claim that this evidence is conclusive. The data are far too limited and the methods are far too crude for that. Uses exist which are not found in this data because the uses did not exist in the areas which were studied. These uses may impose serious external diseconomies. Similarly, those features such as height and area restrictions which are including in zoning ordinances but were not considered here because of the lack of data may also impose negative neighborhood effects. Nevertheless, the fact that externalities could not be identified from the available data raises some serious questions concerning the supposed pervasiveness of neighborhood effects in the urban property market.

The evidence examined here also raises some serious questions concerning the methodology of the modern practices of municipal zoning. If the neighborhood effects do exist but are local so that they could not be observed by the methods used in this paper, then present zoning methods would appear to be less than fully appropriate. Efforts should be made to find restrictions which create independence in the market. It should be mentioned that in Taiwan it is a common practice for upper class residential parcels to be separated from surrounding properties by a high brick wall. It is reported that the Taiwan Provincial Government in an act called "Measures for Implementing Air Defense Dispersion and Methods for Controlling the Construction of Buildings in Major Cities of Taiwan Province" requires this brick wall around homes and other structures of more than one floor in height if they are located in specified districts.[11] It would be interesting to see whether this practice causes full independence in the market.

There would seem to be little doubt but that the evidence reported here suggests that the entire practice of zoning and land planning needs to be reconsidered. Consider the following quotation:

. . . [S]ince the war most European countries, under pressure of reconstruction, have relied more on direct governmental control of development and less on the formalized systems of control. Probably none has gone so far as Britain in abandoning written standards and relying on discretionary control under the general guidance of a development plan. The United States, however, is the one country where the traditional system remains unimpaired, and it is interesting to see the efforts being made to adapt it to the conditions of modern development . . .[12]

While the evidence reported here is not extensive enough to be fully conclusive so that additional studies on this issue are needed, could it be that the European countries are even more mistaken than the United States in not relying more fully upon the pricing mechanism to perform the appropriate allocations in the urban property market?

[11] Yukon Keng, Metropolitan Planning in Taiwan, Republic of China 21-22 (1964).
[12] Delafons, Land Use Controls in the United States 38 (1962).

TABLE A

		3 G + H R4	14A R1A	14A R1	14A R2	17C R3	17C SO	24A SO	24A R2	24A R3	32C R1
No. Observations		41	74	100	29	66	86	79	21	49	195
F Statistic		1.877	1.645	1.655	.276	4.377	5.714	1.575	3.922	1.181	1.961
Multiple R		.728	.475	.377	.238	.767	.713	.490	.792	.510	.295
Constant Term		4.817	4.534	4.418	5.593	3.466	—6.369	2.113	1.489	2.842	3.367
Two-family	B	.339	.060			.141	.092	—.009		—.014	—.222
	T	1.530	1.042			1.178	.756	.368		.306	—1.313
Row Type	B	—.014	.109	.572	—.199	—.191		.088		.081	
	T	.097	1.601	1.946	.356	.694		1.780		1.189	
Multiple Family	B	.187	—.117			.132	.045	.008	.188	—.529	—.058
	T	.786	.002			3.005	.476	.151	.001	—1.436	—1.010
Special Residence	B	—1.736	—.019	.307	.597	2.924					
	T	.514	.001	1.648	.870	.476					
Retail Sales	B					—.069	.844	.075		—2.026	
	T					.000	.495	.657		—1.660	
Comm. Services	B	.446						—.325			
	T	.183						.781			
Comm. Auto Parking	B		—1.567	—.809	.758	.096	.261				
	T		1.489	.856	.128	.347	3.495				
Comm. Wholesaling	B					—.549					
	T					.001					
Light Industry	B	—.147				.105	3.066				
	T	.361				.159	2.410				
Other Transport	B					1.269					
	T					.211					
Railroad	B							—.130	.482		—.115
	T							.691	.041		—1.002

TABLE A (continued)

		3 G + H R4	14A R1A	14A R1	14A R2	17C R3	17C SO	24A SO	24A R2	24A R3	32C R1
Warehousing	B	4.448						.085			
	T	1.915						.530			
Local Government	B			—.205		.184				.177	
	T			—1.403		—1.034				.965	
Public Schools	B		.139			10.141	.209				
	T		1.704			.000	1.195				
Vacant Buildings	B	—.494									
	T	—.889									
Vacant Land	B	—.142	—.104	—.273	.133	.008	—.009	—.027	—.013	—.025	—.031
	T	—.640	—1.636	—2.036	.311	.163	.493	—2.443	—.001	—1.371	—2.562
Time Index	B	.149	.002	.003	.030	—.005	.008	—.002	.022	.004	.005
	T	2.698	.297	.563	.477	—.867	1.756	—.291	2.909	.590	.634
Group Quarters	B	.034		.011			.076			—.027	
	T	.345		1.191			3.540			—1.315	
Deteriorating	B	.307	—.320	—.123		.083	—.165	.001	—.086	.040	.031
	T	2.712	—.001	—1.414		.546	—2.902	.338	—.002	1.056	.400
Dilapidated	B	.238				—.318	—.745	—.010		—.048	.411
	T	2.176				—.247	—3.729	—.303		—.777	.719
Non-White	B	—.409	—.320				.600	—.013			—.091
	T	—2.516	—.000				3.420	—.262			—1.436
Crowded	B	.387	—.040	—.533		—.170	.630	.020	.070	—.025	.071
	T	.995	—.001	—1.653		—.580	2.660	.751	.002	—.231	.678

NOTES FOR TABLE A

Area	Variables omitted	Cor. Variable	Correlation
3G + H, R4	Comm. Auto Parking	Non-White	— .907
	Comm. Wholesaling	Light Industry	.765
		Group Quarters	.703
	Local Government	Warehousing	.945
14A, R1A	Group Quarters	Special Residences	.771
14A, R1	Cemeteries	Multi-family	1.000
	Two-Family	Row Type	.840
	Multi-family	Deteriorating	.851
14A, R2	Local Government	Deteriorating	1.000
		Crowding	1.000
	Deteriorating	Crowding	1.000
	Group Quarters	Special Residences	.991
	Two-family	Special Residences	— .837
	Crowding	Two-family	— .809
17C, R3	Group Quarters	Special Residences	1.000
	Non-white	Public Schools	1.000
17C, S0	Special Residences	Group Quarters	1.000
	Comm. Wholesaling	Comm. Retail Sales	1.000
	Local Government	Group Quarters	.999
	Row Type	Two-family	.785
24A, S0	Local Government	Comm. Services	1.000
	Institutions	Comm. Warehousing	1.000
	Light Industry	Comm. Retail Sales	.901
24A, R2	Comm. Warehousing Institutions	Comm. Retail Sales	1.000
	Retail Sales	Vacant Land	.776
		Dilapidation	.957
		Crowding	.863
	Dilapidation	Crowding	.834
24A, R3	Comm. Services	Comm. Retail Sales	1.000
32C, R1	None omitted		

7

Norman Williams, Jr. and Thomas Norman

EXCLUSIONARY LAND USE CONTROLS:
THE CASE OF NORTH-EASTERN NEW JERSEY

It has been clear for some time that the principal direct public controls over land use (zoning, subdivision control, etc.) are often employed to exclude large groups of people from access to good residential areas on racial and/or on economic grounds. Long a subject for sharp debate, on both moral and constitutional grounds, such exclusionary land-use controls have now suddenly been recognized as a major national problem. There are two reasons for this. The first is the great need for housing, especially for more new low- and moderate-cost housing. The pressure for such housing has obviously been increasing in recent years, but the seriousness of this problem is not generally recognized; from now on this pressure is certain to increase much more rapidly, as more of the children born in the post-war years reach the marriageable and child-rearing ages.[1] Second, most of the vacant land readily available for housing is located in the outer suburban areas, and in recent years most of the desirable new jobs have been gravitating to the same areas. At the same time, the land-use controls which affect the construction of housing and its cost in those suburban areas have become increasingly restrictive. Since the cost of housing has

Most of the data in this article was compiled through a study financed by a grant from the Department of Housing and Urban Development under Section 701.

Norman Williams is a Professor of Urban Planning, Rutgers University.

Thomas Norman is a member of New Jersey Bar.

Mr. Richard Lewis of the Rutgers Department of Urban Planning provided important research assistance in the preparation of this article.

1. For example, in New Jersey the number of births per year jumped in 1946 to over 150 per cent of the average of the 1930's, and grew steadily thereafter, passing 200 per cent in 1955 and reaching a peak of about 220 per cent for the years 1958-1964. While the figure has dropped substantially since, it remains close to 200 per cent. The number of marriages twenty years later has been following a similar curve. The important role of in-migration does not come out clearly is so simple a calculation.

been rising rapidly for several reasons,[2] each additional increment of cost at the present time is increasingly serious in its exclusionary effect. The motivation behind this trend to more restrictive land-use controls is no doubt mixed, probably with some variation both as between different areas and as between different types of potentially exclusionary devices. However, it seems clear that three separate sets of considerations are involved: the desire to retain an open semi-rural environment; dislike of lower-income groups generally; and the desire to avoid the substantial local tax burden which (under our system) is the normal penalty for permitting large-scale residential development. Moreover, not far in the background, major racial issues loom paramount: as is all too obvious, the large concentration of low-income blacks is in our central cities, while the white middle class is increasingly concentrated in the suburbs.

While this problem has been coming to a head for a long time,[3] widespread public realization of its importance is largely a matter of the last year or two. Plenty of broad generalizations are now available on the subject as well as some excellent rhetoric,[4] but there is precious little hard data on the precise nature and extent of the problem and on the precise role played by various devices. It is time—in fact, the time is long overdue—for a detailed land-use and economic analysis of the problem. Such an analysis would (a) determine how much land is suitable and/or available for residential development, (b) analyze the extent to which such land is subject to various potentially exclusionary land-use controls, and (c) determine the actual impact of such land-use controls upon the availability of low- and moderate-cost housing. The data resulting from the first stage of such an analysis has just become available in New Jersey.[5]

---

2. Costs have been rising for all three major factors in housing construction—the cost of labor and materials, the cost of borrowing money, and the cost of land. Under these circumstances, a successful program for low- and moderate-income housing requires much more than making land available. On the other hand, much can be said for the proposition that there is not much point in spending time to work out the financial details of such a program, if there is no assurance that land will be available where such housing can be built.

3. Several commentators caught the essential point fairly quickly after *Lionshead Lake v. Wayne Township*, 10 N.J. 165, 89 A. 2d 693 (1952), *appeal dismissed*, 344 U.S. 919 (1953), cited in n. 32 *infra*. See Crolly and Norton, *Public Health and Minimum House Size*, 72 Regional Plan Association Zoning Bulletin 1 (1954); Haar, *Zoning for Minimum Standards: The Wayne Township Case*, 66 Harvard Law Review 1051 (1953); Haar; *Wayne Township: Zoning for Whom? In Brief Reply*, 67 Harvard Law Review 986 (1954); but compare Nolan and Horack, *How Small a House?—Zoning for Minimum Space Requirements*, 67 Harvard Law Review 967 (1954); Williams, *Zoning and Planning Notes*, The American City Magazine, February, 1951 at 129, October, 1951 at 130, and November, 1951 at 131, all reprinted in Williams, *The Structure of Urban Zoning*, pp. 125-36 (1966). For a discussion of the problem in a broader context, see Williams, *Planning Law and Democratic Living*, 20 Law and Contemporary Problems 317 (1955). For a more typical example of thinking of that period, see McClory, *The Undersized House: A Municipal Problem*, 27 Chicago-Kent Law Review 142 (1949).

4. A number of recent newspaper and/or magazine articles have suggested that the problem derives primarily from requirements for very large residential lots—and, conversely, that if these requirements can be reduced, most of the problem will be solved. The analysis below casts serious doubt on the validity of this approach.

5. The study from which these figures are derived was carried out in the Division of State and Regional Planning of the New Jersey Department of Community Affairs; and many of these figures were published (in a slightly different form) in a recent message sent to the legislature

The generalizations in this article apply only to the area analyzed, the outer suburban ring in north-eastern New Jersey. Similar studies in other areas are much needed, and the conclusions resulting from such studies might (or might not) be somewhat different. In one way it may be true that New Jersey is a special case. The state government historically has played a relatively small role in helping municipalities to finance local services;[6] and so in New Jersey the pressure has been unusually strong for municipalities to engage in "fiscal zoning"—i.e., to use land use controls to attract "good ratables," primarily non-residential development, and to discourage "bad ratables", primarily low- and moderate-cost housing.

Any serious planning analysis depends upon a series of assumptions, stated or unstated. This article proceeds upon the following assumptions:

1. The principal public responsibility—and the principal reason for public concern—in this area is to make sure that land is available for low- and moderate-cost housing. However, because of the prospect of a general housing shortage, the extent to which land-use controls may also restrict the production of housing for higher-income groups is worth mention in passing.

2. A principal dynamic force behind the increased demand for housing in the 1970's and 1980's will be the large groups of young people who will be reaching marriageable age and forming families during that period.[7] The increasing number of old people will also play an important role.

3. Because of the increased costs of housing, multiple dwellings[8] are now the most important form of new housing for low- and many middle-income families, with the possible exception of mobile homes. However, the various restrictions affecting single-family detached housing may be important for some middle-income families; and such restrictions will become very important if public and semi-public programs are enacted to provide such housing for those lower down in the income

---

by Governor William T. Cahill. (A Blueprint for Housing in New Jersey, December 7, 1970). Much credit is due to Governor Cahill for his courage in publicly facing up to a difficult problem. The technical specifications for the study were prepared by the authors of this article, and Mr. Norman was in charge of detailed supervision of the study for a substantial period of time. The actual methodology used is summarized in Appendix A below.

In order to get a clear picture of the nature and the impact of exclusionary zoning, two additional studies are necessary; and preparations for such additional studies are now under way in the Rutgers University Department of Urban Planning. In the first of these studies, the various restrictions revealed by the state's study would be translated into actual housing costs, in order to demonstrate precisely the impact of each device, and to see which devices are the most damaging. The second would analyze the motivation for the adoption of various potentially exclusionary devices, from the political-science viewpoint. In this latter study special emphasis would be given to the ways by which land not originally zoned for multiple dwellings is made available for that purpose—i.e., by rezoning, special permit or variance—and the conditions imposed as the price of such permission.

Until such further studies are completed, the conclusions suggested in this article can be regarded only as reasonable tentative hypotheses.

6. In 1969 New Jersey ranked ninth among the fifty states in municipal expenditure (per capita) for primary and secondary education—and forty-first in state aid (per capita) for such education.

7. See n. 1 *supra*.

8. The term is used here loosely to include various forms of non-single-family detached housing, including garden apartments, town houses, and various as-yet-unknown types of modular housing.

scale—either by revised financing arrangements, or as a result of a major break-through in the cost of housing.

4. There is at least some chance for the development of new types of industrial-ized housing in the next decade or two.

5. In the future, as in the recent past, the main area for the growth of employ-ment, particularly of industrial employment, will be concentrated along the major transportation corridors[9] in the outer parts of the metropolitan area. The growth of industrial employment is of course particularly important to housing demand be-cause of its multiplier effect: that is, one industrial job will support several people, whose needs will normally result in the creation of other jobs, particularly in the service trades, which in turn will support other families with their own needs, etc., etc. In the service trades employment normally expands along with population, even in areas with little industrial employment, but with much less of a multiplier effect; and in the near future such service employment is likely on a statewide basis to expand more rapidly than industrial employment.

6. Residential land located near the principal areas of employment growth is particularly appropriate for residential development to serve those who are working in such areas.

For the purposes of this analysis, then, "exclusionary" land-use controls are defined to include those controls which appear to interfere seriously with the avail-ability of low- and moderate-cost housing where it is needed. Controls which restrict the availability of housing for higher-income groups but do not have a particularly significant effect on low- and moderate-income housing will be referred to as "highly restrictive", but not as exclusionary.

The Four Outer Ring Counties

The survey in question is concerned with the entire state of New Jersey, and (as of the date of writing) has been completed for eight counties. This article summarizes and analyzes the results in the four most important counties in northern New Jersey—Morris, Somerset, Middlesex and Monmouth. In traditional planners' jargon, these counties make up almost all the outer ring around the western edge of the New York-New Jersey Metropolitan area.[10] As indicated in Table I, these counties are dominant in the New Jersey sector of that metropolitan area, both in recent and in probable future growth. Moreover, these counties have by far the largest area of conveniently-located vacant land which is available for future growth of both residence and employment.

Each of these four counties has a distinctive personality of its own. The two northern counties, Morris and Somerset, are located predominantly in the rolling hills of the Piedmont; the other two, Middlesex and Monmouth, lie almost entirely

---

9. More specifically, in those parts of such corridors where public water supply and sewerage are available.

10. Upper Bergen and upper Passaic counties are of course also part of this ring, but are omitted here. Bergen is very important, but is now almost entirely built up. Upper Passaic is remote, hilly, and relatively small. The survey has not completed work on these two counties; if it had, it is unlikely that the results would be materially affected.

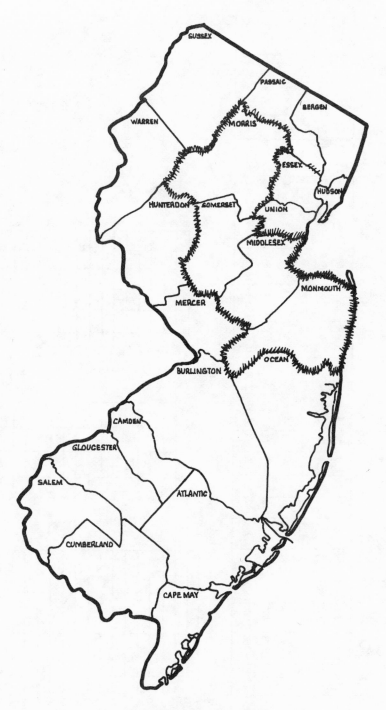

Four-County Area of Analysis

TABLE I
The Four Counties—Relevant Statistics

County	Population[1] (add 000)		Estimated[2]		Dwelling Units[3] (add 000)		Industrial Employment[4] (add 000)				New Industrial Construction[5] (Square feet, add 000)							Medium Family Income[7]				Developable Vacant Land Zoned Residential[8] (Acres)
	1950	1960	1970	1980	1950	1960	1954	1958	1963	1967	1959-65	1966	1967	1968	1969	1970[6]	1966-70	1950	Rank in State	1960	Rank in State	
Morris	164	261	380	571	53	82	17	26	31	38	7,018	1,603	1,006	1,200	840	1,005	5,654	$3,377	(5)	7,696	(3)	106,609
Somerset	99	143	197	283	27	42	15	18	19	28	2,060	667	964	290	1,615	1,255	4,791	3,385	(4)	7,484	(4)	87,479
Middlesex	264	433	576	842	76	125	65	66	76	82	14,245	3,416	2,499	4,287	3,583	3,769	17,551	3,392	(3)	7,054	(5)	56,784
Monmouth	225	334	454	655	82	115	14	14	20	24	3,707	635	564	756	802	422	3,170	2,777	(13)	6,413	(10)	154,923
4 Counties	753	1,173	1,609		240	366	112	125	147	174	27,030	6,321	5,033	6,533	6,840	6,451	31,178					
New Jersey	4,835	6,066	7,089		1,501	1,998	787	794	829	894	85,020	23,040	16,676	18,824	18,798	15,263	92,601	3,285		6,786		

1. Federal Census, 1970.
2. Projections calculated by Bureau of Research and Statistics, Department of Environmental Protection, State of New Jersey, 1969.
3. Federal Census, 1960.
4. Census of Manufactures.
5. An Annual Report of The New Jersey Department of Labor and Industry, State of New Jersey, 1970.
6. This figure represents the first 10 months of 1970.
7. Federal Census.
8. See Table II.

Square feet (800,000) — Middlesex, Morris, Somerset, Monmouth; 36, 33, 31, 29, 27, 25, 23, 21, 19, 17, 15, 13, 11, 9, 7, 5, 3, 1, 0; 1959-1965, 1966 1967 1968 1969 1970

Industrial Employees (000) — Middlesex, Monmouth, Morris, Somerset; 89, 84, 79, 74, 69, 64, 59, 54, 49, 44, 39, 34, 29, 24, 19, 14, 0; 1954, 1958, 1963, 1967

Population (000) — Middlesex, Monmouth, Morris, Somerset; 908, 850, 800, 750, 700, 650, 600, 550, 500, 450, 400, 350, 300, 250, 200, 150, 100, 50, 0; 1950, 1960, 1970, 1980

in the coastal plain. The northern-most county, Morris, is the most diversified. A large area of predominantly hilly terrain contains a wide variety of types of settlement, ranging from rather tired old semi-industrial towns to vast new single-family suburban developments, a substantial estate area, considerable new employment in open areas, and one massive concentration of garden apartments. Somerset County, the next adjacent one, is sharply split in character. The hilly northern part is dominated by an estate area, where fox-hunting reportedly lingers. In the southern part a substantial area of relatively flatter land is still predominantly rural, but with many widely-scattered new suburban subdivisions. The secondary transportation corridors running through both Morris and Somerset counties are being strengthened by construction of interstate highways, and employment has been increasing rapidly in both counties, including a belated but marked pick-up in industrial development in Somerset. Middlesex County, somewhat more homogeneous, is dominated by its location along the east coast's main New York-Philadelphia-Washington transportation corridor. Since the county has both a long industrial tradition and substantial areas of vacant land suitable for industry, Middlesex has become the principal growth area in New Jersey for industrial employment, particularly in the part of the county north of the Raritan River where there is still substantial vacant land. The section south of the Raritan, while still predominantly vacant, is now rapidly building up with both residential subdivisions and a considerable amount of industrial development. In sharp contrast, particularly to Somerset, Middlesex has been primarily a workingman's county; it has long been one of the Democratic strongholds in the state. Monmouth County, comprising the whole northern New Jersey seashore and a large inland area, is also markedly different. Originally a resort area, with scattered pockets of poverty in older towns, it is now rapidly undergoing development with standard subdivisions. While somewhat off-center in terms of primary transportation facilities, Monmouth has much the largest area of available vacant land.[11]

This analysis indicates that the main corridor running through Middlesex County is the most critical area in the New Jersey outer suburban fringe with respect to accommodating the need for low- and moderate-income housing. Since the substantial amount of vacant land available in Middlesex County may still be relatively small,[12] this corridor also necessarily includes adjacent areas in western Monmouth and southern Somerset. A decision on what is the next most important area would depend upon considerations far beyond the scope of this article—essentially upon the decisions involved in a realistic plan for growth of employment in the state. Each of the other three counties has a secondary transportation corridor, and a case can be made for and against each of these three. Morris has the second largest volume of employment, but it is both hilly and remote from the main corridor in Middlesex.

---

11. In most of these counties the principal corridor of development runs roughly through the center of the county; and so, assuming the desirability of providing housing fairly near employment, such housing would normally be accommodated within the same county. A county-by-county analysis is therefore fairly realistic. The exceptions to this are relatively minor: the corridor through Monmouth is near the ocean, and so the result is the same, but southern Somerset is close to the main Middlesex County corridor.

12. As compared to empoyment growth.

Somerset and Monmouth are a bit out of the way, and have long lagged in employ-ment. Yet industrial construction has recently been increasing rapidly in central and southern Somerset, and this trend is likely to continue as transportation facilities improve. On the other hand, the northern part of that county is hilly terrain, and, historically, a high-cost area. Monmouth is a bit off the main line and has had the smallest growth in employment. Yet Monmouth has the largest area of easily devel-oped vacant land, immediately adjacent to southern Middlesex, plus the undoubted attraction of living near the shore.

Six Exclusionary Devices

The New Jersey survey covered what are probably the six most important types of potentially exclusionary suburban land use controls and analyzed the extent to which these are applied to the available vacant land in the state.

1. MINIMUM-BUILDING-SIZE REQUIREMENTS

Minimum-building-size-requirements are normally requirements for minimum floor space. Requirements for a larger house have the most obvious and direct influence on housing costs. For example, assuming average building costs of roughly $20 per square foot for tract housing (which may be optimistic), a requirement for a 1200-square-foot house has practically the same effect as a requirement for houses costing about $24,000.[13] The cost of the lot and of site development must of course be added, so that the actual figure would probably be around $30,000.

2. THE EXCLUSION OF MULTIPLE DWELLINGS: SINGLE-FAMILY RESTRICTIONS

Among those architects and planners who have a special interest in housing costs, there has long been widespread consensus that the most promising opportunity for good inexpensive housing is to be found in some form of multiple dwellings. With the recent sharp rise in housing costs, this is probably even more true nowadays. Such housing may take a variety of different forms, and more may be available in the future—garden apartments, "town houses,"[14] and various developments in "mod-ular housing," which may be coming as a result of the hoped-for industrialization of the building industry.

3. RESTRICTIONS ON THE NUMBER OF BEDROOMS

When multiple dwellings are permitted, the number of bedrooms is often restricted, either by the zoning ordinance or by informal pressure. The most frequent provision requires that 80 per cent of the dwelling units shall have only one bedroom, and permits up to 20 per cent with two bedrooms—and none with more. The fiscal motiva-tion for such restrictions is obvious. Equally obvious, multiple dwellings subject

---

13. As usual, things are not quite that simple. For example, the kitchen is normally the most expensive part of a house, so that adding more bedrooms does not increase the cost exactly in proportion; and there may be economies in framing in a larger space. On the other hand, larger houses may have to have higher-quality features, in order to sell.

14. "Town houses" is simply a more polite term for row houses (single-family attached), which have not conventionally been regarded as a form of multiple dwellings.

to such restrictions do not provide the type of housing needed by most families of normal size.

4. PROHIBITION OF MOBILE HOMES
Such homes now provide the only new inexpensive housing available in most areas,[15] except for some public housing in the cities. They are efficient, readily available, and unnecessarily ugly.[16]

5. FRONTAGE (I.E., LOT WIDTH) REQUIREMENTS
The costs of site development, particularly for street paving and sewers, are fairly substantial, and so requirements for wide lots do affect the cost of housing noticeably. The impact of this factor depends of course upon whether high standards for site development are imposed in subdivision control—and how high they are. Obviously, if curbs and storm sewers are also required, the cost will go up substantially. On the other hand, it is lot width, probably even more than lot size, which tends to preserve that much-desired semi-rural atmosphere.

6. LOT SIZE REQUIREMENTS
While this device has attracted most of the attention, its actual impact is questionable.[17] This point is analyzed at some length below.

The Extent of Exclusionary Zoning

The survey covers all the available vacant land in the four New Jersey counties, and the results are set forth in Table 2. The picture is so clear-cut that it may be summarized rather briefly.

The first and most obvious conclusion is that substantial land is available for continued expansion in the outer ring of metropolitan counties in New Jersey. In these four counties, about 400,000 acres (625 square miles) of developable vacant land are zoned for residential use.[18] Nearly 40 per cent of this total is in Monmouth County; much smaller areas are available in the other three counties, and Middlesex has the smallest of all, with only about 14 per cent of the total. Over and above this total, a substantial amount of additional vacant land (about 40,000 acres, or 10 per cent more) is zoned for non-residential development (industrial, office and research, and commercial), but with residential development also permitted.[19] The

---

15. Though the low initial cost (around $8000-$10,000) conceals the costs involved in rapid obsolescence and low or no resale value.

16. In design, and usually in siting.

17. Larger lots are usually, though not necessarily, also wider—although the two sets of requirements are not always correlated. As indicated above, wider lots do involve a considerable addition to the housing cost; but this is because of the width, not because of the area.

18. From here on, the figures given on the amount of land which is available (or zoned) refer to the amount of readily-developable vacant land which is zoned for residence, except where otherwise specified. The methodology used in the survey is set forth in Appendix A.

19. Both the amount of such land, and the likelihood of its being developed for non-residential instead of residential use, vary as between different counties. In both Middlesex and Monmouth, the additional area of such land is about 10 per cent of the amount indicated in

TABLE II

The Extent of Exclusionary Zoning in Suburban North-Eastern New Jersey

	MORRIS Acres	MORRIS Percentage	SOMERSET Acres	SOMERSET Percentage	MIDDLESEX Acres	MIDDLESEX Percentage	MONMOUTH Acres	MONMOUTH Percentage	TOTAL Acres	TOTAL Percentage
1 Total Land	305,728		195,264		197,626		305,286		1,003,904	
2 Unsuitable for Development	177,200		88,357		93,853		115,305		474,715	
3 SUITABLE FOR DEVELOPMENT	128,528	of Line 3.	106,907	of Line 3.	103,773	of Line 3.	189,981	of Line 3.	259,189	of Line 3.
4 Office & Research	5,993	4.6	3,146	2.8	1,388	1.2	734	0.006	11,261	2.0
5 Commercial	2,985	2.3	1,881	1.8	3,704	3.6	10,854	5.84	19,424	3.7
6 Industrial	12,941	9.9	14,401	13.4	41,899	40.3	23,470	12.3	92,711	17.6
7 RESIDENTIAL	106,609	83.3	87,479	82.0	56,784	44.9	154,923	81.7	405,793	76.7
		of Line 7.		of Line 7.		of Line 7.		of Line 7.		of Line 7.
8 MULTI-FAMILY	1,322	0.8	0	0.0	307	0.006	633	0.004	2,262	0.5
9 MOBILE HOMES	0	0.0	0	0.0	0	0.0	0	0.00	0	0.0
10 SINGLE FAMILY	105,287	99.2	87,479	100.0	56,477	99.04	154,290	99.006	403,531	99.5
11 Minimum Bldg. Size		of Line 10.		of Line 10.		of Line 10.		of Line 10.		of Line 10.
12 Under 700 sq. ft.	0	0.0	14,156	16.1	83	0.1	0	0.0	14,239	3.5
13 700 - 999	13,769	13.0	6,406	7.2	6,572	11.4	1,757	1.1	28,504	7.1
14 1000 - 1199	21,604	20.6	1,689	1.8	17,912	30.9	1,375	0.9	42,580	10.6
15 1200 - 1599	64,059	60.8	62,776	72.3	10,392	20.0	120,019	77.7	257,246	63.8
16 1600 & Over	5,760	5.5	1,971	2.1	21,499	37.6	26,627	17.4	55,857	13.8
17 No Requirement	95	0.09	481	0.5	19	0.0	4,512	2.9	5,107	1.2
18 Minimum Lot Width										
19 50 - 99 linear ft.	1,728	1.5	11,700	13.4	5,194	9.0	1,918	1.2	20,540	5.0
20 100 - 149	47,680	45.3	4,439	5.0	37,496	66.6	14,006	9.0	103,621	25.5
21 150 - 199	30,885	29.3	30,438	34.8	7,150	12.6	11,977	7.7	80,450	20.1
22 200 & Over	24,994	23.9	40,901	46.8	6,637	11.8	122,101	79.4	194,633	48.3
23 No Requirement	0	0.0	0	0.0	0	0.0	4,288	2.7	4,288	1.1
24 Minimum Lot Size										
25 Under 10,000 sq. ft.	359	0.2	218	0.3	2,796	4.9	1,600	1.0	4,973	1.2
26 10,000 - 19,999	4,464	4.1	359	0.4	5,183	9.0	6,033	3.8	16,044	3.9
27 20,000 - 39,999	14,141	13.3	12,140	13.8	26,618	47.1	19,573	12.8	72,472	17.9
28 40,000 - 79,999	52,012	49.8	52,550	60.0	21,880	39.0	98,745	64.0	225,187	55.6
29 80,000 - 119,999	11,277	10.6	658	0.7	0	0.0	26,912	17.4	38,847	9.6
30 3 Acres & More	23,034	22.0	21,554	24.6	0	0.0	1,427	1.0	46,015	11.8

percentage of the developable vacant land which is zoned for industry in three of the four counties (Morris, Somerset and Monmouth) is fairly consistent, ranging between 10 and 13 per cent; the figure for Middlesex, 40 per cent, is strikingly different, and sharply underlines the different character of that county.[20]

MULTIPLE DWELLINGS

As indicated above, from the viewpoint of low- and moderate-income housing, the most important dwelling type for the coming years will be multiple housing. The amount of land zoned for that purpose[21] is miniscule—about thirty scattered vacant tracts, with a total area of a little over 2000 acres or one-half of one per cent of the land. The location of these tracts is shown on Map II. Of this area, just over half is in Morris County,[22] with two-thirds of the remainder in Monmouth, an even smaller amount in Middlesex, and none at all in Somerset. A considerable number of multiple dwellings are being built in New Jersey, and it is probably true that some additional land is made available by rezoning, variance, or special permit.[23] A substantial addition, in fact a somewhat larger area (3300 acres) is potentially available for multiple dwellings, in areas where such construction is permitted in industrial, office-and-research, and commercial districts. Two-thirds of this additional area is in Middlesex County, most of it in a ribbon-commercial zone in one township. In fact, in that county the land available for multiple dwellings in such non-residential zones is more than six times as large as the land where multiple dwellings are permitted in residential zones. The underlying attitude towards apartments and apartment dwellers is clear enough.

RESTRICTIONS ON THE NUMBER OF BEDROOMS

When land in these counties is made available for multiple dwellings, the normal practice nowadays is to restrict the number of bedrooms to one or two per dwelling unit, in an attempt to make sure that such buildings will not be occupied by families

---

Table II above. It seems probable that a substantial part of such land in Middlesex County would end up in industrial use, while this is less clear in Monmouth County. The amount of such additional land in Morris and Somerset Counties is far smaller, about 3 per cent.

20. Over-zoning for industry (and for office and research) is known to be widespread in New Jersey, incuding Middlesex County—so much so that such over-zoning may itself act as a new exclusionary device.

21. In a few other towns the zoning ordinance provides that multiple dwellings may be authorized as a conditional use.

22. In one rural municipality, substantial areas are zoned in widely-varying districts to provide for multi-family use, for 3-acre single-family homes, and for various intermediate-lot-size zones which do not have very high requirements on building size—largely as a result of the unusual attitude and the persuasive abilities of the local mayor. The mayor's attitude was due in part to the fact that his son returned home from the armed services, got married, and then was unable to find a place to live in his own home town. Using this incident as the crux of his argument, the mayor persuaded the town council to establish four districts in the town where garden apartments could be built on vacant land.

23. Individual apartment buildings can be developed on small tracts, with 10,000 square feet or more; and undoubtedly considerably more land is available in scattered vacant tracts (with less than five acres) within developed areas, which were not covered by this survey. On the other hand, development of such small tracts is often less easy, and such tracts are also frequently zond against multiple-dwelling development.

Approximate Locations of Residential Areas in which Multi-Family Housing is Permitted by Right.

with school children.[24] As far as new housing needs for normal-sized families are concerned, such construction is therefore of little help. Of the rather small amount of land zoned to permit multiple dwellings, 83 per cent is covered by such bedroom restrictions.[25] Where such restrictions exist, by far the most common ratio requires at least 80 per cent of the dwelling units to have only one bedroom; up to 20 per cent may have two bedrooms.[26] However, the range of ratios runs from 65-35 to 90-10. A very few towns permit a small number (5-10-20 per cent) of 3-bedroom units.

MOBILE HOMES

Perhaps the most striking fact to emerge from the survey is that in these four counties mobile homes are completely excluded—both as of right and as conditional uses—from every municipality[27] except three.[28] The three exceptions are not significant ones, so no acreage is shown as available on the table. In one remote township, mobile homes with wheels removed are regarded as single-family houses; but almost all of this entire township (except for an industrial zone) is zoned to require that all houses have a minimum building size of 1500 square feet, on one-acre lots, with 200 feet of frontage. In two other townships mobile homes are permitted as conditional uses. In one of these, also in a remote area, mobile homes are a conditional use in all districts.[29] Moreover, a single township in the main corridor through Middlesex County permits mobile homes as a conditional use in a light industrial district, provided that the total area used for mobile homes may in no event exceed 120 acres. The area involved is a strip extending along one of the most heavily-traveled (and ugliest) land-service highways in the East, U.S. Route 1 between New Brunswick and Trenton. A few rather dismal mobile home courts now exist in this area; no one would call this a satisfactory residential environment.

---

24. The ordinance in one town actually limits occupancy in such buildings to one pre-school-age child per dwelling unit, and forbids any occupancy by school-age children.

25. Including all the land so zoned in Morris, and more than half of the land in Middlesex and Monmouth. The percentage covered by such restrictions is even higher in those cases where multiple dwellings are permitted in non-residential districts. Where multiple dwellings are a conditional use, about one-half of the ordinances prescribe similar restrictions; and it seems likely that the same requirements are imposd by informal pressure in other instances. See Williams and Wacks, *Segregation of Residential Areas Along Economic Lines: Lionshead Lake Revisited,* 1969 Wis. L. Rev. 827, 843.

26. Note the ironical result: New Jersey housing policy requires that most single-family houses must be large, and most apartments must be small.

27. Such complete exclusion in New Jersey was explictly permitted by the courts in *Vickers v. Gloucester Township,* 37 N.J. 232, 181 A. 2d 129 (1962), over the eloquent protest of Justice Hall.

The effects of so stringent a zoning policy are apparent state-wide. New Jersey, the eighth largest state and one of the fastest-growing Eastern states, has in recent years fluctuated between no. 36 and no. 44 among the states in the number of mobile home units shipped to dealers in the state. See Bair, *Mobile Homes and The General Housing Supply* (ASPO, 1970) at p. 10.

28. In 1967, 6 townships in these four counties permitted mobile homes, either as of right or as conditional uses.

29. The zoning policy in this township is described in n. 22 above.

MINIMUM BUILDING SIZE

The figures on the minimum building size required[30] for single-family detached houses are equally striking, and almost equally effective in forestalling any possibility of such low- and moderate-cost housing.[31] Only about 10 per cent of the land is subject to requirements of 1000 square feet or less, a requirement much larger than the basic requirement which was upheld in *Lionshead Lake*.[32] However, the really striking conclusion is the large amount of land zoned in districts requiring really substantial houses. Some 77 per cent of the land can be developed only with houses of 1200 square feet or more. The prevalence of this particular requirement varies widely between the different counties. In Monmouth County, the figure is 95 per cent, in Middlesex, 57 per cent, and the other two are in between. Moreover, within this total a not inconsiderable amount (13 per cent of the land) is zoned for much larger houses, with at least 1600 square feet. Again, the prevalence of such larger requirements varies widely as between the different counties. Surprisingly, by far the largest proportional concentration of such larger requirements occurs in Middlesex County (nearly 38 per cent of the total, 21,500 acres); a somewhat larger area is so zoned in Monmouth County (26,500 acres plus, 17 per cent). Such large requirements are relatively rare in Morris and Somerset Counties. The most striking concentration of very stiff minimum-building-size requirements is thus located in the area where these would be most effective in preventing needed new inexpensive housing, lower Middlesex County and adjacent inner Monmouth County.

LOT WIDTH

Analysis of lot width requirements is rather inconclusive without analysis of the accompanying subdivision-control requirements.[33] Only a few comments are in order here. Requirements for very wide lots (150 feet or more) are very common in Monmouth and Somerset Counties (87 and 82 per cent, respectively), but much less so in Morris (about 53 per cent) and especially in Middlesex (about 24 per cent).

LOT SIZE REQUIREMENTS

The requirements on minimum lot sizes are the best known, and most controversial,

---

30. In these four counties, only one per cent of the land is not covered by any zoning requirement on the subject. The figures cited in a previous article, based on a survey made by the state of New Jersey in 1966, therefore represented a substantial understatement of the problem. (It is difficult to believe that such requirements have increased as drastically as that in a few years.) See Williams and Wacks, *Segregation of Residential Areas Along Economic Lines: Lionshead Lake Revisited*, 1969 Wis. L. Rev. 827, 829–30. Note that both the frequency of such requirements and the high standards required are far more severe in their impact on housing than the figures reported by the Census Bureau to the Douglas Commission. See Report of the National Commission on Urban Problems to the Congress and to the President of the United States, *Building the American City*, H.R. Doc. No. 91-34, 91st Cong., 1st Sess. (1968), at p. 215.

31. Assuming that the single-family house still has a role to play in such housing. See assumption 3 on p. 4 above.

32. The leading case nationally on minimum building size is *Lionshead Lake v. Wayne Township*, 8 N.J. Super. 468, 73 A. 2d 287 (L. Div. 1950), *rev'd*, 9 N.J. Super. 83, 74 A. 2d 609 (App. Div. 1950), and 13 N.J. Super. 490, 80 A. 2d 650 (L. Div. 1951), *rev'd*, 10 N.J. 165, 89 A. 2d 693 (1952), *appeal dismissed*, 344 U.S. 919 (1953). Compare n. 3 *supra*. The subsequent history is told in the article cited in n. 30 above.

33. The survey did not cover such requirements.

of all these devices. It is in this area that the difference in zoning policy between Middlesex County and the other three counties is most striking. Compact detached single-family housing, if well-designed, can fit reasonably well on lots between 50 and 75 feet wide, i.e., normally with 5000–7500 square feet.[34] While only 1 per cent of the available land is zoned for such compact development,[35] there is considerable variation between different counties. Over half of the land so zoned is located in Middlesex, where it comprises 5 per cent of the available land. There is a substantial tract so zoned in Monmouth, and practically none in the other two. The next category includes land zoned for lot areas of 10,000 square feet and up, but less than half an acre. Nine per cent of the land in Middlesex County is so zoned (a total of 5,000 acres plus), an area of approximately the same size in Monmouth, and again much less in the others. However, it is in the half-acre zoning[36] that the difference is really striking. Such zones cover about 12–13 per cent in the other three counties, but make up nearly half of the available land in Middlesex County. Put another way, about 60 per cent of the available land in the most important county is zoned for lots of about half an acre or less.

At the other extreme, large-acreage zoning (three acres or more) is a fairly important factor in northern Somerset and southern Morris Counties, covering 24 per cent and 22 per cent respectively of the available land in those counties, almost all located in areas remote from employment growth. No land is so zoned in Middlesex, and only 1 per cent of the land in Monmouth.

Lot-Size Requirements and Housing Costs

A serious evaluation of the real relationship between lot-size requirements and housing costs involves an analysis of the economics of residential development, and is beyond the scope of this article.[37] However, it is possible to draw a few tentative hypotheses on the implications of the above material, with particular reference to the basic theme of this article, the need for low- and moderate-income housing near growing employment areas.

SMALL LOTS

First, let us accept for the moment the assumption that lots of one-half acre or less are less expensive to acquire, to develop, and to maintain than larger lots, and that single-family housing on such lots may continue to play a role in providing moderate-cost housing. The important point here is that a substantial area is zoned for such lots in the most important county (60 per cent of the land in Middlesex, about 34,500 acres), and almost as large an area (about 27,000 acres) in adjacent Monmouth.

---

34. Perhaps 60 feet (and 6000 square feet) would be a more realistic minimum figure. See American Public Health Association, Committee on the Hygiene of Housing, *Planning the Neighborhood* (1948) at p. 37.

35. Plus some scattered vacant land, in small tracts not covered by the survey.

36. A check of the ordinances indicates that the requirements listed in the range from 20,000 to 39,999 square feet are in fact heavily concentrated at 20,000 square feet or half an acre. This is the normal situation throughout the table. See Appendix A below.

37. See n. 5 *supra.*

The area in Morris is smaller, and in Somerset much smaller yet.[38] In a word, there is no shortage of relatively small-lot zoning in the most important area of employment growth.

LARGE ACREAGE ZONING

Turning to large-acreage zoning (3 acres or more),[39] it is clear that—considered strictly from the viewpoint taken in this article—such zoning does not play a particularly important role in suburban north-eastern New Jersey. Such zoning is non-existent in Middlesex, and practically non-existent in Monmouth. A large area is so zoned in a group of contiguous municipalities in southern Morris and northern Somerset; and this zoning raises a different set of problems. This attractive hilly area is far from major employment centers and has always been far from major transportation corridors. Moreover, this area is a traditionally high-cost area, where, even if the land were unzoned, the practical opportunities for producing inexpensive housing are not promising in any event. Yet other factors may now be at work. The expansion of population in this area, and in the nearby secondary transportation corridors passing through Morris and Somerset, will result in an increase in service employment, and so increase the need for low- and moderate-cost housing. Moreover, Interstate 287, the outerring circumferential highway around the western edge of the New York-New Jersey metropolitan region, is presently under construction through the south-eastern part of this area. If this highway should lead to substantial growth of industrial employment,[40] the multiplier effect of the latter would result in a greatly increased need for housing, and the whole situation would change.

As usual with acreage zoning, the important question here is the extent of the mapping for large-acreage development. Some of these towns are almost entirely zoned for large acreage, and some are not. In those towns which are almost entirely so zoned, the disadvantages are obvious—not only in excluding new inexpensive housing needed for local service employment, but also in excluding upper-middle-class housing on smaller lots, in the possibilities for providing public facilities economically, and conceivably even in raising due-process questions as between the

---

38. Though still over 18,500 acres and 12,000 acres, respectively. It should of course be recognized that there is a good chance that much of such land is less well-located than that zoned for larger lots, and that this may discourage development.

39. A somewhat smaller area is zoned in an intermediate acreage category, mostly requiring two-acre lots. There is no clear-cut pattern here; large concentrations of such zoning occur in a few widely-separated spots. Two-thirds of the land in this category is in Monmouth County, where such requirements apply to about 15 per cent of the land. Almost all the rest is in Morris County, in a very different setting. In both these counties, most of the two-acre zoning is in two townships. There is no land in Middlesex zoned for more than one acre; and there is almost no 2-acre zoning in Somerset, where the requirements jump from 1 acre (62 per cent of the County) to over 3 acres (24 per cent).

40. The question has just come up for decision in Bedminster, where Western Electric requested rezoning for a large office development on a 300-acre tract. (Compare the famous case of *Fischer v. Township of Bedminster*, 11 N.J. 194, 93 A. 2d 378 (1952), upholding five-acre zoning for most of the town.) After strong opposition to such rezoning was expressed at the public hearing, primarily by local residents but also by representatives of New York City, Western Electric withdrew its application. See N.Y. *Times*, Jan. 8, 1971, p. 20, col. 1.

towns and landowners and/or developers. On the other hand, other towns have varying zones, providing a considerable choice and range of density, and in these towns such large-acreage zoning, while highly restrictive, is not a particularly important factor in exclusionary zoning as defined here.

ONE-ACRE ZONING

The really widespread use of one-acre zoning raises different questions, and probably more serious ones. A very large area is so zoned, 55 per cent of the total land, varying from 65 per cent in Monmouth and 60 per cent in Somerset to about 50 per cent in Morris and 40 per cent in Middlesex. When the area zoned for multi-acreage lots is added, the figures are 77 per cent of the total land, 82 per cent in Monmouth, 85 per cent in Somerset, 81 per cent in Morris, and 39 per cent in Middlesex.

As suggested above, the motivation for such zoning is complex, involving three different sets of considerations. First, many people do prefer a more open semi-rural environment, with fairly large lots and substantial amounts of private open space located right on their own residential lots. Second, the existing technology of land use control does not provide any generally accepted device for a holding zone to permit communities at the suburban fringe to have some control over (a) the rate and sequence of growth; (b) the cost of the necessary services for new residential development; and (c) the taxes which will have to be levied.[41] There is no doubt that, for lack of any better way, acreage zoning is widely used as a crude technique for these purposes. Third, in some instances acreage requirements are undoubtedly exclusionary in intent. The probability is that such widespread acreage zoning is intended primarily to provide a holding zone, in order to delay development by chasing the developers into a different township. It also appears that, once established, such acreage zoning often does not in fact operate as a holding zone, but rather tends to determine the permanent pattern.[42]

The actual effect of widespread one-acre zoning, while undoubtedly important, is less clear. Obviously, if such zoning does in fact tend to determine the future pattern, so heavy a concentration on requirements for one-acre lots will play a dominant role in determining the future of the whole region, and low-density housing will tend to spread all over the landscape.[43] However, the critical question here is the effect of such zoning on the cost of housing, and this is much more questionable. As indicated above, a sophisticated analysis is needed on the relation between large-lot requirements and housing costs in New Jersey now. Some substantial evidence is available from other states, some years ago; and this evidence does not confirm the oft-stated hypothesis that such zoning is a major factor in preventing low-

---

41. Governor Cahill's forthright and explicit recognition of the influence of tax policy on zoning is as important as his attack on exclusionary zoning, particularly since a special commission is now at work on a reconsideration of New Jersey's entire tax policy.

42. Except in one type of situation. If a substantial area of vacant land in the same community is zoned for much smaller lots, the developers will normally be attracted away from the acreage area and into the area permitting smaller lots. See generally *Josephs v. Town Board of Town of Clarkstown,* 24 Misc. 2d 366, 198 N.Y.S. 2d 695 (Sup. Ct., Rockland, County, 1960).

43. This possibility has been analyzed at length in Regional Plan Association, *Spread City* (1962), with strong emphasis on its disadvantages.

and moderate-cost housing.[44] There are several reasons for this. First, just because land normally costs so much less than enclosed space (i.e., housing), minimum-lot-size requirements inevitably have a far lesser impact in raising housing cost than do minimum-building-size requirements. Second, the implicit assumption in most attacks on large-lot zoning is that the price of land increases more or less *pro rata* with the size of the lot[45] and conversely, decreases *pro rata* for smaller lots. The available evidence does not suggest that this is true. As between different communities, there are substantial variations in the cost of lots of the same size, but, within any given community, the cost of lots does not vary directly with their size or anywhere near that. Larger lots tend to cost more, but far from proportionately more. Moreover, a countervailing factor may be at work. In many communities, more expensive subdivision improvements are required in more intensive subdivisions, frequently starting somewhere in the range from a half an acre to one acre. If such requirements are imposed, the result may even be that, as developed land, smaller lots are actually more expensive than larger lots.

The unfortunate impact of such widespread acreage zoning probably lies elsewhere. In three of these counties, but not in Middlesex[46] one-acre zoning is so dominant that relatively small areas are zoned for smaller lots; and this is likely to drive up the cost of such smaller lots, and thus indirectly affect the cost of housing. In a word, the real objection to acreage zoning is not to the principle, but to the excessive mapping of such restrictions. An area of reasonable size, say less than half of a town, can be zoned for one acre, or for that matter for three or five acres, without having a serious impact on the cost of housing for people in the rest of the town. It does of course have a serious impact on the profits of developers and land-owners, and it is for this reason that the home builders are leading a campaign against large-lot zoning as *the* exclusionary device. Their motivation is obvious: if required lot sizes can be sharply reduced, they can often sell the smaller lots for almost as much as larger lots, and thus receive a fine windfall,[47] but with no benefit to those

44. Three professional studies have been made on the question of whether large-lot requirements are a major factor in raising the cost of housing. All have arrived essentially at the conclusion that the existence of such districts is not an important factor, although the mapping may be. See Urban Land Institute, *The Effect of Large Lot Size upon Residential Development*, Technical Bulletin No. 32, 1958, on the Boston metropolitan area, by the highly respected planning firm of Adams, Howard, and Greeley; Coke and Liebmann, *Political Values and Population Density Control*, 37 Land Economics 347 (1961) on the Philadelphia metropolitan area; American Society of Planning Officials, *New Directions in Connecticut Planning Legislation* (1965).

45. Governor Cahill's message explicitly adopted this assumption (see p. 7). Moreover, the Governor expressed surprise that as much as one acre would be required for a residential lot—in this respect going beyond the similar comments on three-acre zoning in the Pennsylvania decision, *Appeal of Kit-Mar Builders, Inc.*, 439 Pa. 466, 268 A. 2d 765, 767 (1970).

46. One interesting correlation emerges. High minimum-building-size requirements are rather common in the prime areas of industrial growth, and high-acreage requirements are concentrated in more remote areas. As a result, in evaluating the relative importance of these two devices in exclusionary zoning, one important factor is the relative multiplier effect of industrial as compared with service employment. See p. 5 above.

47. It is significant that such circles show little interest in the exclusionary effect of minimum-building-size requirements: the argument is even made that such requirements are not important, because under present conditions no one builds smaller houses anyway. This merely confirms

seeking inexpensive housing. Whether public-spirited liberals should join in this campaign is another question.

Correlation of the Various Devices

The question naturally arises as to whether, and how, and to what extent the standards embodied in these various potentially exclusionary devices have been correlated with one another. For example, do the more extreme requirements on minimum building size appear also in the areas zoned for very large lots, and vice versa? An analysis has been made of those areas zoned for the highest, and the next-to-highest, standards on the three principal devices affecting single-family housing. The following patterns emerge.

THE HIGHEST REQUIREMENTS

First, as for the highest figures on all three devices—at least 1600 square feet for minimum building size, 2 acres, and 200 feet of frontage. In this instance there is little correlation between the various devices: that is, not many ordinances have such high standards on all three devices, and so the existence of one such requirement gives no reason for predicting that the other will occur in the same ordinance. Between pairs of these devices, there is not much correlation, except in one instance. As between large minimum-building-size and large lot-size requirements, there is no significant correlation; some towns have 5-acre zoning and a 600-square-foot minimum building size. There is no apparent correlation at all between large building-size and large frontage requirements. On the other hand, requirements for very large lots and very large lot-width are usually correlated, although there are notable exceptions even here.

NEXT-TO-HIGHEST REQUIREMENTS

In contrast, an interesting pattern does emerge from an analysis of the degree of correlation between standards at the next-to-highest level—that is, a minimum building size of at least 1200 square feet, lot size of one acre, and lot width of 200 feet. In almost every instance, at least one of these requirements is imposed by the municipality. Indeed, this result follows almost automatically from the figures in the table, since about 75 per cent of the available land is zoned for 1200 square feet or more, and a similar amount for one-acre lots or larger. However, the degree of overlap between the two sets of requirements, while necessarily large, is far from complete. The significant point is that quite a lot of land is subject to one requirement and not the other, which of course means that the cumulative impact of these requirements is more effectively exclusionary than the effect of each one alone. Small homes are sometimes permitted on large lots, and large homes on small lots, but usually not small homes on small lots.[48]

---

the point that, if lot sizes were generally reduced, most conventional builders would still not build small houses—and so no great benefit would accrue to middle-income house purchasers.

48. The most important example arises in that 60 per cent of Middlesex County which is zoned for half-acre lots and less; of that 60 per cent over half (about 35 per cent of the total land) is zoned to require high minimum building size (about 1200 square feet), and the remaining 25 per cent, located in relatively remote areas, is zoned for somewhat smaller houses —but not much smaller, about 1000 square feet.

A Note on the Prevailing Law

The law on exclusionary land-use control is evolving so rapidly that a summary of the situation at any given point in time may be obsolete before it is in print. Briefly, two very different lines of arguments are emerging; these might be called the Pennsylvania rationale and the sensible rationale. Taking these in order, in two widely-publicized recent decisions the Pennsylvania court has dealt with two of the critical issues, the complete exclusion of multiple dwellings and large-acreage zoning; and that court (or to put the point more precisely, three or four of the seven judges thereof) has held both of these invalid. In the first decision[49] it was held that every municipality in Pennsylvania must have at least one area where multiple dwellings are permitted. (The case in question involved twin nine-story luxury apartment towers.) The rationale was based upon an extraordinary analogy between excluding apartments and excluding billboards, flashing signs, and quarries. (An unusual approach to analyzing the operations of the housing market.) In the other,[50] anything more than one-acre zoning was apparently also held invalid, in a township where a recent rezoning had eliminated most (but not all) of the previous large-acreage zoning— because large-acreage zoning was assumed to be exclusionary, with no discussion and no definition of that term. Apparently the underlying assumption was either (a) that all townships, (and the entire area of all townships) in or near the metropolitan area are equally subject to the pressure of metropolitan expansion, or (b) that courts could not or should not make distinctions in this respect. If the situation west of Philadelphia is anything like that in northern New Jersey,[51] these decisions will not contribute much to a solution of the problems of exclusionary zoning as defined here. The difficulty with Pennsylvania decisions is two-fold. First they mistakenly assume an identity of interest between developers and those who are excluded from access to good housing, and second they depend upon mechanical formulae (one multiple dwelling zone, more than one acre), instead of an understanding of the actual situation and the complex operations of the housing market. The rhetoric in these opinions is excellent; their only shortcomings lie in their rationale and the precise decision made.

A different and far more useful rationale is beginning to evolve in a series of important decisions from other courts. This evolving rationale is not yet fully articulated in any one decision, but the direction in which these decisions are pointing is clear. Under this approach, in planning for housing needs,[52] local government is under an affirmative duty to make some appropriate provision for all groups in the population, and specifically for low- and moderate-cost housing. This approach would leave it up to the locality to decide which type of such housing is most needed or most appropriate locally—garden apartments or high-rise, mobile homes, etc. Obviously, major elements in this approach remain to be filled in; some of the more important questions are suggested below.

---

49. *Appeal of Girsh*, 437 Pa. 237, 263 A. 2d 395 (1970).

50. *Appeal of Kit-Mar Builders, Inc.*, 439 Pa. 466, 268 A. 2d 765 (1970). The zoning was for two acres along existing streets, three acres elsewhere.

51. One scholarly article of a decade ago suggests that it is, or was then; see Coke and Liebmann, *Political Values and Population Density Control*, 37 Land Economics 347 (1961).

52. To protect public health and safety, and as part of the general welfare.

These cases have come up in a wide variety of situations. The first clear break with the exclusionary-zoning tradition came in the dissent by Justice Hall in *Vickers* v. *Gloucester Township*,[53] arguing that a largely vacant township in the path of development must make some provision somewhere for mobile homes (an opinion which, incidentally, is generally recognized as by far the best of modern zoning opinions.) The more recent cases involve various devices invoked to prevent low- and moderate-cost housing. *De Simone* v. *Greater Englewood Housing Corporation*[54] upheld (against an attack by neighbors) a "d" variance (i.e., a use variance) for a moderate-cost housing project in Englewood outside the local ghetto on the ground that such housing would obviously promote the general welfare. The important point in this decision is a dictum by Hall again, now speaking for a unanimous court, that a refusal of the requested variance would have itself been invalid, which implies some sort of affirmative duty to make such housing possible. Two federal-court opinions arising from somewhat similar fact situations have made fairly explicit statements on the evolving principle. In *Kennedy Park Homes Association* v. *City of Lackawanna*[55] a Federal District Court held invalid a refusal of subdivision approval, with a direct statement in point. The Second Circuit opinion (affirming) praised the lower-court opinion, but laid principal emphasis on the question of racial discrimination involved. *Southern Alameda Spanish-Speaking Organization* v. *City of Union City*[56] held invalid the annulment by referendum of a rezoning to permit a somewhat similar project,[57] again with a strong statement on the point.

Three other recent legal developments are relevant. First, several of the important recent cases on lot-size requirements (outside of Pennsylvania) have been moving towards an analogous position—that on large-lot requirements the critical question is not the basic principle involved in the device, but whether such districts are mapped so widely as seriously to restrict the opportunities for low- and moderate-cost housing.[58] Second, the case law supporting the exclusion of multiple dwellings from private home districts is not as monolithic as it sometimes appears. Apparently no one in recent years has noticed a significant point in the original decisions which upheld the principle of excluding apartment buildings. Three of the four leading cases on the point in the 1920's (there have been none since) contained a rather explicit *caveat*. In response to allegations that such exclusions amounted to a form of economic segregation, these opinions pointed out that, in that state at that time, new

---

53. 37 N.J. 232, 252, 181 A. 2d 129, 140 (1962).

54. 56 N.J. 428, 267 A. 2d 31 (1970).

55. Civil No. 1968-385, W.D.N.Y., August 13, 1970, *aff'd,* Docket No. 35320, December 7, 1970 (2d Cir.).

56. 424 F. 2d 291 (9th Cir. 1970), and on remand, see memorandum of decision, July 31, 1970, Docket No. 51590 (N.D. Cal).

57. But compare the result in a similar situation in *Ranjel v. City of Lansing,* 293 F. Supp. 301 (W.D. Mich. 1969), *rev'd,* 417 F. 2d 321 (6th Cir. 1969).

58. See *Senior v. Zoning Commission of Town of New Canaan.* 146 Conn. 531, 153 A. 2d 415 (1959), appeal dismissed, 363 U.S. 143 (1960), an otherwise fatuous opinion, which in effect established a judge-made rule of law in favor of suburban sprawl in Connecticut; *De Bruler Homes, Inc. v. County of Lake,* 78 Ill. App. 2d 177, 222 N.E. 2d 689 (1966); *County Commissioners of Queen Anne's County v. Miles,* 246 Md. 355, 228 A. 2d 450 (1967); and compare *Clary v. Borough of Eatontown,* 41 N.J. Super. 47, 124 A. 2d 54 (App. Div. 1956); *Grant v. Washington Township,* 1 Ohio App. 2d 84, 203 N.E. 2d 859 (1963).

single-family homes were being built within the reach of the lower income groups so that no such problem arose.[59] If such new housing is no longer available the corollary is obvious. When it finally comes, the great decision drastically limiting the local power to exclude such housing can therefore be phrased, not as blazing the way to new law, but (more comfortably) as a return to first principles. Finally, in *Shapiro* v. *Thompson*,[60] the Supreme Court held invalid a one-year residency requirement on eligibility for public welfare payments, with a clear statement that poor people have a right to move into a community of their choice.

The controlling factor in the background of all these cases is not a legal doctrine at all, but a value judgment rapidly coalescing among thoughtful people, and strongly reinforced by the grim experience of the 1960's, that the time for governmental action of this kind is long past.

As a result, the legal situation on exclusionary zoning today is approaching the situation on racial covenants after the dissenting opinion of Justice Edgerton in *Hurd* v. *Hodge*.[61] After that opinion, serious debate on the basic principle was really over, but the final and controlling decisions had not yet come down. However, in the present situation—once the basic principle is settled—major problems remain to be resolved in rounding out the rationale. Assuming that local governments do have a duty to make some provision for low- and moderate-cost housing, the following questions must be answered:

1. Does this duty apply to all local governments, or are there distinctions (of principle or of degree) between the communities in the path of development and those in more remote areas?

2. How can the extent of such responsibility be quantified, and by whom, in connection with the acceptance of new low- and moderate-income persons not already resident in the municipality?

3. To what extent should the special status accorded to housing for low- and moderate-income groups extend to those farther up the income scale?—and how far?

What is needed is a rationale against exclusionary zoning which has really been thought through, to cover such problems as those above. It would not be difficult, particularly under present conditions in the supply side of the housing market, to develop a rationale which in the real world would lead to large capital gains for land owners, large profits for builders, despoliation of some of the state's remaining attractive landscapes—and no inexpensive housing. It will not be easy to work out a

---

59. See *Miller* v. *Board of Public Works of Los Angeles*, 195 Cal. 477, 234 P. 381 (1925), *appeal dismissed*, 273 U.S. 781 (1927); *Brett* v. *Building Commissioner of Brookline*, 250 Mass. 73, 145 N.E. 269, (1924) (most explicit); State *ex rel. Twin City Building and Investment Co.* v. *Houghton*, 144 Minn. 1, 174 N.W. 885 (1919), *rev'd on rehearing*, 176 N.W. 159 (1920). The fourth decision—*Village of Euclid* v. *Ambler Realty Co.*, 272 U.S. 365 (1926), the leading case on zoning generally—did not discuss this specific issue, but clearly set forth the controlling principle in a different connection:

> It is not meant by this, however, to exclude the possibility of cases where the general public interest would so far outweigh the interest of the municipality that the municipality would not be allowed to stand in the way. (272 U.S. at 390).

60. 394 U.S. 618 (1968). Compare *Edwards* v. *California*, 314 U.S. 160 (1941).

61. 162 F. 2d 233, 235 ff. (D.C.C.A., 1947), *rev'd*, 334 U.S. 24 (1948); and see *Shelley* v. *Kraemer*, 334 U.S. 1 (1948). Edgerton's opinion is the second great classic in American land-use control.

rationale which (together with necessary legislative and executive action) will open the way for more low- and moderate-cost housing. If this is to be done, the hard and serious work lies ahead. The job would tax the abilities of a top-flight group of housing economists and planning lawyers; in actual life, it will probably have to be done by the judiciary.

Conclusion

The overall picture is obvious. In the coming years, the most needed housing types will be multiple dwellings, mobile homes and, perhaps, single-family houses on relatively small lots. The demand for larger houses on larger lots is not insignificant, but it is relatively less important. Realistically, housing policy in suburban northern New Jersey is embodied in, and enforced by, local zoning requirements. The present policy is to prohibit all mobile homes, and practically to prohibit multiple dwellings (especially for normal-size families). As for single-family housing, the policy (except in part of Middlesex County) is to make very little provision for small houses on small lots; about ¾ of the available vacant residential land is zoned to permit only large single-family houses and large lots. Zoning is above all supposed to promote the general welfare; clearly something has gone very wrong. When minimum building size restrictions were first upheld in New Jersey, it seemed likely that if one town could practice exclusion, all the others could, and that they probably would. The facts are now available: almost all the others did, with a vengeance.

In New Jersey, the pattern of exclusionary zoning has been successfully rationalized in court on a highly parochial basis, by relying on the odd notion that the statutory reference to the "general welfare" refers to the general welfare of each individual municipality.[62] Yet in recent years the New Jersey Court has cut the logical basis out from under this whole line of precedent, by deciding explicitly that the "general welfare" should be interpreted on a regional basis.[63] The regional pattern for a large area is clear; the future course for the courts should be equally clear.

Appendix A

A NOTE ON METHODOLOGY

The technique employed in the New Jersey survey was as follows:

---

62. *Lionshead Lake v. Wayne Township*, 10 N.J. 165, 89 A. 2d 693 (1952), *appeal dismissed*, 344 U.S. 919 (1953); *Napierkowski v. Gloucester Township*, 29 N.J. 481, 150 A. 2d 481 (1959); *Vickers v. Gloucester Township*, 37 N.J. 232, 181 A. 2d 129 (1962) (with a maginificent dissent by Justice Hall).

63. *Kunzler v. Hoffman*, 48 N.J. 277, 225 A. 2d 321 (1966), upholding a "d" variance (i.e., a use variance) to permit a hospital for emotionally disturbed persons in a rural area in outer Morris County, and explicitly rejecting the argument that the "general welfare" referred merely to the welfare of the township in question; compare *De Simone v. Greater Englewood Housing Corporation*, 56 N.J. 428, 267 A. 2d 31 (1970), upholding a "d" variance for a moderate-cost housing project in a "white" area in Englewood, as against a protest by neighbors. The regional approach is a strong theme (and not a new one) in New Jersey zoning. Compare *Duffcon Concrete Products v. Cresskill*, 1 N.J. 509, 64 A. 2d 347 (1949); *Cresskill v. Dumont*, 15 N.J. 238, 104 A. 2d 441 (1954).

1. Zoning ordinances effective as of April 1st 1970 were collected and analyzed, and the use districts were mapped on a county map at a scale of 1 inch = mile.

2. In order to determine the amount of land which is both vacant and readily-developable, the next step was to map (and then to black out) all the categories of land unsuitable for development—including built-up areas, publicly-owned land, water and swamps, and land with a slope of 12 per cent or more. The remaining land was considered vacant and developable. The figures given therefore do not take into consideration potential redevelopment. Moreover, since tracts of less than 5 acres were ignored, the figures also do not take into account the existence of scattered vacant land in built-up areas.

3. The number of developable acres in each use district was calculated by the areagraph technique, and this land was classified by zoned use as residential, research and office, commercial and industrial. The developable land in the residential districts was then divided into land zoned for multiple dwellings,[1] mobile homes, and single-family detached houses; and the land allocated to the latter was broken down into the various categories of requirements for minimum building size, lot width, and lot size. The latter requirements were analyzed in terms of ranges, starting with a commonly-used figure and extending upwards almost to the next such figure. In most instances the actual requirements are thus concentrated at the bottom of the range shown. In all instances where requirements vary in different situations—for one- and two-story houses, for developments with and without public water and/or sewer—the survey used the lower figure. The tables therefore understate the severity of the requirements.

4. The maps for each county were checked with the County Planning Office.

Appendix B

The tables appearing in Governor Cahill's message are reproduced for convenient reference. The first summarizes the area available in single-family zones, by various lot sizes, and in multiple dwelling zones. The second sets forth the acreage subject to minimum-building-size requirements of at least 1200 square feet. In both instances these figures lump together land zoned for residence and areas zoned for non-residential development, with residence also permitted, and are therefore somewhat larger than those in Table 2.

---

1. Garden apartments, high-rise structures and residential dwellings providing for three or more families were included in this designation. Two-family districts mapped on vacant land were so rare that these were lumped with the one-family category.

Table A
ZONING OF VACANT LAND THAT PERMITS HOUSING & IS DEVELOPABLE

County	One Acre or More For Each House		1/2 To One Acre For Each House		Less Than 1/2 Acre For Each House		Multi Family Housing		Total	
	Acres	Percent	Acres	Percent	Acres	Percent	Acres	Percent	Acres	Percent
Camden	10,176	21 %	2,144	4%	14,514	29.5%	22,404	45.5%	49,238	100%
Essex	692	9.5%	2,738	38%	3,299	46 %	529	7 %	7,258	100%
Gloucester	41,779	33 %	33,496	27%	22,622	18 %	27,814	22 %	125,711*	100%
Mercer	32,657	45 %	33,436	46%	5,938	8 %	698	1 %	72,729*	100%
Middlesex	23,001	34 %	33,151	49%	9,021	13 %	2,348	3.5%	67,521*	100%
Monmouth	143,943	82 %	19,598	11%	9,809	6 %	1,588	1 %	174,938	100%
Morris	87,473	79 %	15,955	14%	6,016	5 %	1,620	1 %	111,064	100%
Somerset	77,765	85 %	12,737	14%	859	1 %	0	0 %	91,361	100%
Total	417,486	60 %	153,255	22%	72,078	10 %	57,001	8 %	699,820*	100%

*Not including mobile home acreage.

Table B
ZONED FOR A MINIMUM HOUSE SIZE
OF 1,200 SQUARE FEET OR MORE

COUNTY	ACRES	PERCENT OF TOTAL ZONED FOR SINGLE FAMILY DWELLINGS
Camden	20,223	75.5
Essex	5,734	85.2
Gloucester	24,659	25.2
Mercer	33,549	46.5
Middlesex	33,872	52.0
Monmouth	165,706	95.6
Morris	71,131	65.0
Somerset	68,565	75.1
Total	423,439	65.9%

8

George Sternlieb and Lynne Sagalyn

ZONING AND HOUSING

EMPIRICAL FINDINGS AND CONCLUSIONS

Summary of Findings

The statewide survey of new subdivisions in New Jersey provides definitive data on the unavailability of new single-family houses for low to moderate income households in all but select southern counties. The mean characteristics of new housing for each county are presented in Exhibit III-1. New housing under $30,000 and, therefore, within the range of households with $10,000 to $15,000 incomes is available primarily in the southern and western counties - Gloucester, Hunterdon, Cumberland, Cape May, Atlantic, and Ocean. Moderate-priced new housing in new subdivisions is not being built in the urbanized northeast corridor. The mean price of new housing in 1971 in the state was $40,224 compared to $26,000 in 1970 for the United States as a whole, and $32,800 for the northeastern region.[1]

As anticipated, public policy decisions pertaining to minimum zoning requirements are significant factors explaining selling price variation. However, the size of the house - directly affected by the minimum size regulation and indirectly conditioned by minimum lot size requirements - is the single most important factor explaining selling price variation. Lot size and lot frontage specifications are highly significant and highly intercorrelated; (Exhibit III-2) their interaction produces significant cumulative impact. However, the relative importance of each is dependent upon the type of sewage system available within the subdivision and thus the municipality.

---

[1]This average figure for the State represents a weighted figure proportional to the incidence of building permits issued in each county. The county averages generated by the sample were multiplied by the county's proportional share of statewide building permits issued for 1970. The derived value of $40,224 is the sum of these individual products.

Characteristics of New One-Family Homes; 1970, Construction Reports, c25-70-13, U.S. Bureau of Commerce (Washington, D.C.: U.S. Government Printing Office, August 1971), Table 20, page 70.

Several of the expected effects of zoning and subdivision constraints appear to be muted by the aggregation of all sample subdivisions. The regression analyses of complementary sample subsets provide a comparative basis of analysis and understanding. In the instance of sewered and non-sewered subdivisions the importance of the sewage variable is emphasized, although per se the type of disposal system is not statistically significant in explaining selling price variation. The type of sewage disposal system required of the builder by the municipality is important, then, since it conditions other relationships.

The impact of subdivision improvements, given the present uniformity of a high level of standards, does not appear to be statistically significant in explaining selling price variation. However, this is not to say that changes in these requirements concomitant with other changes in policy would not increase the opportunities for lower price housing. There remains the possibility that the costs associated with these improvements reverted to the landowner upon sale to the developer. The only individual requirement which appeared to have any significance was that governing the presence and width of sidewalks. Furthermore, from this survey it appeared that the number of subdivision requirements decreased with decreased density. However, this reduction did not lower the price of the total housing package since more expensive homes tended to be constructed on parcels of an acre or more. Municipal delay associated with subdivision approval proved to be significant only in urbanized areas and in subdivisions with sewer service.

The effect of building code regulations governing wallsheet and cinderblock was significant in explaining price variation. However, relatively, these variables were less important than the zoning constraints or house characteristics.

The socioeconomic status of a municipality as measured by the value of extant owner-occupied housing proved to be the second most significant variable in explaining selling price variation. In urbanized areas, it becomes the single largest factor, whereas in rural areas, it has no statistical significance. The ability of "like" to draw "like" appears to be partially a function of the builder's assessment of the marketplace coupled with existing constraints of lot size, frontage, etc. Underlying this process are the cost realities of land and construction which have substantially eliminated the low and moderate income household from purchasing new housing in New Jersey.

The separate analysis of price variation in urbanized and rural areas re-emphasizes the primacy of certain characteristics associated with growth and a municipal policy of full urban services. For example, municipal administrative delay, gross residential density, the presence of sidewalks, and the social character of the area are decidedly more significant factors in urban areas. By contrast, in rural subdivision, the characteristics of the house and the lot size are more important in explaining price variation.

The following discussion presents a detailed view of the results of the regression analyses. These equations explained between 77 and 92 percent of the selling price variation and had statistically significant F scores at 95 percent confidence level. The full-sample regression equation presented in Exhibit III-3 provides a general understanding of

the major elements underlying selling price variation. This equation
explains 80 percent of the price variation. The most important variables
explaining variation in selling price are livable floor area and socioeconomic status of the community. Together they explain more than 60
percent of the price variation.

Local Public Policy Variables

The minimum livable floor area specified by the zoning ordinance
would have the direct effect of setting a minimum cost for construction.
However, because of the "overbuilding" phenomenon the variable used in
the regression represents the actual living area in the house. It is
the most important variable explaining variation in the selling price of
single-family houses. Exhibit III-3 presents the results of a two-stage
stepwise regression analysis in which livable floor area was entered in
the first step after which the remaining 18 independent variables were
forced into the equation for the second step. This was done to isolate
the magnitude of the floor area variable and assess the additional explanatory power of the residual variables. Variation in livable floor area
accounted for over 57 percent of the variation in selling price. The
regression coefficient of $9.75 means that for each unit increase - one
square foot of livable floor area - the selling price would increase by
$9.75. If the coefficient appears low in comparison with commonly quoted
figures of $15.00 to $20.00 per square foot, it must be remembered that
the equation includes three other variables descriptive of the house and
these are all reflected in the lower floor area coefficient.

Lot size and lot frontage are the next most important public policy
constraint variables. In the above regression, the effects of lot size
and lot frontage are approximately equivalent as revealed by the BETA coefficients of .18 and .16 respectively. That lot size shows a slightly
greater impact upon selling price was to be expected due to the marginal
cost increases of larger lots, although the price increase is not proportional to lot size increase. The relative ability of each to explain
variation in selling price is dependent upon the type of sewage system in
the subdivision. It is interesting to note that this latter variable itself is statistically insignificant in the regression equation. It is the
factors accompanying the type of sewage disposal that create differences
in selling price.

Exhibit III-4 presents the comparative results of the regression
analyses of sewered and nonsewered subdivisions. It is apparent that
these two types embody basic differences. In developments with a private
or public sewer service, lot frontage distances are statistically significant in explaining selling price variation whereas lot size is insignificant; the latter conforms to a priori expectations. Within a given range
of lot sizes, the marginal cost differences between lot sizes are insignificant if it is the minimum size. In this instance the lot size
range is defined by the smallest size marketable and the smallest size
at which individual septic systems become feasible. Conversely, in
developments with private individual septic systems, lot size, rather than
lot frontage, is statistically significant in explaining price variation.

Exhibit III-5 presents the disparities between sample groups; it
is apparent that the major difference between homes in sewered and non-

sewered developments is in the lot attributes. The average house size in nonsewered developments compared to sewered developments is less than four percent smaller and the average lot frontage less than 20 percent larger, while the average lot size is more than 73 percent larger. As expected, subdivision improvement in nonsewered subdivisions -- the presence of curbing and sidewalks, and width of road pavement -- appear to be adjusted for decreased density. Although the average characteristics of these sub-division houses differ, the price differential is small; an average house in the nonsewered subdivision costs approximately an additional $3,245. The net price difference appears to be predominantly a function of the increased lot size.

As expected, the effect of setback requirements upon selling price variation is inconsequential; in addition, it is moderately correlated with lot size and frontage, .66 and .62 respectively. Accordingly it was removed from the equation with other insiginificant variables and the regression analysis was performed again. Exhibit III-6 presents these results. Elimination of the insignificant variables neither alters the explanatory power of the regression equation nor changes its basic relation-ships. It only slightly alters the regression coefficients.

Of the selected subdivision improvements utilized in the equation, only the incidence and width of sidewalks has any statistical significance in explaining selling price variation. The uniformity of the other require-ments -- road pavement width of 28 to 30 feet, the presence of curbing, and the dedication of land for streets -- eliminates the variability of these factors. This is reinforced by the constant insignificance of these vari-ables in both the sewered and nonsewered subdivision regression analyses. Sixty-eight percent of the subdivisions had a road pavement width of 30 feet; 91 percent had some form of street curbing. However, it is important to note that sidewalk incidence and width is only significant in sewered subdivisions (Exhibit III-4) where the mean sidewalk width is more than twice that of nonsewered developments.

The negative sign of the sidewalk regression coefficient confirms a previously stated relationship. The lack of sidewalks in lower-density developments where more expensive housing is the rule rather than the exception emphasizes the importance of the cumulative impact of develop-ment controls. In these cases, it appears that subdivision improvement standards are adjusted downward with decreasing density; however, the higher price of houses is a function of the lot size, socioeconomic char-acter of the area and house amenities. Sidewalks are nonexistent in 64 percent of the subdivisions with lots of one acre or larger. Concomitantly, 61.5 percent of the houses in subdivisions with no sidewalks are priced over $50,000.[2]

Subdivision development fees including special-purpose fees are statistically insignificant in accounting for variation in selling price. Only in one regression, occurring in sewered subdivisions, were they significant; this latter instance was anticipated given the cost pre-

---

[2]These calculations are based on the elimination of houses in sub-divisions fronting on existing roads in which improvements were already in place prior to subdivision. There were 7 subdivisions or 17 house models eliminated.

dominance of sewer tap-on charges within the total fee structure. The
reasoning underlying the negative coefficient sign of this variable is
the same as that previously discussed for sidewalk width. The high price
of expensive houses, which often may be located in municipalities where
builders are subject to fewer such fees, result from other factors. The
regression coefficient means that for every increased dollar of fees, the
selling price will decrease $2.37. However, since this study is concerned
primarily with the nature of the relationship, less weight was accorded to
the equation's predictive ability.

Similarly, municipal delay is statistically significant only in
sewered subdivisions. In these developments an additional month delay in
obtaining subdivision approval would add $80 to the selling price. A further
source of delay can occur at the state level because of an additional level
of plan review by the New Jersey Department of Environmental Protection.
This department is responsible for approving the extension of all new sewer
lines into an existing sewage plant prior to local planning approval.   However, if the lines are for less than 50 houses, the plans can be approved
and implemented on the local level without state approval. If the sewage
capacity of a municipality cannot handle the potential addition, no new
subdivision plats can be approved without expansion and/or fulfillment of
other requirements. A municipality can thereby prevent residential growth
or forestall growth. Morris County, for example, provides evidence of subdivision sections experiencing difficulties with approvals.

After the data reduction process, only two variables describing
code requirements remained in the regression analysis. Both the thickness
of exterior wall sheeting and the size of the cinderblock used in the
foundation are statistically significant in explaining selling price variation. The general requirement for exterior wall sheeting is 1/2" thickness; however in areas with restrictive codes 5/8" or 3/4" is commonly
specified. For this variable, an additional 1/8" of thickness adds $2,254
to house price, an additional 1/4", $4,508. Cinderblock width can be
thought of as a proxy for the extra foundation cost of a brick facade as
well as a restrictive building practice; a 12" block is required in these
cases. Although an 8" block is the standard size block for nonbrick
facades, in our sample 10" was the most prevalent. An increase of two
inches in this variable increases the selling price by $1,203.

Construction Variables

The presence of a full basement is a significant factor explaining
selling price variation. In previous regression analyses prior to data
reduction, a full basement proved to be the second most important variable
descriptive of house characteristics (livable floor areas was the most
important). This relationship persists in the final regressions, which
show that a full basement increases the selling price by approximately
$3,365.

The presence of appliances may attract more consumers and are
additional marketing factors for builders. Larger builders may realize
some economies because of their ability to purchase in large quantities.
Within the regression, this variable is statistically significant, although
as the BETA coefficients show, it is relatively less important than many
others.

Marketplace Variables

The socioeconomic status of the municipality as measured by the 1970 median dollar value of owner-occupied housing is the second most important of all regression variables explaining selling price variation. After assessing the market demand within his building location, a builder incorporates in his houses those amenities and finishes that that market demands and is willing to pay for. The regression coefficient indicates that for every $1.00 increase in the community median value of housing, there is a $.50 increase in selling price; a $5,000 increased differential between communities would mean approximately a $2,500 differential in the average price of new housing between those communities.

A municipality's gross residential density is also a statistically significant variable explaining selling price variation. As expected, it is not significant in the subsets of subdivisions with septic systems where the mean municipal density is 780 persons per square mile compared to 1,752 in sewered subdivisions. According to the BETA coefficients (Exhibit III-7), municipal density is the fifth most important variable explaining price variation. An increase of 100 persons per square mile produces a $138 increase in price; a 500-person-per-square-mile increase would mean an increased price of $690. Although it is important in explaining variation, the price differences do not appear to be major with this level of change. Exhibit A-5 presents the distribution of sample suburban densities; the differences in outlying areas are not major.

This study produced no conclusive findings on the occurence of capitalization of house values as a result of municipal tax rate differential. Although statistically significant in the full regression analysis, tax rate may be functioning for another characteristic. More definitive statements cannot be made without further study.

Builder's Operational Scale Variables

The number of single-family units a builder constructs in a given year is significant in explaining selling price variation. Economies of scale in building construction and land development appear to be passed on to the consumer in the form of lower prices. Such economies are apparent only for large scale builders; there is a price reduction of approximately $6.90 for each additional house built per year. An increase of 100 units results in a $690 reduction. However, the building industry, composed primarily of small and medium-size builders, includes only a few who build more than 500 houses annually.

In prior regression analyses, the size of subdivision development was found to be statistically insignificant in explaining selling price variation. Its insignificance in sewered subdivisions implies that any possible economies of scale in land acquisition in these growing areas are not passed on to the consumer. Only in one of the subsamples -- non-sewered subdivisions -- was any significance noted. For the consumer buying in large developments serviced by private septic systems, an increase of one lot in the development would increase the selling price by $16.83.

Price in Urbanized vs. Rural Area Subdivisions

The price differences between new houses in urban and rural sub-divisions provide further evidence of the effects of development controls. In rural areas house price variation appears to depend upon fewer significant variables and the equation explains a greater proportion of the variation than it does in the urban subsample. The identical set of variables explained 92 percent of variation in the prices of houses in rural subdivisions and 77 percent in the urbanized subsample.

The average sample new house price in urbanized areas was $49,000 compared to $43,230 in rural area subdivisions. Exhibit III-5 indicates considerable variation among other characteristics in these subdivision types. For example, the average lot size in rural areas is almost 50 percent larger than that in urbanized areas -- 28,896 square feet and 19,875 square feet respectively. In addition to the decreased incidence of full basements, houses in rural subdivisions have a smaller average livable floor area. In contrast to these basic house and lot differences, the variables descriptive of subdivision requirements, with some exceptions, show a remarkable uniformity. Average lot frontages are similar. And the incidence of street curbing and sidewalks and the width of road pavements differs only slightly. As expected, the incidence of septic systems in rural subdivisions is greater than that in urbanized areas although the differential is not as large as anticipated.

The results of the regression analyses presented in Exhibit III-8 show that lot size and lot frontage are both significant in explaining price variation in the urbanized subdivisions although lot frontage becomes insignificant in rural areas. The BETA coefficients presented in Exhibit III-7 show that the relative importance of lot size in explaining price variation is greater in subdivisions in rural areas. The unnormalized regression coefficients provide, admittedly, in gross terms, some idea of the differential between rural and urban raw land prices. In urbanized area subdivisions an increase in lot size of 10,000 square feet, or a quarter of an acre, would increase the selling price by $3,300 as compared to $2,000 for the equivalent increase in rural areas.

This set of regression analyses further supports the belief that administrative delay in subdivision approval increases the price of new housing in urbanized areas. A one month delay adds an additional $91 to selling price in urbanized subdivisions.

Conclusions and Policy Implications

Newly constructed single-family housing in suburban New Jersey is effectively out of reach of at least 40 percent of the state's households; these are the families with annual incomes of less than $10,000. In 1970, the median income of all families in the state was $11,407. Since a reasonable purchase price of a house for a family is considered to be between two and two-and-a-half times its annual income, the average family could conceivably afford a house selling between $22,814 and $28,518. However, new single-family housing priced less than $30,000 is available only in a few counties where land costs and zoning requirements are less stringent. These counties, except Burlington County, are not the areas where most employment growth is occurring. Most new single-family housing is therefore financially available to approximately one quarter of the state's households (Exhibit III-9).

Without changes in worker productivity, increases in labor wages are invariably passed along into house selling price despite rises in per capita income. A rate of income increase commensurate with that for higher-income groups would not substantially change the purchasing power of low-income families. "The inability of low-income people to buy new homes is primarily a function of the disparity in incomes among wage-earning classes, not of the absolute level of their incomes."[3]

This study focuses upon the role of public policy in determining the price of single-family housing. How successful are statutory require-ments governing minimum floor area, lot size or lot frontage in establish-ing economic criteria for residence? Would reduction in these policy variables produce economies that could make new housing available to a larger segment of the market? Only to a limited extent will singular changes in these policy variables alter the price range of new single-family housing and thereby increase the effective market of buyers.

Utilizing the regression equation for predictive purposes, we tested changes in several policy variables for their effect upon selling price. For variables other than those selected for studied change, mean values were inserted in the regression equation; then various changes were postulated in the policy variables. In one instance, only the livable floor area was changed; the average sample figure of 2,100 square feet was reduced to 1,200 square feet. Instead of an average sample selling price of $47,434, the predicted selling price was reduced to $38,291. A further reduction of the livable floor area to 800 square feet yielded a selling price of $34,392.

How valid is the assumption that large lot-zoning produces expensive housing? Large lot-zoning alone does not produce expensive housing; the simple correlation between these two variables was .61, a bit higher than Coke and Liebman's findings but nonetheless weak.[4] Interestingly enough, the simple correlation between lot size and livable floor area is also weak - .43; the correlation of floor area with lot frontage is .50. This finding does not contradict the previously cited builder's comment that larger lot sizes necessitate larger houses to make them marketable. It does indicate that there is no continuous relationship. There may be a considerable difference between what the builder constructs on a quarter-acre lot and on a one-acre lot. However, there may be negligible differ-ences between the house size constructed on a half-acre lot, three-quarter acre or an acre lot. Implicit here is a possible step function in the re-lationship between the sizes of lot and house.

---

[3] Marion Clawson, Suburban Land Conversion in the United States (Baltimore: Johns Hopkins Press for Resources for the Future, Inc., 1971) page 83.

[4] James G. Coke and Charles I. Liebman, "Political Values and Population Density Control," Land Economics, Volume 37, 1961, page 357.

In several situations expensive housing was accompanied by large-lot zoning policies. Although large-lot zoning may have contributed to the intended result, from the results of our survey it is more probable that the desirable socioeconomic character of the area was a more significant determinant of sales price. Controlling for the type of sewage disposal system and urban-rural character of the subdivision provides additional understanding.

Provision of public services such as sewer and water lines undoubtedly is a significant factor in determining the location and timing of residential development.[5] The conscious use of these services for guiding suburban development is, however, not commonplace. Nevertheless, the results of this study indicate that the effects of public policy variables embodied in zoning and subdivision ordinances vary under different conditions of sewage disposal. Our results indicate that areas in which sewer service is available provide slightly more flexibility, allowing for changes in public policy that might change sales price.

In urbanized areas, the single most important variable, explaining price variation appears to be socioeconomic level of the community as measured by the value of extant owner-occupied housing in that municipality. Changes in lot size and livable floor area appear to have the same relative effect; lot size is only slightly more important. In rural areas, by comparison the effect of changes in livable floor area upon sales price is much greater than lot size; socioeconomic character of the municipality is insignificant. This prestige factor is relatively unaffected however by local public policies other than those pertaining to school quality. Although state and federal policy decisions regarding matters such as transportation do affect an area's accessibility, they do not necessarily affect its prestige level.[6]

What are the effects upon selling price if the three critical zoning requirements -- lot size, lot frontage, and living area -- are changed? Maintaining the average values for all other variables, the following values were inserted in the equations:

---

[5] It is interesting to note that 28 percent of our sample responses reported that they would not develop in a municipality that did not have an existing sewage disposal system. Also see Paul B. Downing, The Economics of Urban Sewage Disposal, (New York: Praeger, 1969); Grace Milgram and Christine Mansfield, The City Expands - A Study of the Conversion of Land from Rural to Urban Use, Philadelphia 1945-62, (Washington, D.C.,: U.S. Government Printing Office, 1968); F. Stuart Chapin, Jr., and Shirley F. Weiss, Factors Influencing Land Development, (Chapel Hill: Institute for Research in Social Science, 1962); Kenneth B. Kenney, Pre-Development Land Ownership Factors and Their Influence in Social Science, Center for Urban and Regional Studies (Chapel Hill: Institute for Research in Social Sciences, 1965).

[6] The sample correlation of HOUSTOK with accessibility was -.625. For further discussion of the accessibility variable, see Appendix B.

	Type of Sewage Disposal	Lot Size	Lot frontage	Livable floor area (sq. ft.)	Predicted selling price
A.	Septic	one acre	200	1600	$45,442
B.	Septic	one acre	200	1200	39,137
C.	Sewer	15,000 sq. ft.	100	1600	41,059
D.	Sewer	15,000	100	1200	37,609

There is little price difference between the previous instance on page 65 in which only floor area was reduced (to 1,200 square feet) and Example D above. The predicted difference to the consumer between these examples is $682 although the differences in lot size and lot frontage were 7,331 square feet and 13 feet respectively. The importance of the level of municipal services provided is obvious; it is evident that the price differential between the same house (1,200 square feet) constructed on a one-acre lot with a septic system and on a third-of-an-acre lot with municipal sewage is small, $1,528.

The above configurations represent changes based on the full sample data. Additional changes were calculated based on the subsample of subdivisions in urbanized areas only. The average sample values for these variables were: lot size – 19,875 square feet, frontage – 112 feet, livable floor area – 2,214 square feet; the selling price was $49,007.

	Lot Size (sq. ft.)	Lot Frontage (front feet)	Livable floor area (sq. ft.)	Predicted Selling Price
A.	One acre	200	1600	$57,618
B.	15,000	100	1600	42,044
C.	12,000	100	1200	38,053
D.	12,000	80	800	33,843

The changes represented above provide some idea of the possible reductions in sales price when the major policy variables are substantially reduced in urbanized areas. A small, 800 square-foot home on a 12,000 square foot lot with 80 feet of frontage would cost approximately $33,843, providing the appropriate zoning was available and the builder actually built a small house.

Our findings show that changes in zoning policies making land available for higher-density single-family units would not be a sufficient condition to generate housing for low and moderate-income families. However, changes in the major zoning practices would appear to enlarge the effective housing market considerably provided that builders made concomitant reductions in the size and amenities of the housing offered.

Large lot-zoning has been cited elsewhere as an ineffective method of "holding off" land development.[7] Our survey indicates that developers tend to choose those land parcels with both the smallest zoned lot sizes and lot frontages permissible. In Monmouth County, based on the present zoning patterns, the typical lot size expected would be one acre or more; however, the sample figure was 25,000 square feet. It is conceivable that if the smaller lot areas were in closer physical proximity to present development within the municipality, a contiguous development pattern might be fostered.

Another question raised by this research is whether low-density zoning concomitant with a reduced standard of subdivision improvements would substantially reduce the price of housing. Our results show that at reduced densities, subdivision improvement requirements do appear to be adjusted; however, these variables are insignificant in explaining price variation. Sales prices in subdivisions with septic systems are generally higher than those with sewers. More important as a determinant of price is the socioeconomic status of the community as it affects both the price of land and the consumer's expectation of house size and amenities. Furthermore, the effect of subdivision improvement requirements upon the selling price of a house is substantially reduced by the widespread uniformity of these variables.

We did not delve into the cost differentials contingent upon varying engineering specifications for such items as the type of road pavement material. Although there are cost differentials associated with these specifications, they were not discernible from our method of analysis. Furthermore, it is doubtful whether such differentials would significantly change the price distribution of new housing.

Since the builder is presently required to pay for the subdivision improvements, their costs are accordingly either passed on to the consumer in the selling price or passed back to the land seller in the form of a low bid for the raw land. A change in the policy governing financing methods could conceivably influence the builder's locational decision and thereby the patterns of development within the municipality.[8] Such a policy

---

[7] David Heeter, Toward a More Effective Land-Use Guidance System: A Summary and Analysis of Five Major Reports, (Chicago, Ill.: American Society of Planning Officials, 1969); Daniel R. Mandelker, "A Rationale for the Zoning Process", Land Use Controls Quarterly (Vol. 4-1, Winter 1970); The Effects of Large Lot Size on Residential Development, op. cit.

[8] Edward J. Kaiser and Shirley F. Weiss, "Public Policy and the Residential Development Process", Journal of the American Institute of Planners, Volume XXXVI, Number 1, January 1970, page 34.

change could affect selling price by changing the distribution of the cost components in housing cost. Because the land component would be lower in absolute value, a builder might be less compelled to build a large house as a justification for a large land expense.

The effect of the two building code specifications upon selling price is significant but less important than the previously discussed policy variables. In the full sample, the thickness of exterior wall sheeting is more important than the size of the foundation cinderblock. Reducing the requirements of these two variables to 3/8" and 8" respectively from 1/2" and 10.3" - without any other changes in house offering - would signify a $3,871 reduction in sales price. Including these building code changes with respective reductions in lot size, lot frontage, and livable floor area of 15,000 square feet, 100 feet, and 1,600 square feet would yield a sales price of approximately $36,526 - $12,481 less than the $49,007 average.

Local public policies regarding land development significantly affect the extent and nature of suburban residential growth. As a partial consequence, the supply of new single-family housing currently available in New Jersey is restricted to a small segment of economically well-off households. Changes in exclusionary zoning practices through judicial and legislative actions would expand the potential buying market by making land available for higher-density dwellings. This, however, does not imply that low and moderate income households would be able to purchase new housing subsequently constructed on those lands. In addition, while the possibility of a state-wide property tax to finance the costs of local education would substantially remove the fiscal rationalization for exclusionary development controls, it would do little to remove the social intent of many of the local exclusionary practices.

VARIABLES TESTED IN RELATION TO SELLING PRICE

Variable	Definition	Unit of Measurement	Expected Relation To Selling Price
LOTSIZE	lot size	square feet per unit	positive
LOFRONT	lot frontage	front feet per unit	positive
SETBACK	setback	front feet per unit	positive
ROADPAV	road pavement width for interim sheets	front feet per unit	unknown
STREETS	percentage of land dedicated to streets	percentage total subdivision area	unknown
CURBING	street curbing	yes/no	unknown
SIDWALK	sidewalk width	front feet per unit	unknown
SEWAGES	type of sewage disposal	septic/sewer system	negative
DEVFEES	subdivision development fees	dollars per unit	unknown
MUDELAY	municipal delay	number of months	positive
WALLSHT	exterior wall sheeting thickness	fractional inch	positive
CINDERB	cinderblock size	inches	positive
FLOAREA	livable floor area	square feet per unit	positive
FULBASE	full basement	yes/no	positive
APPLIAN	appliances included in selling price	number	positive
DENSITY	municipal density	persons per square mile	positive
TAXRATE	municipal tax rate	equalized dollars	negative
HOUSTOK	municipal housing stock (owner-occupied)	1970 Census dollar median	positive
BUSCALE	builder's scale of operation	annual number of units constructed	negative
DEVSIZE	size of subdivision development	number of units @ completion	unknown

Source: Field Survey, 1971.

EXHIBIT III-1

SAMPLE MEAN VALUES OF SELECTED PUBLIC POLICY VARIABLES

County	n=	Average Selling Price	Variable				
			Average Lot Size (sq.ft.)	Average Lot Frontage (front feet)	Average Setback (feet)	Average Liveable Floor Area (sq. ft.)
All Counties	529	47,434	22,330	113	42	2,137
Atlantic	11	30,518	11,818	103	31	1,776
Bergen	47	67,853	22,845	128	41	2,442
Burlington	27	33,592	11,500	83	31	2,016
Camden	15	38,607	9,580	78	33	2,408
Cape May	4	20,000	9,000	75	15	935
Cumberland	2	19,800	15,000	100	38	915
Essex	18	55,472	16,089	111	33	2,553
Gloucester	3	22,000	7,500	75	35	1,706
Hunterdon	5	36,400	25,000	120	51	1,664
Mercer	18	43,111	16,444	93	36	1,978
Middlesex	49	46,681	12,608	97	32	2,255
Monmouth	56	43,967	24,786	125	51	2,182
Morris	114	52,781	35,081	134	53	2,339
Ocean	68	30,365	9,000	77	30	1,412
Passaic	14	55,228	21,307	118	37	2,300
Somerset	29	61,697	45,307	157	68	2,375
Sussex	10	40,870	20,080	109	38	1,677
Union	23	61,869	22,847	120	45	2,317
Warren	16	44,625	25,025	113	40	2,403

Source: Field Survey, 1971

EXHIBIT III-2

INTERCORRELATION MATRIX
(n=529)

	BUSCALE	LOTSIZE	LOFRONT	SETBACK	DEVFEES	DENSITY	WALLSHT	CINDERB	FULBASE	APPLIAN
BUSCALE	1.00000									
LOTSIZE	-0.12710	1.00000								
LOFRONT	-0.12627	0.80518	1.00000							
SETBACK	-0.23558	0.66437	0.61669	1.00000						
DEVFEES	-0.07685	0.07023	0.09260	0.23764	1.00000					
DENSITY	0.16061	-0.24658	-0.23277	-0.28625	-0.17889	1.00000				
WALLSHT	-0.03906	0.08374	0.18298	0.22983	0.09128	0.13918	1.00000			
CINDERB	-0.04541	0.15254	0.17160	0.20166	0.14953	0.09885	0.17315	1.00000		
FULBASE	-0.25904	0.28310	0.32503	0.33689	0.10736	-0.06588	0.20783	0.24166	1.00000	
APPLIAN	0.20678	0.07251	-0.01184	0.11724	0.06076	0.00546	-0.07012	-0.07625	-0.00884	1.00000

EXHIBIT III-2 (Cont'd.)

INTERCORRELATION MATRIX
(n=529)

	MUDELAY	ROADPAV	CURBING	SIDWALK	SEWAGES	STREETS	HOUSTOK	TAXRATE	FLOAREA	SELPICE
BUSCALE	0.02404	0.04996	0.07297	0.14732	-0.17675	-0.06907	-0.25303	0.15451	-0.14368	-0.26345
LOTSIZE	-0.00278	0.02555	-0.00606	-0.34412	0.25684	-0.34934	0.46790	-0.04787	0.42598	0.61031
LOFRONT	0.02469	0.03519	-0.00280	-0.36573	0.24741	-0.35828	0.48922	0.01416	0.50053	0.64405
SETBACK	-0.05779	0.13764	0.08561	-0.27368	0.13362	-0.28846	0.54423	0.06200	0.44421	0.55873
DEVFEES	0.18187	0.18211	0.21689	0.18157	-0.32833	-0.03204	0.25658	-0.06208	0.20263	0.14969
DENSITY	-0.02338	-0.15919	0.02215	0.08951	-0.26669	-0.00069	-0.00091	0.15974	0.06873	0.05098
WALLSHT	-0.03692	0.05275	0.06173	-0.12341	-0.10503	-0.10467	0.33166	0.29101	0.36025	0.35889
CINDERB	0.09927	0.03757	0.12226	-0.07916	-0.11246	-0.01766	0.28070	0.06723	0.30419	0.34578
FULBASE	0.13977	0.04352	-0.04358	-0.20565	0.11000	-0.15838	0.40202	-0.04791	0.42327	0.50196
APPLIAN	-0.03742	0.07196	0.28015	-0.03954	-0.03904	0.00501	0.02968	0.27835	0.06664	0.05159
MUDELAY	1.00000	0.03368	0.03621	0.14724	-0.04210	0.14977	0.02390	-0.17254	0.18623	0.12244
ROADPAV		1.00000	0.58752	0.31407	-0.14387	0.35312	0.03012	-0.01715	0.08607	0.02592
CURBING			1.00000	0.33328	-0.19562	0.25562	0.13735	0.13992	0.14722	0.08928
SIDWALK				1.00000	-0.36518	0.36706	-0.36724	-0.02601	-0.18904	-0.38205
SEWAGES					1.00000	-0.07573	0.07957	-0.05017	-0.05672	0.07873
STREETS						1.00000	-0.24428	-0.10753	-0.10669	-0.20929
HOUSTOK							1.00000	0.09950	0.57320	0.72032
TAXRATE								1.00000	0.09646	0.01320
FLOAREA									1.00000	0.75733
SELPICE										1.00000

EXHIBIT III-3

STEPWISE EXPLANATION OF SELLING PRICE*

Variable	Unit	Regression Coefficient	t-ratio**	BETA Coefficeint	R²
FLOAREA	square feet per unit	9.75	11.61	.33	.574
BUSCALE	number of houses	-6.89	3.86	-.09	
LOTSIZE	square feet per lot	0.13	4.82	.18	
LOFRONT	front feet per lot	62.43	4.33	.16	
SETBACK	feet per lot	8.21	(.26)	.01	
DEVFEES	dollars per unit	-1.41	(1.19)	-.03	
DENSITY	persons per square mile	1.38	5.15	.12	
WALLSHT	inch	18,233.64	3.45	.08	
CINDERB	inches	601.46	2.89	.06	
FULBASE	yes(1), no(0)	3,364.89	4.09	.10	
APPLIAN	number	761.34	2.19	.05	
MUDELAY	months	70.22	(1.88)	.04	
ROADPAV	width in feet	-85.05	(.53)	-.02	
CURBING	yes(1), no(0)	2,061.39	(1.14)	.03	
SIDWALK	width in feet	-1,012.89	3.91	-.10	
SEWAGES	septic(1), sewer(0)	-1,095.01	(1.08)	-.03	
STREETS	% total subdivision area	100.41	(1.73)	.04	
HOUSTOK	1970 census dollar median	0.53	8.14	.24	
TAXRATE	equalized dollars	-2,324.38	3.46	-.08	

R^2 =   .804
F =
Number of Observations   110   529

* In this and other exhibits of regression results, constant terms are not shown since they have no particular importance for the present study.

** Coefficients in parentheses are insignificant at the .95 level of significance for a one-tail test.

Source: Field Survey, 1971.

EXHIBIT III-4

EXPLANATION OF SELLING PRICE CONTROLLING FOR TYPE OF SEWAGE DISPOSAL

Variable	Regression Coefficient		t – ratios*	
	Sewer	Septic	Sewer	Septic
FLOAREA	8.63	15.76	10.31	6.56
BUSCALE	-9.44	2.62	-5.05	(0.26)
LOTSIZE	0.01	0.16	(0.22)	3.71
LOFRONT	112.25	27.97	5.42	(1.17)
SETBACK	97.81	-45.20	2.95	(-0.62)
DEVFEES	-2.37	-3.29	-2.06	(-0.45)
DENSITY	1.44	1.45	5.92	(1.02)
WALLSHT	-42.16	43,337.22	(-0.01)	2.99
CINDERB	797.22	-609.66	3.91	(-0.97)
FULBASE	3,621.15	1,657.84	4.62	(0.71)
APPLIAN	1,091.49	321.08	3.26	(0.26)
MUDELAY	79.64	-108.04	2.35	(-0.68)
ROADPAV	-298.77	127.65	(-1.70)	(0.38)
CURBING	2,855.70	345.64	(1.31)	(0.08)
SIDWALK	-551.58	-1,067.95	-2.08	(-1.24)
STREETS	96.55	219.43	(1.72)	(1.22)
HOUSTOK	0.46	0.80	6.77	5.06
TAXRATE	-3,391.97	3,624.35	-4.68	(1.66)
DEVSIZE	0.17	16.83	(0.51)	3.21

R^2 = .799 .884
F = 81 41
Number of Observations = 408 121

* Coefficients in parentheses are insignificant at the .95 level of significance for a one-tail test.

Source: Field Survey, 1971.

EXHIBIT III-5

VARIABLE MEAN STATISTICS FOR SAMPLE SUBSETS

Variable	Full Sample Mean (n=529)	Sewered (n=408)	Nonsewered (n=121)	Urbanized (n=385)	Rural (n=144)
FLOAREA	2,136.90	2,155.07	2,075.62	2,213.66	1,931.67
BUSCALE	151.13	172.33	79.61	172.93	92.84
LOTSIZE	22,330.62	19,108.33	33,195.87	19,875.07	28,895.83
LOFRONT	112.99	107.05	133.00	112.35	114.69
SETBACK	42.41	41.12	46.73		
DEVFEES	573.14	637.72	358.76	617.71	453.96
DENSITY	1,529.81	1,752.05	780.44	1,928.40	464.12
WALLSHT	0.51	0.51	0.49	0.51	0.50
CINDERB	10.37	10.49	10.00	10.62	9.71
FULBAS	0.49	0.46	0.59	0.52	0.40
APPLIAN	3.44	3.46	3.36	3.43	3.45
MUDELAY	4.13	4.36	3.36	4.89	2.09
ROADPAV	14.76	14.99	13.97	14.85	14.51
CURBING	0.92	0.95	0.83	0.95	0.85
SIDWALK	2.58	2.93	1.39	2.67	2.29
SEWAGES	0.23			0.15	0.43
STREETS	17.03	17.34	15.99	17.05	16.98
HOUSTOK	28,561.18	28,215.68	29,726.18	29,468.79	26,134.60
TAXRATE	3.19	3.21	3.14	3.22	3.12
DEVSIZE	426.22	506.93	154.07		
SELPICE	47,433.84	46,691.67	49,936.36	49,006.49	43,229.17

Source: Field Survey, 1971.

EXHIBIT III-6

STEPWISE EXPLANATION OF SELLING PRICE: REDUCED VARIABLE SET

Variable	Regression Coefficient	t-ratio	BETA Coefficient	R^2
FLOAREA	10.07	12.25	.34	.57
BUSCALE	-7.34	4.29	-.09	
LOTSIZE	0.13	4.95	.17	
LOFRONT	58.79	4.14	.15	
DENSITY	1.45	5.96	.13	
WALLSHT	18,531.26	3.55	.08	
CINDERB	666.87	3.28	.07	
FULBAS	3,039.37	3.79	.09	
APPLIAN	922.78	2.84	.06	
MUDELAY	68.79	1.89	.04	
SIDWALK	-830.45	3.83	-.09	
HOUSTOK	0.52	8.70	.24	
TAXRATE	-2,361.84	3.56	-.08	

R^2 =   .80

F =   159

Number of
Observations =   529

Source: Field Survey, 1971.

EXHIBIT III-7

BETA COEFFICIENTS FOR REGRESSION ANALYSES*

Variable	Full Sample (n=529)	Sewer Sample (n=408)	Septic Sample (n=121)	Urbanized Sample (n=385)	Rural Sample (n=144)
FLOAREA	.33	.33	.44	.26	.43
BUSCALE	-.09	-.16	(.01)	-.12	-.08
LOTSIZE	.18	(.01)	.26	.27	.38
LOFRONT	.16	.26	(.07)	.14	(-.04)
SETBACK	(.01)	.11	(-.04)		
DEVFEES	(-.03)	-.06	(-.02)	(-.02)	(-.03)
DENSITY	.12	.16	(.05)	.18	(.03)
WALLSHT	.08	(-.00)	.18	.10	(-.07)
CINDERB	.06	.10	(-.05)	(.03)	.22
FULBAS	.10	.13	(.01)	.12	.08
APPLIAN	.05	.09	(-.03)	.11	(-.05)
MUDELAY	(.04)	.06	(.02)	.07	(.03)
ROADPAV	(-.02)	(-.06)	(.01)	(-.04)	(-.03)
CURBING	(.03)	(.04)	(-.07)	(.00)	(.08)
SIDWALK	-.10	-.06		(-.03)	-.18
SEWAGES	(-.03)	(.05)	(.07)	(-.01)	(-.03)
STREETS	(.04)	.23	.33	.07	.12
HOUSTOK	.24	-.14	.09	.32	(.09)
TAXRATE	.08	(.02)	.19	(-.06)	.07
DEVSIZE	—	—	—	—	—

* Coefficients in parenthesis are insignificant @ .95 level of significance for a one-tail test

Source: Field Survey, 1971.

EXHIBIT III-8

EXPLANATION OF SELLING PRICE CONTROLLING FOR URBAN-RURAL LOCATION

Variable	Regression Coefficient		t - ratios*	
	Urbanized	Rural	Urbanized	Rural
FLOAREA	7.48	13.25	7.49	9.13
BUSCALE	-7.43	-14.23	-3.89	-2.21
LOTSIZE	0.33	0.20	4.85	6.93
LOFRONT	60.54	-14.84	2.69	(-0.81)
DEVFEES	-1.10	-1.67	(-0.74)	(-0.71)
DENSITY	1.73	1.37	5.65	(1.05)
WALLSHT	23,587.81	-14,587.73	3.55	(-1.35)
CINDERB	285.62	2,368.59	(1.14)	5.12
FULBASE	3,770.58	3,489.92	4.15	2.04
APPLIAN	1,476.45	-806.56	3.42	(-1.41)
MUDELAY	91.18	189.95	2.37	(1.05)
ROADPAV	-215.97	-195.15	(-1.01)	(-0.86)
CURBING	5.60	4,575.13	(0.00)	(1.68)
SIDWALK	-211.41	-2,122.13	(-0.65)	-4.13
SEWAGES	-508.43	-1,077.71	(-0.39)	(-0.72)
STREETS	153.56	302.35	2.20	2.26
HOUSTOK	0.67	0.20	8.51	(1.86)
TAXRATE	-1,656.50	2,009.93	(-1.88)	(1.54)

R^2 =   .767   .921
F =   67   80
Number of Observations =   385   144

* Coefficients in parenthesis are insignificant @ .95 level of confidence for a one-tail test

Field Survey, 1971.

EXHIBIT III-9

INCOME DISTRIBUTION OF NEW JERSEY FAMILIES: 1970

Income Bracket	State	Central City of SMSA	Outside CC in SMSA	Non-Metropolitan
			Percentage	
Less then $10,000	40.42	58.26	36.20	39.41
$10,000 - $14,999	30.06	25.31	30.73	31.53
$15,000 - $24,999	22.48	13.64	24.57	22.99
$25,000 and over	7.04	2.79	8.50	6.07
Total	100.00	100.00	100.00	100.00
Median Income	$11,407	$8,805	$12,021	$11,480

Source: U.S. Bureau of the Census, Census of Population: 1970, General Social and Economic Characteristics, Final Report: New Jersey (Washington, D.C.: U.S. Government Printing Office, 1972).

IV

The Courts and
Exclusionary Zoning

9

Erwin Elias

SIGNIFICANT DEVELOPMENTS AND TRENDS IN ZONING LITIGATION (excerpts)

Exclusionary Zoning Perspective

At least one of the most significant trends in zoning law is and will probably continue to be a change in attitude toward so-called exclusionary ordinances, provisions, and practices, particularly those intended to have or having the effect of discriminating against minority and low income groups. Included in this category are minimum lot size and floor space provisions and ordinances which exclude multiple dwelling units and mobile homes. Even the definition of "family" found in most zoning ordinances has come under attack on the basis that the resulting limitation on residential use tends to fall hardest on certain classes or groups.[4] This exclusionary aspect of zoning has been the subject of a host of recent studies and articles in law reviews and elsewhere.[5] Almost without exception, these have been highly critical of traditional principles and practices throughout the country and most have advocated drastic changes in present law. Many of these writings are misleading in that the authors tend to draw somewhat unwarranted conclusions from a handful of state and federal decisions.[6] It is too early to assert that all or most common exclusionary ordinances and practices are prima facie invalid, and that one need only bring suit to obtain the desired relief. The law has not developed to this point. Nevertheless the foundations have been laid, some precedent already exists, and it appears likely there will be more and more successful challenges to such ordinances. There is simply too much pressure for change from various sources and directions.

One major impetus has been and will continue to be the implementation of the various federal low income housing programs. The Federal Government is now committed to a policy of dispersing low income housing projects throughout a city or metropolitan area instead of locating such projects in existing ghetto areas. Frequently this policy clashes with local zoning ordinances and practices, and one or the other must yield.[7]

A second impetus is the well-known migration of industries and employers generally from the central cities out to the suburbs and beyond. Efforts by employees to follow and find suitable living accommodations in the vicinity are often frustrated by existing land use regulations. The scope of the problem and the dilemma confronting low income individuals is best illustrated by a few statistics selected more or less at random. According to the National Committee on Urban Problems, in 1969, 25 percent of all metropolitan municipalities permitted no single family homes on lots of less than one-half acre. In Connecticut, 92 percent of all vacant land is zoned for at least one-half acre residences. Two-thirds of the 82,000 acres zoned for single family homes in Cuyahoga County, Ohio, where Cleveland is located, are restricted to lots of one-half acre or up.[8]

Presumably in many of these same areas multifamily dwellings and mobile homes are very restricted or totally excluded. One obvious effect of these restrictions is on the employment situation: The job openings are in the suburbs where the unemployed cannot afford to live. While positions are available in the suburbs, unemployment in the central cities continues to increase together with the size of the welfare roles. Where these conditions prevail, it is readily apparent why such exclusionary zoning measures are looked upon with great disfavor.

A third influence here is the school segregation controversy. Certainly the issue of de facto segregation has focused attention on urban housing patterns and these, in turn, frequently relate to local zoning practices.

Finally, a growing number of state legislatures have enacted or are considering legislation providing for either state or regional control over land use planning and regulation, superceding local authority and prerogatives in this area. This "quiet revolution in land use control"[9] is occurring in at least twenty states[10] and is, in part, a response or reaction to local exclusionary zoning practices and excessive provincialism generally. The message here to municipalities should be clear enough. Either modify prevailing local zoning philosophy and practices or lose authority over local land use.

Before launching into the cases, one other observation should be made. The attack on exclusionary or "snob zoning" appears to represent a basic challenge to traditional objectives of and justifications for zoning laws, particularly the different categories of residential uses. It is apparent that these zoning laws have been employed to serve the best interests of the particular community only and that the predominate purposes have been to protect property values from the impact of undesirable residential use and to protect the local tax base. There is, then, clearly more than a mere superficial conflict between these traditional objectives and propositions to the effect that a municipality owes an obligation to nonresidents and the broader area in regulating land use, that every municipality should be open and available to all economic classes, and that protecting the local economy from low tax, high cost land uses, so-called fiscal zoning, may not be a legitimate object of land use regulation. The conflict does not appear to be susceptible to either easy or popular solutions. One commentator has observed, perhaps correctly, that judicial efforts to resolve the problem will make the school segregation cases appear like simple arithmetic by comparison.[11]

I will now examine developments in the Federal courts.

Federal Precedents

It has been contended that exclusionary ordinances, provisions, and practices are subject to a successful challenge in federal courts on any of the following grounds:[12]

(1) That such laws or practices are violative of the Equal Protection Clause of the Fourteenth Amendment in that they discriminate against racial minorities and the lower income classes. Often, the proponents of this argument equate the two on the basis that most members of minority groups are also in the lower income categories;

(2) That such laws conflict with various federal laws and policies relating to low income housing and that therefore, by virtue of the Supremacy Clause, these ordinances must yield to national policies;

(3) That such laws are in conflict with a somewhat amorphous right to housing derived from the Ninth Amendment to the U.S. Constitution; and

(4) That such laws unduly infringe upon the constitutional right to travel, enter, and abide, in violation of the Privileges and Immunities Clause of the Fourteenth Amendment.

Dicta appearing in a number of recent cases is supportive of one or more of these propositions.[13] Whatever their merit, however, the federal courts have not in fact based a single holding on any one of them and have not struck down a single zoning ordinance or provision because it was deemed exclusionary. There have been a number of successful suits against the Department of Housing and Urban Development and other housing authorities wherein the courts propounded similar theories, but these cases, *Gatreax v. Chicago Housing Authority*,[14] *Shannon v. Romney*,[15] *Fletcher v. Romney*, [16] and *Banks v. Perk*,[17] for example, did not involve zoning ordinances or provisions. The issue in all these cases was whether the governmental entities had obeyed the mandates of the federal law with reference to location of low rent housing projects. The impact on zoning laws and practices is, at most, indirect.

There have been a number of recent decisions where the courts have condemned particular applications of land use regulations but in each of these cases the actions invalidated were rather obviously motivated by racial prejudice. In *Dailey v. City of Lawton, Oklahoma*[18] the district court found that the city council's refusal to rezone a tract to R-4 for the purpose of low income housing was "a direct result of the bias and prejudice on the part of the owners of other property" and was motivated by a desire "to keep a large concentration of Negroes and other minority groups from living in North Addition . . . and the fear of the property owners . . . that . . . such project . . . would bring about a depreciation in property values in the district."[19] The Tenth Circuit Court of Appeals held that the evidence supported these findings.

In *Kennedy Park Homes Ass'n. v. City of Lakawanna, N.Y.*,[20] a frequently cited case, the city rezoned property selected for a housing project to a park and recreation area. The court found that these actions were racially motivated to deny housing to low income and minority groups. Finally, in *Crow v. Brown*,[21] county officials, upon learning of the nature of the project, denied a building permit for low rent public housing projects for blacks in an area zoned for apartments. In each of these cases the purported explanations were found to be wanting. The federal courts have jurisdiction under Section 1983, Title 42, United States Code,[22] and other provisions to grant relief from denials of equal protection, and this, of course, was the basis of these decisions.

Racial zoning as such has been invalid since the 1917 U.S. Supreme Court decision in *Buchanan v. Worley*.[23] Consequently, these three holdings, as such, are hardly extraordinary.

However, the opinions contain language considerably broader than was necessary to the holdings, and this dicta may be indicative of what the future holds. For example, note these quotes from *Crow v. Brown* :[24]

> ''For better or worse, both by legislative act and judicial decision, this nation is committed to a policy of balanced and dispersed public housing . . . in the area of public housing local authorities can no more confine low income blacks to a compacted and concentrated area than they can confine their children to segregated schools . . . (Quoting from *Hobson v. Hansen*, 269 F. Supp. 401 (D.D.C. 1967)). . . . The complaint that analytically no violation of equal protection vests unless the inequities stem from a deliberately discriminatory plan is simply false. Whatever the law was once, it is a testament to our maturing concept of equality that, with the help of Supreme Court decisions in the last decade, we now firmly recognize that the arbitrary quality of thoughtlessness can be as disastrous to private rights and the public interest as the perversity of a willful scheme.''[25]

Economic Discrimination—Relief Denied

To place this all in perspective, perhaps the most important service one can perform in this area, it is necessary to examine what the federal judiciary has declined to do. First, there has been a reluctance, indeed a refusal, to equate exclusion on economic grounds with exclusion on the basis of race or color. The various low income housing referendum cases are in point. In *James v. Valtierra*,[26] the United States Supreme Court upheld the validity of a state constitutional provision which required approval by the majority of the voting electorate in a community as a condition to locating a low rent housing project within the community. The District Court had held that the provision violated the equal protection clause, relying on *Hunter v. Erickson*,[27] where the Supreme Court had invalidated a referendum requirement relating to open housing. In *James*, the majority distinguished *Hunter* on the basis that in that case the referendum placed special burdens on racial minorities.

Here, however, the California law was seemingly neutral on its face. The Court noted that referendum approval is required for "any low-rent public housing project, not only for projects which will be occupied by a racial minority,"[28] and emphasized that mandatory referendum provisions are common in California law. The Court concluded as follows:

"The people of California have also decided by their own vote to require a referendum approval of low-rent public housing projects. This procedure ensures that all the people of a community will have a voice in a decision which may lead to large expenditures of local governmental funds for increased public services and to lower tax revenues. It gives them a voice in decisions that will affect the future development of their cwn community. This procedure for democratic decision-making does not violate the constitutional command that no state shall deny to any person 'the equal protection of the laws.' "[29]

The three dissenters in this case argued that the Fourteenth Amendment also prohibits discrimination against the poor and that the state constitutional provision in question on its face constituted invidious discrimination because it "explicitly singles out low income persons to bear its burden."[30]

Several prior courts of appeals cases had reached the same result. In *Southern Alameda Spanish Speaking Organization v. City of Union City, California*,[31] for example, the court refused to inquire into the motives of the voters in rejecting low income housing.

Preemption—Privileges and Immunities

In *James v. Valtierra*,[32] the Court rather summarily rejected the contentions that the exclusion of low income housing through the referendum process violated the Supremacy Clause and the Privilege and Immunities Clause with the following statements:

"By the Housing Act of 1937 the Federal Government

has offered aid to states and local governments for the creation of low-rent public housing. However, the federal legislation does not purport to require that local governments accept this or to outlaw local referendums on whether the aid should be accepted. We also find the privileges and immunities argument without merit."[33]

Conclusion—Federal Precedents

At first glance, it might appear that the Court in *James v. Valtierra*[34] has rather conclusively rejected the propositions set forth earlier[35] and that further appeals to the federal courts to set aside exclusionary zoning ordinances will be futile unless overt racial discrimination is involved. This may, of course, be the case, and it is understandable that the Court is reluctant to enter this highly explosive area, particularly since state legislatures are beginning to take remedial action. Such an interpretation of this decision may, however, be entirely too broad. It should be noted that in *James*, there was no factual showing of injury to either racial or economic groups. Moreover, a referendum was involved and the Court was unwilling to presume prejudice on the part of the electorate or inquire into their motivation. In a different context, this decision may carry very little weight.[36] While the decision does represent a setback to opponents of "snob zoning" practices, it is not likely that the Court intended to place its stamp of approval on such practices. Where a zoning law or action has a discernible adverse impact on racial minority groups, one must anticipate that the Court will afford a remedy, and it would not be surprising if the Court would do likewise where there is obvious unjustified discrimination between rich and poor. There already exists ample precedent for such a holding.[37]

State Cases

Important developments with respect to exclusionary zoning have occurred in a number of jurisdictions. I will use three recent decisions as a framework for discussion and analysis of trends in the areas of minimum lot size restrictions, multifamily dwellings and mobile homes.

Minimum Lot Size

In *Oakwood at Madison, Inc. v. The Township of Madison*,[38] the New Jersey Court held invalid a township zoning ordinance restricting the number of multifamily buildings and zoning most of the remaining vacant land for one- and two-acre lot minimums, with minimum floor space of 1,500 and 1,600 square feet. The basis of the holding was that such zoning failed to promote a reasonably balanced community, that it ignored the housing needs of the region, and that it constituted fiscal zoning. The town's population had grown from 7,366 in 1950 to 48,715 in 1970. The obvious purposes of the zoning provisions in question were to curb population growth, stabilize the tax rate, and enable the township to "catch its breath."[39] The effect of the ordinance was to exclude the majority of the population from some 8,000 acres of land appropriate for low and moderate income housing. Under the ordinance, the minimum purchase price for a home in this area was estimated at $45,000. The substantial limitation on multifamily dwellings further aggravated the situation.[40]

The plaintiffs had contended that the enabling statute was invalid because it did not expressly include provision for housing needs as one of the purposes of zoning. On this point, the court held that the general welfare concept embraces providing for housing needs, both local and regional. The only issue was therefore the validity of the particular zoning ordinance. After rejecting revenue considerations and population growth control as legitimate justifications for the restrictions, and finding no merit in other justifications relied on by the town, flood control and underground water preservation, for example, the Court concluded as follows:

> "In pursuing the valid zoning purposes of a balanced community, a municipality must not ignore housing

needs, that is, its fair proportion of the obligation to meet the housing needs of its own population and of the region. Housing needs are encompassed within the general welfare. The general welfare does not stop at each municipal boundary. . . ."[41]

The specific basis for striking down the lot size provisions was due process—that these restrictions had no relationship to the general welfare as defined by the Court. In this respect, the rationale differs from a number of decisions on the same issue from Pennsylvania. The most recent case from that state, *In re Kit-Mar Builders*,[42] invalidated two- and three-acre minimum zoning restrictions. At least three of the four man majority in the Pennsylvania cases based their decisions on equal protection considerations. This may be a broader ground than due process for attacking such provisions.

Minimum lot restrictions have generally been upheld throughout the United States although there have been a few previous cases holding the restrictions invalid in a particular situation.[43] The New Jersey and Pennsylvania cases are therefore not really that novel as far as the result is concerned. The explicit rejection of population growth control and revenue considerations as justifications is noteworthy, although a Virginia Court had previously reached similar conclusions in 1959.[44] What is significant, however, is that in part, at least, the decisions were based on the principle that a municipality has an affirmative responsibility for considering and providing regional housing needs for all income groups in exercising its zoning functions.[45]

A great number of local governments are going to be in for quite a shock should this principle spread to other jurisdictions.[46]

Multifamily Housing

Moving into the area of restrictions on multifamily housing, we have another decision out of New Jersey, *Southern*

Burlington County N.A.A. C. P. v. Township of Mount Laurel,[47] decided earlier this year. This was an action for declaratory and injunctive relief against a township zoning ordinance that totally excluded multifamily dwellings from the township,[48] together with trailers and mobile homes. There was an issue of standing raised, but I will postpone discussion on this subject until later.[49] The evidence showed that individual plaintiffs and others lived in substandard housing located within a blighted area of the township, but, despite the fact that some 66 percent of the township is vacant land, no standard dwellings are available for these persons. The minimum building cost for a single family home within the township was more than $23,000, well out of the reach of the plaintiffs and others in their economic bracket.

The court's rationale in striking down this ordinance clearly appears from the following quotation:

> "The patterns and practices clearly indicate that defendant municipality through its zoning ordinance has exhibited economic discrimination in that the poor have been deprived of adequate housing and the opportunity to secure the construction of subsidized housing, and has used federal, state, county and local finances and resources solely for the betterment of middle and upper income persons. The zoning ordinance is, therefore, declared invalid."[50]

This is probably the only decision to date wherein a zoning ordinance has been held invalid specifically on the basis that the ordinance discriminated against the poor either intentionally or through thoughtlessness. The Pennsylvania Court in *Appeal of Girsh*[51] had held that total exclusion of multifamily use was per se unreasonable, but the basis of that decision was due process. The only precedent relied upon by the New Jersey Court is language from dissenting opinions[52] and dicta from recent Federal Court decisions.[53]

Anyone even remotely familiar with the history of zoning litigation in this country is aware of how the United States

Supreme Court characterized multifamily dwellings in *Village of Euclid v. Ambler Realty Co.,*[54] as a predicate for upholding the general concept of zoning restrictions. Such dewllings were described as parasites which in various ways destroy the residential character of a neighborhood and which come very near being common-law nuisances. With this historical background, it is not surprising that exclusion of multifamily land uses have been universally upheld in the past. One can only speculate on whether other jurisdictions will follow the lead of the New Jersey and Pennsylvania courts, but in this connection, the obvious conflict between zoning ordinances banning multifamily dwellings and federal law and policy with respect to dispersion of low income housing is relevant and may be a determining factor.

Appropriate Remedy

One other aspect of the *Mount Laurel Township* decision merits comment. A troublesome issue in zoning cases is the appropriate judicial remedy when an exclusionary zoning ordinance has been successfully challenged. The orthodox approach has been to declare the ordinance invalid and let it go at that.[55] The end result has frequently been that the successful, aggrieved landowner won the battle but lost the war. For example, in the two Pennsylvania cases discussed previously, the municipalities amended the zoning ordinances to comply with the Court's decisions but the property of the particular plaintiffs was not rezoned.[56] To avoid this result, a few jurisdictions have followed a practice of not declaring the ordinance invalid as a whole but granting relief to the particular claimants—judicial spot zoning in effect.[57] In *Mount Laurel,* the New Jersey Court went considerably farther and ordered the township to take affirmative action within parameters established by the court. The defendant was ordered to undertake a study to identify housing needs for persons of low and moderate income residing in the township, those employed within the township, regardless of where they reside, or those projected to be employed in the township in the future, and to then estimate how many low and moderate income units will be required to meet these needs. When this analysis is completed the township shall "develop a plan of implementation, that is, an affirmative program, to enable and encourage the satisfaction of the needs as previously set forth."[58] This task was to be completed within ninety days. Should circumstances arise that will frustrate the implementation of the plan, the township will be under a continuing duty to explain and justify this failure and recommend alternatives.

Note the similarity between this decree and those entered in many of the school segregation cases. Actually the New Jersey court's approach is not unique. The Fifth Circuit has upheld similar decrees in *Crow v. Brown*,[59] a discriminatory zoning case already discussed, and *Hawkins v. Shaw*,[60] involving discriminatory furnishing of municipal services.

Standing

The issue of standing to attack a zoning ordinance or action was briefly referred to previously. In the past, standing has been limited to affected property owners or, in some cases, local taxpayers.[61] A number of recent decisions have expanded the concept to include nonresidents whose property interests outside the zoning entity's boundaries will or may be affected. In *Scott v. Indian Wells*,[62] for example, the California Supreme Court held that a municipality owed a duty to give notice to and hear and consider the views of nonresident objectors to a grant of a conditional use permit for a planned development just within the city limits. Moreover the city owed a duty to consider the proposed development's effect on all neighboring property owners, inside or outside the corporate limits. A similar view was taken by the Missouri Supreme Court in the case of *Dahman v. Ballwin*[63] where nonresident property owners were permitted to challenge a zoning amendment reclassifying a tract of land on the outer edge of the city.

These and similar holdings reflect judicial awareness of the fact that zoning measures may have a substantial impact beyond the municipal boundaries. Note that both decisions involve nonresident property owners. Thus far, no case appears to have extended standing to a nonresident entity or person who does not have an affected property interest.

Mobile Homes

Municipal zoning and building code restrictions on mobile homes and house trailers have been a source of much litigation over the years and the tempo appears to be increasing.[64] This is another area where one can forsee some far-reaching changes in existing laws. Reference has already been made to the fact that the shortage of low income housing in this country has reached crisis proportions. The mobile home industry has grown tremendously in the past decade and has, to some extent, filled the breach. For example, in 1967, 75 percent of all new dwellings starts under $12,000 were mobile homes. By 1969, one-third of all new single family dwellings were mobile homes and 90 percent of all homes sold for less than $15,000 and 98 percent of those under $12,500 were mobile homes.[65] Obviously, this is a highly significant development in the area of meeting the housing needs of low and medium income classes.

Despite these impressive statistics, community resistance to mobile homes remains high. These structures have changed greatly since house trailers first appeared in the 1920s. The great majority of mobile homes sold today differ from conventionally built dwellings mainly in that they are preassembled elsewhere and then moved to the land, rather than being constructed at the site. Once "attached" to the land they are seldom moved again. Nevertheless, the old image lingers and is reflected in zoning laws restricting such dwellings to mobile home parks, excluding them from residential districts, or prohibiting them entirely within the municipality. The latter result may be accomplished by express provision, or, indirectly, by refusal to issue a special permit or by applying restrictive building code provisions. On the whole, the courts throughout the country have upheld and are still upholding these various restrictions.[66] In a few states, however, there has occurred an apparent change in judicial attitude and approach, at least where total exclusion is involved.[67] The Michigan Courts have taken the lead in a series of cases culminating in the 1971 decision in *Bristow v. Woodhaven*.[68] The court there invalidated on due process grounds an ordinance totally excluding mobile homes from a municipality. The rationale was that certain land uses have a preferred status by virtue of overall public policy considerations and ordinances excluding such uses are prima facie invalid. The burden of justifying such exclusion as being in the public welfare is upon the municipality. Included in the category of preferred uses are churches, schools, hospitals, and mobile homes. In discussing the general welfare concept as it applies to mobile homes, the court made the following comments:

> "That term is not a mere catchword to permit the translation of narrow desires into ordinances which discriminate against or operate to exclude certain residential uses deemed beneficial. Citizens of the general community have a right to decently placed, suitable housing within their means and such right must be a consideration in assessing the reasonableness of local zoning prescribing residential requirements or prohibitions. Such zoning may never stand where its primary purpose is shown to operate for the exclusion of a certain element of residential dwellers."[69]

The doctrine propounded by the Michigan court is novel only in its application to housing needs and mobile homes. The courts everywhere have frowned on exclusion of certain land uses, such as for churches, in the past, and in many jurisdictions an ordinance totally zoning out any lawful use is of questionable validity.[70]

It should also be emphasized that restrictions on the location and use of mobile homes not amounting to a total prohibition are still being uniformly upheld throughout the country. One might anticipate some legal challenges to these restrictions on both due process and equal protection grounds in the near future. There appears to be, for example, little justification for excluding such dwellings from residential districts.

Summary—State Developments

The political and other pressures for change I have referred to previously are obviously not present everywhere in the country to the same degree. It may be some time before this development runs its course in all fifty states, and there's always the possibility that either state or federal legislation will preempt the area. It can be safely asserted, however, that a significant trend is emerging, and we haven't seen the last of litigation involving the validity of exclusive zoning ordinances and practices.

NOTES

[4] People v. Skidmore, 329 N.Y.S.2d 881 (1971), ordinance upheld over equal protection argument; Palo Alto Tenants Union v. Morgan, 321 F. Supp. 908 (N.D. Cal. 1970), ordinance upheld against contentions based on freedom of association, equal protection, and due process; Kirsh Holding Co. v. Borough of Manasquan, 59 N.J. 241, 281 A.2d 513 (1971), invalidating family definition designed to prohibit group rental as sweepingly excessive and therefore unreasonable.

[5] See, e.g., Sager, "Tight Little Islands; Exclusionary Zoning; Equal Protection and the Indigent," 21 Stan. L. Rev. 767 (1969); Aloi, Goldberg & White, "Racial and Economic Segregation by Zoning; Death Knell for Home Rule?" 1 U. Tol. L. Rev. 65 (1969); Williams & Wacks, "Segregation of Residential Areas Along Economic Lines; Lyonshead Lake Revisited," 1969 Wis. L. Rev. 27 (1969); Jackson, "Attacking the Affluent Islands: A Legal Strategy for the 70's," 1971 Urban L. Ann. 3 (1971); Aloi & Goldberg, "Racial and Economic Exclusionary Zoning: The Beginning of the End?" 1971 Urban L. Ann. 9 (1971); "Symposium, Exclusionary Zoning," 22 Syracuse L. Rev. No. 2 (1971); Feiler, "Metropolitization and Land Use Parochialism—Toward a Judicial Attitude," 69 Mich. L. Rev. 655 (1971); Freilich and Bass, "Exclusionary Zoning: Suggested Litigation Approaches," 3 Urban Lawyer 344 (1971); Comments—40 U.M.K.C. 24 (1971), 24 U. of Fla. L. Rev. 58 (1971), 81 Yale L.S. 61 (1971).

[6] In addition to the cases discussed in this paper preliminary motions have been adjudicated in a number of cases involving exclusionary ordinances. See, Sisters of Providence of St. Mary of the Woods v. City of Evanston, 335 F. Supp. 396 (N.D. Ill. 1971); Steel Hill Development, Inc. v. Town of Sanbornton, 335 F. Supp. 947 (D.N.H. 1971); English v. Town of Huntington, 335 F. Supp. 1369 (E.D.N.Y. 1970) aff'd 448 F.2d 319 (2d Cir. 1971); Park View Heights Corp. v. City of Black Jack, 335 F. Supp. 899 (E.D. Mo. 1971). The City of Black Jack litigation is discussed in Lefcoe, "From Capitol Hill: The Impact of Civil Rights Litigation on H.U.D. Policy," 4 Urban Lawyer 112 at 113-114 (1972).

7 See Stegman, "National Housing and Land Use Policy Conflicts," 49 J. of Urban Law 629 (1972). The various Federal housing acts and policies are outlined and discussed in the authorities cited in N. 5 *supra*, and the cases cited in Ns. 13-17 *infra*. The applicable site selection rules are set out in, "Site Selection Criteria Regulations, Department of Housing and Urban Development," 37 Fed. Reg. 203 (Jan. 7, 1972).

8 The figures are taken from Maxwell, "The Lawyer in Government," 4 Urban Lawyer 238 at 240 (1972). For similar statistics and a discussion of the impact of exclusionary ordinances on the central city and unemployment, see Aloi & Goldberg, N. 5 *supra* at 12–16.

9 Wall Street Journal, June 28, 1972, p. 1, col. 6, and p. 19, col. 4.

10 *Ibid.* A number of the state enactments are set out and analyzed in Mandelker, *Managing Our Urban Environment, Cases, Text & Problems* 1129–1148 (1971). In Aloi, Goldberg & White, N. 5 *supra*, the authors discuss the potential consequences of such legislation on municipal home rule.

11 Babcock, "The Courts Enter the Land Development Marketplace," 5 City 58 at 61 (Jan.-Feb. 1971).

12 These various propositions are analyzed in most of the articles cited in N. 5 *supra*, particularly Freilich and Bass, and Aloi and Goldberg.

13 See particularly Banks v. Perk, 341 F. Supp. 1175 (N.D. Ohio 1972); Southern Alameda Spanish Speaking Organization v. City of Union, 424 F.2d 291 (9th Cir. 1970); Crow v. Brown, 332 F. Supp. 382 (N.D. Ga. 1971), *aff'd* 457 F.2d 788 (5th Cir. 1972).

14 265 F. Supp. 582 (N.D. Ill. 1967); 296 F. Supp. 907 (N.D. Ill. 1969), *aff'd* 436 F.2d 306 (7th Cir. 1970), *cert. denied* 402 U.S. 922, 448 F.2d 731 (7th Cir. 1971), 457 F.2d 124 (7th Cir. 1972).

15 303 F. Supp. 205 (E.D. Pa. 1969), *rev'd* 436 F.2d (3d Cir. 1970).

16 323 F. Supp. 189 (S.D.N.Y. 1971).

17 N. 13 *supra*.

18 425 F.2d 1037 (10th Cir. 1970).

19 Dailey v. City of Lawton, Okla., 296 F. Supp. 266 at 268–269 (W.D. Okla.).

20 436 F.2d 108 (2d Cir. 1971), *cert. denied* 401 U.S. 1010 (1971).

21 N. 13 *supra*.

22 "Every person who, under color of any statute, ordinance, regulation, custom, or usage, of any State or Territory, subjects, or causes to be subjected, any citizen of the United States or other person within the jurisdiction thereof to the deprivation of any rights, privileges, or immunities secured by the Constitution and laws, shall be liable to the party injured in an action at law, suit in equity, or other proper proceedings for redress."

23 245 U.S. 60 (1917).

24 N. 13 *supra*.

25 *Id.* at 390–391.

26 402 U.S. 137 (1971).

27 393 U.S. 385 (1969).

28 402 U.S. 137 at 140. Note that the majority apparently rejected the thesis that discrimination against low income groups may be equated with discrimination against racial minorities because so many of the latter are poor. See Southern Alameda Spanish Speaking Organization v. Union City, N. 13 *supra*, where the Court appears to equate low income families and racial minorities; Comment, 81 Yale L.J. 61 (1971), particularly pp. 69–71. Compare Lefcoe, N. 5 *supra*.

29 *Id.* at 141.

30 *Id.* at 142.

31 N. 13 *supra*. See also Ranjel v. City of Lansing, 417 F.2d 321 (6th Cir. 1969), *rev'g* 293 F. Supp. 301 (W.D. Mich. 1969), *cert. denied* 397 U.S. 980 (1969).

32 N. 26 *supra*.

33 *Id.* at 140.

34 *Ibid.*

35 See text under Federal Precedents, pp. 7–13.

36 See Comment, "The Equal Protection Clause and Exclusionary Zoning After Valtierra and Dandridge," 81 Yale L.J. 61 (1971), for an analysis of the unarticulated reasons for the majority holding in *Valtierra* and the impact of this decision on future challenges to exclusionary zoning in the Federal courts. Note also the apparent reluctance of the U.S. Supreme Court to adjudicate zoning cases. Not since 1928 in Nectow v. City of Cambridge, 277 U.S. 183 (1928), has that Court granted review in this area, at least where the issue raised was one of due process. *Id.* at 66 n. 21.

37 For example, Harper v. Virginia Bd. of Elections, 383 U.S. 663 (1966), outlawing the poll tax; Griffin v. Illinois, 351 U.S. 12 (1956), holding that indigent entitled to free transcript in criminal case; Douglas v. California, 372 U.S. 353 (1963), holding indigent entitled to free counsel to help prepare criminal cases. Many commentators argue that the right to adequate housing is a fundamental interest protected against discriminatory treatment based on wealth in the absence of a compelling state interest. The authorities cited in Ns. 5 and 36 *supra* all expound upon this thesis to some extent, relying on the various "open-housing" cases such as Jones v. Alfred Mayer Co., 392 U.S. 409 (1968).

38 117 N.J. Super. 11, 283 A.2d 353 (1971).

39 283 A.2d 353 at 355.

40 Multifamily units were restricted by the ordinance to between 500 and 700 additional units, with a maximum of 200 new units per year permitted. Three or more bedroom units were not allowed and two bedroom units could not exceed 20 percent of the total units in any development. The Town conceded that the 200 new units per year limitation was invalid.

41 N. 39 *supra* at 358.

42 439 Pa. 466, 268 A.2d 765 (1970). See also National Land & Investment Co. v. Kohn, 419 Pa. 504, 215 A.2d 597 (1965).

43 See Annots., 95 A.L.R.2d 716, 96 A.L.R.2d 1409.

44 Board of County Supervisors of Fairfax County v. Carper, 200 Va. 653, 107 S.E.2d 390 (Sup. Ct. App. 1959).

45 Prior New Jersey cases had indicated that regional needs are a proper consideration in local zoning, but in a different context. See, e.g., De Simone v. Englewood Housing Corp. No. 1, 56 N.J. 428, 267 A.2d 31 (1970) (variance application).

46 Note, however, that a regional approach can be employed to justify exclusionary zoning. For example, in McDermott v. Village of Calverton Park, 454 S.W.2d 557 (Mo. 1970), the Court upheld single family zoning for the entire community in part because commercial facilities were available in surrounding communities, primarily in the City of St. Louis.

47 119 N.J. Super. 164, 290 A.2d 465 (1972).

48 The ordinance did permit multifamily dwellings on a farm for a farmer, his family, or employees, provided such dwelling was no closer than 200 feet from the boundary line. This limited exception was obviously irrelevant to the issues in the case.

49 See text under Standing, p. 21. The Court found it unnecessary to discuss the standing of nonresident individuals and corporate entities since some of the plaintiffs were present residents of the Township.

50 290 A.2d 465, N. 47 *supra* at 473.

51 437 Pa. 237, 263 A.2d 395 (1970). See Washburn, "Apartments in the Suburbs: In re Appeal of Joseph Girsh," 74 Dickinson L. Rev. 634 (1970).

52 Lionshead Lake, Inc. v. Wayne Township, 10 N.J. 165, 89 A.2d 693 (1952), (upholding five acre minimum); Vickers v. Gloucester Township Committee, 37 N.J. 232, 181 A.2d 129 (1962), (upholding total exclusion of mobile homes).

53 Particularly Southern Alameda Spanish Speaking Organization v. City of Union, N. 31 *supra*.

54 272 U.S. 365 (1926).

55 Note, "Exclusionary Zoning From a Regional Perspective," 1972 Urb. L. Ann. 239 (1972).

56 Strong, Girsh and Kit-Mar, "An Unlikely Route to Equal Opportunity in Housing," 22 Zoning Digest 100a (1970).

57 Daraban v. Township of Redford, 383 Mich. 497, 176 N.W.2d 598 (1970); Lacy v. City of Warren, 7 Mich. App. 105, 151 N.W.2d 245 (1967); High Meadows Park, Inc. v. City of Aurora, 112 Ill. App. 2d 220, 250 N.E.2d 517 (1969); Mangel Co. v. Village of Wilmette, 115 Ill. App. 2d 383, 253 N.E.2d 9 (1969).

58 290 A.2d 465, N. 47 *supra* at 474.

59 457 F.2d 788 (5th Cir. 1972); see text to Ns. 21–25 *supra*.

60 437 F.2d 1286 (5th Cir. 1971).

61 See Freilich and Bass, N. 5 *supra*, particularly pp. 123–129 and authorities cited in Ns. 123–129; Aloi & Goldberg N. 5 *supra* at 47–54.

62 6 Cal. 3d 541, 492 P.2d 1173 (1972).

63 483 S.W.2d 605 (Mo. 1972).

64 See Annots., 96 A.L.R.2d 232, 42 A.L.R.3d 598; Comment, "Mobile Homes in Kansas: A Need for Proper Zoning," 20 Kan. L. Rev. 87 (1971).

65 The figures are exerpted from Comment, N. 64 *supra* at 88.

66 See 2 *Anderson* §§ 11.52–11.54 and authorities cited N. 64 *supra*.

67 In addition to the decisions from Michigan cited in N. 68 *infra*, see Lakeland Bluffs, Inc. v. County of Will, 114 Ill. App. 2d 267, 252 N.E.2d 765 (1971); Town Conover v. Jolly, 177 S.E.2d 879 (N.C. 1970).

[68] 35 Mich. App. 205, 192 N.W.2d 322 (1971). Previous Michigan decisions include Gust v. Canton Township, 342 Mich. 436, 70 N.W.2d 772 (1955) ; Anderson v. Highland, 21 Mich. App. 64, 174 N.W.2d 909 (1969). Note that the courts in reaching these decisions relied in part on the fact that mobile homes were licensed by the state.

[69] 192 N.W.2d 322 at 327–328.

[70] See 1 *Anderson* § 8.16; Note, "Legitimate Use Exclusions Through Zoning, Applying a Balancing Test," 57 Cornell L. Rev. 461 (1972), discussing recent developments in this area.

10

Daniel Lauber

RECENT CASES IN EXCLUSIONARY ZONING (excerpts)

EXCLUSIONARY ZONING CASES: THE FEDERAL COURTS

esented in this table are the exclusionary zoning cases tried in the federal courts and discussed in the text of this report. ses that are only indirectly related to exclusionary zoning are not included. Only cases in which the court has made a ling are included.

a "X" indicates that the particular issue was involved in the indicated case.

COURT CASE (DATE)	EXCLUSIONARY ISSUES INVOLVED						SUBSTANTIVE LEGAL ISSUES INVOLVED				
	Administrative Obstructions	Minimum Lot Size	Public Housing	Referendum	Rezoning		Civil Rights Acts	Due Process	Equal Protection	Standing in Court	Supremacy Clause
el Hill v. Sanbornton (1972)		X			X			X			
rkview Heights v. Black Jack (1972)	X				X					X	
ackshear Residents v. Austin Housing Authority (1972)		X					X		X		
ow v. Brown (1972)	X	X					X		X		
ters of Providence v. Evanston (1971)	X				X		X	X	X	X	
iley v. Lawton (1970)	X				X				X		
nnedy Park Homes v. Lackawanna (1970-71)	X				X		X		X		
nes v. Valtierra (1971)				X					X		X
SSO v. Union City (1970)			X	X				X	X		
njel v. Lansing (1969)			X	X			X	X	X		X

177

EXCLUSIONARY ZONING CASES: THE STATE COURTS

Presented in this table are the exclusionary zoning cases, discussed in this report, in which state courts have ruled. Cases are only indirectly related to exclusionary zoning are not included.

An 'X' indicates that the particular issue was involved in the indicated case.

EXCLUSIONARY ISSUES INVOLVED

COURT CASE (DATE)	Apartments	Exclusion of ...	Burden of Proof	Mobile Homes	Exclusion of ...	Burden of Proof	Limit on number of units built annually	Timed Development	Incompatibility of Multifamily and Single-Family Units	Bedroom restrictions	Minimum construction cost	Cost-elevating requirements	Minimum lot size	Minimum floor area	Variance required	Fiscal Zoning	Regional relief sought from
Pennsylvania																	
Willistown v. Chesterdale (1973)		X													X		
Pennsylvania v. Bucks Co. (1973)																	X
Derry Borough v. Shomo (1972)				X	X	X											
In re Appeal of Kit-Mar (1970)													X				
In re Appeal of Girsh (1970)		X													X		
National Land v. Kohn (1965)													X			X	
New Jersey																	
Schere v. Freehold (1972)													X			X	
So. Burlington Co. NAACP v. Mount Laurel (1972)	X	X															
J.D. Construction v. Freehold (1972)							X								X		
Molino v. Glassboro (1971)										X		X				X	
Oakwood at Madison v. Madison (1971)	X						X			X			X	X		X	
Baskerville v. Montclair (1970)											X			X			
DeSimone v. Greater Englewood Housing Corp. (1970)															X		
Baylis v. Franklin Lakes (no decision - 1973)	X	X		X	X	X									X		X
Michigan																	
Simmons v. Royal Oak (1972)	X		X														
Baker v. Algomac (1972)	X								X								
Bristow v. Woodhaven (1971)				X	X	X											
New York																	
Golden v. Ramapo (1972)								X									
North Carolina																	
Allerd v. Raleigh (1970)	X								X								

11

John Levy

EXCLUSIONARY ZONING:
AFTER THE WALLS CAME DOWN

The case against exclusionary zoning is by now fairly
ll known. Those who oppose it contend that it violates
e equal protection clause of the 14th amendment and
it it represents an unjustifiable use of police power. They
o contend that exclusionary zoning results in a pattern of
ial and economic segregation and that, in concert with
cal policies to encourage commercial growth in suburban
mmunities, it isolates potential jobholders from jobs.
bor shortages in the suburbs and unemployment in
ntral city ghettos become opposite sides of the same coin.
In the light of recent decisions in zoning cases and a
neral tendency of the courts to interpret the equal pro-
tion clause more broadly than in the past, the possibility
a sharp reduction in the amount of suburban land
bject to exclusionary zoning appears to be good.
For example, in a recent New Jersey case, the trial court
und invalid an ordinance which zoned most of the vacant
d in the municipality for relatively low density resi-
ntial use and placed severe limitations on apartment con-
ruction. The court held that a community must plan for
own housing needs and those of the region. "Housing
eds are encompasssed within the general welfare. The
eral welfare does not stop at each municipal boundary."
akwood at Madison, Inc. v. Township of Madison, 283
2d 353 (N.J. trial, 1971). Reported at 23 ZD 570.]
Assume that restrictive zoning is eliminated from a large
rt of the land area of a major metropolitan area through
dicial action, the removal of zoning powers to higher
els of government, or any other mechanism. Assume
ther, that this happens rapidly and in the near future.
rge areas which were formerly zoned exclusively for
gle family houses on large lots are now rezoned for single
nily houses on small lots, garden apartments, row
uses, and high rise apartments.
These areas are not in the older, close-in suburbs, but in
at is often termed "exurbia." In Westchester County,
w York, for example, those municipalities considered to
in the "middle ring" by the area's regional planning
ncies contain little land zoned for lots greater than one
f acre in area and no land zoned for lots larger than one
e. In addition, there is relatively little undeveloped land
ilable for and suitable to residential development in
se municipalities regardless of zoning category.

bn M. Levy, a doctoral candidate in Urban Public Policy Studies
Jew York University, with an M.A. in economics from Hunter
ege, City University of New York, is director of research for the
tchester County Planning Department.

By contrast, in the municipalities in the "outer ring" of
the county, approximately 69 per cent of the total land
area, much of it presently undeveloped, is zoned for single
family houses on lots of one acre or larger. Minimum lot
sizes range up to four acres.

Consider two alternative outcomes:

Outcome A (Best Case). Private builders and public
agencies formerly blocked by local zoning ordinances move
into the exurban areas to produce a rapid expansion of the
housing stock. Consequently there is a large migration of
low- and middle-income people, many of them black, from
the central city. Access to suburban jobs enables these
migrants to make major improvement in their own economic status and at the same time they prove a boon to
suburban industry. Numerou; black and other minority
group children who had formerly attended largely non-
white central city schools are now enrolled in predominantly white suburban schools. The result is a rapid increase
in their educational progress with all that implies.

Those members of the central city's population who
remain behind also benefit. As some members of the central
city's labor force move to suburbia and exchange their city
jobs for suburban jobs, pressure is put on the city's labor
market forcing wages up and unemployment rates down.
(That effect is at least a possibility is suggested by the
fact that suburban unemployment rates are often significantly lower than those of the central city.) Many members
of the working poor are able to better their circumstances
and some city residents who had dropped out of the labor
force in discouragement return to it. These changes reduce
the demands on the city for a variety of poverty-related
services, thus permitting the city to deal more effectively
with other problems and provide a generally higher level of
municipal services.

When all is said and done, both those central city residents who moved and those who stayed behind have bene-
fited. The original suburban residents, if nothing else, at
least have the satisfaction that any distress they may have
suffered has been for a useful purpose and that society as a
whole has been well served by their involuntary sacrifices.

Outcome B (Worst Case). As the barriers of exclusionary
zoning drop, a large supply of housing is constructed in
the affected areas. But it soon becomes apparent that the main
customers for this housing are middle class whites who have
wanted to leave the central city for some time but were not
able to find suitable suburban housing at acceptable prices.
The less affluent central city whites and most central city
blacks can no more afford $40,000 houses on quarter-acre

179

lots than they previously could have afforded $50,000 houses on one-acre lots. Nor can they afford row houses at $30,000 and upwards or garden apartments renting at $250 a month or more. The necessity for an automobile in the "outer ring" areas due to the inadequacy of public transportation is a further obstacle to the migration of lower income families to these areas.

The loss of a significant portion of the central city's remaining white middle class proves to be a severe blow. The impact is particularly great on the public school system, since the out-migration of white families is concentrated among those with school age children. This is hardly surprising, for it is through the schools that many families most acutely feel the pains of class and race conflict. As the percentage of white students in the city school system falls, it becomes impossible to achieve any meaningful degree of integration in the school system.

When firms in the central city see increasing numbers of their middle and lower level personnel moving to exurban areas some miles from the city line (their upper level and many of their middle level people are already there), they too move. Thus the volume of business done in the city shrinks and the receipts from business taxes fall. The market for commercial space softens as a result of the migration of firms causing rents to decline and thereby reducing the property tax burden which commercial real estate can sustain. A comparable effect is noted in residential real estate, for it is often the tenants of the more expensive apartments who move out.

Unfortunately, the central city's lower income groups, especially the minorities, depend upon the blue collar or lower-paid white collar job market, which migrates faster than can the labor force. The result is downward pressure on wages and an increase in unemployment among the very people it was hoped would be the beneficiaries of the elimination of exclusionary zoning.

Financial demands on the city for poverty-related services rise at the same time that the city's tax base is shrinking. The city becomes poorer and progressively less able to cope with its problems and maintain adequate levels of municipal services. The only beneficiaries of the process are the middle class whites who have moved out. The urban blacks find themselves more segregated and in economically more difficult circumstances than before. Their choice of housing is greater than before due to vacancies created by the departure of their more prosperous neighbors, but this is their only gain.

These two extreme cases both contain large elements of reality, and either outcome is possible. Numerous intermediate variations are more likely to occur. The course of events in a community will depend upon several factors. Increased cost and quantity of new housing stock due to the elimination of exclusionary zoning, a "trickle down" effect in suburban and exurban housing markets, and the degree of commitment to central city locations by businesses and manufacturers will all affect the outcome. In some cases poor central city residents may be able to move into the close-in suburbs to replace those moving into newly opened exurban regions. This would occur particularly if the close-in suburbs contained a substantial stock of older multi-family housing. Predicting the outcome in a given area will not be easy. In fact the effect of the elimination of exclusionary zoning will be hard to determine even after the fact because many other social and economic forces will be at work simultaneously.

But one fundamental fact strongly suggests that if even are allowed to take their natural course, the elimination exclusionary zoning will more often tend to favor outcom B than outcome A. This fact is the relationship of white non-white family income in central cities. The 1969 cens figures showed that the median income nationally for blac families in central cities was estimated at $6,794 while f white families in central cities the comparable figure w $9,797. The $10,000 to $14,999 range contained 27.3 p cent of all white families but only 17.1 per cent of all bla families. The $10,000 to $11,999 range contained 13.2 p cent of all white families and 9.2 per cent of all bla families.

Assume that the $10,000 to $15,000 group will accel ate the migration to suburbia because of the elimination exclusionary zoning. Those below the $10,000 line w have great difficulty making the move without assistan while those over $15,000 would be able to move und existing conditions if they so chose.

If the above assumption is valid, then for financ reasons alone the white out-migration attributable to t elimination of exclusionary zoning will be higher than percentage of the central city population as a whole. N financial factors such as discriminatory practices suburban realtors may increase the ratio of white out-mig tion to non-white out-migration still further.

The argument made here is rather schematic and t numbers should not be taken too literally. It mer suggests that the elimination of exclusionary zoning w most likely favor the white population. Only a stro countervailing public policy will prevent a decrease in non-white percentage of the central city's populati following the demise of exclusionary zoning.

Regardless of the effects on the racial composition the central city, the skimming off of large numbers middle income families will increase the percentage of po families. To the extent that growing up in an atmosphere pervasive poverty reduces a child's chance of escaping fr poverty when he becomes an adult, this effect will be v unfortunate.

It is widely believed that lower class black child benefit from being educated with middle class wh children, in part because of an emulation effect. Presu ably, lower class black children also benefit from be educated with middle class black children for the sa reason. Thus the siphoning off of a portion of the cen city's middle class black population may well be de mental to the educational progress of the remaining lo class black population.

The segment of the black population which wou probably gain most from escaping the central city slums of course, that segment with the fewest resources making such a move unassisted.

The equilibrium between outcome A and outcome B be shifted in either direction by a number of public po options. Some are listed below:

Favoring Outcome A.	*Favoring Outcome*
(1) Shifting the emphasis on public housing from the central cities to the suburbs and instituting rent or purchase subsidies specifically aimed at locating central city poor in the suburbs.	(1) Continuing pres policy emphasis.

(2) A "go slow" policy on school and neighborhood integration in the central cities.

(2) Attempting to accelerate school and neighborhood integration.

(3) Altering the present local property tax-based system of supporting local government and public education.

(3) Retaining the present system.

The reasons behind points (1) have already been discussed. The reasoning behind points (2) needs little elaboration. Most middle class whites, regardless of their views on integration as an abstract issue, do not seem to want it for themselves or their school-age children. The liberal who is embarrassed to admit that his children go to a private school is not just a cliche. The vociferous opposition to public housing in Forest Hills and elsewhere needs no belaboring. To push central city integration at the same time that suburban housing development is being freed from long-standing constraints is simply to construct a giant carrot and stick mechanism for moving middle class whites out of the central cities. Points (3) simply reflect the fiscal pressures which cause suburban communities to encourage commercial growth while they resist residential development that will not "pay its own way." A spreading of the fiscal burden would simultaneously lessen the resistance to housing for the less affluent and lessen the attractiveness of commercial growth. Such a change would benefit many central cities which are simultaneously losing jobs and gaining poor residents.

In view of the foregoing, a policy favoring outcome A

would end public housing projects in the central cities; initiate them in the suburbs; slow down integration in the central cities; and replace the local property tax with a broader based instrument such as regional tax sharing.

But the political viability of such a policy is highly questionable. Suburban whites and central city blacks would object. Its main supporters would be central city whites, a group whose numbers are declining in many areas.

·Furthermore, such a policy would produce some painful political contortions. Imagine, for example, New York's Mayor Lindsay seeking a cessation of public housing activity in his city and allowing funds earmarked for New York to be diverted to its surrounding suburban counties.

A "go slow" policy on integration in the central cities would be anathema to many liberals, is highly debatable on its own merits, and might well be ruled out by the courts regardless of the motivation behind it.

There is some prospect for improvement in the local property tax situation as a result of the California Supreme Court's decision in August 1971 (*Serrano v. Priest*) and subsequently other decisions on the financing of public education. However, the time lag between the final judicial decisions and the replacement of the present system may be considerable.

This writer strongly favors the elimination of exclusionary zoning on the grounds that the arguments against it based on law and social justice are overwhelming.

However, the elimination of exclusionary zoning, by itself, will probably not reduce the economic and racial dichotomies which now exist between city and suburb and may in fact increase them. Effective policy to ensure outcome A rather than outcome B is needed now.   ∎

V

More Flexible Controls

12

Jan Krasnowiecki

LEGAL ASPECTS OF PLANNED UNIT DEVELOPMENT IN THEORY AND PRACTICE

In the early sixties, when the planned unit movement got under way,[1] there was a widespread feeling that this form of development was in conflict with traditional zoning and site planning concepts, that it is a "challenge" to traditional ideas and requires a "departure" from them. Since that time most of us have been so busy fashioning our own solutions[2] to the problem that we have had little time to pause and reconsider what the problem really is. That is what I would like to do here.

As you probably know, in 1964 the Urban Land Institute asked me to analyze the legal problems posed by PUDs under the traditional zoning and site planning concepts.[3] This analysis provided the basis for a Model State Enabling Act which was prepared by my friend Dick Babcock with some side line assistance from me.[4] The Model Act has since been adopted, with various modifications, in New Jersey, Pennsylvania and Colorado (in the order of adoption).

The Model Act provides a good foil for my purpose here which is to review the problems as we saw them in 1964; to review the solutions proposed in the Model Act; and finally to reconsider the problems and solutions. For this purpose, I have reproduced the New Jersey version of the Act at the end of this paper. I have chosen the New Jersey version because, though it is identical to the Model Act in most respects, it attempts to extend the PUD approach to commercial and industrial development a feature which sparked some recent litigation that I would like to discuss as well.

185

STANDARD ZONING PROBLEMS AS WE SAW THEM IN 1964.

Case-by-Case Approach to Development Approval.

It was our desire to preserve as much flexibility in design, arrangement and mix of housing types as possible. We felt that planned unit development ought not to be constrained by the minutiae that invariably find their way into standard zoning and site planning control. We recognized that the reason why standard controls tend to become so rigid and so detailed is because they are required to be self-administering[5] — i.e. they must be established in advance of development and must authorize development without giving the local government any opportunity to review each specific proposal. It was clear in 1964 that the courts had shown a preference for the self-administering type of control. Attempts to circumvent this preference by delegating substantial discretion to an administrative agency (e.g. the planning commission) or by reserving this power in the legislative body (through a floating zone or special permit) had come under fire from some courts.[6] Obviously, the courts' preference for the self-administering type of control stemmed from a concern that the power to interpret and apply general standards to particular cases could be abused. The courts, we thought, had expressed distaste for legislative case-by-case control because of a fear that abuse could readily be sheltered from review under the "legislative" umbrella; they had expressed distaste for administrative case-by-case control because of the runaway characteristics of some local administrative agencies (their independence and tenure in office sheltering them from any political responsibility). Accordingly, we felt that a statutory provision expressly authorizing a case-by-case approach to planned unit development would help to dispel some of the above doubts. Thus the Model Act authorized the governing body to designate a "municipal authority" with power to approve "planned unit development" in accordance with standards and conditions prescribed by ordinance. See Section 2(c) and (d), Sections 6 and 9, and Section 11(c) and (d) of the New Jersey Act, *infra*. The Model Act attempts to make clear that the standards and conditions stated in the ordinance should be free from unnecessary detail and should remain flexible. See Section 3, especially Section 3(f) of the New Jersey Act, *infra*. The Model Act did not attempt to prescribe what official or body on the local level should serve as the "municipal authority." Rather, the choice was left with the local governing body, the statue authorizing the local governing body to appoint itself, "or any committee or commission." The New Jersey version has limited that choice to the governing body and the planning board. Section 11(c), *infra*.

The Unitary Permit

One of the obstacles to planned unit development as we saw it in 1964 was the absence of any agency on the local level with power to deal with all, at least the main, elements of a development (i.e. an agency that could decide both "zoning" and "subdivision" matters). By creating a single approving agency on the local level, be it the legislative body or some appointed administrator, we hoped to come as close as possible to the unitary permit concept—a single permit procedure for all elements of the development. Thus the Model Statute expressly combines elements of the development traditionally falling within the zoning power (use, bulk, location of buildings and structures) with elements traditionally falling within the subdivision and site planning control (streets, sidewalks, grading, lighting etc.) by granting to the municipal authority exclusive jurisdiction to approve the development as to all such elements. See New Jersey Act Section 3(e) especially 5(f), *infra*.

"Judicializing" the Approval Process

One of the major reasons why courts, we felt, tended to recoil from "flexible" case-by-case land use control was the absence of any strict procedural setting for these decisions coupled with the immunity from any extensive judicial scrutiny which traditional "legislative" characterization would accord them. Accordingly, the Model Act imposes detailed procedural requirements that treat planned unit applications and approvals as "adjudications" rather than as "rule making" (i.e. as quasi-judicial rather than quasi-legislative in nature). See New Jersey Act, Sections 6 and 7, *infra*.

Continuing Control Taylored to the Approved Proposal

One of the principal characteristics of the "self-administering" type of land use control is that it is, of necessity, pretty indiscriminate of particular locations or design. Thus, for example, under most apartment classifications one can build apartment buildings in a number of different shapes and sizes with different configurations being possible on most sizeable sites. This factor has been one of the problems with getting apartment zoning in the suburbs, questions being legitimately raised whether the developer really proposes to follow the plans which he has submitted (other possibilities being equally open once the zoning has been granted). I have argued for some time that zoning changes granted at the request of a particular applicant can be limited by ordinance to the proposal as described in the plans and oral testimony presented by the applicant in support of his request.[7] Municipal counsels who resort to "contract zoning" obviously do not share my confidence in this proposition since why would they employ covenants where they could do the job directly, by ordinance?

In any event, it was clear to us in 1964 that there was some doubt about whether a developer could be rezoned sensitively to his particular plan of development. If that was so, the conventional zoning concepts were seriously deficient in providing adequate *continuing* control for planned unit development. The particular plan of development is obviously the essence of planned unit development and the idea that a developer might have to be rezoned to some standard district categories leaving him free to reshuffle his plan as he pleased, was obviously unacceptable. Accordingly, the Model Statute elevated the approved plan for planned unit development to the status of a land use regulation. See New Jersey Act, Sections 4, 8 and 9.

Assurances Against Change in Public Requirements

It was clear to us that planned unit development would involve much more "front money" commitment than the standard form of development. Indeed, from a qualitative point of view, it was desirable to encourage an early commitment of sizeable sums of money for improvements on common open spaces and, generally, for better design. We felt that the prevailing doctrine,[8] which would leave the local government free to change its mind on future, if not on current sections, of any approved project, would discourage such commitments. Accordingly, the Model Statute provided extensive protection to an approved plan against impairment by the municipality. See New Jersey Act, Sections 8(b) and 9(f).

Maintenance of Common Areas

Many communities were concerned that developments with

private common areas and facilities might become liabilities if the residents or some private organization should fail to maintain them. The Model Statute sought to provide some additional assurances that the common areas and facilities would not become eyesores at the public expense. See New Jersey Act, Sections 3(c)(1) and (2).

Those were some of the thoughts that led us in 1964 to propose a model law. Since that time, of course, the courts have several times approved PUD controls without the aid of statute.[9] But in those jurisdictions that do not have the statute, financial institutions still have to face some uncertainties: How late can the local government change its mind? How late can protesting neighbors or civic associations file suit?[10] It is no accident, for example, that some of the larger projects in the Chicago area have relied on a special provision of the Illinois annexation law which authorizes the developer and the annexing municipality to "contract" for the zoning against any changes for at least five years.[11] But I did not come here to defend our statute. On the contrary, I simply wanted to describe some of the thoughts that went into it. I now turn to the major burden of my paper.

WHAT IS HAPPENING TO PUD?

I am not going to speak about what "we" thought or did in this part of my paper. I could not presume that my friends who worked on the Model Statute would join me in my remarks. It is clear that I overlooked some problems. I should have listened to Horace when he warned that *"naturam expellas furca, tamen usque recurret"*.[12] Translated loosely it means that when a municipality is set against growth, dressing it up in new language is not going to fool them for long. And when a municipal government is used to passing the buck around, from planning agency to the council, from the council to the mayor, from the mayor to the planning agency, it is hard to persuade them that a single agency is a good thing. But let me back up a little.

In 1964 I thought I could see what was wrong with standard zoning:

(1) the assumption behind standard zoning is that development should be brought under control by self-administering rules set forth in advance of development;

(2) another assumption is that the rules that are established cannot force the assembly of land (except to a minimal extent, e.g.

30,000 sq. ft. per house, 2,000 sq. ft. per apartment unit) and cannot prevent its disassembly (except, again, to a minimal extent through subdivision control). In other words, the assumption is that zoning cannot say "no development in this district unless you assemble 200 acres". A correlative principle of (1) above but one which takes special effect because of assumption (2) is that the municipality must be title-blind when it establishes the rules—that is it cannot zone some land one way because it is assembled and other land some other way because it is disassembled (I am speaking here about basic, standard zoning, not options such as PUD).

Contemplating assumptions (1) and (2), both of which I am prepared to question, I could see why standard zoning tends to divide the municipality into simple-minded districts. Obviously, if you cannot assume that land is assembled under unified ownership, you cannot afford to establish regulations that allow all types of housing at all types of densities, unless you could establish some overall density for the district or a quota for some types of housing, e.g. "no more than 500 apartment units". This brings me to the final assumption of standard zoning:

(3) there was a sense running through standard zoning that you cannot establish regulations for an area that would allow one landowner to deprive the other of a pro-rata share of permissible development: e.g. a regulation providing that in a particular district "no more than 500 apartment units" will be permitted.[13]

I could see in 1964 that as a result of all of the assumptions discussed above, standard zoning would remain simple minded, that it would continue to segregate different housing types into discreet districts and that the only way to arrive at PUD would be to approach it as an optional departure from a standard zoning base. To get there, I could see, that assumption (1) would have to be overcome, and that part of assumption (2), the part which says that one cannot prevent disassembly of land, would have to be modified.

Control Over Growth, Quality

It is clear to me now that I should have paid more attention to assumption (3). For this draws attention to the central problem of zoning: whether you can quota or time development. I started this discussion by saying, belatedly with Horace, that nature cannot be expelled with a pitchfork. I am referring here to the attitude of most municipalities. I should have paid attention to what most municipalities really want:

1. They do not want any more housing.

2. If they have to take in more housing, they want to limit it to some minimal quota, especially when it involves apartments or townshouses. The irony of it is that while standard zoning does not approve of quotas (at least not until the New York court suggested otherwise in *Ramapo*),[14] *the easiest way to run a quota system is to employ standard zoning.* All you have to do is zone all of the undeveloped areas of the municipality at a level which is just below the level at which it is economically safe to develop. If you do the job just right, no one will be able to show that he cannot develop his property yet no one will, in fact, develop until you grant him some change. If a particular landowner calls your bluff and takes you to court, the most that will ordinarily happen is that his land will have to be released for development, the lid staying on tight against the others.[15] Thus by employing standard zoning you can run a quota system without ever stating the principles upon which it is based. The effectiveness of this approach lies in the fact that zoning changes are considered in the standard zoning system to be "legislative"[16] actions—and a legislature does not have to give reasons why it has failed to adopt some proposed legislation. Thus if your quota for the next two years is 200 apartment units, all you need to do is zone everything for single family housing. When the right developer comes along you rezone him for the 200 units. The next one you turn down—you do not have to give him any reasons. You will note that I said "when the right developer comes along". This brings me to the last point that I should have noted:

3. With respect to most forms of intensive development, especially apartment and townhouse, municipalities want to retain the power to discriminate between developers. They want to be able to turn a developer down if he does not have a good track record in terms of financial stability, management, site planning and design work, marketing—generally in terms of reliability and quality.[17] Again the standard approach, which requires a rezoning before you can develop any of the more intensive forms of development, gives the municipality plenary control over this matter.

The ULI Model Statute does not recognize these municipal preferences—in an ideal world perhaps properly so. But we are not living in an ideal world. The fear among municipalities now is that PUD may cause them to lose control over their growth. The East Windsor Township PUD Ordinance under which Twin Rivers[18] was developed describes the PUD as a "district".[19] The purpose, I sense, was to lend credence to the argument that one who meets all of the stated criteria of the ordinance can still be turned down for no reason at all, or for some insubstantial reason. (Because what he is doing is applying for a zoning change.)

There is nothing in the Model Statute that bears on the question whether a PUD can or cannot be made into a district (in the above sense—i.e. so that approval of one project would have little precedential value on an application for another).

The districting question did come up in a different way in *Rudderow* v. *Mount Laurel.*[20] Here the Township had made the PUD approach available in every district in the Township. Opponents of a project which was approved under the ordinance challenged the project and the ordinance on various grounds, among them, the ground that the PUD should have been districted. The trial court held that the PUD must be districted, relying in part on the New Jersey Constitution which states that in the exercise of their zoning powers municipalities *may* divide the municipality into districts.[21] The court read the "may" as a "shall". The Appellate Division reversed the trial court on this point,[22] as well as on some others which I will mention later. So strong is the language of the Appellate Division rejecting the districting idea that it raises the question whether, under the Model PUD statute (which is similar in this respect in New Jersey as well as in the other states that have adopted it) districting is at all permissible.

Most Pennsylvania municipalities, which are operating under the same Model statute, have not limited the PUD to any specific districts nor have they made the PUD itself into a district *a la* East Windsor Township).

There is a growing tendency, however, to limit the densities permissible in the PUD to the same or close to the densities permissible under the standard zoning applicable to the land for which the PUD proposal is made. The reason for this is obvious. Municipalities are scared that PUD represents an open field day on growth.

Concern over this matter is expressing itself in other ways. An absolutely staggering amount of detail is beginning to find its way back into the PUD ordinances. The thought, apparently, is that if you cannot turn a developer down because you do not like his design or because you do not like his record of management or you are not satisfied with his financial responsibility, or because you have approved enough housing for one year, you better arm yourself with a lot of other legitimate "land use" reasons for turning him down. By piling one requirement onto another, you can be practically certain that the developer will have to be a millionaire who will build for millionaires.

My idea of PUD originally was that a procedure should be provided under which a municipality would be encouraged to *throw away the book* and sit down with the developer to negotiate a better product, hopefully a less expensive one for the consumer. I have a feeling this is not happening.

The reason why it is not happening is that local officials do not like the responsibility that comes with a negotiated project, they prefer to find the answers in "the book". Additionally, many of them do not have the professional staff to feel secure that they are entering the negotiations as equals with the developer in terms of knowledge and ability. Use of consultants for this purpose is never as reassuring as availability of inhouse staff. Moreover, it is cheaper to have the consultant review the provisions of the PUD ordinance than to have him involved in the administration of it. As a result, "the book" gets to be the size of the telephone book.

Finally, and this has been my principal contention in this part of the paper, many municipalities feel that they can hold the lid down on growth and get most of the benefits of negotiated development by simply zoning everything too tight, so that all residential development, especially the higher density forms, must come in for a change.

To get things going again in the right direction, it will take more than a few court cases condemning "exclusionary" zoning. My philosophy is "never swim up stream when you can get where you want to go quicker by following the current". I think that NBC has given me the right to claim this as an old Polish saying.

Suggestions

Before we decide to transfer some or all of the land use control powers to the state, I think we should try the following:

(1) Develop a really good data bank at the state or regional level, I don't mean pretty pictures on the wall and colorful pamphlets, I mean hard data that can be employed to evaluate particular development proposals on particular sites, such as market demand, transportation, traffic, data that can serve as a basis for an intelligent cost-benefit analysis. Along with this, the state or regional agencies should have a sufficient staff to detach and assign to a municipality

for evaluation and application of the data, when needed. If your objection is that the public would never shoulder the cost, then I ask you why are so many of you so sure that state land use control is going to produce better results? Certainly on some issues, such as low income housing or the environment, some states might do better than local municipalities have done. But I am not so sure of that either.

(2) My second suggestion is that we legitimate quota and timing controls, subject to certain safeguards against abuse, so as to provide municipalities with the means by which they can approve one high density PUD without being immediately forced to approve the next one. I would also suggest that we allow municipalities to reject PUD proposals on criteria which are not traditionally within the scope of the land use control power—namely the developer's capability to produce and maintain a quality product and his financial capacity to do so.[23] In other words, I would make these considerations legitimate criteria within the land use control power. Let me give an example: Can a municipality today reject a PUD proposal because the developer is unable to release the common areas and facilities from blanket encumberances, or at least so much of them as would make the current phase of development viable on its own? I am not asking you to confuse consumer protection with land use control. But I want you to recognize that the two go hand in hand to some extent. Usually the job that does all right by the consumer is also a good land use job.

I can see that everyone is going to pounce on me now. Developers, those who see salvation in centralized planning, planners (because I'm telling them that the way a development is financed, the way the site is encumbered by liens is more important than physical planning), I don't know who else. But I am going to stand my ground. I think we are all swimming up stream. What I am trying to tell you is this: let the land use control system reflect more nearly what people want to do with it, what they are doing with it surreptitiously, hidden from view by a theory which denies that what's happening is happening. For almost fifty years courts have been dreaming of a world in which land use controls are applied generally and impartially, without reference to any particular developer or any particular site. What nonsense that is. How much development do you know of that has occurred under some long standing zoning classification rather than as a consequence of a zoning change brought about by the developer?

I have this to say to developers: Don't fight an articulated quota system. You are now subject to a rigid quota system that is sheltered from court review because its principles need not be articulated (since we do not believe in quotas). Don't get upset by *Ramapo*.[24] The plaintiffs in *Ramapo* framed a very narrow issue for the courts. They did not present any evidence below. They were content to challenge the validity of Ramapo's phasing ordinance on the record made by the Town.[25]. Thus the truth, accuracy or, more broadly, rationality of the Town's plan was never put on trial on the facts. I feel certain that the courts will place upon municipalities a very heavy burden to justify any timing, phasing quotas when they are challenged on a factual basis.

What about my other suggestion, that developer's submit to standards which test their financial capacity to complete, their management record—generally, their ability to deliver a quality product? My point here is the same as in the case of quotas. Municipalities apply such standards now, sub rosa thus not subject to scrutiny by the courts. In an effort to exclude the "shoe string" developer, they tend to pile on the front end costs (requiring streets to be improved for the whole project at once, sewers to be laid, and so forth). This is not good for developers nor for municipalities. Improvidently located streets or other public improvements may cause economic blight in the future, when the market changes.

In summary, the ULI Model Act provided a good solution to the problem of authorizing, processing and controlling a PUD project. It did not, however, address itself to some of the concerns (fears if you will) of most municipalities: How can we approve one project but turn down another?—has been, perhaps, the central question. As a result, there has been an observable hardening of the arteries. An approach which was designed to encourage flexibility—a negotiated approach to better development—is beginning to look more and more like standard zoning. For example, it is now fairly common to find PUD ordinances that are structured as follows: the ordinance will provide for an overall dwelling unit density (e.g. 5 to the acre) but then it will go on to provide maximum densities for each housing type (e.g. 10 to the acre for apartments, 8 to the acre for townhouses, etc.). In order to administer the individual housing type densities, the ordinance requires the developer to divide the PUD into "use areas" (i.e. apartment use area, townhouse use area, single family detached use area). Why call them "use areas." Why not drop the pretense and call them "districts"? Perhaps there is no escape from this problem, but then Horace was right, was he not?

Larger PUDS—New Town Scale

The ULI Model Act did not really address itself to developments of the New Town scale. New Town developers, even more than smaller scale PUD developers, need assurance that the overall plan of development will not be disrupted by unilateral changes made by the local government. Under the ULI Model, this assurance cannot be given until the developer has submitted plans showing, among other things "(3) the location ... of any common open space ...; (4) the use and the approximate height, bulk and location of buildings and other structures". See New Jersey Act, Section 5(d). A developer whose program stretches over the next fifteen to twenty years cannot provide a plan that gives the height, bulk and location of all of his buildings—even approximately.

Suggestions

I think that there is need to review and revise the statute for developments of the New Town scale. Such large scale projects arguably call for some significant state participation. My earlier remarks about the difficulties experienced by most municipal governments when faced with the negotiated approach to land use control are especially pertinent here. In states such as Pennsylvania and New Jersey, where the power to regulate land use is delegated to the smallest units of local government and where there are no unincorporated or unorganized areas of land, a New Town scale project may well fall within several local zoning jurisdictions and there is often no way in which one can assure that the various municipalities will act in concert.

Non-Residential Uses in PUD

The ULI Model Act limited non-residential uses to those that are "designed and intended to serve the residents" of the PUD. Although I am not qualified to speak as a planner, I think that this was a bad mistake. For a smaller PUD, shopping facilities that are designed to serve the residents only are often times simply not viable. As I recall, the limiting language was inserted in the Model Act purely out of expediency. It was thought at the time that the PUD idea would be opposed if there was any suggestion of extensive commercial or industrial use.

In any event, when Pennsylvania adopted the Model Act it expressly modified the above limitation to permit "those non-residential uses deemed to be appropriate for incorporation in the design of the "PUD.[26] The draftsmen of the New Jersey version went even further. They included references to commercial and industrial developments in the preamble and modified the residential bias of the statute in a number of other places.[27] But they evidently overlooked the old ULI limitation in Section 3(a)(2) of the Act. This oversight represented the central issue in *Rudderow* v. *Mount Laurel.*[28] Notwithstanding that the New Jersey legislature had evidenced its intention to expand the PUD concept to commercial as well as industrial development in numerous portions of the statute, the trial court fastened its attention on that single sentence in the statute and held that a shopping center serving the broader region cannot be approved as part of a PUD. This position has now been reversed by the Appellate Division which stated: "Municipalities, as part of their comprehensive zoning plans, may properly anticipate and provide for the present needs of the public now residing in the areas surrounding the planned community, as well as the reasonably foreseeable future needs of the public they anticipate will move into the area and require servicing". I believe that this represents a sound interpretation of the New Jersey statute as well as an eminently sensible view as to the scope of non-residential use that may be incorporated within an otherwise residential PUD.

SUMMARY AND CONCLUSIONS

When I first came to the problem of Planned Unit control it seemed to me that it was a problem of persuading the courts to approve a "negotiated" approach to land use control. I felt that the courts would do so, if it were surrounded by proper procedural safeguards. I saw that the courts would have to accept a number of modifications in traditional theory. The idea that development ought to be brought under control by self-administering regulations set forth by the legislative body in advance of development, for example, would have to go by the board. Either the courts would have to allow local administrative agencies to play a far more decisive role, or they would have to permit the governing body to reserve to itself a quasi-administrative power (i.e. permit the governing body to reserve the right to translate general standards and policies into detailed application in each particular case). Since the courts have proved themselves willing to accept these departures from traditional theory, there was, in retrospect, very little need for any legislation.

The ULI Model Act provides some advantages over trying to put PUD controls together under the traditional zoning system. For example, it provides assurances that the rules will not be changed in the middle of the game, assurances which are not clearly available under the traditional system. It allows subdivision and site planning approval to be combined with zoning approval in one proceeding, a combination which is difficult to attain when the governing body wants to retain the decisive role on the PUD approval but the state law happens to provide that subdivision and site planning approval lies exclusively with the planning agency. The ULI Model Act also elevates the approved PUD plan to the status of land use regulations, a result which may still be in some doubt when the traditional zoning approach is used.

But these advantages of the Model Act may be outweighed by one of its practical disadvantages: under the Act there is some uncertainty whether PUD must be available to all comers, whether PUD may be confined in districts, and, especially, whether it can itself be made into a district (so that approval would require a rezoning—hopefully, from the local point of view, a completely discretionary legislative action). Mind you, I am not advocating such restraints. But one must be realistic. Fear that PUD may become uncontrollable under the present statutory provisions has led many Pennsylvania municipalities to reject it and has led others to tighten the requirements so as to make nonsense of the idea, as originally conceived.

That is why I urge in this paper that we give some thought to two of the most important needs of the "negotiated" approach to land use control: first, the need of local governments for reliable data and technical assistance; second, the need for some reasonable phasing or quota controls.

NOTES

1. It would be hard to pinpoint an origin for the movement but certainly Eli Goldston and James H. Scheuer deserve credit for giving it a big push: Goldston and Scheuer, *Zoning of Planned Residential Developments,* 73 HARV. LAW REV. 241 (1959).

2. Mandelker, *Controlling Planned Residential Developments,* A.S.P.O. (1966); Frederick H. Bair, Jr., *How to Regulate Planned Unit Developments For Housing—Summary of a Regulatory Approach,* 17 ZONING DIGEST 185, 221 (1965); PLANNED UNIT RESIDENTIAL DEVELOPMENT, Part I, *The Legal*

Aspects, by Krasnowiecki, Part II, *Suggested Legislation,* by Babcock, McBride and Krasnowiecki, Urban Land Inst., Tech. Bull. 52 (1965).

3. See, op. cit. note 2 supra.

4. See, op. cit. note 2 supra, hereinafter referred to as the "ULI Model Act".

5. See, Krasnowiecki, *Basic System of Land Use Control: Legislative Preregulation v. Administrative Discretion,* in the NEW ZONING 3 (N. MARCUS & M. GROVES eds. 1970). I use the words "self-administering" rather than "non-discretionary" because I am talking about rules which are designed to be so dispositive of each individual case as to leave no room for the exercise of discretion *or judgment.* A rule is self-administering in this sense even though it may require that an administrative agency determines compliance in each particular case, so long as the administrative role is intended to remain ministerial in nature.

6. Eves. v. Zoning Bd. of Adj. of Lower Gwynedd Township, 401 Pa. 211, 164 A. 2d 7 (1960) (floating zone), Swimming River Golf & Country Club v. New Shrewsbury, 30 N.J. 132, 152 A. 2d 135 (1959) (delegation to planning agency), Hiscox v. Levin, 31 Misc. 2d 151, 216 N.Y.S. 2d 801 (Sup. Ct. Suffolk County, 1961) (delegation to planning agency). A lot has happened since those cases were decided. *Eves* has all but been repudiated by the Supreme Court of Pennsylvania: Donahue v. Zoning Bd. of Adj., 412 Pa. 334, 194 A. 2d 610 (1963), Cheney v. Village 2 at New Hope, Inc. 429 Pa. 626, 241 A. 2d 81 (1968) (Approving PUD extensive delegation to planning agency). There is every indication that courts have at last recognized the need for the "administrative" approach to land use control: Prince George's County v. M & B Construction Corp.,   Md.   , 297 A. 2d 683 (1972).

7. There are only a few cases that throw any doubt on this proposition, one being Pierson Trapp Co. v. Peak, 340 S.W. 2d 465 (Ky. App. 1960). Indirectly, the cases that have struck down "contract" zoning seem opposed to that power. See, e.g. Montgomery County v. National Capital Realty Corp.,   Md.   , 297 A. 2d 675 (1972); Baylis v. City of Baltimore, 219 Md. 164, 148 A. 2d 429 (1958); Hartnett v. Austin, 93 So. 2d 86 (Fla. 1956). New York took the lead in approving "contract zoning" Church v. Islip, 8 N.Y. 2d 254, 268 N.E. 2d 680 (1960) and Massachusetts and Nebraska followed: Sylvania Electric Products, Inc. v. Newton, 344 Mass. 428, 183 N.E. 2d 118 (1962); Bucholtz v. Omaha, 174 Neb. 862, 120 N.W. 2d 270 (1963). It has always been my position that if a court is willing to approve sensitive rezoning by covenant (i.e. contract zoning) it must really be saying that the local government could sensitively rezone the property by fashioning special regulations for that property and, if so, then contract zoning must be bad since it is far better to do the job by public regulation than by private covenant. On the other hand if the court is not willing to say that sensitive rezoning is valid, then contract zoning is also bad because a local government ought not to be allowed to do indirectly by covenant what it has no power to do directly by zoning. I think the New York court has finally come around to my view that sensitive rezoning (i.e. rezoning to the particular proposal) makes a lot of sense: Albright v. Town of Manlius, 28 N.Y. 2d 108, 268 N.E. 2d 785 (1971).

8. R. ANDERSON, LAW OF ZONING § 4.27 (1968), RATHKOPF, LAW OF ZONING AND PLANNING, ch. 57 (1972).

9. Cheney v. Village 2 at New Hope, 429 Pa. 626, 241 A. 2d 81 (1968), Chandler v. Kroiss, 191 Minn. 196, 190 N.W. 2d 472 (1971).

10. See, Krasnowiecki, *Zoning Litigation and the New Pennsylvania Procedures,* 120 UNIV. PA. L. REV. 1029, 1121-1125, 1133-1137, 1148-1155 (1972).

11. ILL. ANN. STAT. ch. 24 §§ 11-15.1-1 to 11-15.1-5 (Smith Hurd Supp. 1972).

12. Horace, *Epistles,* X. 24.

13. I have been able to find only one case that involved this quota problem: DeMaria v. Enflield Planning & Zoning Comm'n, 159 Conn. 534, 271 A. 2d 105 (1970). The town of Enflield adopted a zoning ordinance which established a quota by limiting the number of apartment units that could be constructed in certain residential districts. In the district in question, the ordinance limited the apartment units to 375. Three developers applied successively for 212, 162, and 112 units respectively. The first and the last applications were approved but the second was denied on aesthetic grounds. On appeal, the Supreme Court of Connecticut held that aesthetic reasons are not sufficient to ground a denial and ordered the second application approved. The court notes that the result of its decision is to annul the third developer's approval. Id. at 542-43, 271 A. 2d at 109. One searches in vain for some indication that the court was aware of the staggering implication of its decision (not the least of which was that the opinion does not indicate whether the third developer was a party to the proceedings). It is noteworthy that in important recent "exclusionary zoning" case of Oakwood at Madison, Inc. v. Township of Madison, 117 N.J. Super. 11, 283 A. 2d 353 (L. Div. 1971), the township conceded the invalidity of an ordinance provision allowing the construction of only 200 multi-family units annually. Id. at 17, 283 A. 2d at 356.

14. Golden v. Town of Ramapo, 30 N.Y. 2d 359, 285 N.E. 2d 291 (1972) discussed in text at notes 24, 25 *infra.*

15. This has been true of all of the "exclusionary" zoning cases that rested on the traditional property-rights/due process argument. Indeed, in most of them the plaintiff landowner himself never got to develop the land in question. See, Krasnowiecki, *Zoning Litigation and the New Pennsylvania Procedures,* 120 UNIV. PA. LAW REV. 1029, 1059-1065, 1076-1083, 1109 (1972). To solve this problem, Pennsylvania recently amended its Municipalities Planning Code to give the court power to order approval of the landowner's proposed development. Pa. Stat. Ann. tit. 53 § 11011 (as amended by Act No. 93, § 19 (Pa. Legis. Serv. 252 (1972)). The Act is reprinted and discussed in Krasowiecki, *op. cit. supra.* Obviously, where the challenge to the zoning is based on equal protection grounds (the argument being that the municipality's entire zoning pattern represents a discriminatory scheme) the power of the courts to order redress must extend beyond a particular site. Such redress was granted in Southern Burlington County NAACP v. Township of Mount Laurel, 119 N.J. Super. 164, 290 A. 2d 465 (L. Div. 1972). However, in Commonwealth v. Bucks County, 22 Bucks Co. 179 (Pa. C.P. 1972) the court held that plaintiffs have no standing to challenge discriminatory zoning practices in the county unless they have a specific site and a housing project in mind. The decision is criticized in Krasnowiecki, *op. cit. supra* at 1103-4. Unfortunately, on April 3, 1973, the

commonwealth Court of Pennsylvania affirmed the lower court's opinion and order, *per curiam*.

16. I have suggested that all amendments designed to respond to particular applicants be treated as "administrative" in nature. See Krasnowiecki, *Model Land Use and Development Planning Code*, Section 208 (2) in MARYLAND PLANNING AND ZONING LAW STUDY COMMISSION, FINAL REPORT: LEGISLATIVE RECOMMENDATIONS, 103-4 (1969).

17. It is not of the fundamental "assumptions" of zoning that such personal characteristics are not within the scope of the land use control power. See Note, *The Ad Hominem Element in the Treatment of Zoning Problems*, 109 UNIV. PA. LAW REV. 992 (1961). I personally believe that this is one of the biggest deficiencies in the effectiveness of our land use control. See Section 204 (d), *Model Land Use and Development Code, op. cit. supra* note 16 at 84.

18. An excellent description of Twin Rivers appears in BURCHELL, PLANNED UNIT DEVELOPMENT, 84-174 (1972).

19. Sections 5 and 6, Ordinance adopted October 2, 1967.

20. Notes, 21 and 22 *infra.*

21. Rudderow v. Township Com. of Twp. of Mount Laurel, 114 N.J. Super. 104, 110-111, 274 A. 2d 854, 858 (L. Div. 1971).

22. Rudderow v. Township Committee of Twp. of Mt. Laurel, 121 N.J. Super. 409, 297 A. 2d 583 (App. Div. 1972).

23. See note 17 *supra.*

24. Golden v. Town of Ramapo, 30 N.Y. 2d 359, 285 N.E. 2d 291 (1972).

25. Discussion with attorneys for Ramapo Improvement Corp. Note also that plaintiffs moved for summary judgment below. Golden v. Town of Ramapo, 30 N.Y. 2d 359, 361, N.E. 2d 291, 293 (1972).

26. PA. STAT. ANN. tit. 53, § 10705 (a) (1) (1972).

27. N.J. REV. STAT. § 40:55-55 (purposes), § 40:55-57 (d) (minimum number of dwelling units and commercial use—original only spoke about dwelling units); § 40:55-66.

28. Rudderow v. Township Committee of Twp. of Mt. Laurel, 121 N.J. Super. 409, 297 A. 2d 583 (App. Div. 1972), see also text at notes 21 and 22 *supra.*

29. Id. at 416, 297, A. 2d 583 at 587.

13

Daniel Mandelker

THE BASIC PHILOSOPHY OF ZONING: INCENTIVE OR RESTRAINT

Zoning is built on the premise that the private market for land use, in a mature urban society, cannot be permitted to make land use allocations without creating severe diseconomies in the urban development pattern. Because land pricing mechanisms do not take account of externalities resulting outside the site, zoning is thought to be needed to curb and, if necessary, prohibit land development decisions that produce externalities considered undesirable. Even before the advent of the zoning ordinance, however, court-made nuisance law operated in much the same manner. In lawsuits brought by private parties, the courts balanced the equities of conflicting uses to award one or the other a preferred claim. Limitations imposed by the very nature of the judicial process probably forced the courts' attention to a comparatively circumscribed arena in assessing the impact of land use conflicts. It was this judicial attention to the immediate area, neighborhood, or zone of influence which the early draftsmen of the zoning enabling act artfully picked up and transformed into the legislatively prescribed zoning district.

The so-called negative character of the zoning process derives from the historic premise on which zoning is based. What underlay the adjudication of land use conflict in the guise of nuisance doctrine was a crudely drawn division of land uses into residential, commercial, and industrial categories, arranged in a pyramid in which the residential use was awarded the preferred position. Potentially harmful externalities occurred as nonresidential uses pushed toward the top, seeking entry into the residential reserve. The courts intervened only as unwanted externalities were produced by upward pushes in development pressures. Where there was no fixed residential development pattern, the courts were reluctant to intervene. Thus, they usually refused to enjoin even noisy and dusty uses such as quarries and cement processing in rural or partially urbanized areas.

THE NEGATIVE AND THE POSITIVE IN ZONING CONTROL

Prohibitory zoning, which prevented developers from capitalizing on substantial increments in development value, has been approved by the courts when justified in the name of externality protection. But the courts have balked when the municipality has sought to add to developer costs increments that could not be justified on the grounds of preventing harm to contiguous and nearby land uses. Only from this perspective is it accurate to say that zoning may be used to prevent developers from visiting harms upon others but may not be used to force the developer to confer benefits on the community as a whole.[1] Good examples are the cases invalidating exactions from subdivision developers for parks and other open spaces, although these cases are clouded by the statutory authority issue and by the failure of the local zoning authority to relate the additional payments to costs generated by the development.[2]

In distinctively urban settings, however, the problems take on a somewhat different cast. The issues become complicated by the need to focus on administrative mechanisms to adjust the constitutional burden and by a partial shift in emphasis from land use to density and intensity of development as the organizing concept in zoning. Here it may be useful to comment on Robert Warren's observation that we may have been misled by the linearity implicit in our organizational models for land use controls: If one conditional use district is good enough for Pocatello, Idaho, then we can solve the problems of Milwaukee, Wisconsin, with ten, and the problems of New York City with—how many?[3] We need to recognize that magnitudes of scale create their own problems and that the limited environmental frame and much greater development intensities characteristic of a city, especially an island like Manhattan, may require an entirely new intellectual apparatus to undergird the land use allocation system. Proposals for air rights transfer and condemnation of holdouts certainly point in this direction. The opportunities for intellectual speculation are endless, but the inquiry in this chapter will be conducted in terms of more conventional zoning doctrines.

But additional words on the developmental setting are in order. In New York, as elsewhere in the nation, interest in positive zoning techniques has been partly triggered by a bullish market for office development which, if undirected, could have serious consequences for the urban fabric. Planners seek solutions to traffic congestion, parking, and pedestrian access problems and

---

[1] *See* Heyman & Gilhool, *The Constitutionality of Imposing Increased Community Costs on New Subdivision Residents Through Subdivision Exactions*, 73 YALE L.J. 1119 (1964).

[2] Other courts have approved subdivision exactions, and some jurisdictions have ruled favorably on "in lieu" provisions. *See, e.g.*, Jenad, Inc. v. Village of Scarsdale, 18 N.Y.2d 78, 218 N.E.2d 673, 271 N.Y.S.2d 955 (1966); Jordan v. Village of Menomonee Falls, 28 Wis.2d 608. 137 N.W.2d 442 (1965); Billings Properties v. Yellowstone County, 144 Mont. 25, 394 P.2d 182 (1964).

[3] Robert Warren is Professor of Political Science, University of Washington, Seattle, Wash.

strive for the creation of visual and other amenities amidst pressures from developers who resist increments to development costs. Often entire neighborhoods or districts must be treated as a unit, in the face of separated ownerships that complicate the problems of unified control. The compulsory land assembly process which was born with urban renewal is a powerful tool in these circumstances, but its use is limited for political, financial, and administrative reasons. In a pluralist society in which centers of control are diffused between the private and the public sector, the answers are not easy to find.

So we seek the carrot rather than the stick. Developers are offered increased densities in return for added increments to cost in the form of dedications for street improvements, additional parking, plazas and pedestrian walkways, and other amenities which, in the historic context of zoning, must be characterized as creating community benefits rather than preventing individual harms and so are suspect. As an answer to possible constitutional objections, density increases are offered as a *de facto quid pro quo* for corresponding increases in development costs. What balance is to be struck between increased density allowances and cost increments to the developer's project is left to the administrative process to determine. Just how this system works is indicated by a brief description of the zoning techniques applied to the private redevelopment of the secondary business center in Rosslyn, Virginia, just across the Potomac River from Washington, D.C.

THE ROSSLYN EXPERIENCE[4]

Rosslyn, Virginia, long a substandard commercial area on the approaches to Washington, moved into the 1960's facing a substantial boom in office development, triggered by increasing government demands for office space available for rent in private buildings. Faced with these pressures and wishing to direct the impending development into a more cohesive and viable pattern, the Arlington County Planning Office embarked on a finely articulated series of zoning strategies. Fundamental to the system of control was the preparation of a tentative development plan for the Rosslyn area, which included a system of linked structures for internal pedestrian circulation. The area was rezoned to a modest commercial zone permitting commercial development at an intensity substantially below what the market was demanding. Rezoning to a greater intensity was possible, but to get it the developer had to submit a site plan for detailed review by the planning commission, agree to provide part of the cost of the internal pedestrian system and connect to it, and assemble a tract of a size sufficient to carry a development that would conform to the plan's intentions. A pattern of small and fragmented sites inhibited large-scale

[4]The material in this section is based on R.C. Ward, "Site Plan Review in Zoning: A Case Study of the Redevelopment of Rosslyn, Arlington County, Va." (Thesis on file in the School of Architecture Library, Washington Univ., St. Louis, Mo. 1968).

redevelopment in Rosslyn, and site consolidation was one of the aims of the planning commission's strategy. Not only were height, setback, and floor area ratio (FAR)[5] standards set by the zoning provisions applicable to the rezone, but the planning commission adopted a policy for the area calling for a mixed daytime-nighttime community and sought to achieve a balance in residential and office use.

As of 1968, the county could credit itself with substantial success. Redevelopment was substantially finished, a substantial degree of tract consolidation had occurred, and most of the new buildings had complied with the pedestrian walkway requirements. But there had been problems. In the process of development, the original mix in land use had been considerably altered in favor of office development. How well the pedestrian access system would function was open to question. A holdout at a strategic point in the development was inhibiting completion. Moreover, the county had to face another critical issue at an interim stage in the area's development. A developer owning a peripheral site not apparently a part of the redevelopment plan sought a rezoning to the more intensive uses contemplated in the redevelopment area. Despite considerable pressure, the county board rejected the rezone, thus maintaining pressure for development in the planned redevelopment area. A decision for development would have seriously weakened the chances of completing the development of the area as it had been projected.

SOME LEGAL ISSUES IN INCENTIVE ZONING

Although the Rosslyn experience does not exactly parallel the problems faced in New York City, partly because the greater intensity and diversity of New York requires even more specialized zoning techniques than those developed for Rosslyn, some of the legal problems likely to be presented by incentive zoning are highlighted by the Rosslyn experience. These will be discussed in turn and some concluding observations offered on the legal acceptability and possible legal character of incentive zoning provisions adopting the trade-off formulas that characterize the Rosslyn effort.

The Right v. Discretion Problem

One initial question is whether density and zone changes under incentive zoning techniques will be available as a matter of right to the developer, or whether the municipality will reserve the decision, in its discretion, to refuse even a developer who conforms to the rezone requirements. On their face, for example, the zone changes devised for the Rosslyn area are available to any

---

[5] A multiple of the size of an owner's lot allowing a maximum amount of floor area which varies in New York City with proximity to its central business district.

developer who complies with the zone requirements in the form of dedications, pedestrian linkages, etc. In an individual case, however, the zoning agency may be reluctant to confer the new zone on a developer for reasons which it may feel intuitively but which are difficult to express. As an example, it may not like the developer's design, even though it complies with all of the formal requirements in the zone change regulations. Unfortunately, we have not reached the point at which design criteria are easy to formulate and make operational, much less apply. It is in circumstances such as these that some observers have called for more explicit procedures as a corrective for substantive ambiguities. Better procedures can help, but they do not provide all of the safeguards that may be needed.

Other problems may be presented by developers who comply formally with the zoning standards, but who do not realize the full potential for the site. The problem has sometimes been acute in urban renewal projects, which are attacked by would-be filling station developers who seek some of the best sites before the entrepreneurship and capital resources for a more intensive development can be mobilized. Some of the same problems may occur in special incentive zones in which realization of goals requires the commitment of substantial capital at risks that are greater than normal. In a significant recent decision, the Michigan Court of Appeals upheld municipal turndown of a filling station developer in an area which the comprehensive plan had earmarked for an intensive civic center-office complex.[6] The problem also can be handled to some extent by minimum tract requirements as a condition to the rezone bonuses, but this solution is not an entire answer when the high intensity of development makes tract size less critical as a control variable. This problem is also less serious when the market is bullish rather than bearish, but in this case the danger may lie in the other direction—developers for more intensive uses may drive out some of the less intensive, but needed, counterparts. Apparently, it was pressures like these which led to the abandonment of some of the apartment zoning in Rosslyn. Given the government's push for office space, office development was a more certain investment.

The Residual Zone Problem

A developer who does not wish to take advantage of the incentives offered to comply with the burdens imposed by the rezone may always attack the underlying zoning classification. If the underlying, or residual, zone is suspect, the entire structure is built on shifting sand. There are several dimensions to this problem. The residual zone may be unrealistic in view of the demands of the market. Developers will thus be encouraged to apply for the rezone and to comply with the rezone requirements that give meaning to the

---

[6]Biske v. City of Troy, 6 Mich. App. 546, 149 N.W.2d 899 (1967), *rev'd*. in part on a slightly different issue, 166 N.W.2d 453 (Mich. 1969).

zoning enterprise, but, as the residual zone moves away from what is realistic, the chances for a successful attack increase.[7] Conversely, a more realistic residual zone makes a successful attack less likely but reduces the incentive to enter the rezone process.

Time brings its own problems. After a series of successive rezones, with development occurring at an intensity substantially in excess of what the residual zone contemplates, the basis for the residual zone grows even more unstable. Of course, a developer is less likely to opt for the residual zone as the viability of development at the higher intensities becomes manifest with time, but the risk should not be underestimated. Indeed, successive administrative departures from the original (and residual) zoning district may of itself make the entire process suspect. In a recent case in which a New Jersey municipality zoned a busy highway as residential throughout its length and then proceeded over the years to give a succession of variances, the court was led to characterize the entire zoning process as patently illegal.[8] The case is, of course, distinguishable because it involved a misuse of the variance power and a blatantly unreasonable zoning classification in the first instance.[9] But the decision gives pause.

The Validity of Density as a Basis for Control

In a developmental setting like that presented by New York or Rosslyn, density is a more important factor than use in the zoning control process. Yet, although density control is authorized by the Standard Zoning Act and has become an integral part of zoning ordinances, the fact remains that use rather than density is the more universal basis for classifying and adjudicating developmental demands and conflicts. *Euclid* talked about use conflicts, not density levels.[10] We have not had nearly enough judicial consideration of density controls, especially in the context of "downtown" and office development, probably because the incentives for compliance with development standards inhibit litigation.

Problems can arise in several ways. One problem is to find a justification for the imposition of density levels in the first instance, since the key to the incentive zoning technique is a density bonus in return for increments to developer costs, which represent the burden of compliance with rezone requirements. In a nonresidential setting, density controls are presumably

---

[7] Although a court will not usually grant a rezoning as part of its decree, in an attack of the kind described here, they are likely to do just that. *See* Daraban v. Township of Redford, 166 N.W.2d 453 (Mich. App. 1969).

[8] Wilson v. Borough of Mountainside, 42 N.J. 426, 201 A.2d 540 (1964).

[9] For a treatment of "The Role of the Amendment" in the zoning process, *see* Krasnowiecki in this volume, Chapter 1.

[10] Euclid v. Ambler Realty Co., 272 U.S. 365, 47 S.Ct. 114 (1926).

needed to control and avoid excess traffic congestion. (I am not considering, at this point, the relationship between density, bulk controls, and siting requirements.) The assumption is that increased site densities are reflected directly in increased traffic flow and circulation problems. The courts are becoming more sensitive to traffic considerations in zoning controversies; many of the cases have arisen in suburban areas in circumstances in which a proposed new use would have meant a demonstrably qualitative difference in traffic impacts. A recent New York case, in which a suburban town down-zoned a corner location from commercial to residential to prevent the construction of a restaurant, may be instructive on this score.[11] The lot in controversy was near a large regional shopping center, and the court, in reaching its decision, was impressed with the fact that it was "enmeshed" in one of the largest and most successful shopping complexes on Long Island. In the circumstances, although and perhaps because traffic congestion was already considerable, the court was unwilling to uphold a zoning decision that would simply have prevented the addition of a relatively small and incremental use.

These decisions may not prove controlling in a decidedly more intensive city center location, but they are certainly worth considering. One problem is that the increments to traffic flow will become less identifiable as development in any one area or "special" district nears completion, so that public control in the name of traffic flow may weaken as the area is developed and the objectives of the special control realized.

Another problem arises out of those provisions of the Rosslyn and similar ordinances which seek street widenings and other public dedications in return for density bonuses and other incentives. Here again, our closest analogy is to subdivision control in suburban areas. The New York courts have been able to extend the customary dedication for streets and like facilities to include parks and other open spaces in a subdivision setting, but the transferability of this doctrine outside the subdivision control context is not clear. To the extent that the subdivision cases turn on the fact of subdivision rather than on some notion of cost-benefit linkage, the municipality will not be able to use the mere incidence of development as an opportunity to exact land and other dedications from the developer. If the courts will generally take the position of a line of California cases and extend the rationale of subdivision exactions to any discretionary zoning decision that permits an increase in the intensity of development with corresponding traffic effects, these difficulties may decrease somewhat. In California, street widenings have been linked to the increased traffic flow generated by the new development.[12] Again, however, these developments generally occurred at land use intensities low enough that any more intensive increment was readily identifiable as contributing to traffic problems. In the context of Manhattan or Rosslyn, these increments to traffic and congestion problems may be more difficult to identify.

---

[11] Stevens v. Town of Huntington, 20 N.Y.2d 352, 229 N.E.2d 591, 283 N.Y.S.2d 16 (1967).

[12] See, e.g., Southern Pac. Co. v. City of Los Angeles, 242 Cal.App.2d 38, 51 Cal. Rptr. 197 (Dist. Ct. App. 1966), appeal dismissed for want of a substantial federal question, 385 U.S. 647 (1967).

Yet another way of looking at the issues is to consider the density and other incentives offered to the developer as a *de facto quid pro quo* for related dedications and other expenditures that lessen the public burden. This technique is beginning to receive judicial sanction in the context of planned unit development regulation, and there is no reason to believe that the underlying rationale is not transferable to a more urban setting provided the density bonus is real and is not manipulated from a false base. As I have pointed out elsewhere, the problem here is perhaps less that of judicial risk than of a corresponding risk that the zoning agency will manipulate the system by setting density standards unreasonably low, utilizing paper increases to coerce dedications and other exactions from the developer.

Maintaining Public Commitment Over Time

Running through these comments has been a concern over the ability of the zoning agency to maintain its commitment to the purposes of incentive zoning procedures over the long period of time it will usually take to realize the objectives of the zoning process. What has been said, furthermore, reflects to some extent the special problems of an area like Rosslyn, in which the planning commission had very definite developmental objectives which were reduced to a tentative development plan for the site. Although incentive zoning need not always involve the realization of a private redevelopment plan, it would appear that much of the interest in special zoning districts derives from a similar motivation. Certainly the special district proposed for the Lincoln Square area in New York City bears some of the earmarks of the Rosslyn plan in its attention to specific development objectives.

Nor is the problem made any easier by land assembly and resale through the urban renewal process, as recent studies have indicated. Pressures on the renewal agency as described in Nashville and St. Louis studies led to substantial departures from the original development plan as demand built up for results in the local renewal program.[13] Changes in intended land use in these cities were the product of weaknesses in the local market, which did not support the original renewal objectives. In a New York or Rosslyn setting, the possibilities lie in the other direction, as more intensive land users seek to push out less intensive development which the municipality seeks to protect. Apparently, not even the Champs d'Elysée is exempt!

Substantial modifications in the developmental objectives may mean significant windfalls for those developers who bide their time and then seek special concessions from the local zoning agency. These pressures may be hard to resist, and they increase the incentive for holdouts. A secondary business center like that in Rosslyn has been developing in Clayton, Missouri, adjacent to St. Louis, and there are some indications, in the decision to allow a second

---

[13]Mandelker, *The Comprehensive Planning Requirement in Urban Renewal,* 116 U. PA. L. REV. 25 (1967).

high-rise office tower, that the municipality is beginning to lose control. Certainly the parking and circulation systems have not kept pace with the new development. In the urban renewal context, the disposition decisions of the renewal agency may be difficult to upset, but the private developer has more leverage through the zoning ordinance. Nor is effective control guaranteed by insitutional legal changes. The answer lies, if anywhere, in the commitment of the zoning and planning agencies. Here the problem is complicated by the fact that some changes over time may be justified, especially as new possibilities and opportunities are revealed as experience with the ordinance accumulates. How to distinguish the arbitrary change from the necessary and even beneficial accomodation is not easy.

CONCLUSION

Lest we be thought to have painted too dark a picture, we should conclude with the observation that discretionary controls of the kind envisioned in incentive zoning formulations do not always run as many risks as a cautious analysis may indicate. In New York, the courts have been sympathetic to administrative zoning techniques, and the structure of zoning controls very often forecloses any serious challenge. Even in Rosslyn, a dissatisfied developer was reluctant to take the planning agency to court, for the pressure to comply when the monetary stakes are high is considerable. Furthermore, in the context (at least) of a commercial area the possibilities for a so-called neighboring challenge are limited if not nonexistent.[14] Finally, administrative decisions by the zoning agency will usually be accorded considerable judicial respect if the criteria are adequate and reasonable and if the finding is well supported.

Unless we take the English New Town approach and place the planning, development, and management of commercial and semipublic centers in public hands, we will always need some method of accommodating the public and private interest in land development. A shift to more complex administrative and incentive techniques simply exposes some of the complex problems of control and coordination that are either hidden or compromised in the more conventional, preset regulations. Adequate and justifiable developmental criteria, fairly exercised, are the best assurance against over-reaching and downright temptation. Some of us are not entirely convinced that the necessary criteria are readily at hand. I suspect that the tendency to apply special controls to areas of special quality, such as historic districts and cultural centers, represents an attempt to seek substantive support in a committed environment as an alternative to reliance on operational legislative criteria which are difficult to formulate. But experience teaches best, and I am likewise not ready to admit that our intellectual resources are not up to the challenge.

---

[14]*See* Mandelker, *Control of Competition as a Proper Purpose in Zoning*, 14 ZONING DIGEST 62 (1962).

14

Robert Freilich

INTERIM DEVELOPMENT CONTROLS: ESSENTIAL TOOLS FOR IMPLEMENTING FLEXIBLE PLANNING AND ZONING (excerpts)

I. THE CONCEPTUAL PROBLEM

A. *The Need For A General Theory of Interim Development Controls*

Underlying the entire concept of zoning is the assumption that zoning can be a vital tool for maintaining a civilized form of existence only if we employ the insights and the learning of the philosopher, the city planner, the economist, the sociologist, the public health expert and all the other professions concerned with urban problems.[1]

This brings us to the second requisite of an adequately inclusive point of view toward land use. This is the view of land use as a constantly evolving and continuously changing phenomenon—an evolutionary scheme which through the medium of development policies is progressively adjusted in the flow of time to take account of unpredictable elements of technological and social change.[2]

We are living in the age of the urban crisis, which involves some of the most severe domestic problems of our society and is the cause of great social and economic unrest. In the long-range view, however, it may not prove to be the explosive problems of our cities which are most difficult to resolve, but rather the reduplication of these problems in the land surrounding our metropolitan areas through inability to utilize intelligent and far-reaching land development policies.[3]

---

1. Udell v. Haas, 21 N.Y.2d 463, 469, 235 N.E.2d 897, 900 (1968).
2. F. CHAPIN, URBAN LAND USE PLANNING 98 (2d ed. 1965).
3. H. GANS, PEOPLE AND PLANS: ESSAYS ON URBAN PROBLEMS AND SOLUTIONS 57 (1968): Although the city planning profession and the city planning agency are inventions of the

Rational land development policies cannot, however, be accomplished unless our society is willing to understand that intelligible planning must precede the adoption of permanent land use controls. In this regard we have been totally remiss in failing to provide legal mechanisms to protect and nourish the planning process and as a result we have almost totally failed to incorporate planning into the chaotic development of our communities.

The nexus between planning and incorporation of planning into legal implementing measures lies in the use of little known legal tools—interim development controls. Stated simply these controls can be used to prevent land development, during the formulation of planning policies, which would conflict in any way with permanent legal controls implementing the basic planning policies. With planning so protected, there is no longer the need for hasty adoption of permanent controls in order to avoid the establishment of nonconforming uses and structures. Of even far greater importance are the corollary effects of such protection. Firstly, the planning process can be brought out into the open for full democratic debate and citizen participation; thus, assuring a greater relationship to the real goals and needs of the people. Secondly,

---

twentieth century, city planning has existed since men began to build towns and to make decisions about their future. In most societies, but particularly in America, there has been little consensus about these decisions. The diverse classes, ethnic groups, and interest groups who live in the city have different conceptions of how the city ought to grow and change, what aspects of city development ought to be encouraged or discouraged by public policies and who should benefit from policy and allocation decisions.

See also Gans, *Regional and Urban Planning*, 12 INTERNATIONAL ENCYCLOPEDIA OF THE SOCIAL SCIENCES 129 (1968). The problem was well stated by the National Commission on Urban Problems appointed by President Johnson:

The United States is expected to have a population increase of about 100 million persons between 1967 and the end of the century. Ninety percent of these new people will be living in cities. Unless a program for building new towns is carried out 75 to 80 percent of the population growth is likely to take place in our metropolitan areas. This means we will need to construct and provide additional housing and urban facilities equal to what now exists in every American city of 25,000 or more persons.

While some of the additional population may be housed in existing central cities, it would be a reversal of the trend of the past 20 years for any substantial portion to be so housed. We must assume that the increase in population thus will require that new land be converted from nonurban use—principally agriculture—to urban uses.

A conservative estimate of the new land required for urban development by the year 2000 is 18 million acres, or 28,125 square miles—an area approximately equal to the total area of the states of New Hampshire, Vermont, Massachusetts and Rhode Island.

This rough calculation established the gross dimensions of the situation. It presents, in itself, the first great problem in land-use regulation, the sheer magnitude of undertaking to carry out rational regulation of development on 18 million acres of land. There is the added complication that these regulations will be devised and administered—assuming continuation of present practice—by several thousand different local governments.

NATIONAL COMMISSION ON URBAN PROBLEMS, RESEARCH REPORT NO. 2: PROBLEMS OF ZONING AND LAND-USE REGULATION 6 (1968).

continuous amendment and revision of the planning policies of the community can be, for the first time, successfully accomplished. Long term essentially static planning is no longer feasible in our rapidly urbanizing society. New flexibility in planning has become essential as evidenced by the growing use of new town development, "cluster zoning," "bonus and incentive zoning", "floating zones", and "planned unit development".[4] With the use of interim development controls a flexible system of planning, continuously updated and current, can be utilized to provide the tying rod for an effective and complete system of total environmental protections. The distinct possibility exists in fact that by extensive use of interim development controls implementing flexible and continuous planning the legal systems of zoning and land use control in the United States can be significantly modernized to perform a more useful role.

Interim development controls, however, do not exist as such in American planning and legal literature. The author has had to analyze and collect judicial precedents, statutes, ordinances and land use practices which occur under numerous diverse and inconsistent nomenclature, into the single term 'interim development control'—a term borrowed from the British and Commonwealth systems. The lack of any single identifying name for these legal controls has left their use to scattered application and ineffective utilization of the separate devices, primarily a limited use of "stop-gap" zoning techniques.[5] It is the purpose of this article to demonstrate that a general theory of interim development controls can be stated and that the establishment of a broad based general theory can be utilized to institute an entirely new dimension to the planning process and to land development controls. To further that end a model state enabling statute has been drafted to help unify the support and practices of this vital land use control device.

B.   The Implementation of Planning

The failure to protect and incorporate the planning process in our society is amply demonstrated by the fact that the principal tool of land development policy, zoning, is handled in each metropolitan area by hundreds of fragmented local governments without conscious commitment to the concept that principles are essential to the

---

4.   See Heeter, *Toward a More Effective Land Use Guidance System: A Summary and Analysis of Five Major Reports,* AMERICAN SOCIETY OF PLANNING OFFICIALS (A.S.P.O.), PLANNING ADVISORY SERVICE REPORT NO. 250, 8 (1969).

5.   The literature in this area has been scanty and mainly in the narrow field of stop-gap zoning. *See* Note, 18 SYRACUSE L. REV. 837 (1968); Note, 14 W. RES. L. REV. 135 (1962); 136 A.L.R. 844 (1942); 86 A.L.R. 662 (1933). Considering the vast amount of judicial decision-making concerning interim controls, the lack of any meaningful commentary and analysis of an important land use control is surprising indeed.

establishment of meaningful land development policies[6] and that rational planning of land use must be incorporated in the legal controls which are adopted to regulate the use of land. These legal controls should encompass many areas other than zoning, since the planning of the environment is concerned with the totality of physical, social and economic policies.[7] Effective implementation of planning, at a very minimum, requires intelligible subdivision controls, open space, provision for public facilities, drainage and flood controls, building and housing codes and complementary tax policies.

The master plan is the traditional planning basis for all implementing legal tools. Authorized by the Standard Planning Enabling Act of the 1920's,[8] which has been adopted by most states in identical or equivalent form,[9] the purpose of the master plan in modern terms designated as the "comprehensive" plan, is to provide:

> . . . a co-ordinated, adjusted and harmonious development of the municipality and its environs which will, in accordance with present and future needs best promote health, safety, morals, order, convenience, prosperity and general welfare in the process of development . . . the promotion of good civic design

---

6. R. BABCOCK, THE ZONING GAME xiv (1966): Since the early days of zoning, thousands of communities have been disposing of zoning disputes without any significant awareness that they were participating in a law-making process which might embrace a body of principles. If this is because there are no principles by which the execution of zoning law is capable of being measured, then it is time to acknowledge this dreary fact. If, however, there are such principles, then it is time to put them out where they can be subject to scrutiny, not in separate and isolated municipal forums but in a political arena where as large a consensus as possible may weigh their usefulness in a democratic society.

7. In Grosso v. Board of Adjustment of Millburn Township, 137 N.J.L. 630, 631, 61 A.2d 167, 168 (1948), the court stated: "Planning is a science and an art concerned with land economics and land policies in terms of social and economic betterment. The control essential to planning is exercised through government ownership or regulation of the use of the locus." POOLEY, PLANNING AND ZONING IN THE UNITED STATES, 6-7 (1961). The author states: "Planning is thus much broader than zoning. It embraces all facets of the municipality's development. Zoning is concerned merely with the orderly control of the physical growth of the municipality." See also Mansfield and Swett, Inc. v. Town of West Orange, 120 N.J.L. 145, 198 A. 225 (1930), for a particularly enlightened early view of this distinction. On the economic and social aspects, see Bauer, Social Questions in Housing and Community Planning, 7 J. So. ISSUES 1 (1951); Perloff, New Directions in Social Planning, 31 J. AM. INST. PLANNERS 297 (1965); Davidoff, Advocacy and Social Concern in Planning, 31 J. AM. INST. PLANNERS 331 (1965); Webber, Comprehensive Planning and Social Responsibility, 29 J. AM. INST. PLANNERS 232 (1963).

8. U.S. DEPT. OF COMMERCE, ADVISORY COMM. ON CITY PLANNING AND ZONING, A STANDARD PLANNING ENABLING ACT (1928); U.S. DEPT. OF COMMERCE, ADVISORY COMM. ON ZONING, A STANDARD STATE ZONING ENABLING ACT (rev. ed. 1926).

9. See A MODEL LAND DEVELOPMENT CODE (Tent. draft no. 1, 1968) (hereinafter cited as MODEL CODE). Appendices "A" and "B" set forth the text of both the Standard Planning Enabling Act and the Standard Zoning Enabling Act. See also U.S. HOUSING AND HOME FIN. AGENCY, STATE PLANNING LAWS (2d ed. 1958); Haar, The Master Plan: An Impermanent Constitution, 20 LAW & CONTEMP. PROB. 353 (1955).

and arrangement, wise and efficient expenditure of public funds and the adequate provisions of public utilities and other public requirements.[10]

In preparing the comprehensive plan the planning commission proceeds to develop maps, plats, charts, descriptive materials and planning policies which will form the basis of the implementing legal tools of zoning and subdivision regulations, official maps for streets, parks, and drainage, and a long term financial program, usually designated as the "capital budget."[11]

The requirement of comprehensive planning was carried over to the standard Zoning Enabling Act which provides that "such regulations shall be made in accordance with a comprehensive plan."[12] The presumption that the legislation had in mind the master plan prepared by the planning commission in requiring zoning ordinances to conform to a "comprehensive plan" is shattered by the discovery that about half the cities which have adopted zoning have no master plans at all.[13] The courts have concluded from this that the comprehensive plan of the zoning enabling act has no reference to the master plan, and one court has gone so far as to suggest that the requirement means nothing more

---

10. MODEL CODE, § 9 *Purposes In View, Standard Planning Act.*

11. *Id.,* Appendix "B".

12. *Id.* The importance of the comprehensive plan to the entire concept of zoning is emphasized by the holding of the Court of Appeals of New York in a recent decision:

This fundamental conception of zoning has been present from its inception. The almost universal statutory requirement that zoning conform to a "well-considered plan," or "comprehensive plan" is a reflection of that view . . . that consideration must be given to the needs of the community as a whole following a calm and deliberate consideration of the alternatives, and not because of the whims of either an articulate minority or even majority of the community . . . . The comprehensive plan is the essence of zoning. Without it, there can be no rational allocation of land use. It is the assurance that the public welfare is being served and that zoning does not become nothing more than just a Gallup poll.

Udell v. Haas, 21 N.Y.2d 463, 469, 235 N.E.2d 897, 900 (1968). *See also* Haar, *In Accordance With A Comprehensive Plan,* 68 HARV. L. REV. 1154 (1955); Dunham, *City Planning: An Analysis of the Content of the Master Plan,* 1 J. LAW & ECON. 170 (1958). Note, *Spot Zoning and the Comprehensive Plan,* 10 SYRACUSE L. REV. 303 (1959). The holding of the Udell case is also emphasized in Speakman v. Mayor of North Plainfield, 8 N.J. 250, 256, 84 A.2d 715 (1951); "the specific requirement of a comprehensive plan is extended to avoid an arbitrary, unreasonable, or capricious exercise of the zoning powers."

13. B. POOLEY, PLANNING AND ZONING IN THE UNITED STATES 6 (1961); Haar, *supra* note 12, at 1157. Pooley points out that as a matter of historical record zoning has preceded planning in most communities. *See also The* NATIONAL COMMISSION ON URBAN PROBLEMS, RESEARCH REPORT NO. 2, PROBLEMS OF ZONING AND LAND USE REGULATION 29 (1968). One well known planner, Frederick P. Clark, stated: "I believe the largest part of the problem of land-use controls comes from municipalities devising and amending these controls on an ad hoc bases, without any clear, long-range community development plan in mind." *See also* Chapin, *Taking Stock of Techniques for Shaping Urban Growth,* 29 J. AM. INST. OF PLANNERS 76 (1963): ". . . until the '701' Program came along, the instances where the general plan was used as an instrument of decision-making by local government were not many."

than having a rational, integrated zoning ordinance with no prior planning.[14]

If the legal tool of zoning need not be shaped by long-range planning, the other implementing tools suffer the same defect, despite the provision for preparation of these tools in the standard planning enabling act. Subdivision controls are usually adopted independently of the master plan.[15] Nor has the official map any legal relationship to the master plan. Some cases mistakenly refer to the master plan as the "official map," but in no case has there been any requirement that the official map be predicated on the master plan.[16] To conclude the point,

---

14.   Kozesnik v. Montgomery Township, 24 N.J. 154, 166, 131 A.2d 1, 7 (1957):
There has been little judicial consideration of the precise attributes of a comprehensive plan. Our own decisions emphasize that its office is to prevent a capricious exercise of the legislative power resulting in haphazard or piecemeal zoning. Without venturing an exact definition, it may be said for present purposes that "plan" connotes an integrated project of a rational process and "comprehensive" requires something beyond a piecemeal approach, both to be revealed by the ordinance considered in relation to the physical facts and the purpose authorized by the [state enabling act]. Such being the requirements of a comprehensive plan, no reason is perceived why we should infer the legislature intended by necessary implication that the comprehensive plan be portrayed in some physical form outside the ordinance itself. A plan may readily be revealed in an end-product—here the zoning ordinance—and no more is required by statute.
15.   Just as in the case of the "comprehensive plan" for zoning, one court was able to piece together the requirements of an official map plan simply from existing conditions despite the fact that an ordinance required a master plan before disposition of subdivision controls:
. . . subdivision design and improvement obviously include conformance to neighborhood planning and zoning, and it may properly be said that the formulation and acceptance of the uniform conditions in the development of the district constitute a practical adoption of a master plan and zoning requirements therefore.
Ayres v. City Council of Los Angeles, 34 Cal.2d 31, 41-42, 207 P.2d 1, 7 (1949). See discussion of this case in Nelson, The Master Plan and Subdivision Control, 16 MAINE L. REV. 107, 108 (1964):
Municipalities have tried to remedy irresponsible and unplanned development by promulgating subdivision regulations, but the regulations tend to deal with practical matters like the size of curbstones and the thickness of pavements. When they do venture into the more sophisticated areas of design and public interest denial, the regulations operate without regard to related community problems. The only place where all these factors are considered is in the formulation of the master plan. Nevertheless, up to now, subdivision regulation and master planning have followed separate paths.
See also THE ADVISORY COMMITTEE ON CITY PLANNING AND ZONING, MODEL SUBDIVISION REGULATIONS 36, n. 7 (1936):
Even in cases where (completion of a master plan or official map) is not a legal requirement, such plan should be available if really effective and intelligent control over subdivisions is to be exercised, good principles realized, and justice assured to the subdivider. The study and consideration required, in master planning is a prerequisite to an intelligent understanding of the principles which should obtain in wise subdivision control.
16.   MODEL CODE. A New York statute, N.Y. Town Law § 277 (1938) provides:
In approving such plans the planning board shall require, that the streets and highways—if there be an official map or master plan,—shall be coordinated so as to compose a convenient system conforming to the official map and properly related to the proposals shown by the planning board or the master plan."

few, if any municipalities adopt a capital budget, the fourth principal tool which reflects the requirements of an updated master plan.[17]

The initial relationship we have explored between planning and the legal tools for implementation has been the general failure of local governmental bodies to utilize planning, or where planning is performed, to integrate such planning into land development regulations. As shall be subsequently explored, a substantial reason for this failure lies in the haste of municipalities to eliminate future non-conforming uses and their failure to utilize interim controls during the planning stage to protect against such future uses. By such failures municipalities have by-passed meaningful planning and have entered into permanent controls with the good faith intention of amending the controls at a later date. The results are generally disastrous.[18]

Beyond this, however, the whole mechanism of planning should be conceived not as static decision, but as dynamic process.[19] So conceived the planning process consists of two different facets. First, the

---

See also N.Y. Town Law § 270 (1956):

> The town board may establish an official map of that part of the town outside the limits of an incorporated city or village showing the streets, highways and parks theretofore laid out, adopted and established by law and drainage systems may also be shown on such map. Such map shall be final and conclusive with respect to the location and width of streets and highways, drainage systems and the location of parks shown thereon. Such official map is hereby declared to be established to conserve and protect the public health, safety and general welfare . . . ."

There is no requirement for any adherence to the Master Plan which is established by the planning board and not the governing board. N.Y. Town Law § 272-a (1938).

17. "Another important area is the relation of land-use regulations to the capital improvement program of a city, to assure that the city's investments are not nullified by outmoded regulations that do not reflect the changes implied by the proposed capital investment itself." (Testimony of William Doebele before the Douglas Commission, *supra* note 13, at 29). Needless to say, the requirements of a capital program do not include coherence to any plan. N.Y. Gen. Mun. Law § 99-g (1962).

18. The failure to plan for the growth of our urban areas was well stated by the court in Mansfield and Swett, Inc. v. Town of West Orange, 120 N.J.L. 145, 150-51, 198 A. 225, 229 (1938):

> The baneful consequences of haphazard development are everywhere apparent. There are evils affecting the health, safety and prosperity of our citizens that are well-nigh insurmountable because of the prohibitive corrective cost. To challenge the power to give proper direction to community growth and development—is to deny the vitality of a principle that has brought men together in organized society for their mutual advantage.

Similarly the New York Court of Appeals cited the importance of planning to urban development in Village of Lynbrook v. Cadoo, 252 N.Y. 308, 314, 169 N.E. 394, 396-397 (1929):

> Town planning is a new field of legislation comparable with the recent development of zoning law and regulations. Its purpose is to preserve through a governmental agency a uniform and harmonious development of the growth of a village and to prevent the individual owner from laying out streets according to his own sweet will without official approval.

19. *See Process Planning: A Symposium on the New Urban Planning,* 4 J. Am. Inst. Planners (1965); Davidoff & Reiner, *A Choice Theory of Planning,* 28 J. Am. Inst. Planners 103 (1962). Hayes, *Analytical Techniques in Urban Planning and Renewal,* American Society of Planning Officials (A.S.P.O.), Planning 68-80 (1964).

responsibility of the planner is not only to see that planning is performed, but to see that planning is effectively implemented and that the plan adapts to the physical, social and economic changes in the environment. Planning in this sense, leaves no choice between planning and not planning. Planning has been defined as the intelligence function of man, the rational adaptation of means to ends.[20] In government, specifically, planning brings to fruition the long-term comprehensive point of view designed to achieve the purposes and goals of the community. Planning then becomes a process because by continuous and systematic study and appraisal of conditions and by periodic check-up on the extent to which action is effective, planning attempts to guide the making and execution of important decisions co-ordinated with established objectives.[21] Where the planning process intersects with land development policies, the fulcrum continues to be the comprehensive plan.[22] It is of the highest importance, therefore, that this plan, which is the basis of all the land development policies and implementing legislation, be continuously reviewed and amended as part of the planning process and that each proposed amendment to the zoning ordinance, the subdivision regulations, official map and other controls be carefully weighed against the policies and goals of the plan to avoid its

---

20. *See* DIRECTIVE COMM. ON REGIONAL PLANNING, YALE UNIV., THE CASE FOR REGIONAL PLANNING WITH SPECIAL REFERENCE TO NEW ENGLAND, Chap. 1 (1947).

21. M. MCDOUGAL & D. HABER, PROPERTY, WEALTH AND LAND 456 (1948). In their work the authors divide the planning process into four tasks: (1) Clarifying and Defining Objectives—standards and goals, the needed resources and services, alternation of practices and institutions and synthesis into effective programs of action; (2) Study Determining Conditions—develop realistic understanding of the conditions which determine the limits of possible achievements of goals; (3) Devise Appropriate Means to Secure Goals—this is the function of government—to recommend the action, of the appropriate kind and level, and to supply the framework in which development can flourish within the specific goals of the community; and (4) Assist in Carrying Recommendations Into Action—The contribution of implementation is as important as the contribution of conception. This process of evaluation is indeed a part of [the planner's] general function of determining the conditions which affect the achievement of specific goals and basic values and here leads directly to subsequent recommendations for action. It is exactly for this reason that the planning process is a continuous one and the role of the planner a permanent one. The purposes of planning cannot be achieved in one blow by a single exercise of the four separate steps involved in the process of planning. The continuing achievement of the major values of any community requires a continuous exercise of all its powers of foresight and rational decision. *Id.* at 461. *See also* CHAPIN, *supra* note 2, at 30, who indicates that the cycle consist of four phases: (1) experiencing of needs and wants, (2) defining of goals, (3) planning alternative courses of action, and (4) deciding and acting.

22. Chapin, *Taking Stock of Techniques For Shaping Urban Growth,* 29 J. AM. INST. PLANNERS 76 (1963):

> The general plan—variously known as the comprehensive plan, master plan, guide plan, development plan is perhaps the oldest of the techniques for guiding urban expansion in use today. . . . In recent times especially in the Western World, the effectiveness of a plan in guiding development has been dependent on how well related it is to the decision making process of governing bodies. This dependence has given rise to the emphasis that today is placed on the planning process and the function of planning in government.

piecemeal destruction after adoption.[23] Thus the process of change is made by continuously examining the plan and in issuing periodic supplemental reviews. It is not the planning process if changes such as zoning amendments do not come from goals generated by the plan but are the result of pressure exerted by private property interests.[24]

---

23.   In testimony before the Douglas Commission, it was stated that this in fact is the single most important problem of land use control:

There should be a major separate emphasis on the need to base land-use controls on a community development plan and of continuing to maintain a relationship to such a plan in determining which of the various proposed amendments should be adopted. I believe the largest part of the problem of land use controls comes from municipalities devising and amending these controls on an ad hoc basis, without any clear, long range community development plan in mind. Even where communities have such long range plans, many do not known how to use them effectively.

Testimony of Frederick P. Clark, Planner, NATIONAL COMM'N ON URBAN PROBLEMS, RESEARCH REPORT NO. 2, PROBLEMS OF ZONING AND LAND USE REGULATION 29 (1968).

24.   Most of the elected officials and members of the public seem to look on the zoning ordinance as a device for protecting individual property rights, not as a device for carrying out a public policy or a comprehensive plan. Although initial development of the zoning ordinance, with or without a previous comprehensive plan, may have been related to some general concepts, the damage comes in progressive changes, which are applied to each piece of property as a private matter. One partial antidote is to force prior adoption of the comprehensive plan and to require statements of conformance with the plan for each zoning change. The plan necessarily has a more general, public construct and substance.

Testimony of Morton Lustig, NATIONAL COMM'N ON URBAN PROBLEMS, RESEARCH REPORT NO. 2, PROBLEMS OF ZONING AND LAND USE REGULATION 30 (1968).

New stimulus to the planning process has come from the American Law Institute's MODEL LAND DEVELOPMENT CODE, *supra* note 9. In § 2-105 the drafters call for the adoption of a comprehensive land development plan and in § 2-106 have called for continuous review of the plan in periodic land development reports which must be submitted at intervals of no greater than five years after adoption of the plan. MODEL CODE 46, 47.

This section provides for periodic reports to be prepared by a designated agency . . . . The reports are to state the then existing problems, changes in the assumptions upon which the plan was based, recommended amendments and most importantly a new short term program of action. The section also requires an evaluation of the prior short term program and an analysis of the feasibility and consequences of the new problem.

These reports are the central mechanisms for an on going planning process. If the plan (the original framework for the process) is considerably out-of-date because of technological, economic or demographic changes, or is the infusion of new ideas, or analyses of past community goals, the preparation of a new Land Development Plan should be recommended. Otherwise corrective amendments should be proposed.

Id. at 48. A similar proposal but one calling for a periodic review within every two to three years was recently suggested for incorporation in the regulatory process by the American Society of Planning Officials. NOBLE, A PROPOSED SYSTEM FOR REGULATING LAND USE IN URBANIZING COUNTIES 21 (1967).

The A.I.I. proposal has come under some mild criticism for adopting the position that a land development plan and the subsequent land development reports are not required for standard Euclidean zoning ordinances, while requiring the planning process for more advances tools of flexible zoning such as floating zones and planned unit development.

See Schulman, *The American Law Institute's Model State Planning and Zoning Statutes,* 1968 LAND USE CONTROLS 1. Schulman finds that the five year requirement for a periodic report presents a confusing conflict with existing capital program requirements. He further believes that the drafters have created the wrong incentives and deterrents. If irrespective of a plan in existence, a

The second facet of the planning process concerns a discernible broadening trend toward the subject matter and in the scope of concern of the planning profession. In the early stages of development the concept of planning embraced only the physical properties of the environment. The man credited with the growth of planning in this country, Frederick Law Olmstead, Jr., described the general plan as a single complex subject—the intelligent control and guidance of the physical growth and alteration of the cities.[25] During the 1930's, Edward M. Bassett, a leader in the zoning movement, was still describing the master plan in terms of streets, parks, public building sites, public reservations, zoning districts and bulkhead lines.[26] The physical emphasis of planning proved to be too limited to account for dynamic forces exerting influence on the metropolis. First, the physical concept was tied to the "neighborhood"[27] and the bursting of the city into a regional urban complex shattered any hope that such simplistic models would offer effective solutions for urban problems.[28] The frustrations of the early years of urban renewal and redevelopment[29] finally forced planners to realize that the problems of metropolitan minority groups require employment, health and education opportunities and led legislators to enact broad social legislation such as the Economic Opportunity Act, the Model Cities Act and the Housing and Urban Development Act of 1968. The concept of planning emerging from these

---

municipality may undertake all the common regulatory devices—zoning, sub-division regulations, variances and special permits—then the carrot offered to communities to encourage them to plan is "unlikely to excite the provincial political palate. So what if we can't have floating zones (whatever they are) or approve fancy plans by big time developers?" On the other hand, Schulman believes that the requirement to plan may be a disincentive to the flexible devices. For a different point of view, see Babcock, The Lawyers Are At It Again, 7 A.S.P.O. NEWSLETTER 34 (Aug. 1968), who believes that the carrot of flexible devices will in fact encourage municipalities to plan and that for the simplistic regulation there is at least the cardinal virtue of certainty.

25. See T. KENT, THE URBAN GENERAL PLAN 28-30 (1964); see also MANDELKER, MANAGING ON URBAN ENVIRONMENT, 459 (1966).

26. E. BASSETT, THE MASTER PLAN 65 (1938). The physical orientation is emphasized by Olmstead's belief that the master plan could be designed for a period of twenty-five to fifty years in the future. See also SCOTT, THE HISTORY OF CITY PLANNING (1970).

27. See Perry, The Neighborhood Unit, in 7 REGIONAL SURVEY OF NEW YORK AND ITS ENVIRONS 22-140 (1929); J. DAHIR, THE NEIGHBORHOOD UNIT PLAN (1947); H. HOYT, THE STRUCTURE AND GROWTH OF RESIDENTIAL NEIGHBORHOODS IN AMERICAN CITIES (1939); see Haar, The Content of the General Plan: A Glance at History, 21 J. AM. INST. PLANNERS 66-75 (1955), Dunham, City Planning: An Analysis of the Content of the Master Plan, 1 J. LAW & ECON. 170-186 (1958).

28. See Isaacs, The Neighborhood Theory: An Analysis of Its Inadequacy, 14 J. AM. INST. PLANNERS 15 (1948); Fagin, The Penn Jersey Transportation Study: The Launching of a Permanent Regional Planning Process, 29 J. AM. INST. PLANNERS 9 (1963).

29. See M. ANDERSON, THE FEDERAL BULLDOZER: A CRITICAL ANALYSIS OF URBAN RENEWAL 1949-1962 (1964); Bauer, Social Questions in Housing and Community Planning, 7 J. SOC. ISSUES 1 (1951); Dyckman, National Planning for Urban Renewal: The Paper Moon in the Cardboard Sky, 26 J. AM. INST. PLANNERS 49 (1960).

measures, including the extension of economic and social opportunities, bears little resemblance to traditional planning solutions; the planning process is no longer envisaged solely in terms of a master plan, but as pyramidal or developmental programs that will improve social as well as physical conditions and will be coordinated in the ongoing planning process.[30]

---

30. *Cf.* WEBBER, THE PROSPECTS FOR POLICIES PLANNING, THE URBAN CONDITION 319 (L. Duhl ed. 1963). A system of social and rational planning has developed which incorporates the new concepts. A leading sociologist describes the new theories:

> The social scientists and the rational programmers owe no allegiance either to the master plan or to physical determinism. Aided by research findings which indicate that the portions of the physical environment with which city planners have traditionally dealt do not have a significant impact on people's behavior and by studies of social organization which demonstrate that economic and social structures are much more important than spatial ones, the rational programmers devote their attention to institutions and institutional change, rather than to environmental change.

H. GANS, PEOPLE AND PLANS: ESSAYS ON URBAN PROBLEMS AND SOLUTIONS 69-71 (1968). The new social planning has had its impact on traditional land use planning although it has not entirely changed its direction. The drafters of the American Law Institute Model Land Development Code are frank to admit that it is possible to have planning and planning law which is focused primarily or directly on social and economic factors and not on land development, but they have chosen to concern themselves with the physical development of land; proper location and intensity of activities which use land and the type, design and location of structures and facilities that serve these activities. The drafters have taken ample note of the direction of the new planning:

> To state that physical development is emphasized is not to say that land planning ignores social and economic objectives. It is rather to state that land planning seeks to identify the physical factors which can influence significantly realization of social and economic objectives. Land planning results in programs or policies for physical development which maximizes the opportunity to realize social and economic objectives.

MODEL CODE xvi, at n.9. Nor have the drafters adopted the inflexible map approach to land planning. As previously noted they have been willing to adopt new flexible techniques for development to fit the environment which is commonly known as the "policies plan." The approach taken seems to be a middle ground which has been resolved by planners and generally supported by planning lawyers. Perhaps this middle ground was best expressed by Norman Williams in an article which foreshadowed much of the controversy yet to come:

> In planning, primary emphasis is on the physical environment, yet the social environment is also involved in many ways—the distinction between the physical and the social environment is really an artificial one anyway, since the arrangement of the physical environment has a decided impact upon social conditions, and vice versa.
>
> This process of conscious and purposeful control over the development of the physical and social environment in a relatively free society is something rather new in history. Moreover in such a society the development of techniques to forecast probable future trends, and thus to ascertain and evaluate the range of possibilities within which control may be exercised is a difficult process at best. The development of effective methods of exercising such control is even more difficult. Any consideration of planning for techniques must therefore start with a realization that planning for the future environment is still in the experimental stage, and that the techniques available, while extremely useful are still rather crude. It is a truism to say that even the best plans must be subject to constant review in the light of changing conditions. Moreover, what techniques are available have generally not been thought out in terms of all their implications for the whole environment.

Williams, *Planning Law and Democratic Living,* 20 LAW & CONTEMP. PROB. 317-318 (1955). Babcock, *The Lawyers Are At It Again,* 34 A.S.P.O. NEWSLETTER No. 7, August 1968, at 1:

> It will disturb many that the definition in the Code of a plan—or the planning

In this process of developing planning techniques and planning goals, the use of interim development controls assumes wide significance. Not only are such interim controls an essential ingredient of the master plan for protection of long-range planning goals during the continuous review of community needs, but in light of the broadened social and economic perimeters of the planning concept, interim controls make possible the selection of community programs in a democratic manner by opening up the proposed plan to public hearing and preventing nonconforming uses from arising during this process. In Federal legislation alone there are the Urban Renewal and Model Cities programs, whose housing, social and economic goals must be protected during the process of formulating general plans required by the "workable program" requirements of the laws.[31] Similar requirements have been made for federal transportation aid,[32] open space, sewer, water and air pollution, beautification and other programs.[33]

---

process—still emphasizes the physical rather than the social. To my view, the decision on balance is right. The drafters recognize that our urban sickness cannot be cured by a model land development code. Until Congress and state legislatures are prepared to shake up our miserable local tax structure and to be tough auditors in financing of housing, open space, highway construction, and 701 programs, it seems a bit harsh to complain about a model land development code that does less than propose a total reconstruction of our urban system.

31. A brief summary of the requirements of some of the federal legislation recognizes the need for comprehensive planning in these areas. The Urban Renewal Program, 42 U.S.C. § 1455 (1964), requires that all urban renewal plans conform to a general plan for the community as a whole and this provision is inserted in all contracts for loans or capital grants. In defining an urban renewal plan, 42 U.S.C. § 1460 (1964), requires that the plan conform to the general plan of the locality and to the "workable program" required by 42 U.S.C. § 1451 and shall be consistent with broadened local objectives. The Community Renewal Plan, the latest proposal preceding the Model Cities Program, requires unification of renewal programs on a community-wide basis and must be adopted in conjunction with a comprehensive plan. See Testimony of William Slayton, Urban Renewal Administrator, Hearings on Urban Renewal Before the Subcomm. on Housing of the House Comm. on Banking and Currency, 88th Cong., 1st Sess. 394-402 (1963). No project in any of these communities will be approved unless a "workable program" is adopted by the community which includes comprehensive planning, comprehensive codes in health, plumbing, sanitation, housing, building and electrical, and detailed plans for community facilities, including social, health and recreation. 42 U.S.C. § 1451(c), as amended, 79 STAT. 474 (1965). In the Model Cities program a concentrated attack on social and economic conditions as well as physical blight is required to be made with tremendous financial inducements for the community making the effort. To aid in the establishment of comprehensive planning, the government adopted the Urban Planning Assistance Program, 40 U.S.C. § 461, known as the "701" program, which gives grants to communities to establish comprehensive plans and planning staffs.

32. See 23 U.S.C. § 134 (1964); G. SMERK, URBAN TRANSPORTATION: THE FEDERAL ROLE (1965).

33. Open space programs, scenic design and beautification, and other sewer, water and air pollution programs require comprehensive planning processes. See e.g., 42 U.S.C. § 1500(b), Supp. 1965. See also Blession, Urban Design and Its Relationships to the Comprehensive Planning Process, HIGHWAY RESEARCH RECORD No. 137, 1-4 (1965).

II. Constitutional and Statutory Problems in the Use of Interim Development Controls

A.   The Nature and Purpose of Interim Controls

Taking into account the principles of the planning process, the courts have validated legal measures to protect that process during its formulation. This is the first and perhaps the most important aspect of interim development controls.[34] The protection of the planning process is by no means limited to initiation of the first general plan of the community. The continuing planning process requires periodic review of the goals of the plan and of the implementing controls, and the courts have granted the same protection to the continuing planning process as to its commencement.[35]

Corollary to the first purpose of protecting the planning process is the prevention of new non-conforming uses during the planning process. As the first purpose is essential to insure that planning itself takes place, so this second purpose assures that the effectiveness of the planning shall not be destroyed before it has been implemented. The problem of the non-conforming use has long been a thorn in the side of meaningful zoning. The early exponents of zoning, fearful of constitutional attack

---

34. [N]o where . . . is there any express requirement that a master plan be adopted before zoning ordinances can be passed. Undoubtedly it is desirable that this be done as early as possible so that zoning can be carried out in accordance with some systematic design. But there are good reasons why interim zoning should not have to wait until that is accomplished.

As the name indicates a master plan would have to be comprehensive and the preparation of its details may be unavoidably slow; and the rate of growth may change from time to time. If no zoning regulation were possible until the master plan was completed and adopted, in counties where fast growth was-occurring, it might do so in an incongruous and uncontrolled manner which the planning commission would find difficult or perhaps impossible to keep abreast of, or to devise a master plan that would be of much benefit; thus the whole purpose of effective zoning would be frustrated.

Gayland v. Salt Lake County, 11 Utah2d 307, 309, 358 P.2d 633, 635 (1961). Similarly early California cases upheld interim zoning during the process of formulating master plans: Miller v. Board of Pub. Works, 195 Cal. 477, 234 P. 381 (1925), cert. den., 273 U.S. 781 (1926): "Therefore we may take judicial notice of the fact that it will take much time to work out the details of the plan and that obviously it would be destructive of the plan, if during the period of its incubation, parties seeking to evade the operation thereof should be permitted to enter upon a course of construction which might progress so far as to defeat, in whole or in part, the ultimate execution of the plan"; Lima v. Woodruff, 107 Cal. App. 285, 200 P. 480 (1930). See Haar, *In Accordance With a Comprehensive Plan,* 68 Harv. L. Rev. 1154, 1163 (1955).

35. See e.g., Campana v. Clark, 82 N.J.Super. 392, 197 A.2d 711 (1964); Monmouth Lumber Co. v. Ocean Township, 9 N.J. 64, 68, 87 A.2d 9, 14 (1952):

It is entirely consistent with the theory of planning to provide, after study of the conditions of the community, a means of preventing changes in the character thereof which might be opposed to the theory of planning and zoning pending the formulation of a detailed and complete "comprehensive plan" for the municipality, either new or in substitution for an outmoded plan.

on the due process elements of zoning procedure,[36] protected non-conforming uses and, if in the early days control was exercised, it was by way of prohibition on extension, repair or replacement of such uses.[37] Not only has the expectation that such uses would ultimately wither away been proven wrong, but zoning boards have continued to grant many variances,[38] permitting creation of additional non-conforming uses. Unless some effort to prevent the proliferation of non-conforming uses is successfully made, the whole concept of zoning may prove to be futile.[39] The traditional policy of the courts has been to express firm acceptance of control of non-conforming uses and to reaffirm the need for interim development controls to protect against their encroachment.

> Given the objective of zoning to eliminate non-conforming uses, courts throughout the country generally follow a strict policy against their extension or enlargement—by interpreting the (interim type ordinance) to protect only those permits which have become final, however, we enable municipalities to deter the vast majority of last minute efforts to race through the gamut of permit procedures. . . .(the court does not) intend to frustrate this method of discouraging the exploitation of the delays in the municipal legislative process. Under the circumstances of this case the private interest of the developer must yield to the public interest in the enforcement of a comprehensive zoning plan.[40]

---

36. The first comprehensive zoning ordinance was adopted by the City of New York in 1916 and it was not until 1926 that the doubts as to the constitutionality of the procedure were finally laid to rest by the Supreme Court in Village of Euclid v. Ambler Realty Co., 272 U.S. 365 (1926). See M. ANDERSON, ZONING LAW AND PRACTICE IN NEW YORK STATE 21 (1963): "The draftsmen of the initial New York City resolution were conversant with these decisions. They were sensitive to the constitutional hazards, and aware of the judicial skepticism which is invoked by novel legislation. Accordingly they sought to draft around the known obstacles and to hedge against quick judicial condemnation of zoning." See also C. BERGER, LAND OWNERSHIP AND USE 639-40 (1968); J. METZENBAUM, THE LAW OF ZONING 114-15 (1930); McCormack, A Law Clerk's Recollections, 46 COLUM. L. REV. 710 (1946).

37. See E. BASSETT, ZONING 26-27 (1940).

38. Many commentators see non-judicial administration of zoning ordinances as an acute problem: Norton, Elimination of Incompatible Uses and Structures, 20 LAW & CONTEMP. PROB. 305 (1955); Mandelker, Prolonging the Non-conforming Use, 8 DRAKE L. REV. 23 (1958); Anderson, The Nonconforming Use—A Product of Euclidean Zoning, 10 SYRACUSE L. REV. 214 (1959).

39. B. POOLEY, supra note 13, at 101. Many new types of controls are being used against non-conforming uses: elimination as common law or public nuisances, Standard Oil Co. v. City of Tallahassee, 183 F.2d 410 (Fla.), cert den., 340 U.S. 892 (1950); widening of the previously described restrictions on enlargement, Molnar v. Henne & Co., 377 Pa. 571, 105 A.2d 325 (1954); amortization, Harbison v. City of Buffalo, 4 N.Y.2d 553, 152 N.E.2d 42 (1958); but c.f. Hoffman v. Kineally, 389 S.W.2d 745 (Mo. 1965).

40. Russian Hill Imp. Assoc. v. Board of Permit Appeals, 66 Cal.2d 34, 56 Cal. Rptr. 672, 423 P.2d 824 (1967). See also County of San Diego v. McClurken, 37 Cal.2d 683, 234 P.2d 972 (1951).

The battle between the onrushing developer seeking to build the non-conforming use and the municipality seeking in hasty determination to adopt a zoning ordinance or amendment has been termed "a race of diligence" and the courts, recognizing the existing problem of non-conforming uses, have been loathe to permit the creation of new ones.[41]

The third objective of interim development controls is the promotion of public debate on the issues, goals and policies of planning and of the development controls proposed to implement the plans. The studies, drafting, deliberations and public airing, with changes and revisions of proposed controls, required to prepare and enact comprehensive development controls mean that a considerable period will almost certainly elapse between the time when deficiencies in land use planning are recognized and the effective date of implementation of remedial controls.[42] The failure to institute democratic discussion leads not only to hasty and improvident adoption of plans but also to the failure to utilize planning itself.[43] Essential public involvement will often prevent the kind of planless implementation too often found in our communities when action is precipitated without public participation.[44]

---

41.   The expression "race of diligence" was made famous in the leading case of Downham v. City Council of Alexandria, 58 F.2d 784, 788 (D.C. Va. 1931). *See also* Hasco Elec. Corp. v. Dassler, 143 N.Y.S.2d 240 (1955), *aff'd on other grounds,* 1 App.Div.2d 889, 150 N.Y.S.2d 552 (1956). Roselle v. Moonachie, 49 N.J. Super. 35, 42 (1958), "a race of technical advantage between the individual and the community's representatives." The extent and nature of the rush for building permits to acquire vested rights before the adoption of the permanent controls making the proposed use non-conforming should never be overlooked or under-estimated. In one borough of the City of New York alone, the pendency of the new Building Zone Amended Resolution of the City of New York, which became effective on December 15, 1961, resulted in an increase in applications for construction of apartment house buildings from 364 buildings costing $441,900,000 in 1960 to 1,266 buildings costing $1,560,000,000 in 1961. C. RATHKOPF, THE LAW OF ZONING AND PLANNING 57-84 (Supp. 1965). *See also* J. METZENBAUM, THE LAW OF ZONING 1703 (2d ed. 1951).

42.   F. HORACK & V. NOLAN, LAND USE CONTROLS 48 (1955).

43.   Plager, *Participatory Democracy and the Public Hearing: A Functional Approach,* 21 ADMINISTRATIVE L. REV. 153 (1969).

44.   The new policy of citizen participation and control in public affairs raised by the words "maximum feasible participation" of the public in neighborhood poverty programs, in the demand for "decentralization" of public schools in large urban centers, has also become quite apparent in the demand for greater neighborhood control over building, zoning, housing and plumbing codes and for meaningful participation in urban renewal, planning and model cities. See Cahn & Cahn, *The War on Poverty: A Civilian Perspective,* 73 YALE L.J. 1317 (1964); Wilson, *Planning and Politics: Citizen Participation in Urban Renewal,* 29 J. AM. INST. PLANNERS 242 (1963); Babcock & Bosselman, *Citizen Participation: A Suburban Suggestion for the Central City,* 32 LAW & CONTEMP. PROB. 220 (1967). Of particular interest is the comprehensive program of decentralization called for by Herbert Gans: "Neighborhood municipal offices must be established to create better communication between city hall and the ghetto; and neighborhood planning offices, staffed in large part by residents to be trained in planning techniques, are essential if the ghetto is actually to rebuild itself. Such offices cannot however, be mere branches of central agencies, for the ghetto must have power to implement its demands, and authority to develop plans for its future." H. GANS, PEOPLE AND PLANS: ESSAYS ON URBAN PROBLEMS AND SOLUTIONS 294 (1968). *See* ALTSHULER, COMMUNITY CONTROL: THE BLACK DEMAND FOR PARTICIPATION IN LARGE AMERICAN CITIES 183 (1970).

The public will ask the questions: Why regulate? For what purpose? The need for public participation has become so strong that a California court has held that a master plan must be submitted for a public referendum.[45] The adoption of interim controls, with the attendant hue and cry from affected landowners, interested lay citizens and citizens' organizations, helps to stimulate public discussion.

During the early years of zoning an inadequate theory of interim controls hampered their development. The early "interim ordinance" was not a true interim control designed to protect the planning process until the adoption of the permanent control, but a quickly prepared ordinance, without a map, designed to preserve the status quo until complete regulations with a map could be established.[46] Such ordinances, however, were permanent, hasty controls adopted within the confines of the zoning enabling act and were usually designed to put aside comprehensive planning.[47] The point to be demonstrated is that it is not sufficient for a permanent ordinance to be thrown together, without proper planning safeguards or time limitations, to be justified as an "interim control". Such an ordinance should be measured by the standards of a permanent control. An interim control is designed to protect and enhance the planning process and the courts will insist upon such planning to be evidenced with the interim control and for the latter

---

45. O'Loane v. O'Rourke, 231 Cal.App.2d 774, 42 Cal. Rptr. 283 (1965). Fletcher v. Porter, 203 Cal.App.2d 313, 21 Cal.Rptr. 452 (1962), involved public participation in the planning process. The court approved the submission of an initiative petition by the electorate to present an ordinance for adoption by the city council or adoption by referendum, requiring (a) preparation of a master plan and (b) interim control of zoning and rezoning of property: "[W]e do not believe the legislation fails on appellant's theory that, pending the formation of a master plan, the council, and not the electorate, may exclusively exercise the power. . . . The electorate through the initiative possesses no less power. So long as the Charter itself does not preclude such "freezing," the electorate may exercise the legislative prerogative to protect a proposed master plan from interim destruction during its period of incubation." Id. at 323, 21 Cal.Rptr. 452, 458.

46. E. BASSETT, supra note 37, at 87.

47. Id. at 88: "If enforced, [interim controls] usually result in unfairness to property owners and often delay or embarrass the adoption of a comprehensive and non-discriminatory plan. The defect of all interim ordinances is that their districts are so ill-defined and their regulations are so general that a large proportion of the requirements are unreasonable in their application to specific lots." Bassett's citation indicates that he was actually condemning hastily prepared ordinances of a permanent character. The nature of the controls of some of these earlier ordinances bears out this point: no store or factory shall be built unless the owners within a specified distance consent, City of Stockton v. Frisbie & Latta, 93 Cal.App. 277, 270 P. 270 (1928); Deitenbeck v. Village of Oak Park, 331 Ill. 406, 163 N.E. 445 (1928); no factory shall be built near "a majority of buildings which are dwellings" City of Tucson v. Arizona Mortuary, 34 Ariz. 495, 272 P. 923 (1928); Kirkwood Bros. v. City of Madisonville, 230 Ky. 104, 18 S.W.2d 951 (1929); a percentage of owners must consent in writing, City of Des Moines v. Manhattan Oil Co., 193 Iowa 1096, 184 N.W. 823 (1921).

to be in effect for only such period of time as is necessary to achieve its designated purposes.[48]

Some of this confusion, although surprisingly little in view of the large number of cases which have dealt with the subject, is still carried over to modern court decisions. In two recent decisions the word "interim" was used simply to describe hasty permanent ordinances, although both ordinances were held to be valid. The confusion is amply demonstrated in *Town of Lebanon v. Woods*,[49] where a rural residential town without water or sewage systems adopted a zoning ordinance requiring all development on lots one acre or more in size and where only residential uses were permitted. The ordinance was adopted to stall a land developer seeking to develop quarter-acre lots. The town attempted to classify the ordinance as "interim" to justify its lack of standards, although it had a single district, set back, side and rear yard and height standards, and was to be effective pending the adoption of a master plan and zoning regulations. In upholding the ordinance the court made the following statement indicating its confusion between a properly drafted interim ordinance and a permanent zoning scheme:

> Indeed, all zoning regulations are in a sense "interim" because they can be amended at any time, after proper notice and subject to certain limitations.[50]

Similarly, a Georgia court upheld an ordinance, which failed to zone all the property in the municipality, under the false name of "interim," although it was quite apparently simply an emergency measure of a permanent nature.[51]

---

48. Bassett failed to understand this point as demonstrated by his statement that such ordinances were not adopted with proper planning:

> State enabling acts usually require a municipality to appoint a zoning commission to prepare the ordinance, make a preliminary report and later a final report to the local legislature, holding public hearings at different stages of progress. These requirements have done much to prevent interim ordinances.

E. BASSETT, *supra* note 37, at 89, citing State *ex rel.* Kramer v. Schwartz, 336 Mo. 932, 82 S.W.2d 63 (1965), a case which did not condemn interim controls but held that they must be authorized by a state enabling act before the municipality could proceed.

49. 153 Conn. 182, 215 A.2d 112 (1965).

50. *Id.* at 187, 215 A.2d at 115. The dissent blistered the majority for having treated a permanent regulation without any requirement for comprehensiveness or standards. "In my judgment the opinion in this case will set back zoning in Connecticut for many years." *Id.* at 198, 215 A.2d at 120. But the dissent went on to make the same blurred distinction between interim controls, and permanent ones that the majority made: "Interim regulations must be measured by the same yard stick as regular ones." *Id.* at 203, 215 A.2d at 122.

51. Taylor v. Shetzen, 212 Ga. 101, 102, 90 S.E.2d 572, 574 (1955):

> The fact that the comprehensive ordinance recited that it was adopted because of "an emergency in the county" and refers to the regulations as "interim" regulations does not render it void. . . .
> [M]unicipalities and counties which have had conferred upon them the power to zone

B. *Constitutional and Statutory Authority*

If there is any turmoil involving the use of interim zoning controls that turmoil does not stem from any doubts concerning the constitutionality of such controls; it relates solely to the statutory power which restricts the manner in which zoning controls may be exercised. Although the courts of eight states have held that interim zoning ordinances are statutorily barred by the procedural requirements of the particular zoning enabling statute enacted by the state,[52] it is clear that these decisions are against the case law of the great majority of states and have for seven of the eight states been reversed by statutory authorization of interim zoning or by judicial authorization of interim control of building permits at the time of public hearing of proposed zoning controls.[53] In no case, however, has a state court held that a municipality was constitutionally barred from exercising interim development controls.[54] Moreover, even in states that prohibit interim development controls, a municipality which has received a delegation of the police power through home rule or charter government may still have the independent power to enact such legislation despite the existence of

---

property cannot always at one and the same time enact such a comprehensive scheme of zoning and planning as will particularly describe and embrace every piece of property by metes and bounds in the entire area of the county or municipality. . . .
See also State ex rel. Lightman v. City of Nashville, 166 Tenn. 191, 199, 60 S.W.2d 161, 163 (1933), where the court invalidated an "emergency" ordinance which had established three crudely designed residence districts. The court stated that "nothing on the face of the ordinance indicates that it was intended as an emergency measure," and the ordinance was invalidated for failing to hold a public hearing as required by the enabling act.

52. *See e.g.*, Phillips Petroleum v. City of Park Ridge, 16 Ill.App.2d 555, 149 N.E.2d 344 (1958); Downey v. Sioux City, 208 Iowa 1273, 227 N.W. 125 (1929); Krajenke Buick Sales v. Kopkowski, 322 Mich. 250, 33 N.W.2d 781 (1948); State ex rel. Roerig v. City of Minneapolis, 136 Minn. 479, 162 N.W. 477 (1917); State ex rel. Fairmount Center Co. v. Arnold, 138 Ohio St. 259, 34 N.E.2d 777 (1941); Kline v. City of Harrisburg, 362 Pa. 438, 68 A.2d 182 (1949); State ex rel. Lightman v. City of Nashville, 166 Tenn. 191, 60 S.W.2d 161 (1933); State ex rel. Kramer v. Schwartz, 336 Mo. 932, 82 S.W.2d 63 (1935).

53. Minnesota and Michigan have reversed by statutory authority. MINN. STAT. § 394.34 (1961); MICH. COMPILED LAWS ANN. § 125.285(15); Judicial approval of public hearing controls appears in: Illinois, Chicago Title & Trust Co. v. Village of Palatine, 22 Ill.App.2d 264, 160 N.E.2d 697 (1959); Lancaster Dev. Ltd. v. Village of River Forest, 84 Ill.App.2d 395, 228 N.E.2d 526 (1967); Iowa, Brackett v. City of Des Moines, 246 Iowa 249, 67 N.W.2d 542 (1954); Missouri, Fleming v. Moore Bros. Realty Co., 363 Mo. 305, 251 S.W.2d 8 (1952); Ohio, State ex rel. Davis Inv. Co. v. City of Columbus, 175 Ohio St. 337, 194 N.E.2d 859 (1963); State ex rel. Cahn v. Guion, 27 Ohio App. 141, 160 N.E. 868 (1927); Pennsylvania, A.J. Aberman, Inc. v. City of New Kensington, 377 Pa. 520, 105 A.2d 586 (1954). There is also some doubt as to whether Illinois prohibits interim zoning since the Phillips Petroleum Case, *supra* note 52, dealt only with a resolution prohibiting the issuance of building permits, and the Ohio decision may in fact be a reversal of State ex rel. Fairmont, *supra* note 52, but the issue was complicated by the fact that the Davis case dealt with a charter city. The Ohio case of Cahn, also permitted interim zoning.

54. *Infra* note 56.

the standard state enabling act for the non-charter or non-home rule municipalities or unincorporated areas.[55]

Most states have affirmatively declared that interim zoning is constitutionally permissible and that it is permissible for a municipality to enact such legislation under the standard zoning enabling act. The exercise of temporary restrictions pending the adoption of permanent zoning controls is the exercise of the police power and will be presumed to be valid unless the particular exercise itself is unreasonable or not related to the health, safety or general welfare of the community.[56]

> We are not disposed to define the police power . . . so narrowly that it would exclude reasonable restrictions placed upon the use of property in order to aid the development of new districts in accordance with plans to advance the public welfare of the city in the future . . . .
> We are not required to say that a merely temporary restraint of beneficial enjoyment is unlawful where the interference is necessary to provide the ultimate good either of the municipality as a whole or of the immediate neighborhood. . . . If we assume that the restraint may be permitted, the interference must not be unreasonable, but on the contrary must be kept within the limits of necessity.[57]

---

55. *Infra* notes 84 and 85; *see* State *ex rel.* Davis Inv. Co. v. City of Columbus, 175 Ohio St. 337, 194 N.E.2d 859 (1963).

56. Downham v. City Council of Alexandria, 58 F.2d 784 (E.D. Va. 1932). In Monmouth Lumber Co. v. Ocean Township, 9 N.J. 64, 87 A.2d 9 (1952), the New Jersey Supreme Court upheld interim zoning under the Standard Zoning Enabling Act as a valid exercise of the police power, stating the rule cited by most courts:

> Aside from the necessity for compliance with specific constitutional and statutory provisions proscribing the limits of the exercise of the power, the requisite test for validity of a municipal ordinance of this nature is that it be reasonable, and the burden of proof is upon those who attack the ordinance to show that it is unreasonable in the relation of the regulation to the health, safety, morals, or the general welfare of the community . . . .
> Such action is within the intent and purposes of the statutes relating to planning. . . . It is entirely consistent with the theory of planning to provide, after study of the conditions of the community, a means of preventing changes in the character thereof which might be opposed to the theory of planning and zoning pending the formulation of a detailed and complete "comprehensive plan" for the municipality, either new or in substitution for an outmoded plan.

Id. at 71, 75, 87 A.2d at 12, 14. *See also* Mang v. County of Santa Barbara, 182 Cal.App.2d 93, 5 Cal.Rptr. 724 (1960); Town of Lebanon v. Woods, 153 Conn. 182, 215 A.2d 112 (1965); Taylor v. Shetzen, 212 Ga. 101, 90 S.E.2d 572 (1955); Chicago Title & Trust Co. v. Palatine, 22 Ill.App.2d 264, 160 N.E.2d 697 (1959); K.G. Horton & Sons, Inc. v. Board of Zoning Appeals of Madison County, 235 Ind. 510, 135 N.E.2d 243 (1956); State *ex rel.* Dickason v. Harris, 158 La. 974, 105 So. 33 (1925); Deal Gardens, Inc. v. Board of Trustees of Village of Loch Arbour, 48 N.J. 492, 226 A.2d 607 (1967); Rubin v. McAlevey, 29 App.Div.2d 874, 288 N.Y.S.2d 519 (1968); McCurley v. El Reno, 138 Okla. 92, 280 P. 467 (1929); McEachern v. Town of Highland Park, 124 Tex. 36, 73 S.W.2d 488 (1934); Gayland v. Salt Lake County, 11 Utah 2d 307, 355 P.2d 633 (1961); Walworth County v. City of Elkhorn, 27 Wis.2d 30, 133 N.W.2d 257 (1965).

57. Arverne Bay Const. Co. v. Thatcher, 278 N.Y. 222, 229-30, 15 N.E.2d 587, 590-91

Just as there is a presumption of validity of the regulatory ordinance,[58] the good faith of the municipality in enacting the ordinance will not be subject to challenge, nor can there be any assertion that the council did not proceed in good faith to the enactment of the planning proposals in some reasonable form.[59] A liberal rule of construction will be applied not only to the ordinance itself, but to the power of the municipality to adopt it,[60] and the court will not scrutinize its reasonableness with the same degree of care given to a permanent control.[61]

The Supreme Court over forty years ago established the principle that zoning is an exercise of the police power, analogizing the use of zoning to the elimination of nuisances.[62] If the ordinance was unreasonable in its application to specific property owners, the Court would grant individual relief but would still hold the basic ordinance valid and constitutional.[63] Moreover, decisions show clearly that the amount of pecuniary harm resulting to any particular plaintiff will not weigh heavily and that once the public purposes for which the ordinance was passed have been established and its reasonableness shown, it makes no difference how many property owners are affected unless a total deprivation amounting to a taking is shown.[64] The courts are reluctant to

---

(1938); Westwood Forest Estates v. Village of South Nyack, 23 N.Y.2d 424, 297 N.Y.S.2d 129 (1969). Similarly, the Supreme Court of Illinois, in Chicago Title & Trust Co. v. Village of Palatine, 22 Ill.App.2d 264, 160 N.E.2d 697 (1959), found such procedures within the health, safety and general welfare of the police power:

The theory underlying these statutory provisions is that in order to achieve such results there should be a careful and scientific study made by a competent commission and that after the commission has reached a conclusion there should be an opportunity afforded to the public to express their views and make objections if they have any concerning the proposed enactment so that the commission can balance the objections against the advantages and reach a sound final conclusion. . . . It would be utterly illogical to hold that, after a zoning commission had prepared a comprehensive zoning ordinance or an amendment thereto, which was on file and open to public inspection and upon which public hearings had been held, and while the ordinance was under consideration, a court could by merely filing an application compel the municipality to issue a permit which would allow him to establish a use which he either knew or could have known would be forbidden by the proposed ordinance, and by so doing nullify the entire work of the municipality in endeavoring to carry out the purpose for which the zoning law was enacted.

Id. at 269-70, 160 N.E.2d at 700.

58.   See e.g., Mang v. County of Santa Barbara, 182 Cal.App.2d 93, 5 Cal.Rptr. 724 (1960); City of Dallas v. Meserole Bros., 164 S.W.2d 564 (Tex., 1942).

59.   Miller v. Board of Pub. Works, 195 Cal. 477, 234 P. 381, cert. den., 273 U.S. 781 (1925).

60.   See e.g., Fowler v. Obier, 224 Ky. 742, 7 S.W.2d 219 (1928).

61.   See e.g., McCurley v. El Reno, 138 Okla. 92, 280 P. 467 (1929).

62.   Village of Euclid v. Ambler Realty Co., 272 U.S. 365 (1926). In earlier cases the Court showed itself sympathetic to municipal control and land usage through exercise of the power to forbid nuisances Hadacheck v. Sebastian, 239 U.S. 394 (1915).

63.   Nectow v. City of Cambridge, 277 U.S. 183 (1928); Gorieb v. Fox, 274 U.S. 603 (1927).

64.   See e.g., Vernon Park Realty, Inc. v. Mount Vernon, 307 N.Y. 493, 121 N.E.2d 517 (1954).

interpose or substitute their judgment for that of the legislature, particularly in regard to planning for future growth,[65] and will strongly support interim development control measures on this basis.[66] The validity of an interim development control is measured by its reasonableness in supporting the community's right to govern its life and growth through rational planning and reordering of the pattern of the land. There is no eternal vested constitutional right to continuation of an existing zoning classification of land.[67] An interim ordinance is drafted with the same care as a permanent ordinance so as to provide administrative relief for the singular case of hardship which would justify the granting of a variance, and variance procedures are carefully engrafted into such controls by the prudent draftsman to avoid constitutional problems.[68] Except for some statutory problems in a few jurisdictions, it can safely be stated that the validity of interim development controls has been secured.

---

65. Berman v. Parker, 348 U.S. 26, 33 (1954):

The concept of the public welfare is broad and inclusive. The values it represents are spiritual as well as physical, aesthetic as well as monetary. It is within the power of the legislature to determine that the community should be beautiful as well as healthy, spacious as well as clean, well-balanced as well as carefully patrolled.

66. See e.g., Hunter v. Adams, 180 Cal. App. 2d 511, 520, 523, 4 Cal.Rptr. 776, 780, 784 (1960):

It is difficult for us to conceive how an intelligent integrated plan can be formulated if, while it is under study and planning, the area is in a constant state of flux with new building construction and improvements. . . . If the injury is the result of legitimate governmental action reasonably taken for the public good and for no other purpose, and is reasonably necessary to serve a public purpose for the general welfare, it is a proper exercise of the police power.

Thus, the Michigan Supreme Court held: "The people of the community, through their appropriate legislative body, and not the courts, govern its growth and its life." Robinson v. City of Bloomfield Hills, 350 Mich. 425, 431, 86 N.W.2d 166, 169 (1967).

Many a property owner has relied on Nectow v. City of Cambridge, 277 U.S. 183 (1928) to challenge the constitutionality of interim zoning. The Nectow case held that the zoning of a strip of property residential while all surrounding property was unrestricted commercial and industrial was unconstitutional in so far as the ordinance related to the individual property. The difficulty in applying this argument to interim zoning lies in the nature of interim zoning itself. By protecting the planning process and working for the elimination of non-conforming uses, the municipality is trying to achieve rationality, purpose and conformity in the zoning plan. Thus, the court in Downham v. City Council of Alexandria, 58 F.2d 784, 787 (E.D. Va. 1932) in rejecting the Nectow argument stated:

In this case we have just the reverse. If plaintiff is given the relief prayed for, he will be permitted to use his parcel of property for commercial purposes while all of the adjoining properties and all the property in that immediate vicinity is restricted to residential purposes. Here it is manifest that the restrictions complained of do bear a very real and substantial relation to the public health, safety, and welfare.

67. See Standard Oil Co. v. City of Tallahassee, 183 F.2d 410 (5th Cir.), cert. den., 340 U.S. 892 (1950); Rodgers v. Village of Tarrytown, 302 N.Y. 115, 96 N.E.2d 731 (1951).

68. Cf. e.g., Hasco Elec. Corp. v. Dassler, 143 N.Y.S.2d 240 (1955); Rubin v. McAlevey, 29 App.Div. 2d 874, 288 N.Y.S.2d 519 (1968).

•   •   •

III.   A COMPREHENSIVE THEORY OF INTERIM DEVELOPMENT CONTROLS

A.   General Considerations

Any comprehensive approach to interim development controls should take into account three factors. The first is the timing of the introduction of the controls, permitting interim controls to be placed on land use either at the very commencement of the planning process or when the planning process has led to formal proposals advertised for public hearing. The introduction at the public hearing stage assures that definite standards exist in the form of the planning proposals which have actually been drafted. Introduction at the public hearing stage recognizes two forms of interim control: administrative withholding of building permits from the time that notice is furnished to the public for public hearing, and standard interim legislation effective at public hearing. What is new in this "theory" is not a recognition of administrative control of building permits as an interim control but a recognition that in one form or another almost every state has adopted a theory and concept of interim development controls which is applicable at the public hearing stage. Every municipality in the nation should then become aware of the possibility of effectuating the planning process at least at the public hearing stage.

Second, the new approach should consider methods of utilizing interim controls at the commencement of the planning process by adoption of more rational and explicit standards than are presently required either by statute or judicial determination. If the legal and planning professions turn their attention to this problem, greater safeguards from arbitrariness can be erected and new methods of flexible

---

municipalities to adopt controls. In Ayres v. City of Los Angeles, 34 Cal.2d 31, 207 P.2d 1 (1949), a requirement of dedication of a strip of land was held to be "supplemental" and "consistent" with the act. It could also have been interpreted as a "municipal affair" in which event for a charter municipality, the Map Act would be inapplicable; Heyman, *Open Space and Police Power, Open Space and the Law,* INSTITUTE OF GOV'T. STUDIES 19-20 (1965). *See also* Adler v. Deegan, 251 N.Y. 467, 491, 167 N.E. 705, 714 (1929) where a liberal definition of "consistency" under a home rule grant, permits a municipality to "work in harmony" with state law. Hyman, *Home Rule in New York,* 15 BUFF. L. REV. 335 (1965); *Home Rule and the New York Constitution,* 66 CAL. L. REV. 1145 (1966). A corollary to this rule concerns the cases authorizing municipalities to regulate the building construction activity of state agencies; RHYNE, SURVEY OF THE LAW OF BUILDING CODES 55 (1960); *Municipal Power to Regulate Building Construction and Land Use by Other State Agencies,* 49 MINN. L. REV. 284 (1964).

zoning, taking into consideration the continuity of the planning process, can be considered as a meaningful substitute for the Euclidean zoning of the present day.

Finally, the third factor is the use of interim development controls to regulate whole new aspects of the planning process including non-zoning matters, to control the resources of the environment which involve and affect the social, economic and physical well-being of the community.

B.   Timing of the Introduction of Controls

There seems little doubt that controls may be introduced either at the commencement of the planning process or at the public hearing stage. In our earlier discussion of the planning process it was apparent that interim controls not only protect planning in process, but also provide a very important stimulant to planning itself in that such controls avoid the hasty adoption of permanent controls designed principally to ward off non-conforming uses on an "emergency" basis. The interim control statutes which have been enacted, as distinguished from the zoning enabling acts, have generally provided for the use of interim development controls at the beginning of the planning process. Similarly, the case law supports the use of interim development controls at the initiation of planning.[89]

The courts, however, have also recognized the use of interim controls to be effective at the public hearing on the planning proposals,[90] and this rule has been held to apply to administrative denial of permits at the public hearing stage.[91] It is obviously constitutionally safe that the

---

89.   The earliest case conceived of the interim ordinances as an integral part of the planning process and therefore essential to the commencement of the preparation of the plan. Miller v. Board of Pub. Works, 195 Cal. 477, 496-97, 234 P. 381, 388 cert. denied, 273 U.S. 781 (1925):

It is a matter of common knowledge. . .(and) we may take judicial notice of the fact that it will take much time to work out the details of such a plan. . .That being so. . .that the ordinance in question, being, as it declares, an initial unit in the general zoning of the city, is part and parcel of a comprehensive plan which has relation to the welfare of the city as a whole and, therefore, it must be held that the ordinance in question is a valid exercise of the police power.

See also Downham v. City Council of Alexandria, 58 F.2d 784 (E.D. Va. 1932): Fowler v. Obier, 224 Ky. 742, 7 S.W.2d 219 (1928); Butvinik v. Jersey City, 6 N.J. Misc. 803, 142 A. 759 (1928); McCurley v. El Reno, 138 Okla. 92, 280 P. 467 (1929).

90.   Thus, California has recognized interim development at the public hearing stage. Lima v. Woodruff, 107 Cal.App. 285, 290 p. 480 (1930). See also Couch v. Zoning Comm. of Town of Washington, 141 Conn. 349, 106 A.2d 173 (1954); Hasco Elec. Corp. v. Dassler, 143 N.Y.S.2d 240 (1955): "The Court is inclined to the opinion that the local legislative body was vested with the authority to enact reasonable stop-gap or interim legislation prohibiting the commencement of construction for a reasonable time during consideration of proposed zoning changes." See also 1 YOKLEY, ZONING LAW AND PRACTICE 161, 164, 165 (2nd Ed. 1951).

91.   Sharrow v. City of Dania, 83 So. 2d 274 (Fla. 1955); Chicago Title & Trust Co. v. Village

ordinance be effective at the time of public hearing,[92] but there seems to be no valid reason why the adoption of the ordinance at the commencement of the planning process is not also authorized so long as the period set for the completion of the plan is reasonable.[93] Most of the statutes have authorized a two-year period and the courts have accepted two years as valid. It matters not whether the planning process is originating a plan or is amending an existing plan. The rule of reason should apply.[94]

One factor which should be kept in mind with reasonableness is that public debate and discussion is an important justification of interim controls and there should be no need for the planning commission or consultants to prepare the plan in secrecy. Open public discussion should eliminate costly errors and the possibility of meeting a hostile or indifferent public attitude which jeopardizes adoption and implementation of the plan.[95] This process, however, requires a

---

of Palantine, 22 Ill.App.2d 264, 160 N.E.2d 697 (1959); A.J. Aberman, Inc. v. City of New Kensington, 377 Pa. 520, 105 A.2d 586 (1954).

92.   Note, *The Administration of Zoning Flexibility Devices: An Explanation For Recent Judicial Frustrations,* 49 MINN. L. REV. 973, 1015 (1965):

A Court ought, and doubtless would be much more inclined, to find a stop-gap zoning measure valid where its effectiveness is expressly limited to a reasonable period of time and where it forbids only uses which are prohibited by the provisions of the pending zoning ordinance. The latter restriction would prevent the use of interim devices until the prepared comprehensive zoning ordinance is sufficiently developed to indicate the uses which would be permitted in various areas. This point of development no doubt would vary somewhat among localities, depending on the procedures followed in enacting comprehensive zoning ordinances. Nevertheless in most cases it would seem likely to yield a fair compromise.

93.   *See* Haar, *In Accordance With A Comprehensive Plan,* 68 HARV. L. REV. 1154, 1163 (1955), where the author states that interim zoning should be upheld so long as the period of duration is reasonable. The court should condemn only the indefinite suspension. Thus the court sustained a two year period of time in Darlington v. Frankfort 282 Ky. 778, 140 S.W.2d 392 (1940), but disapproved an excess of two years in Deerfield v. Hague 8 N.J. Misc. 478, 151 A. 373 (1930).

94.   In Campana v. Township of Clark, 82 N.J. Super. 392, 395-97, 197 A.2d 711, 713-14 (1964), the Court stated an appropriate rule:

The question thus arises as to whether the passage of 31 months during which time this interim ordinance has been in effect, constitutes an unreasonable exercise of the police power. . .We can take judicial notice of the fact that it requies considerable time to prepare and put into effect a worthwhile and comprehensive zoning plan. . .However, zoning, like every exercise of police power, must be contained by a rule of reason. . .

In some instances the municipalities have been allowed in excess of two years, the courts finding that in such cases definite progress was being made toward the goal of adopting a new zoning ordinance. . .

In the instant matter the "temporary" ordinance has been in effect for more than two years. However, as has been seen, the mere passage of time alone is not the sole determining factor of the reasonableness or unreasonableness of the "stop-gap" ordinance. We must also look to the progress of the study being made, its nearness to completion and the prospects for passage of a new zoning ordinance, keeping in mind at the same time that such a comprehensive zoning plan requires considerable time for preparation and study.

95.   Plager, *Participatory Democracy and the Public Hearing: A Functional Approach,* 21 ADMINISTRATIVE LAW REV. 163. (1969).

reasonable period of time to unfold a representative plan. The courts should not be unduly restrictive in limiting this process. A balance should be achieved, carefully weighing the deprivation to the property owner against the legitimate needs of the community.

C. *Standards for Controls at the Commencement of the Planning Process*

While interim zoning has long been accepted at the commencement of the planning process as a valid police power measure, the cases lend little guidance to appropriate standards to be used in controlling uses during the planning process and prior to formulation for public hearing. At the public hearing stage no such difficulty presents itself since the completed plan or amended plan serves as its own standard to determine the conformity of the use. The only standard that has been utilized for pre-public hearing controls is the requirement that the controls be in effect for a reasonable period of time—usually not in excess of two years. The statutes authorizing interim controls furnish little other guidance except to indicate that multiple dwellings and business, commercial or industrial uses may be excluded during the planning process.

In recent years planners have been moving toward adoption of more flexible zoning theories, for example, the floating zone, site plan review, the planned unit development, incentive zoning and the performance standard for industrial users. If zoning is moving away from rigid controls toward a degree of flexibility in the plan itself, there seems little reason why such flexibility cannot be incorporated into interim development controls. Since the planning process is under continuous review, the use of interim development controls with flexible policy planning may very well be the zoning ordinance of the future.[96] If the

---

96. The British system has moved precisely in this direction. Beginning with the Interim Development Acts of 1932 and 1943, the Town and Country Planning Act of 1962 and the Land Commission Act of 1967, the nation required that all municipalities (principally at the county level) prepare flexible plans, and while the plans were in progress, fashioned a complete set of interim development controls. As the plans were adopted, the control of land continued to be on an ad hoc basis in which maps were drawn for the larger county facilities but development within the villages and towns was guided by a written statement. Jay, Fines & Furmidge, *Village Planning,* 114 U. PA. L. REV. 106 (1965). The policies for settlement have been classified:

    (a)   Major expansion—"growth points"

    (b)   Minor expansion—"some expansion permitted"

    (c)   Rounding-off—"settlement contained"

    (d)   Infiling—"settlement on existing streets only"

    (e)   Restricted—"single family dwellings based on local needs"

Id. at 109. Thus, within broad guidelines, policies have been determined and then individual planning permissions are granted. The continuing planning process is demonstrated by the following statement: "Despite the trend toward regional planning, county and county borough councils remain the statutory planning authorities primarily responsible for the preparation of development plans and for day to day development control. . . .Such flexibility, which is one of the distinctive

planning profession is turning away from the mapped master plan showing specific locations of land use and toward the policies plan in which the municipality states the basic policies which should guide the particular location of land uses,[97] flexible policies utilizing interim development controls can be shaped. Thus, Chapin rejects the unitary approach in favor of the adaptive approach—an evolutionary scheme in which the flow of development controls can be shaped. Chapin also points out that in the progressive planning approach planning analysis calls for policy-making sequence in which the first step is to make a broad general plan.[98] The broad outlines of policy are first developed and the details filled in at later stages. This would certainly leave sufficient standards to guide an interim development policy. Courts have not hesitated in recent years to accept the floating zone where broad policy considerations determine whether industry or apartment uses should be established in residential areas,[99] and one court has accepted the planned unit development.[100]

---

features of the British system, ensures that plans are adapted to meet advances in technology and the changing goals of society." *Id.* at 107. In America the movement is toward "planned unit development." The use of planned development must be based on a Comprehensive Development Plan; however, no longer need it be a "land use map," but rather the development of general goals and the formulation of objectives for physical and social needs. Risse, *Regeneration in Developed Areas,* 32 PLANNING NEWS 3, 7 (1968):

> There are no preconceived notions about what may be desirable beyond the general goals of the comprehensive plan, the administrative procedures and guidelines and the limitations imposed by site and environment.

See also Perrin, *Noiseless Secession from the Comprehensive Plan,* 33 J. AM. INST. PLANNERS 336 (1967).

97. Babcock & Bosselman, *Citizen Participation: A Suburban Suggestion for the Central City,* 32 LAW & CONTEMP. PROB. 220, 226 (1967); Aschman, *The Policy Plan in the Planning Program,* PLANNING 1963, 105 (1963).

98. F. CHAPIN, URBAN LAND USE PLANNING 98 (1963).

> Develop a first estimate of existing conditions and significant trends in the urban area. In scope this estimate encompasses the full range of planning studies; as to detail, it is abbreviated and general, to be progressively rounded out as the program proceeds.

Id. at 351, *See generally* NATIONAL RESOURCES PLANNING BOARD, ACTION FOR CITIES (1965).

99. *See, e.g.,* Huff v. Board of Zoning Appeals, 214 Md. 48, 133 A.2d 83 (1957); Rodgers v. Village of Tarrytown, 302 N.Y. 115, 96 N.E.2d 731 (1961).

100. *See* Cheney v. Village No. 2 at New Hope, Inc., 429 Pa. 626, 241 A.2d 81 (1968), *reversing,* Eves v. Zoning Bd. of Adjustment, 401 Pa. 211, 164 A.2d 7 (1960), *commented on in* Haar & Hering, *The Lower Gwynedd Township Case: Too Flexible Zoning or An Inflexible Judiciary?,* 74 HARV. L. REV. 1552 (1961). *See also* Krasnowiecki, *Planned Unit Development: A Challenge to Established Theory and Practice of Land Use Control,* 114 U. PA. L. REV. 47, 67 (1965).

> Perhaps Richard Babcock has put it best: This current restlessness with segregating the uses reflects, in part, a growing disenchantment with the validity of the visual or mapped master plan. No longer do all planners believe that it is both necessary the possible that the law forecast the precise direction and kind of growth. The increasing substitution of verbal plans—statements of municipal objectives—for mapped or graphic master plans refects an awareness that precision in prediction is not feasible, and classification by use not so simple a guide to sensible urban development. BABCOCK, THE ZONING GAME 130-31 (1966).

The American Law Institute has adopted, in its Model Land Development Code, a procedure for the use of highly flexible zoning devices where the municipality has a comprehensive plan and current revisions at least every five years. This alternate procedure measures the individual development proposals against the land development policies applicable. The model section, however, requires a more extensive statement of criteria than does the English legislation.[101] For example, the criteria may be the attainment of industrial development with residential-commercial development to provide housing for industrial workers, or realization of certain population densities or consistency with stated performance standards relating to noise, traffic and appearance.[102] There will inevitably be difficulties in preparing policies of this kind and securing their adoption. The fact that most local government bodies used a fixed map has tended to remove pressure to adopt broader policies. There is also the certainty which comes with mapped planning and a fear that broader policies may lead to corruption and favoritism in disposing of individual applications. While there is little precedent to assist the form and content, there is no urgency to rapid policy formation; rather this should be a continuing process, benefiting from experience gained in the process.[103]

---

101. MODEL CODE 61-62: "This section, together with 3-105 concerning applications, enables localities which have an ongoing planning process to handle most development proposals in accordance with criteria which permit both departures from otherwise applicable regulations and a greater degree of individualized treatment than is possible in most jurisdictions today."

102. *Id.* at 62-63. The reporters state:

It is probable that a local government utilizing comprehensive development procedures, would also adopt general development ordinances covering all of its territory. This section permits, however, the designation of areas where the comprehensive process must be used for any proposed development. . . . It is possible, although unlikely, that the process would be used for nearly all development. It is also possible for a jurisdiction which has adopted [a land development plan] containing relatively definite provisions governing future development to use the [land development plan] as the basis for a comprehensive regulatory scheme.

103. The policies, like land-use decisions, should advance only as fast as our current understanding of development processes clearly permits. NOBLE, A PROPOSED SYSTEM FOR REGULATING LAND USE IN URBANIZING COUNTIES 20-21 (1967). Supporting the use of "locational criteria" for apartment housing, *see* Finney v. Halle, 241 Md. 224, 239, 216 A.2d 530, 538 (1966):

In essence, the criteria which we use currently for locating apartment zoning would evolve around the fact that the apartment building project is on a major thoroughfare, with good accessibility to the area within the region, so to speak, by the road system, or that it is in close proximity to community facilities, most usually shopping centers facilities so that this higher density can take advantage of accessibility features and service features. The Planning Board would also like to see these higher density residential zones, that apartment zoning is within our current context of the regulations, generally at the edge of a residential area rather than in the middle of such an area.

15

Fred Bosselman

CAN THE TOWN OF RAMAPO PASS
A LAW TO BIND THE RIGHTS
OF THE ENTIRE WORLD?

I. INTRODUCTION

In the famous case of *Buchanan v. Rucker*[1] the plaintiff sought to collect in the English courts on a default judgment issued by the Island Court of Tobago against the defendant. The defendant claimed that he had never been to Tobago and was not subject to the jurisdiction of the Tobago court. Lord Ellenborough refused to recognize the Tobago court's judgment:

> Supposing however that the Act had said in terms, that though a person sued in the island had never been present within the jurisdiction, yet that it should bind him upon proof of nailing up the summons at the Court door; how could that be obligatory upon the subjects of other countries? *Can the island of Tobago pass a law to bind the rights of the whole world?* Would the world submit to such an assumed jurisdiction?[2]

One of the most important issues in the United States today is the question of who gets to live where. Our present system of laws lets each individual local government determine who may live within its borders through the use of a wide variety of indirect but very effective regulatory techniques. Like the Island of Tobago these local governments pass laws that affect the "whole world" by limiting the right of outsiders to live in the community.

In 1969 the town of Ramapo, New York, adopted a relatively new legal technique that allows local governments to limit severely the amount of new residential development. This technique, known generally as "development timing," gives local government an even more powerful tool for determining who will live within its borders than had heretofore been available.

This article expresses the opinion that, based on past experience, each town can be expected to exercise this and similar techniques as if it were an island independent of other towns; that the resulting

---

1. 103 Eng. Rep. 546 (K.B. 1808).
2. *Id.* at 547 (emphasis added).

impact on metropolitan growth patterns will have serious social and environmental consequences; and that the results will force the legislatures and courts to realize that the laws of individual towns and cities, such as Ramapo, must not be allowed to bind the whole world without adequate state supervision.

II. GROWTH CONTROL AS A LOCAL CONCERN

Unlike virtually every other modern nation we seem to have adopted the position that the control of growth is primarily of concern to local rather than state or federal government. How did we arrive at this position?

The United States began in an historical context that made growth control seem wholly irrelevant. The colonists arrived in a land that seemed to stretch endlessly beyond the western horizon, occupied only by what they viewed as a few tribes of wandering savages. Concern about overpopulation was hardly foremost in their minds. Nevertheless the nation had barely been settled when problems of too rapid growth in the cities were perceived. The concentration of immigrants in the new colonial cities, as contrasted with the sparse population of the countryside, "created a host of problems unknown or little felt in rural communities."[3]

Concern with fire, crime and sanitation led the cities from the beginning to enforce regulations restricting population growth by attempting to exclude the poor. "Boston established the pattern for the exclusion of poor and undesirable strangers in May, 1636, when the Selectmen forbade any inhabitant to entertain a stranger for more than two weeks without official permission."[4] By the end of the seventeenth century almost every sizable town was making some effort to exclude the "indigent or undesirable stranger."[5] Nevertheless, by mid-century all of the major colonial cities faced problems of fire, water supply, crime, mob disorder, disease and indigence, much of which was attributed to overcrowding.[6]

Urban problems were thus as old as colonial settlement itself, but the "antagonism of the country bumpkin toward the city slicker mounted from the late 1750s onward."[7] Many in the dominant rural population echoed the sentiments of Thomas Jefferson: "The mobs of great cities add just so much to the support of pure government,

---

3. A. SCHLESINGER, THE BIRTH OF THE NATION 112 (1968).
4. C. BRIDENBAUGH, CITIES IN THE WILDERNESS 79 (1938).
5. *Id.* at 231.
6. *Id.* at 407.
7. C. GREEN, THE RISE OF URBAN AMERICA 47 (1965).

as sores do to the strength of the human body."[8] De Tocqueville opined that "I look upon the size of certain American cities, and especially the nature of their population, as a real danger." He predicted that democratic government would perish "unless the government succeeds in creating an armed force, which, while it remains under the control of the majority of the nation, will be independent of the town population, and able to repress its excesses."[9]

Throughout the eighteenth century the problems of crime, disease and poverty were associated with the cities, while rural areas were popularly thought to be free of such problems. Most of these ills were attributed to the hordes of indigent people who flocked to the cities to compete for the industrial jobs available there. Although the large cities recognized that exclusion of poor people would increase the cost of labor, there was nevertheless great popular pressure to improve the lot of the poor or remove them from the cities. As a consequence, most of the larger cities made some attempt to control the number of homes built for poor people through fire and building regulations, but not without some ambivalence in these attempts.[10]

No such ambivalence was found in the growing suburbs of the late nineteenth century. Here there were few industrial jobs demanding cheap labor, and the well-to-do could be increasingly restrictive in designing communities to exclude the poor. The very existence of the suburbs as separate local governments was based on the idea of combining the city's conveniences with the rural area's freedom from urban problems. This rapid proliferation of the suburbs coincided with the massive foreign immigration that filled the cities in the latter part of the nineteenth century.[11]

Luther Gulick described the rapid emergence of a wide variety of local legislation restricting the use of urban land as a natural reaction to overcrowding. "The problems arise in acute form because of congestion. The individual cannot protect himself against the dangers or discomforts arising from the free acts of others. Therefore, the community establishes rules of action to maximize welfare by rationing freedom."[12] It was in this context of rapid urban and suburban growth, around the turn of the century, that the city planning movement

---

8. Jefferson, *Notes on Virginia*, in M. WHITE & L. WHITE, THE INTELLECTUAL VERSUS THE CITY 14 (1962).

9. A. DE TOCQUEVILLE, 1 DEMOCRACY IN AMERICA 289 n.1 (rev. 1945).

10. *See generally* Babcock & Bosselman, *Suburban Zoning and the Apartment Boom*, 111 U. PA. L. REV. 1040 (1963).

11. R. WOOD, SUBURBIA: ITS PEOPLE AND THEIR POLITICS 34 (1958).

12. Gulick, *Metropolitan Political Developments*, in THE METROPOLIS IN MODERN LIFE 66, 70 (R. Fisher ed. 1955).

began to become popular. The problems with which the city planning movement was trying to cope were the problems associated with the rapid migration of large numbers of people to the urban areas. This increasing congestion, coinciding with the disappearance of the frontier, spawned the city planning movement, with its attendant regulatory legislation.[13]

Because the problems were perceived as urban, and because the state legislatures were traditionally dominated by rural interests, the state legislatures typically delegated to local governments the power to regulate land. Professor Ernest Freund summarized the attitude prevailing during that period:

> The exercise of the police power for safety and health is of the greatest importance in closely populated districts. This part of the police power has therefore chiefly grown up in cities, and there today finds its most extensive application. This fact is recognized by an ample delegation of powers of local legislation in this field by the state to incorporated municipalities. . . .
> . . . The principle of delegation seems to be to make the municipal police power co-extensive with local dangers arising from the close aggregation and contact of persons and property in a limited space or territory.[14]

So well accepted became the idea of state delegation to local governments of the power to regulate the use of land, that when Edward Bassett wrote his evaluation of the first twenty years of zoning law he began chapter one by stating that "[m]unicipalities must obtain their power from the state"[15]—it being obvious that only the municipalities were interested in exercising this power.

Until recent years, therefore, our political system assumed without serious question that land development and urban growth problems were local in nature and occurred only in cities—or in communities that threatened to become cities. It seemed natural that such problems should be resolved by voluntary local action of any local government troubled by these problems—thus the enabling act approach to land use controls.

Despite the wide use by local governments of their powers to control the development of land,[16] the casual observer usually finds little evidence that the exercise of these powers has significantly di-

---

13. *See* S. TOLL, ZONED AMERICAN 117-19 (1969).
14. E. FREUND, THE POLICE POWER 130-31 (1904).
15. E. BASSETT, ZONING 13 (1936).
16. *See generally* A. MANVEL, LOCAL LAND AND BUILDING REGULATION (National Commission on Urban Problems, Research Report No. 6, 1968).

verted the process of urban growth from the directions it would have taken in the absence of regulation. Developers will build only that which they think the market will support; they cannot be forced to build something else merely because the local regulations desire another type of development—thus the old cliché that land use regulation can stop growth but not create growth.

But until recently there has not been much stopping of growth either. Although local governments have on paper had wide-ranging and autonomous powers to control growth under the zoning and related enabling legislation generated by the city planning movement, in reality the impact of these local regulations has been dampened by two important factors. First, the political process in outlying communities was frequently dominated by real estate and local business interests that perceived increased growth of the community as beneficial to their financial interest.[17] Second, court decisions held that local governments had no power to stop development in outlying areas where there were few immediate neighbors to be directly affected.[18] As a result, the energies of suburban communities were traditionally devoted not to stopping growth but to controlling its nature, *i.e.*, keeping out developments that might bring in poor people or minority groups.

The political situation is now changing rapidly. The business and real estate interests increasingly find themselves outweighed by other residents who do not perceive increased growth as beneficial. There is a new mood evident in the public attitude toward urban growth, and its message is "stop." If courts should begin to permit local governments to use their existing regulatory powers to stop the development of outlying areas, these new political forces are likely to assure that those powers are extensively used. It was in this context that the New York courts considered the new regulatory system adopted by the town of Ramapo.[19]

III. THE RAMAPO ORDINANCE

The town of Ramapo is located a few miles west of the Hudson River, just north of the New Jersey line, in Rockland County, New York. The opening of the Tappan Zee Bridge made the town an "easy 25-mile commute from the heart of New York City," and brought a rapid increase of development activity.[20] The sudden increase

17. R. WOOD, *supra* note 11, at 180-82.

18. *See, e.g.*, Arverne Bay Constr. Co. v. Thatcher, 15 N.E.2d 587 (N.Y. 1938).

19. Golden v. Planning Bd., 285 N.E.2d 291, 334 N.Y.S.2d 138 (1972) [hereinafter referred to as the *Ramapo* case].

20. Brief for Respondents-Appellants at 3, Golden v. Planning Bd., 285 N.E.2d 291, 334 N.Y.S.2d 138 (1972).

in activity stimulated the adoption by the town of a development plan in 1966. The plan declared the town's policy to preserve its "rural, semi-rural and suburban character" by keeping the population increase at a moderate level.[21] It projected a total ultimate population for the area within the town's jurisdiction of 72,000 people living in 20,000 residences.[22]

The plan further expressed the town's policy that the areas of greatest residential density should be developed in and surrounding the existing urban areas.[23] Under the plan, however, no part of the town's jurisdiction was deemed suitable for multiple-family dwellings. Although the town's zoning ordinance had previously provided for apartments at a density of eight to ten units per acre, the 1966 plan's highest proposed density was four units of single-family housing per acre.[24] In conjunction with the development plan, the town also adopted a capital improvements program, that set up an eighteen-year schedule for sewerage and drainage facilities, parks and recreation areas, school sites, roads and firehouses.

In 1969 Ramapo adopted a new zoning ordinance imposing "sequential development limitations" on residential subdivision development to "eliminate premature subdivision, urban sprawl and development without adequate municipal and public facilities." The ordinance requires a subdivision developer to obtain a special "residential development use permit" from the Town Board prior to receiving any building permit, special permit from the Board of Appeals, subdivision approval or site plan approval from the Planning Board. The standards for issuance of the special permit are based on the availability of or proximity to (1) public sanitary sewers or an approved substitute, (2) drainage facilities, (3) improved public parks or recreation facilities including public school sites, (4) state, county or town roads, and (5) firehouses.[25] The relationship of each public facility to the proposed development is rated on a sliding point scale: the more immediate the availability or proximity of the facility to the subdivision the greater the number of points allocated, to a maximum of five per facility.

Development is permitted only when a subdivision accumulates fifteen points under this system. The capital improvements program projects sufficient public facilities to provide the needed fifteen points

---

21. RAMAPO PLANNING BOARD, DEVELOPMENT PLAN 20 (July 1966).

22. *Id.* at 24. The incorporated villages located within the boundaries of the town are not within the town's jurisdiction. References to "the town" in this article refer only to the area within its jurisdiction unless otherwise noted.

23. *Id.* at 21.

24. *Id.* at 22. Interview with Manuel Emanuel, Planning Consultant to the Town of Ramapo, N.Y., Aug. 24, 1972.

25. Brief for Respondents-Appellants, *supra* note 20, at 11.

for all land in the town at some point during the eighteen-year life of the program.[26] Therefore, if the capital improvements program is followed, the town will never need to deny an application for a development permit, but can merely delay the effective date of the permit until such time as the needed facilities are to be constructed.[27]

The Planning Board may grant variances from the point requirement in case of hardship.[28] A procedure is provided by which developers may request the town to acquire a development easement in order to reduce the tax assessment if valuation is affected by the temporary use restriction, although there is apparently no assurance that the request would be granted.[29]

Finally, a key provision of the ordinance allows the developer to advance the date of authorization by agreeing to provide such improvements as will bring the development within the required number of points for earlier or immediate development.[30] Thus, if a developer is willing to construct the needed major roads, firehouses, trunk sewers and treatment plants, and provide the park and school sites at his own expense, he can presumably build anywhere in the town immediately.

A coalition of landowners and homebuilders brought suit in the New York state courts challenging the validity of the ordinance on the grounds that it was ultra vires and void because the power to control growth through sequential development limitations had not been delegated to the town; that it was unconstitutional as an invasion of property rights because it operated to destroy the value and marketability of the property for residential use; and that it uncon-

---

26. The ability of the town to insure that its plan will be followed does not seem completely certain. Sewers are provided by a special district although the district's governing board is apparently identical to the Town Board. *See* ROCKLAND COUNTY PLANNING BOARD, ROCKLAND COUNTY WATER AND SEWER STUDY 60 (1971). Firehouses are also provided by separate fire districts. Most of the roads in the town are under the jurisdiction of the state or county, and schools are constructed by independent school districts. Interview with John Keogh, Administrative Assistant to Town Boards and Commissions, Town of Ramapo, N.Y., Aug. 23, 1972. Moreover, as a practical matter, construction of many of the facilities may depend on referendums or on applications for federal assistance.

27. The *Ramapo* majority opinion apparently gave great weight to the fact that the ordinance only permitted the Planning Board to condition, not to deny, applications for permits. 285 N.E.2d at 298-300 & n.7, 334 N.Y.S.2d at 149-50 & n.7.

28. RAMAPO, N.Y., ZONING ORDINANCE § 46-13.1 (1966). The town has granted occasional variances for developments in the 12-14 point range, especially when the developer is promising to provide the needed public facilities. Interview with Emanuel, *supra* note 24.

29. 285 N.E.2d at 296, 334 N.Y.S.2d at 144.

30. *Id.*

stitutionally excluded new residents from the community in a manner that violated the equal protection of the laws.[31]

The case was argued for the town by the draftsman of the ordinance, former town attorney Robert Freilich, now a professor at the University of Missouri-Kansas City School of Law, and the editor of *The Urban Lawyer*.[32] On May 3, 1972, the court of appeals upheld the validity of the ordinance. Judge Scileppi's majority opinion received the concurrence of four other members of the court. Judge Breitel wrote a dissenting opinion in which Judge Jasen concurred.

The majority stated that "[t]he undisputed effect of these integrated efforts in land use planning and development is to provide an over-all program of orderly growth and adequate facilities through a sequential development policy commensurate with the progressing availability and capacity of public facilities."[33] It found the ordinance a legitimate exercise of the zoning power for the purposes of avoiding undue concentrations of population and of facilitating adequate provision for transportation, water, sewerage, schools, parks and other municipal facilities.

The court conceded that insularity of many communities results in distortions of metropolitan growth patterns and the crippling of regional and state-wide efforts to solve the problems of pollution, decent housing and public transportation. Although it recognized the need for regional planning, the court held that the authority to phase growth as envisioned in the Ramapo ordinance was within the ambit of the state's enabling legislation.[34]

Although stating that it would not countenance exclusionary zoning, the court found that sequential development and timed growth were not exclusionary but were attempts to "provide a balanced cohesive community dedicated to the efficient utilization of land. The restrictions conform to the community's considered land use policies as expressed in its comprehensive plan and represent a bona fide effort to maximize population density consistent with orderly growth."[35]

---

31. Brief for Petitioners-Respondents, Golden v. Planning Bd., 285 N.E.2d 291, 334 N.Y.S.2d 138 (1972).

32. Professor Freilich is so confident that the Ramapo ordinance represents the wave of the future that he has asked the National Science Foundation to fund a $450,000 project to replicate it across the country. *Hearings Before the Subcomm. on Urban Affairs of the Joint Economic Comm. on Regional Planning Issues*, 92d Cong., 1st Sess., pt. 3, at 460-70 (1971). (The proposal is reprinted as an appendix to Professor Freilich's testimony.) *Cf.* Freilich, *Interim Development Controls: Essential Tools for Implementing Flexible Planning and Zoning*, 49 J. URBAN LAW 65 (1971).

33. 285 N.E.2d at 296, 334 N.Y.S.2d at 144.

34. *Id.* at 300, 334 N.Y.S.2d at 150.

35. *Id.* at 302, 334 N.Y.S.2d at 152.

With respect to the taking of property issue, the court held that since the restrictions were only temporary in nature they could not be considered, on their face, as an unconstitutional taking of the landowner's property. The court pointed out that the landowner's loss is also mitigated by the ordinance's provision for a reduction in tax assessment and for voluntary construction of the necessary facilities by the developer.[36]

Judge Breitel, in a dissenting opinion, found Ramapo's sequential development ordinance to be beyond the scope of powers either delegated or implied in the state's enabling legislation. He suggested that the ordinance was exclusionary in effect, even if not exclusionary in motive, and that it caused the landowner to suffer substantial economic loss without compensation.[37] An attempt by a single community to deal in isolation with economic, social and political problems of regional significance, without the benefit of regional institutions or understanding, could be justified only if specifically authorized by state legislation. "Legally, politically, economically and sociologically, the base for determination must be larger than that provided by the town fathers."[38]

The significance of the *Ramapo* decision goes beyond the particular technique of development timing endorsed by the court. An earlier case[39] held that local governments could not preclude development in outlying areas where there were no neighboring uses to be injured by the development. The court now holds that when a community has a sound plan for the development of its entire jurisdiction—and whether this plan incorporates development timing or not is perhaps irrelevant—it can preclude development inconsistent with that plan in outlying areas. Before examining the importance of this holding, however, it will be helpful to look in more detail at the theoretical basis for the development timing concept embodied in the Ramapo ordinance.

IV. THE DEVELOPMENT TIMING CONCEPT

The concept of "development timing"—controlling the rate at which development occurs according to an established schedule—has been discussed for many years,[40] but Ramapo is the first town in which

36. *Id.* at 303-05, 334 N.Y.S.2d at 154-56. The effectiveness of the tax assessment reduction features of the ordinance were questioned by Justice Hopkins in his concurring opinion in the Appellate Division. 324 N.Y.S.2d 178, 187-88 (App. Div. 1971).

37. 285 N.E.2d at 310, 334 N.Y.S.2d at 163 (Breitel, J., dissenting).

38. *Id.* at 311, 334 N.Y.S.2d at 165.

39. Arverne Bay Constr. Co. v. Thatcher, 15 N.E.2d 587 (N.Y. 1938).

40. *See* Cutler, *Legal and Illegal Methods for Controlling Community Growth on*

a complex development timing ordinance, based on a master plan for capital improvements, has received the approval of an appellate court.[41] Underlying the idea of development timing is a rather simple planning concept: development is desirable if it is the logical extension of an existing urban area and can be served by incremental expansion of existing public facilities. Development farther removed from existing urban areas is undesirable.

So conceived, city planning is little more than the translation of basic principles of civil engineering into suggested guidelines for development that minimize the cost of public facilities. This type of plan assumes that a continued extension of the status quo is desirable, and projects the method of achieving this extension with the least expenditure of public funds. It partakes of the flavor of the early city planning movement, which saw no need to examine the impact of its plans on different population groups and their ability to find jobs and housing, on the provision of social services, or on the protection of natural resources or environmental quality.[42]

Given the assumption that a continued gradual extension of present patterns of development according to a well-prepared engineering study would be socially desirable, this pattern of development can be regulated neatly through the use of the development timing technique. Sewers and streets can be most economically constructed if the construction takes place in increments, with each increment of urban growth being directed to the next concentric circle beyond the last existing subdivision. This vision of a gradually expanding urban organism duplicating itself with increased beauty and economy with each succeeding expansion brings to mind the famous crustacean of Doctor Holmes' poem:

> Build thee more stately mansions, O my soul,
>   As the swift seasons roll!
>   Leave thy low-vaulted past!
> Let each new temple, nobler than the last,
> Shut thee from heaven with a dome more
>   vast,
>   Till thou at length are free,
> Leaving thine outgrown shell by life's unresting sea![43]

---

the Urban Fringe, 1961 Wis. L. Rev. 370; Fagin, Regulating the Timing of Urban Development, 20 Law & Contemp. Prob. 298 (1955); Schmandt, Municipal Control of Urban Expansion, 29 Fordham L. Rev. 637 (1961).

41. For a list of lower court cases involving earlier attempts at development timing, see N. Williams, The Structure of Urban Zoning, and its Dynamics in Urban Planning and Development 50-51, 153 (1966).

42. See M. Scott, American City Planning Since 1890, at 108, 228, 255-60 (1969).

43. O. Holmes, The Autocrat of the Breakfast Table 97-98 (1886). Cf. L. Mum-

It seems anomalous today to consider as a goal of planning that the New York metropolitan area and its constituent parts should continue to reproduce, expanding in successive increments by building new chambers each similar to the last but larger, growing gradually through "domes more vast." Considering the environmental degradation and racial segregation that has been fostered by our present patterns of development, almost any alternative would be an improvement over the present pattern.

Of course, the technique of development timing need not necessarily imply merely an incremental expansion of the status quo. In theory the technique could be used to channel development in any intended direction and to encourage specific types of physical development that might be considerably different from the existing pattern. Thus, for example, development timing could be used to shut off all incremental development in favor of the development of large new towns.[44]

But any sophisticated use of development timing requires enforceable regional planning policies. If development timing is undertaken by individual local governments, each concerned with the engineering economies involved in the construction of its own public facilities, these economies will inevitably point toward an incremental expansion of existing development patterns.

Under control techniques available prior to *Ramapo*, local governments had a wide range of discretion in determining the character of development that could be constructed but had no power to prevent or delay development entirely.[45] Thus developers have typically had the choice of a wide range of vacant land available for sale for development purposes. After the land is purchased the developer uses an ingenious variety of means to provide municipal services, including private utilities, special districts, or gerrymandered annexations.[46] Developers will often go beyond the areas of most logical development to isolated locations on the urban fringe where they can find land at reasonable prices.[47]

These isolated subdivisions or apartment complexes must be served

---

FORD, THE CITY IN HISTORY: ITS ORIGINS, ITS TRANSFORMATIONS, AND ITS PROSPECTS 552-54 (1961).

44. *See* Slayton, *The Need for New Mechanisms,* in THE NEW CITY 119, 122 (D. Canty ed. 1969).

45. *See* Babcock & Bosselman, *supra* note 10.

46. *See* M. CLAWSON, SUBURBAN LAND CONVERSION IN THE UNITED STATES 141-65 (1971).

47. *See* F. BOSSELMAN, ALTERNATIVES TO URBAN SPRAWL: LEGAL GUIDELINES FOR GOVERNMENTAL ACTION 5 (National Commission on Urban Problems, Research Report No. 15, 1968).

by water, streets and sewers. Their remote location means that water and sewer lines must be extended over great distances, resulting in higher costs for these services. Existing public schools in the undeveloped area are inadequate to handle the greatly increased population, resulting in overcrowded classrooms and schools located great distances from pupils. New schools must be constructed, resulting in unwanted taxes for existing residents. Unplanned traffic is created as the new scattered populations make their way to the increasingly distant city. The existing roads are inadequate to handle these problems, and become clogged with traffic, forcing the construction of massive new highway projects. Having constructed these new highways and water and sewer facilities, the governmental agencies then encourage more development that can be assessed to help pay for the facilities.[48] This entire "leapfrogging" process creates a pattern around the edges of urban areas that is aptly characterized as urban sprawl.

That urban sprawl is costly and unaesthetic seems certain. That development timing systems will change the existing pattern of sprawl also seems certain. But this does not demonstrate that every alternative to urban sprawl is an improvement.

V. The Overall Impact of Local Development Timing

Consider the probable impact of numerous communities in a metropolitan area, each controlling substantial vacant land situated in the path of future development and each permitting housing only on the land located near its existing urban area for which sewers and other facilities are planned for the near future. What will happen to land prices? It has been pointed out that where a narrow urban-limits policy is adopted "the impact on land development will be considerable. Competition among developers for the potential sites will be more intense, as their number is more limited. More competition for fewer sites will inflate prices, increase densities, or both."[49]

If the density of housing permitted on the land were allowed to increase in a ratio comparable to the increase in land value, the impact on housing costs might be minimal.[50] The capital improvement

---

48. *See* Williams, *The Three Systems of Land Use Control*, 25 Rutgers L. Rev. 80, 85-87 (1970).

49. D. Mandelker, The Zoning Dilemma 42 (1971).

50. Housing costs, however, may still be increased because the effect of the Ramapo-type ordinance will be to increase public facilities costs borne by new residents. Public construction of such facilities usually must be preceded by either a bond issue to be voted on by local referendum or by application for a federal grant from an agency which at the present time receives many more applications than it has funds to disburse. The local government's plan, therefore, is likely to be contingent either on the approval

plans on which the regulations are based, however, will not permit any increased density because the public facilities are sized for the densities currently projected. Since the whole system is designed to fit the proper size of the streets and sewers, if the system is to have any validity the local government must maintain roughly the same density as currently projected.

Although urban planners have been advocating narrow urban-limits policies for many years, few actual examples can be found in this country for studying the effect of such a policy. Perhaps the best example is in Honolulu County, Hawaii, where the combination of a statewide land use law and countywide zoning and planning has succeeded in implementing a policy of narrow urban limits.

The Hawaiian Land Use Law[51] created the State Land Use Commission and authorized it to divide the state into four zoning districts, only one of which—the urban district—permitted intensive development for housing or other purposes. The policy of the Commission has been to keep the urban district boundary restricted to the general outlines of the already urbanized area and to promote the filling in of vacant land within the urban district before permitting rezoning of land outside the existing urbanized area. Furthermore, when rezonings

---

of the voters at a subsequent election or on the receipt of a grant of federal funds. Since the voters are increasingly likely to reject such referendums, and because the amount of money available from federal agencies is quite limited, developers are likely to be told that the timetable shown in the plan would permit development of their land if only someone—like, say, the developer—would build the trunk sewer. Under existing law the prevailing rule allows local governments to force developers to pay for only those costs of public facilities that are directly generated by their proposed development. See D. HAGMAN, URBAN PLANNING AND LAND DEVELOPMENT CONTROL LAW 253-58 (1971); Van Alstyne, Taking or Damaging by Police Power: The Search for Inverse Condemnation Criteria, 44 S. CAL. L. REV. 1, 56-57 (1971). See also Associated Home Builders v. City of Walnut Creek, 484 P.2d 606, 94 Cal. Rptr. 630 (1972). This rule is more of an academic proposition than a realistic assessment of what goes on. In fact, developers are frequently forced to pay additional sums into particular funds or build facilities of greater capacity than those needed for their own projects, but they find the alternative of litigation so expensive and time-consuming that they forbear from enforcing their legal position. Under the Ramapo decision, however, their presently weak legal position will deteriorate even further. The developer will have three choices. First, he can wait until the voters or the federal agency or both take the necessary action to approve the funds. Secondly, he can build the trunk sewer himself, adding the cost into the price of the housing he constructs. Thirdly, he can go to the court and attempt to prove that the town did not, as the majority in the Ramapo decision put it, "put its best effort forward in implementing the physical and fiscal timetable outlined under the plan," a burden of proof that would be quite imposing, given a complex fact situation similar to the one described.

51. HAWAII REV. STAT. ch. 205 (Supp. 1972).

are permitted they are typically restricted to land immediately adjoining the outer boundary of the existing urban area.[52]

Because Hawaii's insular location creates additional transportation costs for building materials and provides only a tightly constricted labor supply, there seems little doubt that housing costs in Hawaii would be somewhat higher than on the mainland, regardless of any impact caused by the narrow urban-limits policy. This is true even though the Hawaiian climate makes it unnecessary to provide heating or insulation in most housing. But when one looks at the magnitude of the difference between housing costs for Hawaii and those for the nation—the median value of owner-occupied housing in Hawaii in 1970 was $35,100 as compared to the national median of $17,000—one can hardly help but attribute a large share of these increases to the narrow urban-limits policy and the housing shortage that it has produced.[53]

Outside of Hawaii, however, there is scarcely any single local government having authority to control the use of land whose jurisdiction includes an entire housing market. The metropolitan areas of the country are expanding so rapidly that individual local governments can best be thought of as occupying one small portion of a giant "urban field" that includes most of the northeast United States.[54] The city "has not just grown bigger than its boundaries—it has outgrown the concept and vocabulary of the city itself."[55]

The Commission on Population Growth and the American Future recently pointed out that the territory of metropolitan America has expanded even faster than its population, producing ever lower population densities over the total urbanized area.

> Roads and communications extend the reach of today's metropolitan areas deep into their hinterland. Villages and towns become part of the city-system, grow, and the metropolis expands . . . the most extensive depopulation in the contemporary United States is occurring in central cities of metropolitan areas. . . .
> . . . Declining central cities lost more people in the 1960's than were lost by declining rural counties. . . . Continuing dispersal and

---

52. *See generally* F. BOSSELMAN & D. CALLIES, THE QUIET REVOLUTION IN LAND USE CONTROL 22-24 (1971).

53. *Id.* at 25-28.

54. Friedmann & Miller, *The Urban Field*, 31 AM. INSTITUTE OF PLANNERS J. 312 (1965). *See also* J. GOTTMANN, MEGALOPOLIS (1961); J. PICKARD, U.S. METROPOLITAN GROWTH AND EXPANSION, 1970-2000 (Commission on Population Growth and the American Future, 1972).

55. Ylvisaker, *The Shape of the Future*, in METROPOLIS: VALUES IN CONFLICT 63, 68 (Elias, Gillies & Riemer eds. 1964).

expansion means that the density of the central cities and of the great metropolitan areas as a whole is falling slightly as the border gets pushed further and further outward.

The territorial expansion of metropolitan areas has resulted from the movement of business and the more affluent and white population out of the central city, and from a shift in the locus of new growth—residential, industrial, commercial—to the expanding periphery. . . . The suburban resident has a decreasing need to come into the city. Many work at industries along the beltways circling many cities.[56]

Ramapo and its counterparts will increase this trend. If more and more towns adopt development timing a major increase in housing costs can be expected. This will effectively exclude all but upper income groups from the areas that adopt development timing by restricting the amount of land available for housing and increasing its cost. Development will be forced farther and farther into the rural areas that form the fringe of the urban field.

Ironically, Ramapo defended its ordinance as a means of preventing urban sprawl, and the majority of the court of appeals accepted it on that basis.[57] But, by preventing urban sprawl within its own borders, Ramapo is contributing to the far more serious problem of megalopolitan sprawl. This means the loss of usable open space and the need for more major highway construction.

Supporters of local stop-growth movements argue, however, that stopping growth can be justified as the first step in a general rebellion against the present patterns of development. The ideological leadership of the movement is provided by the Sierra Club and other organizations that see the imposition of limits on growth as a general corollary to the zero population growth movement.[58] One who witnesses one of these public meetings where grandmother and granddaughter stand shoulder-to-shoulder agreeing perhaps for the first time on one thing—that all their problems are caused by the nasty developer—can hardly avoid a feeling of open-mouthed amazement.

That the imposition of local limitations on growth is a foolish response to a serious problem seems so self-evident that it would be hardly necessary to spend time arguing the point were it not for the tremendous increase within the past year of the popularity of the stop-

---

56. COMMISSION ON POPULATION GROWTH AND THE AMERICAN FUTURE, POPULATION AND THE AMERICAN FUTURE 31-32 (Bantam ed. 1972).

57. 285 N.E.2d at 295, 334 N.Y.S.2d at 143.

58. See Luten, *Progress Against Growth*, SIERRA CLUB BULLETIN, June 1972, at 22.

growth movement.[59] Obviously, the overall growth of the nation depends on the number of people who are born, immigrate, emigrate and die. Stopping the growth of Livermore or Boulder or Palm Beach does not reduce the nation's population growth; it merely directs it somewhere else. While it may be in the self-interest of the existing residents of a particular municipality to divert the problems caused by growth onto other areas and other people, it is fraudulent to justify this diversion on the grounds of environmental improvement unless some impartial source has evaluated the environmental impact of the various alternatives. The wolf of exclusionary zoning hides under the environmental sheepskin worn by the stop-growth movement.

The majority of the court of appeals were obviously concerned that the elaborate mechanism of the Ramapo ordinance might conceal an exclusionary purpose.[60] The court was impressed, however, with the town's argument that it had not only built "biracial low-income family housing,"[61] but had even defended its proposals for such housing against litigation brought by some of its own residents.[62]

Interviews with local officials indicate that this housing has now been completed. It consists of approximately 200 units, seventy-five percent of which are designed for and occupied by the elderly, all of whom are white. About fifty units are occupied by low-income families, ten to twenty percent of which are black. No further low-income housing is contemplated.[63]

Without denying the noble intentions of the town's officials, evidence such as this hardly justifies the court's assertions that Ramapo seeks "to provide a balanced cohesive community dedicated to the efficient utilization of land," that it has made "a bona fide effort to maximize population density consistent with orderly growth" and that it seeks "to maximize growth by the efficient use of land."[64] The town permits no multiple-family dwellings at all, and insists on large lot sizes for single-family homes.[65] The average lot size under the

---

59. *See, e.g.*, NEWSWEEK, Aug. 21, 1972, at 40; BUSINESS WEEK, Aug. 26, 1972, at 12; HOUSE AND HOME, May 1972, at 28; Los Angeles Times, Aug. 20, 1972, at 28, col. 1.

60. 285 N.E.2d at 302, 334 N.Y.S.2d at 152-53.

61. *Id.* at 295 n.2, 334 N.Y.S.2d at 143 n.2. *See* Brief for Respondents-Appellants, *supra* note 20, at 7.

62. *See* Fletcher v. Romney, 323 F. Supp. 189 (S.D.N.Y. 1971); Farrelly v. Town of Ramapo, 317 N.Y.S.2d 837 (App. Div. 1970).

63. Interview with Keogh, *supra* note 26.

64. 285 N.E.2d at 302, 334 N.Y.S.2d at 152.

65. The majority cites recent decisions of the Pennsylvania Supreme Court holding invalid a complete prohibition of multiple family dwellings, Appeal of Girsh, 263 A.2d 395 (Pa. 1970), and minimum lot sizes exceeding one acre, Appeal of Township of Concord, 268 A.2d 765 (Pa. 1970), but distinguishes the Ramapo ordinance because it "does not impose permanent restrictions upon land use." 285 N.E.2d at 302, 334 N.Y.S.2d

zoning ordinance is 40,000 square feet, or approximately one acre, and many areas are restricted to two-acre lots.[66] In general, the ordinance seems to have succeeded in limiting the number of building permits to the level of 300 to 350 housing units per year as contemplated by the master plan; the prices of these homes start at $40,000 to $45,000.[67]

The court stated that "[w]e only require that communities confront the challenge of population growth with open doors."[68] But a door that is open just a crack will apparently suffice.[69] And if Ramapo can obtain immunity from judicial inspection of the exclusionary effects of its regulation by providing homes for five or ten black families in a town that projects its ultimate population as 72,000, there are few other communities that would be unwilling to make the same "sacrifice." If the court is willing to accept this degree of tokenism, adoption of the Ramapo approach by other towns is not likely to be impeded by a judicial finding of exclusionary intent.

Summarizing at this point, then, ordinances of the Ramapo type, if they become commonplace, will encourage the clustering of new development around the fringes of existing settlements and the excluding of new development from large areas where it now typically takes place. The impact of a proliferation of such ordinances would be to create a series of communities made increasingly exclusive by raised housing costs and to exaggerate the trend toward megalopolitan sprawl. The current mood of the suburban population and the lack of vigilance expressed by the court of appeals is likely to produce a wide proliferation of Ramapos not only in New York but throughout the country.

What can be done? Three approaches seem worth considering, a discussion of which will form the basis for the rest of this article: (1) affirmative intervention in the land market to counteract the effects of exclusionary zoning; (2) additional litigation designed to induce the courts to apply new judge-made standards to local zoning actions; and (3) state legislation that would provide some sort of regional planning review of suburban zoning.[70]

---

at 152. It is hard to see why an ordinance that allows large lot development over a whole township is more exclusionary than one that gives the developer a choice between large lot development and no development at all.

66. Interview with Keogh, *supra* note 26.

67. Interview with David Silverman, Attorney for the Rockland County Builders Association, New City, N.Y., Aug. 23, 1972; Interview with Emanuel, *supra* note 24.

68. 285 N.E.2d at 302, 334 N.Y.S.2d at 153.

69. The record contained little evidence of this issue since the challenge was directed to the ordinance on its face. This makes it hard to see how the majority could have expressed its conclusions with such certainty.

70. Other alternatives are obviously possible, *e.g.*, voluntary action by suburban

VI. LAND BANKING

One means of counteracting the effect of widespread use of development timing for exclusionary purposes would be an extensive program of land banking that would acquire and make available to potential developers sufficient land to serve as a ceiling on land prices. Such a program might hold down the upward spiral of housing costs likely to be engendered by the *Ramapo* decision.

Proponents of this type of land banking program frequently cite the experience in Sweden and the Netherlands where for many years the large cities have been in the business of acquiring land for future developments.[71] Stockholm, in particular, is the city that has used the land banking system to the greatest extent. It has purchased large tracts of land in the suburban area and thereby precluded the typical suburban development that characterizes the outlying areas of most cities.[72] Instead, Stockholm has developed a number of new communities, often cited as models of gracious living, linked with a central city by mass transit.[73]

Many students of urban planning who have examined the Swedish system have advocated its use in this country. John Reps is one of the most persuasive advocates for the creation of such a land banking system:

> Land at the urban fringe which is to be developed for urban uses should be acquired by a public agency. Acquisition, in fact, should run well ahead of anticipated need and include the purchase or condemnation of idle and agricultural land well beyond the present urban limits. The public agency, therefore, should be given territorial jurisdiction which includes not only the present central city and surrounding suburbs but a wide belt of undeveloped land.[74]

The advantages of a land banking system were excellently summarized in a recent paper prepared for the House Subcommittee

---

communities, direct federal intervention and complete abolition of zoning; but these latter measures seem less practical.

71. Note, *Public Land Banking: A New Praxis for Urban Growth*, 23 CASE W. RES. L. REV. 897, 908-12 (1972).

72. As of 1966 Stockholm owned seventy-four percent of the land within the city limits and large tracts outside its boundaries. Passow, *Land Reserves and Teamwork in Planning Stockholm*, 36 AM. INSTITUTE OF PLANNERS J. 179, 180 (1970).

73. *See* Cribbet, *Some Reflections on the Law of Land—A View From Scandanavia*, 62 Nw. U.L. REV. 277, 305-09 (1967).

74. Reps, *The Future of American Planning: Requiem or Renascence?*, 1967 PLANNING 47, 49. *See also* A. DOWNS, URBAN PROBLEMS AND PROSPECTS 15-17 (1970).

on Housing.[75] Such a land bank would stabilize the land market in much the same way as the Federal Reserve Bank stabilizes the money market. It would reduce land price fluctuations and improve the functioning of the private land market by releasing land from its inventories according to an overall plan of development.[76] The Douglas Commission recommended that state governments enact legislation enabling the acquisition of land in advance of development for the following purposes: "(a) assuring the continuing availability of sites needed for development; (b) controlling the timing, location, type, and scale of development; (c) preventing urban sprawl; and (d) reserving to the public gains in land values resulting from the action of government in promoting and servicing development."[77]

Is it feasible to consider a land banking program within an urban field the size of that surrounding New York City? In New York State, the vehicle for a land banking program is already theoretically available in the Urban Development Corporation, which has the power to acquire and develop or sell for development land throughout the state.[78] It is questionable however, whether the Urban Development Corporation could realistically expect to find either funds or political support sufficient to undertake the massive land banking effort needed to counteract a severe constriction in the supply of land available for development. The Urban Development Corporation is currently attempting to provide housing sites in Westchester County on a much less extensive scale than would be necessary to provide the market-influencing function said to characterize land banking. The strength of the adverse reaction to these limited efforts leads one to suspect that large-scale land acquisition by the Corporation would be greeted with violent opposition by the residents of the suburban area.[79] Nevertheless, this alternative certainly deserves serious consideration.

---

75. Haar, *Wanted: Two Federal Levers for Urban Land Use—Land Banks and Urbank*, in PAPERS SUBMITTED TO SUBCOMM. ON HOUSING PANELS OF THE HOUSE COMM. ON BANKING AND CURRENCY, 92d Cong., 1st Sess., pt. 2, at 927, 934-36 (Comm. Print 1971).

76. *Id.* at 935. *See also* Reps, *supra* note 74, at 51-52.

77. NATIONAL COMM'N ON URBAN PROBLEMS, BUILDING THE AMERICAN CITY 251 (1968). Similar proposals may be found in the reports of other urban policy task forces. *See* PRESIDENT'S COMM. ON URBAN HOUSING, A DECENT HOME 144-46 (1969); PRESIDENT'S COUNCIL ON RECREATION AND NATURAL BEAUTY, FROM SEA TO SHINING SEA 115-16 (1968); PUERTO RICO PLANNING BD., URBAN LAND POLICY FOR THE COMMONWEALTH OF PUERTO RICO 95-106 (1961); NEW YORK STATE URBAN DEVELOPMENT CORP. AND NEW YORK STATE OFFICE OF PLANNING COORDINATION, NEW COMMUNITIES FOR NEW YORK 64-66 (1970).

78. N.Y. UNCONSOL. LAWS § 6251 (McKinney Supp. 1972). *See* Reilly & Schulman, *The State Urban Development Corporation: New York's Innovation*, 1 URBAN LAWYER 129, 131-32 (1969).

79. *See* N.Y. Times, June 21, 1972, at 1, col. 2 (city ed.); N.Y. Times Jan. 17, 1973, at 1, col. 7 (city ed.).

VII. Greater Judicial Scrutiny

Judge Breitel, in his dissent, concluded that the majority's "unsupportable extrapolation from existing enabling acts" to uphold the Ramapo ordinance "without considering the social and economic ramifications for the locality, region, and State . . . is unsound as well as invalid."[80] The majority's refusal to force Ramapo to support its assertion that it sought a balanced community[81] is consistent with the judicial attitudes in most states. The courts have generally given local zoning decisions a presumption of validity.[82] Many courts say they will uphold the local action if it is "fairly debatable" or unless some other extraordinary burden of proof is borne by the plaintiffs.[83]

When the plaintiff has the usual complaint that he is being unfairly treated in regard to his neighbors or that his property values are being reduced by an unwarranted amount, the quantum of relevant facts is at least manageable.[84] But a truly herculean burden is encountered when he seeks to demonstrate what Judge Breitel described as the "social and economic ramifications for the locality, region and State."[85]

In recent years the advisability of this allocation of the burden has increasingly been questioned. In *Vickers v. Township Committee*,[86] the majority of the New Jersey Supreme Court, relying in part on the

---

80.   285 N.E.2d at 309, 334 N.Y.S.2d at 162.

81.   "Ramapo, far from excluding the poor, has fought to make available hundreds of units of public housing, which is integrated, and for low and moderate income families." Brief for Respondents-Appellants, *supra* note 20, at 39.

82.   285 N.E.2d at 301, 334 N.Y.S.2d at 151. *See generally* 3 R. Anderson, American Law of Zoning § 21.16 (1968).

83.   Of course, the extent to which courts will inquire into local decisions varies from state to state and over time. As Norman Williams has pointed out:

The proper role of the courts . . . is of course a standing controversy; and in the rapid flux of current zoning law, attitudes on this problem have almost reversed themselves. Twenty years ago, the principal problem was to keep the courts from arbitrarily upsetting almost all zoning regulations; and in some states—for example Michigan, and sometimes Illinois—this is still problem no. 1. Yet in other states—notably New Jersey, and sometimes California—the courts have gone almost to the opposite extreme, automatically and uncritically approving any local action on which someone has pinned the label "planning."

N. Williams, *supra* note 41, at 55.

84.   Plaintiffs do at times succeed in persuading the courts that the local decision is invalid. David Trubek has commented that "One of the most striking things about the area of judicial review of state zoning powers is not how *few* cases the courts take—which is what one would predict from the existence of the presumption of validity—but rather how many they take, and the number of times that local restrictions are overturned." Trubek, *Testimony Before the U.S. Commission on Civil Rights*, Exhibit No. 32, at 841 (June 16, 1971).

85.   285 N.E.2d at 309, 334 N.Y.S.2d at 162.

86.   181 A.2d 129 (N.J. 1962).

presumption of validity of municipal action, upheld an ordinance prohibiting trailer camps in certain areas of the town. In his influential dissenting opinion, Justice Hall attacked this reliance. "Judicial scrutiny has become too superficial and one-sided. . . . '[T]he presumption of validity . . . is only a presumption and may be overcome or rebutted not only by clear evidence *aliunde*, but also by a showing on its face or in the light of facts of which judicial notice can be taken, of transgression of constitutional limitation or the bounds of reason.' "[87] Justice Hall suggested that municipalities be given the burden of justifying their actions when there is a possibility that they have gone to a doubtful extreme.[88]

The Supreme Court of Pennsylvania, Justice Roberts writing for the court in *National Land & Investment Co. v. Kohn*,[89] also recognized that the presumption of validity has a dubious base in logic:

> [W]e must also appreciate the fact that zoning involves governmental restrictions upon a landowner's constitutionally guaranteed right to use his property, unfettered, except in very specific instances, by governmental restrictions. The time must never come when, because of frustration with concepts foreign to their legal training, courts abdicate their judicial responsibility to protect the constitutional rights of individual citizens. Thus, the burden of proof imposed upon one who challenges the validity of a zoning regulation must never be made so onerous as to foreclose, for all practical purposes, a landowner's avenue of redress against the infringement of constitutionally protected rights.[90]

A recent decision of the Michigan Court of Appeals reached a similar result in regard to a refusal to rezone land for a mobile home park.[91] In view of the "massive nationwide housing shortage," the court held that mobile home parks occupied a "preferred or favored" status, causing the burden of proof to shift to the municipality whenever it sought to exclude a park.

These courts are correct in removing the presumption of validity and shifting the burden of proof in any case where local regulations are not based on an effective system of regional planning. The constitutional issues inherent in these cases are too important to be allowed to escape effective judicial review.[92] It has been argued that

---

87. *Id.* at 143-44.
88. *Id.* at 144.
89. 215 A.2d 597 (Pa. 1966).
90. *Id.* at 607. *See also* Appeal of Township of Concord, 268 A.2d 765 (Pa. 1970).
91. Bristow v. City of Woodhaven, 192 N.W.2d 322 (Mich. Ct. App. 1971).
92. It would unduly lengthen this article to discuss the nature of the constitutional

detailed review of the factual circumstances of local zoning decisions is a function for which the courts are ill-equipped because of the lack of legislatively-stated policies on which to base decisions, the political implications of the subject and the complexity of the fact and value issues presented.[93]

> [I]t would be unwise for anyone to assume that the state courts will take on the issue except in extreme circumstances, and wrong to establish a policy that would try to make them do this without a major legislative change of the basic land use control system which would create standards and rules that courts might usefully apply.[94]

It is unquestionably difficult for courts to fashion the type of simple standards usually thought appropriate for interpreting constitutional provisions and to enforce the standards in a manner that will have a beneficial impact on the urban growth process. The land development business has so many complex facets that enforcement of simple "rules of thumb" may produce complex and unexpected results. Consider, for example, the elimination of large minimum lot size requirements. Assume that the court eliminated all density requirements.[95] Developers could now put as many dwelling units on an acre of land as they wished. But low-income housing developers must operate on a very strict budget, and the land that has sewer and water utilities sufficient to support such housing may be too expensive for them. The owners of any land that is even remotely susceptible to future high density development can be expected to ask a price beyond the means of the low-income developers; but it will be a price they can reasonably expect to receive because of the great demand for sites for other types of housing.

Observation will reveal that most low-income housing outside central cities is built on land originally zoned for low densities and rezoned at the request of the developer. If that is true, then, in one sense exclusionary zoning is the best ally the low-income housing developer has—the more exclusionary the better. It keeps the price of land down to where he can afford it. The best way for a community

---

issues that are raised by local exclusionary efforts. The subject has received extensive attention in the law reviews. A good general summary of the constitutional arguments is found in Aloi & Goldberg, *Racial and Economic Exclusionary Zoning: The Beginning of the End*, 1971 URBAN L. ANN. 9. The assumption is made that if the courts seriously examine the factual context of current zoning practices they will find them in violation of one or more constitutional or statutory provisions.

93. *See* Trubek, *supra* note 84, at 851.

94. *Id.* at 853.

95. *Cf.* Appeal of Township of Concord, 268 A.2d 765 (Pa. 1970).

to avoid low-income housing might be to zone all its land not for five-acre lots but for quarter-acre lots; then no low-income developer could touch it.

Or consider the standard apparently adopted by the Ninth Circuit in *Southern Alameda Spanish Speaking Organization v. Union City*.[96] In this case the plaintiff sought to construct low-income housing to serve Mexican-American residents of the community who were being displaced by code enforcement and by freeway projects. The court said:

> Surely, if the environmental benefits of land use planning are to be enjoyed by a city and the quality of life of its residents is accordingly to be improved, the poor cannot be excluded from enjoyment of the benefits. Given the recognized importance of equal opportunities in housing, it may well be, as matter of law, that it is the responsibility of a city and its planning officials to see that the city's plan as initiated or as it develops accommodates the needs of its low-income families, who usually—if not always—are members of minority groups.[97]

The court seems to be saying that if a community has existing residents who are poor or members of minority groups, it has an obligation to see that housing is made available for them. While this principle may sound appealing, its converse implications are appalling. It implies that a community that has managed so far to avoid any low-income residents may continue to avoid them in the future, and that low-income residents have a "right" to remain in the communities in which they now reside.

It seems likely that the enunciation by the courts of simple and basic principles that sound appealing on their face may have results far different than originally intended when applied to land development. Consequently fears of judicial incapacity to resolve these problems seem well warranted. But one can agree completely that it is desirable for courts to serve as permanent arbiters of local planning decisions and still believe in the desirability of judicial intervention mainly as a catalyst to secure the ultimately more desirable legislative action. "As in the passionate areas of school segregation and reapportionment, legislative action in the agitated field of private land use will probably be forthcoming only when the bench challenges the current posture of the law."[98] The political resistance to effective regional planning is very powerful. Additional impetus in the form of

96.   424 F.2d 291 (9th Cir. 1970).
97.   *Id.* at 295-96.
98.   Babcock & Bosselman, *supra* note 10, at 1090.

court-imposed sanctions might be extremely helpful in persuading local officials of the desirability of significant regional policies.

VIII. REGIONAL PLANNING MECHANISMS

Both the majority and dissenting opinions in the *Ramapo* case suggested with unusual frankness that the legislature should pass new laws that would extricate the courts from the dilemma that the instant case presented.[99] The majority extolled the virtues of regional planning:

> Of course, these problems cannot be solved by Ramapo or any single municipality, but depend upon the accommodation of widely disparate interests for their ultimate resolution. To that end, State-wide or regional control of planning would insure that interests broader than that of the municipality underlie various land use policies.[100]

But in reality regional planning has been frequently extolled and rarely implemented.

Planning in the United States in the early part of this century was conceived as synonymous with city planning.[101] The problems for which planning was seen as a solution were viewed as local problems susceptible to local solutions. Beginning late in the nineteenth century, however, the growth of most central cities by annexations slowed and the creation of separate and independent suburbs increased. People began to think of the central city and its associated suburbs as a single region. Gradually the recognition grew that problems pervaded the entire region, but the mutual antagonism of the central city and its suburbs overcame any desire they might have had to find common solutions.[102]

Regional planning in the United States began outside of any governmental framework with the growth of citizen-sponsored regional planning societies.[103] Gradually most states passed enabling legislation

---

99. 285 N.E.2d at 300, 334 N.Y.S.2d at 149; 285 N.E.2d at 309, 334 N.Y.S.2d at 162 (Breitel, J., dissenting).

100. *Id.* at 300, 334 N.Y.S.2d at 150.

101. S. TOLL, *supra* note 13, at 120-22. *See also* JOINT CENTER FOR URBAN STUDIES OF THE MASSACHUSETTS INSTITUTE OF TECHNOLOGY AND HARVARD UNIVERSITY, THE EFFECTIVENESS OF METROPOLITAN PLANNING 44 (1964), *presented at Hearings Before the Subcomm. on Intergovernmental Relations of the Senate Comm. on Government Operations*, 88th Cong., 2d Sess. (1964) [hereinafter cited as JOINT CENTER STUDY]. *See generally* M. SCOTT, *supra* note 42.

102. M. SCOTT, *supra* note 42, at 174-76.

103. B. MCKELVEY, THE EMERGENCE OF METROPOLITAN AMERICA, 1915-1966, at 61 (1968). The Regional Plan Association in the New York area began as a voluntary organization made up of "leading citizens" who were interested in the growth of the New York

for the creation of agencies to undertake regional planning. But these government-authorized regional planning commissions tended to follow a typical pattern: they were advisory bodies made up of leading citizens interested in planning, appointed by the heads of local governments.[104] The commissions were given the function of preparing regional plans, but neither the plans nor the commissions had the powers necessary to make them effective.[105]

When the federal government began to develop the interstate highway program in the late 1950's, it became apparent that the absence of effective regional planning would seriously hamper the highway network. All too often the federal and state highway agencies could find no one who could even predict, much less control, the location where future development would take place. In response, Congress attached to the Federal Aid Highway Act of 1962 a requirement that regional transportation planning be undertaken for metropolitan areas.[106] At about the same time, Senator Edmund S. Muskie's subcommittee instituted a series of studies of metropolitan planning in the United States that found that the existing system of metropolitan planning was largely ineffective.[107] The studies concluded that the power to control major decisions lay with the elected officials of local governments, but that the existing regional planning agencies had little influence on these local governments.[108]

Out of these studies came a federal recommendation that the metropolitan planning agency should be a Council of Governments made up of elected public officials from the local governments in the metropolitan area—a requirement that was designed to squeeze out the typical, metropolitan agency based on the "leading citizen" model.[109]

---

area. It undertook the preparation of regional planning studies, educated the public in the need for planning and criticized the plans of local governments if they overlooked the regional interest. But RPA's function from the beginning has been purely advisory, and its plans and recommendations have no legal force and effect. *See* M. SCOTT, *supra* note 42.

104. JOINT CENTER STUDY, *supra* note 101, at 52.

105. *Id.* at 62-65.

106. 23 U.S.C. § 134 (1970).

107. HOUSING AND HOME FINANCE AGENCY FOR THE SUBCOMM. ON INTERGOVERNMENTAL RELATIONS OF THE SENATE COMM. ON GOVERNMENT OPERATIONS, 88th Cong., 1st Sess., NATIONAL SURVEY OF METROPOLITAN PLANNING (Comm. Print 1963); HOUSING AND HOME FINANCE AGENCY FOR THE SUBCOMM. ON INTERGOVERNMENTAL RELATIONS OF THE SENATE COMM. ON GOVERNMENT OPERATIONS, 89th Cong., 1st Sess., 1964 NATIONAL SURVEY OF METROPOLITAN PLANNING (Comm. Print 1965). *See also* ADVISORY COMM'N ON INTERGOVERNMENTAL RELATIONS, GOVERNMENTAL STRUCTURE, ORGANIZATION AND PLANNING IN METROPOLITAN AREAS (1961).

108. *See* JOINT CENTER STUDY, *supra* note 101, at 88, 121-22.

109. Charles Haar, then Assistant Secretary for Metropolitan Development, explained

The federal impetus for metropolitan planning remained academic and received little attention in the early 1960's because federal law gave metropolitan planning agencies no explicit function. This changed with the creation of the A-95 program (so called because its guidelines are set forth in Budget Bureau Circular No. A-95).[110] Originally established under the Demonstration Cities and Metropolitan Development Act of 1966,[111] the A-95 program requires applicants for grants-in-aid under certain federal programs to submit their applications to the appropriate metropolitan planning agency for review and comment.[112] Typically the applicants are local governments or special districts seeking federal aid to construct public facilities. The comments of the regional planning agency are not binding on the federal agency that awards the grant, but because the federal agency typically has more applicants than funds, an adverse comment from a regional planning agency is often the kiss of death.

Unfortunately, however, this program of regional planning has not proven to be very effective. After reviewing the performance of the regional planning agencies for the Presidential Task Force on Governmental Reorganization, Melvin Mogulof concluded that these Councils of Governments are generally weak and ineffective because the member governments do not want them to emerge as an independent source of regional influence but prefer to view them as coordinators that serve to ensure the continued flow of federal funds.[113] The operation of a regional agency has been described as "backscratching." "I'll vote for whatever you want in your county because I expect you to vote for whatever I want in my county."[114]

---

the rationale:

The problems to which metropolitan planning is addressed are public problems. Public action is required for their solution . . . . But, where public action is desired, public money is required. And our political credo since the days of the Stuart kings has been that gathering and spending public money is the duty and responsibility of elected officials, and of those nearest the electorate at that. . . . [E]lected officials have tended to look beyond the fairly circumscribed interests of professional planners. The necessity of returning to their constituency makes officials more responsive to public needs. It makes them more inclined to seek practical means of meeting those needs.

On the whole, I think it is probably valid to assume that councils of governments tend to be more realistic citizen planning agencies. They do not tackle many of the grand issues professional metropolitan units have faced. But they get more done, albeit by sticking to more limited and perhaps more feasible issues.

Haar, *What Are We Learning About Metropolitan Planning?*, 1969 PLANNING 33, 46-47.

110. Bureau of the Budget Circular No. A-95 (July 24, 1969).

111. Act of Nov. 3, 1966, Pub. L. No. 89-754, 80 Stat. 1255.

112. Bureau of the Budget Circular No. A-95 (rev. Feb. 9, 1971).

113. Mogulof, *Regional Planners, Clearance, and Evaluation: A Look at the A-95 Process*, 37 AM. INSTITUTE OF PLANNING J. 418 (1971).

114. O'Harrow, *Metropolitan Planning—Now or Later*, 37 PLANNING 14 (1971). *See also*

The weaknesses of the currently popular system of regional planning have caused many commentators to demand more powerful and effective methods.[115] Some areas have taken steps toward creating a strengthened agency for regional planning. The Metropolitan Council of Twin Cities in Minnesota is the leading example of a regional planning agency, the members of which are appointed by the governor with the advice of the legislature. It exerts strong and independent powers to control metropolitan growth in the twin cities area.[116] The Atlanta region also seems to be moving in this direction,[117] but the difficulties encountered by attempts to force strong metropolitan planning have been great.

When a metropolitan area includes parts of more than one state (Ramapo's includes substantial segments of three states—New York, Connecticut and New Jersey), the problems are doubly severe. In 1965, in response to the demands of federal highway legislation, a Tri-State Transportation Commission was created for the New York metropolitan area by interstate compact and implementing legislation from the three states.[118] The Commission's primary function was planning new highway locations for the region. When the A-95 program was instituted, the Commission was the only agency capable of undertaking any regional planning function.[119] To comply with the A-95 requirements, the compact legislation was amended to change the Commission's name to the Tri-State Regional Planning Commission.[120]

At the present time, the Commission still functions primarily as a transportation planning agency.[121] Nevertheless, it has begun tentative steps toward a broader planning approach. A staff-prepared housing plan has been prepared and will be presented to the Commission in 1972-1973. The plan seeks to allocate the annual need for each subregion by structure type and income class. [122] The staff, however, pro-

---

ALI Model Land Development Code 57-58 (Tent. Draft No. 3, 1971).

115. Babcock, *Let's Stop Romancing Regionalism,* 38 Planning 120, 121 (1972).

116. F. Bosselman & D. Callies, *supra* note 52, at 136-53.

117. Buckner, *Atlanta Broadens Its Regional Base,* 38 Planning 144 (1972).

118. N.Y. Sess. Laws 1965, ch. 413; Laws of New Jersey 1965, ch. 12; Conn. Gen. Stats., ch. 291 (1966); Interview with Richard Deturk, Deputy Executive Director, Tri-State Regional Planning Commission, Aug. 25, 1972.

119. The Metropolitan Regional Council is a voluntary association of mayors of local governments in the region, but it has never undertaken any regional planning.

120. N.Y. Sess. Laws 1971, ch. 333; 1972, ch. 269; Laws of New Jersey 1971, ch. 161; Connecticut Laws of 1971, Public Act No. 450.

121. Of a proposed budget of about $11.5 million for 1972-1973, all but about $1.5 million is for transportation related programs. Tri-State Regional Planning Commission, Continuing Comprehensive Planning Program and Joint Regional Planning 150 (1972).

122. *Id.* at 34. At the present time it is estimated that perhaps eighty percent of

poses no system for enforcing compliance with its plan, and the Commission is prohibited from involving itself in actual land use decisions under the terms of the interstate compact by which it was created.[123]

Insofar as the A-95 program is concerned, the Commission has concluded that its geographical area is too vast to allow review by the Commission or its staff of most applications for federal funds. Consequently, it has delegated to the county planning agencies its authority to review applications except for those projects that its staff classifies as of regional significance.[124] Approximately eighty-five to ninety percent of local applications are approved without any difficulty, and the remaining applications are usually approved after modification.[125]

Meanwhile, the state of New York was working on its own program of regional planning. Governor Rockefeller created the Office of Planning Coordination, an agency that became the most powerful state planning organization in the country. It embarked on a massive project of reorganizing state programs through a planning-programming-budgeting system.[126] As part of its project it created eleven multi-county regional planning districts within the state[127] and proposed legislation that would give these regional agencies power to review new development decisions affecting certain areas of critical state concern.[128] The Office of Planning Coordination wanted county and regional planning agencies to review all "public and private actions which, because of their size or nature, would directly or indirectly affect more than one municipality . . . ."[129] During 1971, however, the legislature abolished the Office of Planning Coordination[130] and its proposed legislation has remained dormant.

The Office of Planning Coordination issued, as one of its last acts, the New York State Development Plan, which projects extensive

the vacant land in the region is reserved for about twenty-five percent of the population. Davidoff & Davidoff, *Opening The Suburbs: Toward Inclusionary Land Use Controls,* 22 SYRACUSE L. REV. 509, 525 (1971).

123.   Interview with Deturk, *supra* note 118.

124.   Interview with J. Douglas Carroll, Jr., Executive Director, Tri-State Regional Planning Commission, Aug. 25, 1972; Interview with Deturk, *supra* note 118, at 31.

125.   Interview with Carroll, *supra* note 124.

126.   Fletcher, *From PPBS to PAR in the Empire State,* 45 STATE GOVERNMENT 198 (1972).

127.   *See* NEW YORK STATE OFFICE OF PLANNING COORDINATION, NEW YORK STATE DEVELOPMENT PLAN-I, at 84 (1971).

128.   NEW YORK STATE OFFICE OF PLANNING COORDINATION, NEW YORK STATE PLANNING LAW REVISION STUDY (Study Document No. 4, February 1970).

129.   NEW YORK STATE OFFICE OF PLANNING COORDINATION, *supra* note 127, at 86.

130.   *New York Planning Metamorphoses,* 37 PLANNING 83 (1971).

population growth for the area in Rockland County occupied by Ramapo, designating it for population densities in the range of 2,000 to 10,000 persons per square mile. "By virtue of its key location, this sector of the New York urban area will experience great population increase in the coming decades. Development pressures, now so evident in the southern end will move progressively north [to the Ramapo area] as the state gives priority to providing facilities to sustain this growth."[131]

The state plan, like the various regional plans, has no force and effect. No private developer nor governmental agency has any legal obligation to pay it any attention whatsoever. It seems fair to say, therefore, that the impact of regional planning on Ramapo—or any other town in the region—is minimal. If a town chose to embark on a massive development program, it might be forced to negotiate with the county and regional agencies to obtain the federal funds necessary to finance the development. If, however, its goal is to exclude development, it has the legal power to implement these policies regardless of the opinions or plans of any state, regional or federal agency.

Both the majority and dissenting opinions in *Ramapo* proclaim the need for regional planning and cite the tentative drafts of the American Law Institute's Model Land Development Code as an example of a statute that authorizes development timing, but in a context of regional planning.[132] If it is reasonable to assume that the enabling legislation will soon be revised to provide a stronger role for regional planning, then fears of the adverse effects of the *Ramapo* decision may be unfounded.

Much of the existing enabling legislation for planning, zoning and subdivision control remains based on model statutes that were drafted by the Department of Commerce in the 1920's.[133] In the mid-1960's the American Law Institute concluded that it was advisable to begin a project of drafting new model legislation to supplant these forty-year old models. The new legislation was designated a "Model Land Development Code." Five tentative drafts have appeared to date, covering in all about three-fourths of the total material eventually to be encompassed within the Code.[134]

The draftsmen of the Model Code have tried to weight evenly the

---

131. NEW YORK STATE OFFICE OF PLANNING COORDINATION, *supra* note 127, at 54.

132. 285 N.E.2d at 296-303, 334 N.Y.S.2d at 145-53; 285 N.E.2d at 306, 334 N.Y.S.2d at 158 (Breitel, J., dissenting).

133. *Reprinted in* ALI MODEL LAND DEVELOPMENT CODE Appendices 1 & 2 (Tent. Draft No. 1, 1968).

134. Tentative draft number one was published in 1968, number two in 1970, number three in 1971, number four in 1972 and number five in 1973.

need for state or regional participation in land use decisions, the values of participatory democracy that our existing system has done so much to foster, and the risk that any regulatory process can become too costly and time-consuming. They attempted to resolve these conflicting values by defining the major development problems and providing for state or regional participation in only these major decisions, leaving the great majority of cases within the sole jurisdiction of local government. In addition, by providing that the state shall participate only on appeal from an initial decision of any agency of local government, the Code drafts preserve the expertise of local people to solve local problems. The time and expense of state review is conserved by limiting it to major decisions and by providing that the review shall be of the record made at the local hearing, thus eliminating the need for duplicate hearing procedure.

Identifying what constitutes "major" development decisions, which invoke state level review, is obviously a difficult problem. The Code drafts have adopted a threefold definition authorizing state or regional participation in: (1) all development proposals in certain districts declared to be "districts of critical state concern"; (2) all decisions regarding certain types of development alleged by the developer to be "development of state or regional benefit"; and (3) all decisions involving "large scale development" having a state or regional impact.[135]

The tentative drafts also recommend a substantially increased state participation in planning for land development. The state planning agency would be authorized to prepare state land development plans, which might cover the whole state or any region thereof, or a multi-state region if approved by an interstate compact.[136] Each plan would be a comprehensive plan rather than a plan concentrating on any single function.[137] Within this framework, however, most of the planning and regulation would continue to be handled at the local level.[138]

The tentative drafts of the Model Land Development Code would authorize local governments to tie the issuance of "development permits" (a combined procedure that replaces existing zoning and subdivision control permits) to a land development plan using a system of development timing.[139] The exercise of these powers by local governments is, however, limited by the authorization for state and re-

---

135. ALI MODEL LAND DEVELOPMENT CODE §§ 7-201, 7-301, 7-401 (Tent. Draft No. 3, 1971). *Cf.* FLA. STAT. §§ 380.05-.06 (Supp. 1972).

136. *See generally* ALI MODEL LAND DEVELOPMENT CODE art. 8 (Tent. Draft No. 3, 1971).

137. *Id.* § 8-402.

138. ALI MODEL LAND DEVELOPMENT CODE § 3-101 (Tent. Draft No. 2, 1970).

139. *Id.* §§ 3-202, -105.

gional planning and by the supervision of local regulations found in articles seven and eight of the Model Code.[140] Thus, section 8-405 authorizes the state planning agency or any regional agency designated by it[141] to prepare state or regional land development plans for any region of the state.[142] Once a state or regional plan is adopted, any local land development plan that the state agency finds inconsistent with the state or regional plan is not entitled to any weight in support of the validity of any local government action.[143] Thus, once a state or regional plan is adopted, the local government can enforce a development timing mechanism only if its own local land development plan is consistent with the state or regional plan.

Under article seven of the Code, the state may become involved even more directly in certain types of land development decisions. Thus, certain portions of the state can be designated as "districts of critical state concern."[144] Certain types of development may be designated as "development of state or regional benefit,"[145] or as "large scale development."[146] If any application for a development permit is within an area so designated or involves development of the type designated, the local decision in regard to the development permit must include a consideration of the overall impact of the development on the surrounding region.[147] Additionally, such decisions are appealable to a state land adjudicatory board, which may review the local government's decision in regard to a regional impact of the development.[148] Under the system proposed by the Code, local governments could be authorized to use systems of development timing with confidence that they would fit into an overall state or regional planning system.[149]

---

140. *See generally* ALI MODEL LAND DEVELOPMENT CODE § 8-102 (Tent. Draft No. 3, 1971).

141. *Id.*

142. *See id.* § 8-405(2) & note. This section provides that such plans are adopted when they have been submitted to the legislature and no action is taken to disapprove the plan within ninety days. At the annual meeting of the American Law Institute in 1971, however, it was agreed that the next draft of the Code would include two alternative proposals for methods of adopting the plans; the first being a full scale submission to the legislature for approval; the second being an adoption of the plan by gubernatorial action without any legislative approval. Future drafts of the Code will contain these three alternatives.

143. *Id.* § 8-502 (3).

144. *Id.* § 7-201.

145. *Id.* § 7-301.

146. *Id.* § 7-401.

147. *Id.* § 7-502.

148. *Id.* §§ 7-701 to 704.

149. Although the Model Code is still over a year away from publication of a final draft, the state of Florida recently passed the Environmental Land and Water Management Act of 1972, FLA. STAT. ch. 380 (Supp. 1972), which provides for supervision

Federal legislation currently pending in Congress would provide grants-in-aid to the states to work on state and regional planning programs containing similar types of control by state or regional agencies over local decisions. On June 21, 1973, the Senate passed S. 268;[150] similar legislation is under consideration by the House Interior Committee and passage is expected in the 1973 session of Congress. The legislation is expected to contain provisions requiring the states to establish some system to ensure that development of state or regional benefit is not excluded through the actions of local governments.

The trends clearly seem to indicate that state legislation will increasingly give state or regional agencies a supervisory role over major land use decisions made by local governments. Whether or not this legislation follows the format of the ALI model, it appears likely that some form of state supervision will be a key element of future legislation.

IX. Conclusion

Local government's assertion of the power to undertake development timing might be at least partly beneficial if any of three conditions existed: an effective system of regional planning, an extensive program of land banking, or detailed judicial scrutiny of the effects of development timing. None of these now exists. Consequently, authorizing local governments to exercise development timing power might be analogized to giving dynamite to a baby. It is a risky business, but at least it induces the parents to watch the child more closely.

---

by the state planning agency of areas of critical state concern and development of regional impact in a manner similar to article seven of Tentative Draft Number Three.

150.   119 CONG. REC. 11655 (1973). For legislative history see *Hearings on S. 3354 Before the Senate Comm. on Interior and Insular Affairs,* 91st Cong., 2d Sess., pts. 1 & 2 (1970); *Hearings on S. 632 and S. 992 Before the Senate Comm. on Interior and Insular Affairs,* 92nd Cong., 1st Sess., pts. 1 & 2 (1971); *Hearings on S. J. Res. 52 and Title II of S. 1618 Before the Subcomm. on Housing and Urban Affairs of the Comm. on Banking, Housing and Urban Affairs,* 92d Cong., 1st Sess., pts. 1 & 2 (1971).

16

Jerome Rose

FROM THE LEGISLATURES: PROPOSED DEVELOPMENT RIGHTS LEGISLATION CAN CHANGE THE NAME OF THE LAND INVESTMENT GAME

Proposed Development Rights Legislation Can Change the Name of the Land Investment Game

Legislation has been introduced into the Maryland legislature (Senate Bill No. 254, 1972) and similar legislation is being considered in a number of other states, including New Jersey, that could change the current basic rules of land investment and development. The proposed legislation seeks to control land development and preserve open space by the use of a legal concept, well-known to the British, called *development rights*.

The legislation does not create development rights; a development right has always existed as one of the numerous rights included in the ownership of real property. It may be compared to mineral rights (i.e., the right to mine and remove minerals from the land) or to air rights (i.e., the right to utilize the air space above

the surface of the land). A development right is nothing more than the right that permits an owner to build upon or to develop his land.

As one of the many rights of land ownership, it is subject to reasonable regulation under the police power and is also subject to the governmental power of eminent domain. It may be separated from other rights and regulated by government or sold by the owner and transferred separately. For example, an owner of land may sell his mineral rights or air rights and still retain ownership and use of the surface of the land. Similarly, an owner may sell his development rights separately while continuing to own and use the land for such purposes as farming. The development rights, once sold, may be conveyed to and from persons other than the owner of the remaining rights to the land.

Development rights legislation seeks to utilize the separability and transferability of development rights as the basis of a technique to induce owners of undeveloped land to preserve their land in open space. The owners of *preserved open space land* are compensated for their deprivation of use by the sale of development rights to developers of other land in the jurisdiction. To make such sales possible it is necessary to establish a system that creates a market for development rights in which owners of *developable land* must buy development rights from owners of *preserved open space land* as a prerequisite for development.

Development rights legislation seeks to create such a market with any one of many variations on the following system:

(1) Each local government would prepare a land use plan that specifies the percentage of remaining undeveloped land in the jurisdiction and that designates the land to remain undeveloped as *preserved open space land*. The land use plan would also designate the land to be developed and would specify the uses to which the developable land may be put. A zoning law would be enacted to implement this plan.

(2) The planning board of each local government would prescribe the number of development rights required for each housing unit and for each square foot of commercial and industrial space to be developed. On the basis of this numerical assignment the planning board would then compute the number of residential, commercial, and industrial rights required to develop the jurisdiction in accordance with the land use plan. (Other legislative proposals are limited to residential development.) The local government would issue certificates of development rights (ownership of which would be recorded) in the exact amount so determined.

(3) Every owner of undeveloped land in the jurisdiction would receive certificates of development rights in an amount that represents the percentage of acreage (or assessed value) of his undeveloped land to the total acreage (or assessed value) of all undeveloped land in the jurisdiction. (An alternate plan would give development rights *only* to owners of *preserved open space land*.)

(4) An owner of *developable land,* who does not have enough development rights to fully develop his land would have to buy additional development rights, on the open market, from those who have acquired such rights from either original distribution or subsequent purchase.

(5) Thus, owners of *preserved open space land* would be able to sell their development rights to owners of *developable land*. In return for the compensation derived from this sale, owners of *preserved open space land* will have sold their rights to develop their land in the future. Their land will thus be preserved in open space and the owners will have been compensated without any capital costs to government.

(6) Development rights will be

subject to ad valorem property taxation as a component of the total assessed value of the developable real property in the jurisdiction.

To attorneys for investors in and developers of raw land, development rights legislation may become a source of many novel and interesting legal questions. A sampling follows:

(1) Does the deprivation of the right to develop *preserved open space land* constitute a harsh and unreasonable exercise of the police power in violation of the due process clause of the Fourteenth Amendment? Does the substitution of certificates of development rights for the right to develop overcome this objection?

(2) Does the deprivation of the right to develop *preserved open space land* constitute a de facto "taking" within the meaning of the federal and state eminent domain provisions? Does the substitution of certificates of development rights constitute "just compensation" within the meaning of those provisions?

(3) What is the value of *devel-opable land* for the purpose of tax assessments and eminent domain when the owner of the land also owns sufficient certificates of development rights for intensive development? What is the value of certificates of development rights for tax assessment purposes when the owner does not also own *developable land?*

(4) To what extent will conveyances of real property be complicated by the separation of development rights from the rest of the fee?

The answers to the above and numerous other questions must await enactment of specific legislation. This column is intended to be an early warning of the creation of a new device of land use regulation that has captured the imagination and enthusiasm of many urban planners and promises to provide new challenges and opportunities for investors in and developers of raw land. After passage of development rights legislation, the *Real Estate Law Journal* will provide a more detailed anlysis of the legal issues arising therefrom.

VI

Greater Regional Control and Intervention

17

Paul Davidoff and Neil N. Gold

THE SUPPLY AND AVAILABILITY OF LAND FOR HOUSING FOR LOW- AND MODERATE-INCOME FAMILIES (excerpts)

Eliminating Legal and Institutional Barriers to Equality of Access to Land and Housing

Eliminating racial discrimination in housing will not in itself bring about an end to racial segregation in our urban areas. Access to land and housing is not to be understood as involving only equality of opportunity in regard to the existing housing supply. It involves also the elimination of legal and institutional barriers that in the name of the conservation of municipal expenditures prohibit the development of low- and moderate-cost housing on the bulk of the metropolitan vacant land supply. Preeminent among these barriers are zoning ordinances, subdivision regulations, and building codes, which:

1. Raise the price of land and housing beyond the financial reach of families in need of adequate shelter, and beyond the financial reach of low- and moderate-income families generally.
2. Preclude construction or emplacement of housing types that are necessary to meet the shelter requirements posed by households of varying sizes and incomes.
3. Reduce the holding capacity of in-lying vacant residential land through low-density zoning, which effectively excludes 75 to 80 percent of families in need of shelter from access to the urban land base.

Strategies to overcome the disabling effects of fiscally motivated zoning ordinances, subdivision regulations, and building codes must involve a realignment of authority and responsibility for the enactment and administration of these land use and housing controls. This is not to say that localities should have no voice in the promulgation of reasonable land use standards. It is to say that the test of reasonableness must be based upon a metropolitan rather than a local definition of the term.

In the case of zoning ordinances, the process of defining reasonable standards would involve, first, the making of annual surveys of housing needs for metropolitan areas in terms of race, income, and household size of needy households; second, as in Chapters I to III, metropolitan housing needs should be plotted against the metropolitan supply of vacant residential land to draw up a balance sheet, so to speak, that relates the impact of local zoning policies to metropolitan housing problems.

A third step would involve developing a series of projections as to the future holding capacity of various sectors of the metropolitan area. Holding capacity, as used here, does not refer to the zoned capacity of a particular section, but, rather, to the physical capacity of the land for residential development, taking into account, soil conditions, access to transportation, topography, and so forth.

The fourth step would involve development of model zoning, subdivision, and building codes that set forth assigned densities for every community in the metropolitan area, with slight variations in density permitted on the basis of previous land use trends, and differences in assigned holding capacity. Wherever possible, however, minimum lot size requirements should be uniform for topographically similar areas. The objective would be to eliminate the competition between communities for high-valuation development by removing the mechanisms whereby such high-valuation development is rendered inevitable.

In the case of restrictive and costly building codes, a slightly different approach to the problem of cost reduction is called for. As we pointed out in Chapter IV, many areas of the country have already adopted so-called Model Building Codes that are based upon performance standards. Too often, however, the administration of these codes and their gaps in coverage compromise the intent of the legislation. For this reason, an effort should be made to further simplify building codes to accelerate the introduction of new materials and new processes as they become available.

Shifting responsibility and authority over zoning from municipalities to counties and metropolitanwide agencies raises serious questions as to the substance of the powers to be granted to these higher levels of government. Should county and metropolitanwide agencies be empowered to preempt local zoning? Or, should they be given only review and approval powers over municipal planning and zoning actions? Second, is it politically realistic to attempt a shifting of responsibility in the area of zoning away from local government? Third, what is the nature of the sanctions that would have to be employed by county or metropolitan zoning agencies to secure local acceptance of imposed changes in residential holding capacity? One alternative would be for the states to enact legislation providing for county review and approval of municipal zoning and planning action for municipalities of say, 50,000 population. A second would involve the enactment of state legislation authorizing metropolitan planning agencies to review and approve local zoning and planning policies in line with existing or proposed metropolitan land use, transportation, or housing plans. Still a third alternative would involve the enactment of state legislation creating new areawide land development agencies empowered to regulate all phases of land use and development with a metropolitan area.

One of the virtues of the first alternative is that by vesting authority at the county level instead of at a more distant governmental level, opposition to loss of local control over zoning might be considerably reduced. Adoption of the second alternative would entail the risk of granting metropolitan planning agencies more power than they would be able to employ effectively; for it is common knowledge that metropolitan planning agencies are by and large politically ineffective in overcoming the parochial self-interests of their constituent public bodies. The third alternative, the creation of areawide land development agencies, would require a degree of commitment to metropolitanwide solutions to intraurban social and economic disparities that is not likely to be present in most suburban communities, for reasons intrinsic to the competitive nature of local government in urban areas.

With regard to possible sanctions that could be employed to secure local acceptance of compulsory zoning changes, it is likely that nothing short of preemption of the zoning power or the withholding of needed Federal and state aid could convince localities to change their zoning ordinances to facilitate racial and income desegregation in the metropolitan area.

Assuming that a state determines to vest authority over zoning, subdivision regulations, and building codes in metropolitanwide or county agencies, what standards should be promulgated by these agencies in attempting to bring about a fair balance in population and land use in a given metropolitan area?

1. Minimum lot sizes for single-family dwellings should be limited to a half acre, except in nonurbanized portions of metropolitan areas. Other forms of density zoning, such as elimination of multi-family housing from an entire district, should also be eliminated, particularly in metropolitan areas suffering from a shortage of low- and moderate-cost housing.

2. Minimum house size requirements and occupance permits that control the number of persons who can legally reside in a dwelling unit should also be eliminated, unless it can be shown that they serve to protect the public health and safety. In such cases, the burden of proof would lie with the municipalities.

3. Communities should not be permitted to zone out certain structural building types that can make significant additions to the supply of low- and moderate-cost housing. Of particular importance is the need to rule out prohibitions against development of all forms of low-density multi-family housing from suburban areas.

4. Mobile homes should be permitted throughout suburban areas in so-called mobile home parks, in which the mobility is sacrificed for larger lot sizes and permanent placement. Municipalities should also be denied the opportunity to prohibit trailer parks or other forms of accommodations for mobile homes from their jurisdictions.

5. The principle of maximum access between homes and jobs should be required to be placed in all zoning ordinances so that communities that seek to encourage the development of new industrial growth would be compelled to permit the development of new moderate-cost worker housing reasonably close to the job sites.

Minimum lot sizes have been increasing steadily in recent years to the point where the bulk of the land supply in some of the nation's largest urban areas is reserved for very low density single-family home construction. To the extent that these increasing lot sizes represent the actual desires of the American people, a case can be made for maintaining them intact in areas not suffering from a housing shortage or from substantial substandard dwellings. However, there is some doubt as to the views of the American people on this question. The University of Michigan's Survey Research Center, in a report issued some years ago on the housing desires of the American people, found that 85 percent of American families wanted to live in free-standing, single-family homes, on lots of up to half an acre. Yet, as we have seen, lot sizes are increasing so rapidly in suburban areas that one-acre, two-acre, and four-acre zones are now quite common. In the New York region, as we have seen, more than half of the zoned vacant land supply is reserved for single-family homes on lots of more than half an acre. Not only do these high minimum lot size requirements increase raw land costs, land development costs, and housing costs in urban areas, but, by sharply decreasing residential densities, they threaten to create artificial land shortages in the nation's urban areas.

For all of these reasons we question whether density controls constitute a valid use of the police power in urban areas. In our view the adoption of a reasonable lot size requirement of say, half an acre, better comports with the growing demand for urban land, while, at the same time, posing no threat to those who wish to purchase more than one lot to maintain privacy and exclusiveness.

Minimum house size requirements also constitute an arbitrary method of regulating the type of household that may be permitted to reside in political jurisdiction or neighborhood. In the name of upholding standards, high minimum house size requirements serve mainly to prevent the development of the type of housing that was instrumental in alleviating the housing crisis of the late 1940's, that is, the bungalow type structure with 800- and 900-square-foot interior space designed for the nuclear family, with the possibility of adding more rooms at a later date. In our view, government has a positive responsibility to foster the development of a variety of house sizes that can accommodate the many types and sizes of families that prefer to live in free-standing single-family homes. To the extent that minimum house size requirements impede the development of such a variety of house sizes, they bar effective resolution of metropolitan housing problems.

Still more critical from the point of view of the unmet housing needs of low- and moderate-

income families are the numerous and subtle devices whereby communities exclude precisely those types of dwelling units that can accommodate families of restricted incomes. The word subtle is chosen to illustrate the fact that few zoning ordinances specifically exclude low-density multi-family housing, which can be developed at reasonable costs, from their communities. However, by overzoning for single-family housing, these communities put a premium on land that is zoned for multi-family development, thereby creating pressures for high-density high-rise zones in which land costs can be allocated over a larger number of dwelling units. This type of situation makes it extremely difficult for multi-family builders to bring in units at rents or prices affordable by low- or moderate-income families, with the result that new housing tends to be limited to costly single-family units and equally costly multi-family units.

An example of more direct exclusion of low- and moderate-cost housing is provided by zoning ordinances that prohibit families from living in mobile homes, whether on single lots or in mobile home parks. Yet mobile homes constitute one of the least costly forms of housing in the United States. A fully furnished 700-square-foot mobile home, for example, may be purchased for less than $5,000. Similarly, a fully furnished 1,400-square-foot mobile home—equivalent to a large four-bedroom single-family house—may be purchased for less than $9,000: this should be compared with $20,000 and $30,000 price tags on equivalent nonmobile homes. However, for what can best be described as snob reasons, municipalities from one end of the country to the other exclude mobile homes from their jurisdictions. Again, the intent is to uphold standards. In our view, mobile homes ought to be permitted in every section of every metropolitan area, and their wider use ought to receive encouragement from public agencies. Certainly, local government should not be permitted to exclude such units for arbitrary reasons.

Finally, the inclusion of the principle of maximum access between homes and jobs in all zoning ordinances is critical to the development of needed job-linked housing programs in the nation's metropolitan areas. Precedent for this recommendation exists in the statement on findings of the Demonstration Cities and Metropolitan Development Act of 1966, and in the *Guidelines*, issued by the Department of Housing and Urban Development for the legislation in which recognition is given to the need to overcome housing and job location imbalances in urban areas and also to the need to revise zoning ordinances and other laws and regulations that impede resolution of program objectives, among which is "better access between homes and jobs." At a minimum, the adoption of this proposal could result in local acknowledgment of responsibility for building housing along with jobs in land-rich sections of metropolitan areas. At a maximum, it could lead to comprehensive planning for manpower and housing development for a section or for the whole of a metropolitan area.

Before concluding this section on strategies to eliminate legal and institutional barriers to the development of low- and moderate-cost housing, we should point out that financial incentives must be provided to communities that will be affected by an influx of new families in order not to tax unfairly the existing residents of the community. Such incentives should take the form of tax structure awards for radically and economically inclusive land use planning. The specifics of these incentive proposals are discussed in our section on proposals to aid in the diffusion of population.

Reducing Land Development Costs

Since land development costs play a major role in pricing the bulk of the urban land supply beyond the reach of low- and moderate-cost housing developers, proposals to lower land development costs are a necessary element in promoting equality of access to urban land and housing. It will come as no surprise to learn that subdivision regulations and building codes tend to shift backward to the purchasers of new houses costs that in many cases are properly public, but which, because of their expense, cannot and will not be borne by local governments. This is somewhat different, at least in degree, from the attempt of many suburban communities to secure sidewalks, decorative street lighting, wide access roads, storm sewers, and so forth, from developers of new housing, and also from the equally prevalent attempt of many communities to have developers dedicate land for open space, parks, schools, and other public purposes. In these latter instances there is doubt as to the fairness of requiring such abrogation of property rights as the price for securing a building permit.

Reducing the land development costs in suburban areas requires a threefold strategy:

1. Reduction in the width (frontage) of building lots, either through lowering minimum lot size standards, or through developing cluster zoning or planned unit developments in lieu of free-standing single-family homes on large lots.

2. Preemption of local powers over subdivision regulations, and the vesting of such powers in county, state, or metropolitan-wide agencies authorized to prescribe uniform subdivision regulations based upon generally accepted definitions of the public as well as the private aspects of the preparation of residential land.

3. Absorption by state and/or Federal agencies of all or part of the cost of land preparation in low- and moderate-cost housing developments in suburban areas (for which precedent exists in the inclusion of land development costs as eligible project expenses in connection with Title I urban renewal grant programs).

Implementation of this strategy could reduce the costs of land development for single-family homes to the point where these expenditures would account for no more than 8 or 10 percent of total housing costs. The elements of this strategy apply as well to the problem of land development controls in multi-family housing. The proliferating tendency for suburban communities to require multi-family developers to provide high land requirements per unit, in addition to full fireproofing, covered garages, black-top paving, and utility piping, to say nothing of elevators, pools, solaria, playgrounds, and so forth, has already raised site costs in some suburban multi-family housing developments to single-family site cost levels. Hence, the promulgation of uniform subdivision regulations and building codes covering multi-family as well as single-family developments could prevent communities from imposing upon developers the obligation to provide such amenities, thereby opening new lands to low- and moderate-cost housing developers otherwise excluded from such areas.

The local character of the housing construction industry, in particular, the fact that most builders operate entirely within one metropolitan area, suggests that uniform subdivision regulations would tend to equalize land development costs for comparable housing types within a metropolitan area. However, the widespread practice of withholding approval of applications for building permits, as a means of compelling land on the outskirts of the nation's major central cities, compared with the unavailability of vacant residential land within these cities, and on the other, the seemingly universal desire of families with young children to live in low-density environments that are, by and large, not reproduceable within these large central cities.

While the imbalance in land supply will insure that central city populations will not increase substantially in the coming years, it is difficult to predict the population changes that may take place in these cities as a result of the movement of rural families, particularly Negro and Puerto Rican families, from the farms to the cities. In the long run, if present land use patterns are permitted to continue it is likely that Negroes, Puerto Ricans, Mexican Americans, and other minority groups, such as the elderly and the white poor, will come to dominate the populations of the major central cities, with severe economic consequences for these groups, for the cities in which they live, and for the nation as a whole. For concomitant with the continuing movement of middle-income families out of the cities will occur the continuing movement of blue-collar and gray-collar jobs and economic opportunities away from these cities to more economically advantaged sections of the metropolitan area and of the nation. Thus, it is not solely a matter of freedom of choice whether the concentration of these minority groups in central cities should be permitted to continue. Far more than is currently recognized, the diffusion of population generally, but of disadvantaged groups in particular, throughout suburban parts of metropolitan areas has passed beyond the realm of freedom of choice. The real issue, as we view the problem, is whether the postwar trends in employment and population location can be reversed. If not, if industry cannot be brought back in sufficient numbers to overcome the loss of jobs it may become necessary to develop new courses of action to bring together within reasonable distances of each other jobs and people who need jobs in our urban centers.

The question of the concentration of population in urban configurations as a whole is perhaps more significant in terms of its long-range impact upon American life than is the builder acquiescence to the construction of these amenities, would have to be faced. Accordingly, we propose:

1. An amendment to state zoning enabling legislation to abrogate the powers of local governments to withhold building permits from prospective developers meeting all necessary zoning, building code, and subdivision requirements, for a period in excess of six weeks.

2. A further amendment reducing the discretionary power of local planning and zoning commissions to authorize multi-family housing only on a conditional or special basis, thereby avoiding the need to create a permitted multi-family zone.

3. A further amendment establishing de facto multi-family residential zones in any zoning district that contains 10 percent or more of a community's post-1950 multi-family housing supply. The purpose of these amendments would be to unmask the subterfuges by which multi-family units are placed in more desirable single-family zones by special permission of the local planning and zoning agency in return for builder agreement to abide by the subdivision regulations desired by local officials.

18

Fred Bosselman and David Callies

THE QUIET REVOLUTION IN LAND USE CONTROLS (excerpts)

Hawaiian Land Use Law

Hawaii began the quiet revolution in land use control by passing its Land Use Law in 1961. The primary motive of the draftsmen was to preserve Hawaii's agricultural land. On the island of Oahu much of the state's best agricultural land came under tremendous pressure from developers as the City of Honolulu expanded greatly during the 1950's. Further concern over the urban sprawl that would result from future expansion of the City of Honolulu was another major motivating factor in the adoption of the Land Use Law.

The Land Use Law created a state Land Use Commission and directed it to divide the entire state into four districts-- conservation, agricultural, rural and urban. Land in the urban district was to be used for whatever purpose was permitted under the local zoning regulations. Land in the agricultural and rural districts were to be used only in compliance with the regulations of the state Land Use Commission. Lands in the conservation district were to comply with the regulations of the state Department of Land and Natural Resources.

The Land Use Commission controls urban growth by drawing the boundaries of the urban districts. Only land so zoned is available for any intensive form of development. Although the Commission has in theory included enough land in the urban district to meet future needs for a 10-year period, in fact it appears that much of the vacant land zoned urban is not readily available at prices developers are willing to pay. Consequently, the Commission receives a large number of petitions from developers seeking the rezoning of land from agricultural or conservation to the urban district classifica- tion.

The Commission's decisions on such applications constitute the most controversial aspect of the regulatory program. Developers complain that insufficient land is

285

available for housing, while conservationists grumble that
too little land is being preserved for agricultural and
conservation purposes.

It is probably to the Commission's credit that it
is not too popular with either the builders or the conservationists. While its actions have not been based on clearly
enunciated planning policies, it would appear that the
Commission is attempting to reconcile three basic planning
principles: (1) prime agricultural land should be preserved
for agricultural use; (2) tourist-oriented development should
be encouraged without disturbing the attractions of the natural
landscape; and (3) compact and efficient urban areas should be
provided where people can live at reasonable cost.

Since tourism has clearly replaced agriculture as
the major source of income to the state, it can be argued that
the importance of preserving agricultural lands has lessened
in the past 10 years. Nevertheless, the importance of preserving agricultural land is a principle that has received strong
acceptance by the Hawaiian public, and although the long-run
competitive position of Hawaiian sugar and pineapple on world
markets may be questionable, crop production presently provides
employment for a large portion of the population.

Conservationists also support the principle of preserving agricultural land, not so much for its economic impact,
but because of the development that would take place if the
preservation of agricultural land were abandoned. Their opposition to development has increased substantially, particularly
in recent years with the boom in the tourist industry. To the
dismay of the more ardent environmentalists in their number,
the Law has been administered in a manner that strongly
encourages the development of tourist facilities in many
natural or agricultural areas of the state. While the state
has attempted to control such development in ways calculated
to preserve the natural environment, many conservationists
argue that these controls nevertheless have been insufficiently
strict to accomplish their purpose.

In deciding applications for rezoning, the Commission
has attempted to confine new development to narrow areas immediately adjacent to the existing urban districts. This policy
of restricted urban limits has succeeded in avoiding the type
of urban sprawl so typical in many parts of the country.
While the Commission has granted one new town proposal somewhat
removed from Honolulu, and is considering two others, general
development has progressed only through the progressive widening of the boundaries of urban Honolulu.

Opponents of this narrow urban limits policy argue
that it has seriously increased the cost of housing. Developers
are forced to purchase land on the immediate outskirts of
Honolulu. By thus creating a shortage of land the narrow urban
limits policy has increased its value and forced development

onto the slopes of the mountains, where site improvement costs are extremely high. The land shortage has furthermore resulted in an absence of competition, thereby encouraging each segment of the housing industry to increase its profit margins. The overall consequence is that housing costs in Hawaii are more than double the national average.

Conservationists argue, however, that this increase in housing costs is a small price to pay for preserving the natural environment of the state. The destruction of the beautiful Hawaiian scenery, they argue, would not only destroy the island's mainstay tourist industry, but also make the state an undesirable place to live at any price. Furthermore, high housing costs could serve as a brake on a rapid increase in immigration, which they fear will reduce the state's desirability as a place to live.

Strong conflicts between development and conserva- tion are inherent in Hawaii's present condition. The Land Use Law provides a mechanism by which the state can resolve these conflicts according to a statewide policy. The decision-making process would probably be more effective, however, if more closely tied to a state planning process that provided the regulators with more current data and better analyses of the relevant policy considerations.

Vermont Environmental Control Law

A boom in second homes and ski resorts that accompanied the construction of interstate highways created a growing concern about the impact of this recreational explosion on the rural character traditionally associated with Vermont. The result was the adoption in 1970 of a com- prehensive Environmental Control Law (Act 250) creating an Environmental Board, assisted by seven regional commissions, which passes on all major proposals for development in the state. Any residential subdivision involving lots of less than 10 acres, any commercial or industrial development of substantial size, and any development above the elevation of 2500 feet requires a permit from the Environmental Board. Applications for permits are reviewed by an Agency 250 Review Committee, consisting of representatives of certain state agencies. This Committee then sends recommendations to one of the seven district commissions, which holds a public hear- ing, at which comments may also be offered by local or regional planning commissions. The district commission's decision is based on a series of rather general environmental criteria spelled out in the statute, and may be appealed to the Environmental Board.

The Environmental Control Law further requires the adoption of a series of statewide plans which will become additional criteria for decisions on applications for permits. The first such plan, an interim land capability plan, was produced by the State Planning Office in the summer of 1971 and is currently pending adoption by the Environmental Board. This plan provides a preliminary classification of the lands of the state by physical limitations on development, capability for agriculture, forestry or mining, and the existence of unique or fragile environmental conditions. By 1973 two additional plans will be prepared which will provide even more comprehensive criteria for determining desirable locations for development.

Since the Vermont Environmental Control Law has been in effect for only two years, and decisions to date have not been based on the contemplated statewide plans, it is obviously too early to obtain any final evaluation on the Law's operation. The Law's careful attempt to insure that future regulation will be based on comprehensive state planning is a laudable goal, but it means that the full operation of the Law will be delayed until the completion of the planning process.

At the present time the Board's work consists primarily of requiring the environmental upgrading of development by attaching conditions to permits. The Board has been attempting to promote some interim planning policies, such as the creation of broad greenbelts alongside the interstate highways, but its consideration of individual applications has reflected more the existing policies of other state agencies than any overall comprehensive view of future growth.

The mixture of enforcement and persuasion in the administration of the Vermont Law is evident from the Ryder Pond case. A District Commission denied an application for permission to drain and dredge a beaver pond pursuant to the creation of a recreational lake, to be developed in aid of a residential construction project. An appeal was taken to the Environmental Board, but before arguments were heard the head of the Agency 250 Review Board convinced the developer that the cost of creating the recreational lake would exceed his increased profit from selling lakefront lots. Moreover, as an "old Vermonter," the developer was persuaded to develop around the pond, thus preserving a piece of "original Vermont" which would in itself have value to would-be home purchasers.

The Vermont Law appears to provide an efficient administrative process in which both local and state interests can participate. The combination of this regulatory process with an extensive planning program offers the potential of a well-reasoned framework for evaluating development proposals. Whether this potential will be realized will depend on the quality of the plans that will evolve over the next two years.

San Francisco Bay Conservation and Development Commission

In the early 1960's public attention was drawn to

the rate at which San Francisco Bay was being filled by developers. In 1965 the legislature created a San Francisco Bay Conservation and Development Commission and authorized it to prepare a plan for the future of San Francisco Bay. The Commission completed this plan in 1969 and submitted it to the legislature. The legislature responded by adopting the plan and requiring that anyone seeking to develop within or along the shoreline of the Bay must obtain a permit from the Commission.

The San Francisco Bay plan is a model of organization and readability. By focusing on the Bay and its immediate shoreline the plan kept the issues easily comprehensible to the public, thereby attracting broad support. By offering a well-reasoned program that balanced both conservation and development it defused much of the potential opposition.

The Commission's primary power is to pass on all proposed development in or along the Bay. The Commission has taken a rather firm position opposing all development for other than water-oriented uses. This has brought it into conflict with a number of the local governments in the Bay area which have sought to promote development for a variety of other purposes. An early controversy with the City of Oakland was settled through a compromise that was not wholly acceptable to conservationists in the Bay area. A current controversy between the Commission and the City of San Francisco, however, finds the Commission showing strong opposition to San Francisco's hopes to redevelop its waterfront area. The Commission has flatly denied permission for construction of a hotel-office-recreational complex known as Ferry Port Plaza, on the ground that most uses in the project are not water-oriented. The city, county, and port of San Francisco--but not the developer--have all filed suits to compel the issuance of a permit.

But the disputes that have surfaced do not reflect the true impact of the Commission. The mere creation of the Commission forestalled development proposals that would have involved miles of shoreland and the filling of many thousands of acres of Bay land--proposals on which substantial planning had already been completed but which have never been formally tendered.

The San Francisco Bay Conservation and Development Commission has been extremely successful in achieving the purposes for which it was created. In the long run, however, a more comprehensive approach is needed. The crucial question is whether the Commission's success can lead to systems of state or regional planning and regulation that have broader goals, or whether it will become merely a regulatory version of a single-function special district.

Twin Cities Metropolitan Council

As in many metropolitan regions, the Minneapolis-

St. Paul region experienced a housing and population boom
after World War II. Area-wide problems such as sewage
disposal, public transportation, pollution and police
protection were being inadequately handled at the local
government level. Sewage disposal in particular reached
crisis proportions in 1959 when it was discovered that a
substantial portion of wells in the area were drawing from
recirculated sewage.

In 1967 the Minnesota Legislature created the
Metropolitan Council of the Twin Cities Area as an administrative agency to coordinate the planning and development of
the metropolitan area. The Council is directed to prepare
a comprehensive plan for the region and implement this plan
by coordinating the proposals for most major public facilities
to be constructed by government agencies in the region.
Several segments of this plan, called the Development Guide,
are already prepared and binding upon the various agencies
required to submit plans to the Council.

The key to the Council's regulatory power lies
in its authority to review plans of various agencies, such
as the Metropolitan Sewer Board, which may not act without
an approved plan. The Council also has some rather inadequate powers to delay certain other plans, such as those
submitted by counties and municipalities in the metropolitan
region, upon which it is required to pass. The Council also
has the power to pass on private land use proposals within
a substantial area around the site of the new airport
which is to be proposed for the Twin Cities region.

The Council's power to thus coordinate the construction of public facilities remains far from complete,
however. While the Metropolitan Sewer Board has been
established as an agency of the Council, not all of the
Council's attempts to obtain control over similar major
agencies constructing public facilities in the region have
been successful. In particular, the Metropolitan Airports
Commission has steadfastly fought what it regards as Council
intrusion on its prerogatives. Moreover, with increasing
power the Council has found increasing friction with local
government. Rural portions of the metropolitan region feel
the Council is being used to promote urban programs at their
expense. Other local governments fear that the Council will
become increasingly involved in purely local affairs, despite
the Council's professed disinterest in such matters.

This increasing friction led to the defeat in the
1971 session of the legislature of the Council's proposals
to create a Metropolitan Housing Board and to expand the
functions of the Metropolitan Parks Board. The legislature
also refused to grant the Council increased control over
the relatively autonomous Metropolitan Airports Commission
and the Metropolitan Transit Commission. Highway planning
also remains relatively independent of the Council.

Finally, some legislators worry that they are creating an agency so powerful that it competes with the legislature itself. This concern, together with the opposition of local governments, was responsible for the defeat of the proposal to provide for direct election of members of the Council, in lieu of the present system by which members are appointed by the Governor from legislative districts.

The Council did achieve passage of one major piece of legislation in 1971--the fiscal disparaties bill which provides that each local government in the region must contribute 40% of the net growth of commercial and industrial property tax valuations after 1971 to the Council for redistribution to the various local governmental units according to population and need. Operation of this law will be viewed with interest throughout the country.

The Council clearly hopes to remain in the policy-making sphere and avoid being drawn into the implementation of functional programs on a day-to-day basis. But until the Council obtains a more complete system of land use control in the metropolitan region, the Council's power to implement its planning policies will remain somewhat limited.

Massachusetts Zoning Appeals Law

As in many other metropolitan areas, it is difficult to find land in the suburbs of Boston on which local regulations permit the construction of low- and moderate-income housing. This problem stimulated concern on the part of the state legislature that was manifested in the Massachusetts Zoning Appeals Law.

The Law authorizes developers of low-income housing to apply to local zoning appeal boards for a "comprehensive permit" in lieu of all other permits required under all other local regulations. If the application is denied, the developer can appeal to a Housing Appeals Committee created at the state level. The Appeals Committee is authorized to reverse the local decision if it was not "reasonable and consistent with local needs." This latter term is defined in the form of quotas which authorized the denial of a permit where the number of housing units or the total land area used for low-income housing would exceed certain percentages of the total number of housing units or land area in the town.

The drafting of the Law left a number of ambiguities, as even its proponents concede, for they have proposed amendatory legislation which would clarify the responsibilities of the local boards and the powers of the Appeals Committee. Despite these ambiguities, however, the state's Department of Community Affairs has moved forward to implement the Law as best it can, issuing regulations to clarify

the provisions of the Law. In its initial major decision,
Country Village Corporation v. Board of Appeals of the Town
of Hanover, the Appeals Committee ended 15 months of application and appeals by ruling in favor of the developer, while
interpreting the Law in a manner to avoid as many of the
legal complications as possible. This initial decision is
now being appealed to the courts.

Because many developers have refused to take advantage of the Zoning Appeals Law due to the doubts concerning its legal validity and interpretation, a court decision
will be of great benefit in encouraging increased use of the
Law. Even prior to such a decision, however, a substantial
number of additional communities have undertaken studies of
housing problems as a result of the Law's passage, and
others have taken appeals to the Committee. Nevertheless,
any real evaluation of the Law's merits must await either a
court decision or amendatory legislation clarifying the
way the Law is to operate.

Maine Site Location Law

In 1970 several firms proposed major oil terminals
in areas in the State of Maine where local governments had
adopted no land use regulations. Realizing how little protection it had against these developments, the state
responded by passing a package of environmental legislation
including a new Site Location Law that requires approval by
a state agency of certain types of new development.

The Law requires large commercial and industrial
developments to obtain permits from the State Environmental
Improvement Commission. Also covered by the bill are residential subdivisions in excess of 20 acres and other residential developments that would require effluent discharge
permits from the state.

In 1971 the Environmental Improvement Commission
was placed within a new Department of Environmental Protection
--an umbrella agency designed to coordinate all of the state's
functions in regard to environmental protection. Also included
within the Department is the Maine Land Use Regulation Commission, recently created to plan and regulate the use of land
in the "unorganized counties" which make up the largely unoccupied northern half of the state.

The Site Location Law operates with a meager budget
and small staff. Applicants are required to carry their
application forms around to a variety of other state agencies
to obtain their approval prior to the filing of the application.
Decisions of the Commission are to be based on the financial
capacity of the developer, the effect on traffic and the
natural environment, and the suitability of the soil conditions.

The Commission's first major test case was the application by Maine Clean Fuels, Inc. to build a large oil terminal in the Searsport area. The Commission rejected the proposal and the applicant has indicated that it may appeal. No other proposals for oil terminals have reached the application stage (except a preexisting proposal that the courts ruled exempt under a grandfather clause).

The Commission's real workload, however, has been the processing of permits for residential subdivisions. About 83% of the applications have been for the construction of housing, and about half of these were for seasonal housing. The Commission has granted most of these permits, but has attached conditions preventing the use of septic systems and otherwise encouraging a better quality of development. Home-builders suggest that these conditions have forced many small builders out of business, but on the other hand, the conservationists argue that the Commission has failed to adequately enforce the conditions attached to the permits.

In the long run the Site Location Law may be seen as more of a stopgap remedy than a permanent solution. The absence of any overall state planning process that provides a rational basis for regulation, and the reliance on clearly inadequate criteria for decision-making, must eventually weaken the program's effectiveness. The major question for the future is whether the state can expand the Site Location Law into a more comprehensive land regulatory system that leaves the local issues to local governments but deals with major development proposals in the framework of a broader conception of state planning than the current law contains.

Massachusetts Wetlands Protection Program

Beginning in 1963 Massachusetts adopted a series of statutes designed to control the development of both coastal and inland wetlands. The initial 1963 statute required the issuance of a state permit for any development in coastal wetlands areas. In 1965 the system was supplemented by a more comprehensive program of protective orders to be issued by the Massachusetts Department of Natural Resources. These protective orders define the boundaries of the coastal wetland areas and prohibit any development except under carefully controlled circumstances. The orders are filed in the title records and become binding restrictions on the use of land. To date about one-third of the state's coastal wetlands have been covered by protective orders and another one-third are in various stages of public hearings.

Tentative development orders are first prepared by field personnel of the Department. A public hearing is then held in the affected town and the individual landowners are given the opportunity to negotiate regarding the exact

boundary of the wetlands. Once negotiations with landowners
are complete, the Department's draftsmen plot the boundaries
of the order on copies of the local assessor's maps and
record these maps with copies of the written order as conservation restrictions against the land. If the landowner
fails to appeal within 90 days he forfeits his right to
challenge the order. In practice only about 20 owners of
the several thousand affected by coastal protective orders
have gone to court.

One case, however, has gone against the Department
in Massachusett's Superior Court, involving a 60-acre tract
held by a construction company. If the Supreme Judicial
Court sustains the decision, it could well trigger other
challenges. However, time is on the side of the Department.

Protection of the inland wetlands is governed by
two separate statutes, one requiring permits for development
on inland wetlands and the other paralleling the protective
order system of the coastal wetlands law. In neither case,
however, do the inland laws provide as complete protection.
The administration of the inland wetlands act has been
seriously hampered by the physical difficulty of locating
the inland wetlands which are estimated to occupy more than
300,000 acres scattered throughout the entire state. Permits
for filling inland wetlands may not be denied but may only be
conditioned to minimize damage to the natural environment.
Broad exemptions also weaken the inland permit law.

The system for adopting inland protective orders
is so cumbersome that the Department has not yet adopted its
first inland protective order. The statute defined inland
wetlands in a restrictive way with broad exemptions making
it difficult to determine the area validly affected by the
order. The act gives a one-year veto power to the local
governments in the area affected by the wetlands order.
Furthermore, the statute gives any objecting landowner the
right to veto a protective order merely by sending a regis-
tered letter to the Department within 90 days, thereby
requiring the Department to acquire the property by eminent
domain. Thus, the Inland Wetlands Act appears in reality
to be little more than an authorization to the Department
to negotiate with landowners for a voluntary sale or gift
of their development rights to the state.

Despite all these handicaps the Department is
planning to move ahead on the administration of the act and
has scheduled its initial public hearings. After the first
few orders have been processed it will determine whether the
act provides a workable method of regulation.

The protective order system of the Coastal Wetlands
Act provides much more protection than the permit requirements of either the inland or the coastal acts. Barring
unfavorable court decisions the coastal wetlands protective

orders should provide substantial future protection for the state's salt marshes.

Wisconsin Shoreland Protection Program

Wisconsin has long been noted for the water-oriented recreation associated with its more than 8,800 ponds and lakes and 1,500 streams and rivers. Increasing development of the shorelines of these lakes and rivers threatens to pollute the waters and destroy the scenic advantages that the state possesses.

In 1966 the state adopted a Water Resources Act which required counties to enact regulations for the protection of all shorelands in unincorporated areas. In cases where the counties failed to adopt such regulations the Act authorized the state Department of Natural Resources to impose its own regulations on the shorelands areas of the county.

The Department of Natural Resources prepared a model shoreland protection ordinance which has been used as the basis of regulation by many of the counties in the state. The ordinance controls filling and dredging, requires setbacks from shorelines, regulates the cutting of trees, and controls minimum lot areas in subdivisions that are not served by public sewers. It also authorizes the classification of shoreland areas into a number of use districts.

Although the Department has the authority to compel the adoption of shoreland protection ordinances, it has no authority to enforce them. The Department has worked closely with the county zoning administrators from around the state to insure that they are aware of the Department's goals and know what to look for in evaluating an application. Relations with the county legislative bodies, however, have not always been smooth. Some are unhappy that they must implement what they view as the state's regulations, thus taking the blame from landowners which they feel is more properly directed at the state. Thus, the county zoning administrator is often put in an uncomfortable position of enforcing regulations that do not have the enthusiastic support of his employer. The Department is concerned that this may lead to lax enforcement of the shoreland ordinances, and has supported proposals to require applications for variances under the ordinances to be reviewed by the Department. The Department has also sought authority to pay part of the salary of the county zoning administrators.

The shoreland protection program has succeeded in directing the attention of county governments toward the problems created by shoreland development, and has achieved a fair measure of success. All parties agree, however, that

the system is less than perfect and might well be replaced
by a more comprehensive program.

New England River Basins Commission

        The federal Water Resources Planning Act authorized
the creation of interstate River Basins Commissions to provide
coordinated water resources planning. The commissions are to
consist of representatives of various federal and state governments, and are to report to the cabinet level Water Resources
Council, which has the responsibility for guiding the nation's
planning effort in the water resources field. The New England
River Basins Commission was created in 1967 and has probably
the most extensive experience of any commission created under
the Act.

        The Commission consists of representatives from
10 federal departments, seven states and six interstate commissions, and a chairman appointed by the President. Federal
and interstate members are responsible to their parent agencies,
which usually have specific programs and goals that they wish
to be considered by the Commission. State representatives must
attempt to maintain contact with and present the views of all
of the various agencies within their state as well as the
metropolitan and local government interests in the state.

        The Commission has undertaken a number of studies
of particular problems such as flood plain regulation and
power plant siting. It also reviews and comments on individual projects and performs general coordinating and public
relations activities and provides for the exchange of information between agencies.

        Eventually, however, the Commission's main goal is
to create a comprehensive plan for coordinated federal-state
management of water and related land resources in the New
England region. At this point the Commission is still at an
early stage of preparing the various elements of the plan.
The element of the plan that has proceeded the farthest is
the Connecticut River Basin Plan which has been circulated
in draft form. The first draft was primarily based on an
extensive study that had been begun by the Corps of Engineers
prior to the creation of the Commission and was continued
under the Commission's jurisdiction but with the Corps of
Engineers continuing to do most of the work. The initial
draft was rather severely criticized by a citizen review
committee appointed by the Commission which felt that the
plan was too strongly oriented toward the building of structures by the Corps of Engineers. The citizen committee
recommended greater emphasis on land use controls to minimize
flood damage by preventing construction in flood plains. As
a result of the citizen's committee report, the Commission
is proposing an extensive additional study of the basin to
provide a more comprehensive basis for planning.

Based on its past experience the Commission is shifting away from a watershed-oriented approach toward a state-by-state approach. It intends to prepare a plan for each of the individual states within the region in order to facilitate adoption by the states of the Commission's recommendations and give the states greater incentive for participation in commission activities. It anticipates that future planning will more strongly emphasize non-structural and environmental matters and will involve more participation by public officials and citizens in all stages of the planning process. It has found that although state boundaries do not necessarily make sense from a geographical standpoint, the programs necessary to implement plans are controlled at the state level, and only plans recognizing the existence of state boundaries can be easily implemented by the states.

The Commission suffers from the lack of any formal controls to ensure implementation of its plans and its suggestions for coordination. Its recommendations are advisory only and are disregarded more frequently than the Commission would like. Substantial reevaluation of the Commission's structure and powers is required if it is to be an effective planning and regulatory instrument.

Other Innovative Legislation

The nine programs studied in detail do not make up the entire output of recent innovative state legislation involving land use control. A number of other laws might be characterized as "critical area legislation" designed to control the use of land in particular sections of the state, and similar in that respect to the San Francisco and Wisconsin statutes.

The Tahoe Regional Planning Agency, though a bi-state agency created by interstate compact, is an example of the critical area approach. The Agency was empowered to adopt a development plan for the Tahoe Basin and implement this plan with land use regulations. Although the Agency has been buffeted by strong conflicts over the desirability of development and conservation in the Basin, it expects to adopt a plan and implementing regulations by the end of 1971.

The Hackensack Meadowlands Development Commission offers another approach toward critical areas. The Hackensack Meadowlands are largely undeveloped wetlands just across the Hudson River from Manhattan. The State of New Jersey created a Hackensack Meadowlands Development Commission with the responsibility of preparing a plan and exercising control over all development in the Meadowlands. The Commission has released a proposed master plan recommending that a substantial segment of the area be placed in a marshland conservation zone, and that other portions of the area are to be reserved

for high-density housing, industrial facilities, and a variety
of other uses.

In 1971 the New York Legislature created an Adirondack Park Agency responsible for the preparation of a
comprehensive plan for the use of land in Adirondack Park,
much of which is privately owned. Until the plan is completed
the Agency has interim regulatory powers to prohibit development that would have a substantial and lasting adverse impact
on the park. When finally adopted the master plan is to
establish regulations to control the intensity of land use
and development in each portion of the area.

Delaware, in response to proposals to build new oil
terminal facilities in the state, passed a Coastal Zone Act
which seeks to prohibit new heavy industry along the entire
coast of the state. Requests for permits are made to the
State Planning Office whose decisions may be appealed to a
newly created State Coastal Industrial Board.

A number of other states have created land use
study commissions looking toward complete modernization and
overhaul of the state's land regulatory systems. The
Colorado Land Use Act creates such a commission and also
authorizes interim regulatory powers over certain types of
development. The Washington Land Planning Commission has
been directed to recommend a model land use code for the
State of Washington which allows statewide interests to be
considered in future land development. Alaska has also
created a planning commission and directed it to prepare a
statewide plan for its land resources.

A substantial number of states have adopted wetland protection laws. A number of these authorize the
adoption of regulation defining the use that may be made
of wetlands--North Carolina, Rhode Island and Connecticut
offer examples of this type. A number of other states,
such as Maryland and Georgia, offer more limited protection
through statutes requiring permits for dredging and filling
of wetlands areas.

19

David Listokin

FAIR SHARE HOUSING DISTRIBUTION: WILL IT OPEN UP THE SUBURBS TO APARTMENT DEVELOPMENT

Introduction

Although a regional approach to planning[1] and housing has long been advocated, it is only in recent years that such an approach has begun to attract serious interest. At this writing, at least sixteen governmental and quasi-public bodies have either implemented or proposed regional housing allocation strategies, and their number is constantly growing.

But what exactly is fair share? Why has it generated so much recent attention? What are its criteria for housing distribution? What effect have these regional housing strategies had in the past? And what can be expected of them in the future? We shall attempt to answer all of these questions here.

Fair-Share Plans: Objectives and Background

Fair-share housing plans typically determine where housing—especially low- and moderate-income units—should be built within a region, according to such criteria as broadening the economic mix in communities and the placement of housing in environmentally suitable locations.

The following governmental and institutional bodies have either implemented or proposed fair-share plans:[2] Dade County Metropolitan Planning Board;[3] Delaware River Valley Regional Planning Commission;[4] Fairfax County, Va.;[5] The Greater Hartford Process, Inc.;[6] the State of Massachusetts;[7] Metropolitan Washington Coun-

---

[1] See Friedmann, "The Concept of a Planning Region—The Evolution of an Idea in the United States," in Friedmann & Alonso, *Regional Development and Planning* p. 497 (1964).

[2] For an excellent overview of the existing and implemented fair-share plans, see Mary Brooks, "Lower-Income Housing: The Planners' Response," ASPO Rep. (No. 282 July-Aug. 1972); "Fair-Share Idea Begins to Spread," *16 NCDH Trends in Housing*, (No. 2 July-Aug. 1972). Much of the first part of this article was derived from Brooks' analysis.

[3] Metropolitan Dade County Planning Dep't, "Housing in the Metropolitan Plan: Dade County, Florida—Final Report" (undated).

[4] Delaware Valley Regional Planning Comm'n, "Equal Share Housing Allocation: Criteria, Assumptions and Methodology," Working Paper No. 4 (June 30, 1972).

[5] Amendment 156, Fairfax County Zoning Ordinance, effective Sept. 1, 1971.

[6] See, "Concerted Action in Hartford Region," *16 NCDH Trends in Housing,* at 1. (No. 4-Dec. 1972).

[7] Mass. Gen. Stat. 40B §§ 20-23, inserted by State 1969, Ch. 774, § 1.

cil of Governments;[8] Metropolitan Dade County Planning Department;[9] Metropolitan Council of the Twin Cities Area;[10] Miami Valley Regional Planning Commission;[11] Middlesex County (N.J.) Planning Board;[12] the State of New Jersey;[13] New York State Urban Development Corporation;[14] Sacramento Regional Area Planning Commission;[15] and the San Bernardino County Planning Department.[16] Others developing fair-share mechanisms have included the University of Pennsylvania's Fels Center of Government[17] and the St. Louis Metropolitan Section of the American Institute of Planners.[18]

Although it is difficult to pinpoint the exact reasons for the recent proliferation of fair-share plans, we can isolate a number of precipitating factors, chief among which is the growing recognition of the need for regionalism in land-use and housing decisions. Many urbanologists, attorneys, and governmental officials have been pressing for a regional approach as opposed to a local perspective. The National Commission on Urban Problems, for exam-

----

[8] Metropolitan Washington Council of Governments, "A Fair-Share Housing Formula for Metropolitan Washington," (Jan. 1972).

[9] Metropolitan Dade County Planning Dep't, "Housing in the Metropolitan Plan" (undated).

[10] Metropolitan Council of the Twin Cities Area, "Metropolitan Development Guide, Housing Policy Program," (1972).

[11] Miami Valley Regional Planning Comm'n, "A Housing Plan for the Miami Valley Region" (July 1970).

[12] John Kim (Principal Planner Middlesex County Planning Board), "Outline for Study on Low and Moderate Income Housing in Middlesex County, New Jersey Analysis Forecast and Allocation of 1975" (undated).

[13] Assem. Bill No. 1421 (introduced Nov. 13, 1972).

[14] New York State Urban Development Corp. Programming Unit, "Five-Year UDC Development Programs Guide for the Central New York Region" (Dec. 1971).

[15] Sacramento Regional Area Planning Comm'n, "An Approach to the Distribution of Low- and Moderate-Income Housing" (Aug. 1972).

[16] San Bernardino County Planning Dep't, "Government Subsidized Housing Distribution Model" (Jan. 20, 1972).

[17] University of Pennsylvania, The Fels Center of Government, Standards for Suburban Housing Mix, Bucks County, Pennsylvania (1971).

[18] American Institute of Planners, St. Louis Section, "St. Louis Housing: A Regional Problem" (1973).

ple, has stressed the importance of formulating and evaluating zoning statutes and housing policies according to regional considerations.[19] Similarly, Norman Marcus, in a recent law review article, concluded that unless the state's remaining vacant land is allocated according to a set of sound regional priorities, it may be impossible to undo the mistakes which already have been made in central cities.[20] This sentiment has been echoed by Governor William Cahill of New Jersey[21] and by participants in the National Conference on Housing.[22]

Contributing significantly to the mounting support for regionalism is an increased awareness that piecemeal, local actions in housing and zoning can have an adverse impact upon the environment. Another important reason is the growing recognition that local housing and zoning decisions are dichotomizing our society into white suburban enclaves and minority group cities with adverse racial, social, and economic effects.[23] Many of the fair-share plans are based on concern for increasing the housing availability and choice of those who currently are ill-housed. The Dade County regional allocation strategy, for example, lists among its objectives the substantial improvement of the quality of newly built and rehabilitated low- and moderate-income housing units, and the provision of open occupancy, low- and moderate-income housing in suitable, new locations.[24]

---

[19] National Commission on Urban Problems, *Building the American City* 222-24 (Government Printing Office, 1968).

[20] Norman Marcus, "Exclusionary Zoning: The Need for a Regional Planning Content," N.Y. L. Forum No. 4 740 (1970).

[21] Cahill, "New Horizons in Housing," pp. 27, 33 (March 1972).

[22] See addresses by Eugene Moody, "Regional Housing Issues," and Richard Dusen, "Regional Leadership and Housing," in National Conference on Housing: *Regional Issues and Strategies: Summary of Proceedings* at 6 and 17 (Aug. 8-10, 1971).

[23] Sager, "Tight Little Islands; Exclusionary Zoning; Equal Protection and the Indigent," 21 Stanford L. Rev. 767, (1969); William & Wacks, "Segregation of Residential Areas Along Economic Lines; Lionshed Lake Revisited," Wis. L. Rev. 27 (1969); James Coke & John Gargan, *Fragmentation in Land Use Planning and Control,* National Commission on Urban Problems Research Rep. No. 18 (Washington, D.C., 1969); Norman Williams & Thomas Norman, "Exclusionary Land Use Control: The Case of North Eastern New Jersey," 22 Syracuse L. Rev. 476 (1970-71); Frank Aloi & Arthur Goldberg, "Racial and Economic Exclusionary Zoning: The Beginning of the End," 1971 Urban L. Annual 9 (1971).

[24] See note 3 *supra*.

Fair Share: Variations

There are many differences among the fair-share plans. One variation is generated by the type of body selected to formulate or implement the specific strategy. Our enumeration of fair-share plans shows variously that states, e.g., Massachusetts, New Jersey; counties, e.g., Dade County, Fla., Middlesex County, N.J.; Councils of Government (COGs), e.g., Metropolitan Washington COG; and regional planning agencies, e.g., Delaware River Valley Regional Planning Commission, have adopted or are considering strategies for regional housing allocation.

Another variation arises from the geographical areas encompassed by the fair-share plans. These can range from groups of adjacent states, e.g., in those plans considered by regional planning commissions, to much smaller areas, such as individual counties.

But, the most important differentiations in fair-share plans involve these questions: What type of housing is being allocated? What are the criteria for housing allocations? Who is responsible for building the fair-share housing? And, last, will compliance be enforced?

Variations in the Types of Allocatable Housing[25]

Some fair-share programs, e.g., the Miami Valley Regional Planning Commission plan, project the *total* number of low- to moderate-income units needed in the region. Others, e.g., the Washington COG plan, allocate only those units *subsidized* by the federal, state, or local governments.

The advantage of projecting the total number of housing units needed (both subsidized and unsubsidized units) is that this projection provides a more accurate estimate of the region's need for low- and moderate-income housing than can be obtained by merely calculating the number of subsidized units to be built. But, on the other hand, it is probable that in suburban areas, low- and moderate-income families could afford only subsidized housing. Hence, in a fair-share housing formula, it may be more realistic to project only the subsidized housing units, as in the second example, and then to allocate these units to districts or muncipalities within the region.

---

[25] See Brooks, note 2 *supra* at 18.

Variations in the Allocation Criteria

The most frequently mentioned criteria[26] for fair-share housing allocations are based on considerations of *equal share, need, distribution,* and *suitability.*

Equal Share

One way to achieve the objective of equal housing distribution might be to establish equitable minimum percentages of low- and moderate-income housing to be contained in each community. The rationale for this strategy is that all areas within a region have the same obligation to meet the region's housing needs.

Such an approach has been adopted by the Massachusetts fair-share plan, which establishes boards of review empowered to overrule local zoning bodies which refuse to allow the construction of low- to moderate-income housing. Local decisions can be overturned when the review board finds that a proposed housing project poses no environmental problem and in cases where the locality is not meeting its minimum percentage requirements. The minimum standard specifies that 10 percent of the community's housing be comprised of units subsidized for low- or moderate-income families, or that such housing should occupy 1.5 percent of the community's local land area minus public lands, whichever is less. These long-term guidelines are supplemented by annual standards specifying that the review boards cannot permit the construction in any one year of a low- to moderate-income housing development that would occupy ten acres or .3 percent of the town's land, whichever is larger. These annual guidelines were instituted to assure communities that they would not be inundated by housing they did not want.

Fairfax County, also has opted for an equal share approach. In 1971, it passed an amendment[27] stipulating that applicants for rezoning in its Planned Development Housing District must provide, or cause others to provide, that at least 6 percent of the total housing units initiated would be for low-income families, and an additional 9 percent must be allotted to moderate-income units. Developers of fifty-unit or larger tracts in the county's residential Garden Court district must provide the same percentages of low- and moderate-income housing units.

---

26 *Id.,* at 20.

27 See note 5 *supra.*

One advantage of an equal-share requirement is that no one community can charge that it is being forced to do more than its sister communities. Another benefit is that it facilitates calculating the number of units to be assigned.

But, equal share has several serious drawbacks. In most instances, the minimum equal-share percentages are chosen arbitrarily, thereby negating the rational objectives of fair share. Such was the case in Massachusetts, where considerable criticism was provoked.[28] The legality of the equal-share approach has also been questioned—Fairfax County's plan was overturned by the Virginia Supreme Court[29] and the constitutionality of the Massachusetts plan was also challenged,[30] although this challenge was subsequently defeated.

Need

In contrast to an equal-share strategy, one could allocate housing to regions where there is the greatest need. These might be areas with large numbers of dilapidated or deteriorating units, neighborhoods with extensive, overcrowded housing and geographical sectors, and areas that offer attractive employment potential. Such an approach, especially if the primary aim is to improve the quality of the housing stock, usually results in more housing units being allocated to urban areas than to suburban locations and to more units in slum neighborhoods within these urban enclaves, as opposed to higher housing quality neighborhoods.

Distribution

An alternative strategy is to allocate low- and moderate-income units to areas lacking such units in order to achieve a greater income and implicitly racial mixture in those communities. For example, most of the low- to moderate-income housing units could

---

[28] See Nathaniel Taylor, "Reconsidering the Massachusetts Suburban Housing and Zoning Reform Law: The Need for Change," Paper Submitted at American Institute of Planners Conference, Boston 1972 (mimeo).

[29] The Board of Supervisors v. DeGroff Enterprises, Inc., 198 S.E.2d 600 (1973).

[30] Board of Appeals v. Housing Appeals Comm., Board of Appeals of Concord v. Housing Appeals Comm. (both cases heard together) 294 N.E.2d 393 (1973).

be allocated to those communities with the lowest number of families on welfare, or the highest incomes, or the least amount of subsidized housing. Such a fair-share strategy would allocate the most housing to wealthy white suburban areas and the least to urban areas with high percentages of nonwhites and low-income families.

Suitability

Another guideline for allocating housing is the selection of areas containing the most suitable housing sites, e.g., those that are already serviced by sewer and utility lines, or that contain adequate vacant land for development. In addition to physical suitability, there is the matter of a subregion's financial capacity to service additional housing. When financial capacity is of prime concern, then most of the housing units are allocated to subregions with a high property tax base behind each student or resident, since these communities are better able to bear the additional municipal and school expenditures incurred by new housing construction.

Although we have discussed each of the four allocation criteria separately, it is important to realize that these criteria can be interdependent. For example, in allocating housing to areas where there are jobs, one may well achieve the additional goal of housing distribution since expanding job opportunities are largely in the suburbs. Similarly, if the most suitable housing sites, e.g., those with a well-developed infrastructure, are in urban areas, then the allocation of housing to urban sites may well result in the assignment of housing to areas of greatest need.

Moreover, many fair-share plans are explicitly designed to achieve several objectives. The Massachusetts fair-share plan, for example, stresses the equal-share approach, but also specifies that the zoning review boards be guided by such suitability considerations as open space and the health and safety of local residents. That other fair-share plans also have chosen to combine several criteria is illustrated in Exhibit 1.

Responsibility for Building the Fair-Share Housing

The third major variation among fair-share plans involves their implementation. In some cases, the body that formulates the plan builds the housing. For example, the Urban Development Corporation's housing allocation plan is primarily a corporate planning instrument for its own use in deciding where it should build low-

and moderate-income housing units.[31]   Similarly, the Chicago Housing Authority's plan for a wider distribution of public housing units throughout the city was designed for its own use.[32]

In instances where the body formulating and promulgating the fair-share plan does not construct the housing itself, the question of just precisely who is responsible for implementing the fair-share plan is often left unanswered. In the opinion of Mary Brooks, a leading authority,[33] those allocation plans establishing priority areas for housing development (rather than allocating specific numbers of housing to subregions) are predominantly directed towards developers to try to orient them to focus this construction in the priority locations. But, since the specifics of how developer compliance is to be insured is often rather vague, there is some doubt about the viability of such a strategy. In contrast, the fair-share plans that allocate specific numbers of units to communities make the locality primarily responsible for seeing that the allocated housing is built. The community can either construct the allocated housing itself or arrange for or encourage others, e.g., non-profit housing sponsors, to do so.

Local compliance with the fair-share plan is insured by the agency effecting the fair-share plan using both persuasive and coercive strategies. The first strategy is useful when opposition to the construction of low- and moderate-income housing is based on unfounded fears that such activity will quickly destroy neighborhoods. In many instances, the fair-share agency can reduce opposition to their plan by attempting to persuade and demonstrate to the antagonists that the entry of lower-income housing will not have an adverse impact.

But since persuasive strategy proves ineffective where the opposition is deeply rooted, many agencies have resorted to more coercive methods in order to assure compliance. For example, a regional unit of government, e.g., county government, may withhold financial aid unless a municipality agrees to build low- and moderate-income housing. But, by far the most popular instrument

---

[31] Interview with James D. Wiley of the UDC, February 1973; also see forward, New York State Urban Development Corporation, Program Development Division, Programming Unit, "Five-Year UDC Housing Development Program Guide for the Central New York Region (Dec. 1971).

[32] Chicago's public housing distribution action was prompted by Gautreaux v. Chicago Housing Authority 436 F.2d 306 (7th Cir. 1970).

[33] Note 2 *supra* at 19.

EXHIBIT 1. ALLOCATION CRITERIA OF SIX FAIR-SHARE PLANS

	IMPLEMENTED				PROPOSED	
	Metropolitan Washington Council of Governments	Miami Valley Regional Planning Commission	San Bernardino County, Cal.	Metropolitan Council. Minneapolis-St. Paul	Sacramento Regional Area Planning Commission	New Jersey (Assembly Bill 1421, 1972) Voluntary Distribution
Need Allocation Criteria	(1) Number of households of less than $10,000 annual income with commuters into the area (the greater the number of households, the greater the share of new units) (2) Number of overcrowded housing units (the greater the number of units, the greater the share of new units) (3) Number of deficient housing units (the greater the number of units, the greater the share of new units)	(1) Share of households of less than $10,000 annual income ($7,000 in rural areas) (the greater the number of households, the greater the share of new units)	(1) Deficient housing units within income group level appropriate (the greater the number of units, the greater the share of new units) (2) Number of jobs (the greater the number of jobs, the greater the share of new units) (3) Number of households with annual gross income less than $10,000 (the greater the population in this category, the greater the share of new units)		(1) Total population in the area as a percent of the regional population (share is in proportion to the population) (2) Number of households in the 0-$5,000 category as a percentage of the total regional low-income households (the greater the number of such households the greater the share of new units) (3) Number of households in the $5,000-$8,000 income bracket (see 2) (4) Number of jobs in the area as a percent of the total region's jobs (the greater the number of jobs the greater the share of new units)	(1) Substandard housing in the municipality (2) The number of low and moderate income households as a percentage of households in the municipality.
Distributive and Equal Share Allocation Criteria	(4) Percent of jobs within 45 minutes of area (used as a modifier)	(2) Equal Share (3) Proportion to the population	(4) Equal share (5) Number of households (share is in proportion to the population)	(1) Percentage of existing low- and moderate-income housing (the higher priority is given to lower percent)	(5) Inverse of (3) in urban areas	(3) Proximity to existing and projected locations of low- and moderate-income employment

	IMPLEMENTED					PROPOSED
	Metropolitan Washington Council of Governments	*Miami Valley Regional Planning Commission*	*San Bernardino County, Cal.*	*Metropolitan Council, Minneapolis-St. Paul*	*Sacramento Regional Area Planning Commission*	*New Jersey (Assembly Bill 1421, 1972) Voluntary Distribution*
Suitability Allocation Criteria	(5) Percent of units less than $25,000 or $250 rent (used as a modifier) (6) Potential per capita fiscal resources (used as a modifier)	(4) Inverse of (1) (the greater the number of households, the smaller the share of new units) (7) Number of acres of vacant serviced residential land (the greater the amount in acres, the greater the share of new units) (8) Number of vacant housing units (the greater the number of units, the greater the share of new units)	(5) Assessed valuation per pupil (the higher the valuation, the greater the share of new units) (6) Overcrowding in schools (the greater the overcrowding, the smaller the share of new units)	(2) Amount of land currently developed (the higher priority is given to areas with more development) (6) Assessed valuation of pupil average daily attendance (the higher the value the greater the share of new units) (7) Existing additional school capacity (the less the capacity, the less the share of new units) (8) Vacant residential land valued at $10,000 per acre or less (the more acres in vacant land, the greater the share of new units)	(6) Elementary school district assessed valuation per household as a percentage of the assigned valuation in urban area (for Marysville-Yuba City and urban areas only) (the higher the assessed valuation the greater the share of new units)	(4) Availability of sites for construction of low- and moderate-income housing. Uniformity with state development plan and county and municipal master plans. (5) Availability of land and open space areas and their intended use (6) Existence of and feasibility and estimated cost of providing local and regional public services and facilities to support proposed housing. Impact on local taxation. (7) Effect on the community and impact on existing land use development regulations

Note: Following Brooks' approach proximity to jobs was considered as a distributive criterion. The proposed New Jersey plan did not specify whether the allocation would be manipulated inversely or directly.

Source: Brooks, *Lower Income Housing: The Planners' Response*. Planning Advisory Service Report No. 282 (July-August 1972), and fair share reports.

used by regional governments to insure municipal compliance has been using their A-95 review power.[34] This sanction requires that municipal proposals for federal assistance for public facilities—especially for sewer and water facilities—be first evaluated by regional planning bodies as to their necessity and regional impact. Currently, also subject to such review are all local applications to federal agencies for subsidies or mortgage insurance for subdivisions of over fifty lots, multifamily and public housing projects of over 100 units, and mobile home courts of over 100 spaces.

Frequently, the agencies formulating and effecting the fair-share programs also are empowered to conduct the A-95 review. Therefore, they have considerable leverage in persuading municipalities to comply with fair-share requirements; since these municipalities often cannot construct sewers and other facilities without federal aid, they tend to avoid doing anything that would incur the wrath of the review bodies. The effectiveness of this review power is corroborated by Dale Bertsch, executive director of Dayton, Ohio's fair-share program, who reports that the A-95 review power of Miami Valley Regional Planning Commission is his most important tool for insuring compliance with fair-share objectives.[35]

Fair Share: Potential Impact

Because fair-share plans are still in their infancy, it is too early to conclusively gauge their impact. But, we can attempt a preliminary evaluation by discussing their potential impact and then examining their performance to date and the prospects for their future.

Fair-share plans are designed to substantially increase housing choice and housing mix in suburban areas. The Washington, D.C., COG fair-share plan illustrates this. Back in October 1971, almost 60 percent of the federally subsidized housing units in the metropolitan Washington area were allocated for the District of Columbia.[36] Many subregions had few or no subsidized units—Fairfax County, for example, had only 6 percent while Arlington contained none. The COG plan would markedly change this uneven

---

[34] See David Myhra, "A-95 Review and the Urban Planning Process," 50 J. Urban L. No. 3, p. 449 (Feb. 1973), and William Brussat, "Knowing Your A-95," Urban Land, pp. 13 (March 1973).

[35] Bertsch, in National Conference on Housing, note 22 *supra* at 49.

[36] See note 8 *supra* at II and 10.

distribution by allocating only 20 percent of the future subsidized units to the District of Columbia—i.e., one-third its current total. Conversely, suburban areas would be given a much larger share of the region's low- and moderate-income housing. Fairfax County, for example, would be allocated 24 percent, while Arlington's share would be 9 percent. The projected impact of the Washington COG fair-share plan throughout the region is shown in Exhibit 2.

Marked changes were also envisioned by the Sacramento Regional Area Planning Commission's plan which would, if effected, significantly increase the percentage of subsidized housing units allocated in many of the region's suburbs.[37] This projected impact is not surprising, for the goal of many fair-share plans is to increase housing opportunities in the suburbs. Progress has been made in achieving this objective, but not without some difficulty, as we shall demonstrate shortly.

Fair Share: Impact to Date

Fair share has had a mixed but promising track record to date. The Metropolitan Council (Minneapolis-St. Paul) and Washington COG fair-share plans have both begun auspiciously and have elicited widespread approval. The Dayton Plan, having confronted and solved numerous problems, is quite successful today. But some fair-share strategies—namely the Fairfax County, UDC, and Massachusetts plans—have encountered significant problems.

Before we examine the individual performance records, we must reemphasize that because fair share has just started, our conclusions about its results can be regarded as only tentative.

Metropolitan Council and Washington COG Plans:
Auspicious Beginnings

Both the Metropolitan Council (Minneapolis-St. Paul)[38] and Washington COG fair-share plans[39] have gained strong support in their areas. The former has generated considerable suburban acceptance, as well as actual construction of low- and moderate-income housing; some suburban communities had even complained

---

[37] See note 15 *supra* at 5.

[38] Telephone interview with Metropolitan Council Staff, Oct. 1973.

[39] Telephone interview with Washington COG Staff, Oct. 1973.

EXHIBIT 2.   IMPACT OF
WASHINGTON COG FAIR-SHARE PLAN

Jurisdiction	1971 Distribution of Subsidized Housing Units	Percent of New Federally Subsidized Housing Units to be Allocated to Indicated Jurisdiction under the Fair-Share Plan
Alexandria	3.5	2.6
Arlington	.0	9.0
Bowie	.0	.2
College Park	.3	.8
District of Columbia	59.6	20.3
Fairfax County	5.9	24.4
Fairfax City	.2	.6
Greenbelt	.0	.6
Loudon County	.5	1.4
Montgomery County	7.8	26.7
Prince George's County	18.1	10.9
Prince William County	2.2	.2
Rockville	1.3	1.0

Source: Metropolitan Washington Council of Governments, "A Fair Share Housing Formula for Metropolitan Washington (1972) at II and 10.

that they were not allocated sufficient housing. At least ten suburban communities already have established public housing authorities and have issued bonds to finance these authorities. Some localities have even gone so far as to adopt a Fairfax County strategy, requiring private large-scale developers to construct certain minimum percentages of low- and moderate-income housing.

The Washington COG fair-share plan also has received considerable initial support from both the Department of Housing and Urban Development and the COG's constituent members. The former agreed to subsidize over 6,000 housing units under the 221(d)(3)-236, 235, rent supplement, Project Rehab, Operation Breakthrough, and public housing programs. About 1,800 of these units were granted as a bonus by HUD in recognition of the COG's innovative regional allocation strategy. The COG's members cooperated in many ways—agreeing occasionally to construct public housing and granting property tax abatements on the projected subsidized housing that would be built.

To date, however, little subsidized housing has been built under the Metropolitan Council and especially the Washington COG fair-share plans. One reason for their low output is their relatively short existence—both plans were adopted in early 1972. Other restraints have been the high cost of undertaking housing without financial aid, combined with the uncertainty of obtaining housing subsidies.

Dayton Plan: Initial Difficulties Overcome

The Dayton plan was formulated in cooperation with local public officials, planning consultants, and community groups.[40] This team approach, coupled with favorable press coverage during its gestation period, resulted in the Dayton plan's unanimous adoption in September 1970 by elected officials of the Miami Valley Regional Planning Commission (MVRPC).

Its smooth beginning led to the expectation that the Dayton Plan could be effectuated without opposition. However, such optimism was unfounded, according to the account of one observer:[41]

Consensus [in adopting the Dayton Plan] did not mean mandate. Now the struggle is taking place over finding flat sites for real housing units. And if emotion did battle with reason in getting the plan accepted that was only a skirmish compared with the difficulties of implementation.

Not surprisingly there is resistance in white suburbs. There is also passionate resistance in a middle income black suburb. There is trouble too when MVRPC tries to stop proposed projects.

Resistance to the Dayton Plan was often vociferous. Some of its supporters were roundly defeated in the November 1971 election. Two counties and ten municipalities even threatened to secede from the MVRPC.[42] And when the MVRPC proposed a 166-unit for Miamisburg, a blue-collar suburb of Dayton, a local ad hoc committee was formed to oppose it. The committee's persuasive arguments that the proposed housing would increase local taxes and overburden schools, sewers, and transportation facilities, resulted in overwhelming defeat for the Miamisburg housing plan.

---

[40] Dale Bertsch & Ann Shafor, "A Regional Housing Plan: The Miami Valley Regional Planning Commission Experience," Planners Notebook at 2-5 (No. 1, April 1971).

[41] Lois Craig, "The Dayton Area's 'Fair Share' Housing Plan Enters the Implementation Phase," 1972 City 50 at 54 (Jan.-Feb. 1972).

[42] Id., at 56.

Today such opposition has largely died down.[43] The reasons for the sudden change in attitude are not clear. Among the mitigating factors might be the MVRPC's established reputation, the dynamism of its executive director, Dale Bertsch, and the willingness and patience of the MVRPC's staff in explaining the fair share's intentions to hostile communities. The decline in opposition is reflected in the fact that no county or municipality ever made good on its withdrawal threats. Furthermore, there was a sharp rise in the Dayton plan's construction pace; whereas a 1972 report[44] revealed that 800 units had been built since the plan's inception, there were 3,000 completed as of early 1973 (over 4,000 if we include housing built under HUD's 235 and 502 subsidy programs). The Dayton Plan, then, after weathering stiff opposition, now seems on its way to dispersing considerable numbers of low- and moderate-income units in the region's suburbs.

The Massachusetts Plan: Limited Success

During fiscal years 1971 to 1973, almost 50,000 low- and moderate-income housing units were constructed in Massachusetts under subsidy programs from HUD, Massachusetts Department of Community Affairs (MDCA), Massachusetts Housing Finance Agency (MHFA), and other agencies.[45] Although much of this housing has been built in the major cities, especially Boston, there has been considerable construction in suburban areas as well. In the opinion of MacDonald Barr, MCDA's Coordinator of Planning and Program Development, this construction has significantly broadened Massachusetts' suburban housing mix.[46]

This dispersion has not been effected through the Massachusetts zoning review plan, however. Rather, it has resulted from the independent efforts of private developers. The state's fair-share strategy has in itself accomplished very little.

Two 1972 reports[47] corroborate the Massachusetts fair-share

---

[43] Telephone interview with Ann Shafor of the Miami Valley Regional Planning Commission, Oct. 1973.

[44] Craig, note 41 *supra* at 53.

[45] Telephone interview with MacDonald Barr of the Massachusetts Department of Community Affairs, October 1973.

[46] *Id.*

[47] See Taylor, note 28 *supra* and MacDonald Barr, "The Massachusetts Zoning Appeals Law: Lessons of the First Three Years," Paper submitted at American Institute of Planners Conference, Boston 1972 (mimeo).

plan's slow pace. The state plan provides two levels of zoning review—one by local zoning boards of appeals and another by a state Housing Appeals Committee. As of mid-1972, only nineteen appeals had been received by the latter group and perhaps more significant, a total of only thirty-five applications had been filed before the former group. Of this thirty-five, eighteen had been denied and subsequently appealed, twelve were still awaiting a decision, and only five had resulted in permits to build.[48] Of these five approvals, two were stalled until recently by court action, and the remaining three resulted in the construction of 364 units, all for the elderly. Clearly, the Massachusetts track record has not been impressive.

Why such a slow pace? One explanation is that until recently, the entire Massachusetts fair-share plan was under a legal cloud.[49] And there have been substantive problems as well—poorly defined administrative procedures and high out-of-pocket costs for developers who submit to the zoning review process.[50] The following account summarizes the defects:[51]

"The Massachusetts suburban housing and zoning reform law is not working. Its failure can be summarized in the following manner: first its approach to the problem of inadequate housing and exclusionary zoning is negative. Rather than attempting to implement an affirmative housing strategy, the law seeks only to break down exclusionary suburban barriers where they conflict with the construction of low and moderate income housing.

Second, it establishes a nundesirable adversary system between developers of subsidized housing on the one hand and suburban communities which are generally opposed to such housing on the other. This increases the risk of financial loss to developers, puts communities unprepared to accept such housing in the defensive, requires an almost automatic appeal to the state, and diminishes the legitimacy of the entire housing effort. . . .

Third, the law provides insufficient policy direction, planning standards and state legislative mandate by which conflicts can be resolved at the local level. . . ."

---

[48] Barr, note 47 *supra* at 6-7.

[49] See note 30 *supra*.

[50] Barry, note 47 *supra* at 9-12.

[51] Taylor, note 28 *supra* at 1.

The UDC Plan: Stalled by Opposition

The New York State Urban Development Corporation (UDC), established in 1969,[52] had tremendous potential for dispersing large numbers of low- and moderate-income housing in the state's suburbs. It had a dynamic executive director, Edward Logue, and strong support from Governor Nelson Rockefeller. Moreover, as a fair-share plan, it was unique on two counts: It had its own financing capability and was legally empowered to override local zoning restrictions. Yet, despite its commendable achievements— the construction of more than 30,000 housing units[53] and the implementation of such innovative projects as industrial condo- miniums—the UDC has done little in the way of housing dispersal.

Opposition to the UDC has been most vehement in Westchester County. The state's fair-share approach was initiated in this county through a UDC proposal for the construction of 900 units in the unincorporated areas of the towns of Westchester,[54] with no more than 100 units to be built in any one town or school district. The 900-unit objective was established after analysis of the UDC's statewide construction capability in relation to both the overall needs of Westchester County and to the specific requirements of the UDC's current and proposed programs in the cities and villages.

Anticipating vigorous opposition by many Westchester com- munities, the UDC made special conciliatory efforts. Not only would the scale of the housing projects be small (100 units each), but they would be of low density with each development situated on no less than ten acres. In addition, each site would be provided with its own recreation spaces. And the UDC also recommended state reimbursement to those communities incurring cost-revenue deficits because of the projects.

Despite all of these concessions, the UDC projects were vocifer- ously opposed. In September 1972, Governor Rockefeller imposed a moratorium on the UDC Westchester projects so that both UDC and local Westchester officials could further discuss the proposed housing units.[55] The present status of the UDC Westchester pro-

---

[52] See Reilly & Shulman, "The State Urban Development Corporation: New York's Innovation," 1 Urban Lawyer 129 (1969).

[53] Telephone Interview, with New York State Urban Development Cor- poration staff, Nov. 1973.

[54] See New York State Urban Development Corporation, "Fair Share" at 6 (undated).

[55] The New York Times, Dec. 27, 1972.

posals remains unclear; no housing has been built to date; and in light of continued protest, there is some doubt whether the UDC is still committed to building these projects. The strength of the opposition is evident in the successful pressure brought to bear upon the New York legislature to strip the UDC of its power to override local zoning—a move that many feel resulted from the UDC's fair-share efforts.[56] Although it would be premature to conclude that the UDC will abandon future fair-share efforts, its experiences to date clearly reveal the potential difficulty of such undertakings.

The present impact of fair share, then, is mixed—widespread acceptance by communities in the Minneapolis-St. Paul and greater Washington areas, belated success in Dayton, and limited success in Massachusetts and New York. But what about the future? Will we be likely to see more regional allocation strategies? And what will their impact be?

Future of Fair Share

Current trends indicate increasing adoptions of fair-share plans in the future. With racial and environmental problems intensifying, there will be increasing pressure to centralize zoning-housing decisions through such instrumentalities as fair share. A growing advocacy for regional review of zoning-housing policies underlies both the American Law Institute land-use revisions[57] and National Land-Use Bill(s).[58] Such sentiment undoubtedly will encourage the further adoption of regional housing allocation strategies.

We can expect support for fair share from at least three groups: developers, the courts, and suburban communities themselves. Housing developers, seeking expanding business opportunity in the suburbs, already have sided with antiexclusionary zoning groups, e.g., the Suburban Action Institute;[59] this same motive may

---

[56] "UDC Zoning Power Cut," in NCDH 17 *Trends in Housing* (July-Aug. 1973).

[57] American Law Institute, "Model Land Development Code" (Tentative Draft No. 3, 1971).

[58] See Vance Hartke, "Toward a National Growth Policy," 22 Catholic U. L. Rev. 279 (1973); William Reilly, "New Directions in Federal Land Use Legislation," 1973 Urban Law Annual 29.

[59] See Geoffrey Shields & L. Sanford Spector, "Opening Up the Suburbs: Notes on a Movement for Social Change," 6 Yale Rev. L. & Social Action 300 (1972).

also prompt developers to support fair share. Many courts involved in exclusionary zoning suits have voiced their support for a legislatively established regional housing and zoning plan that would free them from their current duties as "super planning agencies." [60] This sentiment, which has already been echoed by political leaders, points to further adoption of fair-share plans. And, finally, suburban communities themselves may well support fair share, viewing it as a lesser evil when compared to court challenge and possible overruling of their present zoning-housing policies.

Although we can expect the spread of fair-share plans, we cannot confidently predict their success in dispersing significant amounts of housing. A major restraint is the federal housing subsidy moratorium, which already has stalled many fair-share plans. Almost no housing has been built under the Washington COG fair-share plan, for example, because the area's high housing costs would place unsubsidized units beyond the reach of low- and moderate-income families. [61] The continued success of the Dayton Plan is also jeopardized by federal housing subsidy cutbacks. [62] And, although increased state subsidies might compensate for federal cutbacks in most cases, state housing aid does not match recent federal housing subsidies.

With fair-share plans addressed primarily to housing location rather than to housing finance, their success, assuming their elimination of local opposition, depends largely upon the availability of housing subsidy funds. Lacking adequate housing subsidies, regional allocation strategies can have little impact upon the distribution of low- and moderate-income housing units in suburban areas.

Another possible obstacle to fair share is its conflict with nongrowth sentiments. [63] Such a hold-the-line position may well be a convenient justification by suburban communities for retaining their exclusive nature; but whatever its origins, its spreading popularity and its underlying conservatism pose a direct threat to fair-

---

[60] National Land and Investment Co. v. Board of Adjustment 419 Pa. 504, 521, 215 A.2d 597, 607 (1965).

[61] See note 39 *supra*.

[62] See note 43 *supra*.

[63] See Finkler, "Nongrowth as a Planning Alternative," *ASPO Report* No. 283 (Sept. 1972).

share programs. Whereas the latter strategy advocates rapid housing production within a regional plan, the nongrowth position completely rejects the desirability of speedy construction maintaining instead that housing production should be reduced, and in some cases, halted entirely. It is upon the outcome of this philosophical-social conflict and the availability of subsidies that the future of regional housing allocation depends.

Conclusion

If widespread interest is a reliable indicator, then the fair-share plan is an idea whose time has come. A marked change from the status quo requires careful analysis of the variations in such plans as well as their drawbacks and potential impacts. This article has attempted to facilitate such analysis.

20

Richard Babcock

COMMENTS ON MODEL LAND DEVELOPMENT CODE

In law, land use planning and policy have moved to center stage. What was once a matter calling for planners to putter with zipatone and for lawyers to fret over gas stations has now become an issue to which such prestigious and diverse national institutions as the Sierra Club, the NAACP, the ACLU, the Audubon Society, the UAW, and the National Association of Home Builders direct their energies.

We are at a watershed. The dominant role the municipalities struggled to achieve in the last four decades is being challenged, not just in the scholarly journals but in the courts, the legislatures, and the market place. We may expect that local land use regulations, particularly as they affect low and moderate income housing, will become the occasion for legal struggles in the seventies on the same scale that school desegregation was in the sixties.

One would be rash this early in the contest to predict the outcome and that is not my purpose tonight. Rather I want to describe to you an ongoing effort to restate in model form the statutory framework within which the use of private land has been regulated by municipalities for almost five decades. I refer to the effort of the American Law Institute to draft a Model Land Development Code[1] usable in whole or in part by states which decide it is time to revise the rules

† The following is from an address by Mr. Richard F. Babcock to the 1971 URBAN LAW ANNUAL staff on April 23, 1971.

* Partner, Ross, Hardies, O'Keefe, Babcock, & Parsons (Law firm, Chicago, Ill.); A.B., Dartmouth College, 1940; J.D., University of Chicago, 1946; M.B.A., University of Chicago, 1950.

1. MODEL LAND DEVELOPMENT CODE (Tent. Draft No. 3, 1971) [hereinafter cited as MLDC].

by which land development is to be regulated. The reporters for this project are Professor Allison Dunham of the University of Chicago Law School and my partner, Fred Bosselman. I am Chairman of the Advisory Committee to the Reporters. I declare all this so my bias, if apparent, is at least explained.

I propose to describe the scheme of that part of the ALI code dealing with the relationship between the state and the municipalities. It appears in Tentative Draft No. 3.[2] However, some premises on which the Code is based:

First, land use regulation should be left to local decision-makers except where those decisions may impose external costs. Most decisions on land use development do not have an extra-municipal impact, as anyone who has nodded through the interminable agenda of boards of appeal and plan commissions knows. Besides, there are important benefits in having power exercised as close to the people as possible—an issue, by the way, on which the suburbanite and the ghetto resident share common ground. It follows, therefore, that the machinery of local administration, while crying for a major overhaul, should not be abandoned.

Second, to the extent that there should be a voice in some decisions that can speak for a constituency greater than the municipality, the state is the appropriate authority. This implies a rejection of at least two alternatives, the national government and metropolitanism of some sort.

I can only pause on the reasons behind our choice of the state—an elaboration of why we rejected these other alternatives is an evening's task in itself. Let it be left like this: The appropriate role of the federal government is to reward states that do demonstrate a willingness to take responsibility for growth policy, not to take on the hopeless role of decision-making in Washington. Metropolitanism, in its most innocuous forms—regional planning agencies or councils of governments—is on balance an exercise in futility, a "talk-talk" role that is bound to fail. America's experiments in the eighteenth and nineteenth centuries with policy making by confederation were notable for their inability to gain victory in tough conflicts, and I see nothing to suggest that such a system can do any better at the end of the twentieth century in the tense social and political arena of land

---

2. Tentative Draft No. 3 has not as yet been endorsed by the ALI. Copies may be obtained from American Law Institute, 4025 Chestnut Street, Philadelphia, Pa. 19104.

development policy. In short, planning without the attributes of sovereignty—the power to tax, to regulate, and to condemn—is nothing.

If, on the other hand, by metropolitanism we mean some new layer of general government that does enjoy those sanctions, then we have an entirely new ball game. The ALI reporters acknowledge the pitiful record of state government that leads some to demand a new system, but they suspect that the evils, if they do exist, will emerge under any system. Further they see evidence that the long sleep of the states is over; and they have reason to suspect that metropolitan government can be used—as the blacks in Atlanta so eloquently put it—to give the white suburbanites a last chance to hang on to power in the central city just when the blacks are about to seize it.

Tentative Draft No. 3 gives the state a voice in selected areas of land use development but does not require that the state first have prepared or have in process a state plan.[3] This scheme of state regulation may be faulted for the same reasons that 40 years of municipal regulation have been attacked: unprincipled regulation without guidelines. Indeed, the Code itself is internally inconsistent since Article 3 conditions a municipality's power to exercise some sophisticated types of regulation upon the existence of a planning process.

This charge is well made and the only answer takes the form of a plea in abatement. The crisis of excessive localism in land use policy is immediate and serious. The sin is not that there is no planning but that there is too much planning by a multitude of local governments, each one trying to save for itself all the "goodies of life" in the metropolis while palming off on others as many of the "cheap cuts" as possible. What is needed now is an opportunity for a wider consensus to be injected into some areas of the decision-making even if that greater voice does not speak with the benefit of a five-year "study of the problem." One is tempted to speculate about the fate of this country in 1933 if Roosevelt's 100 days of reform by legislation had been put off for 1,000 days while a plan was being conceived. In any event, the drafters had to make a choice and I, for one, share their skepticism about the usefulness of a legislative model that would postpone all regulatory reform while the planners plan. The draft provides authority for comprehensive state planning in Article 7, but it does not withold the state's regulatory powers under Article 8 until the planning is completed.

---

3. This premise may be of little significance to the lawyers but may be the occasion for substantial critical comment from the planning profession.

Those, then, are what I see as the major premises. Now to the Code itself.

The system proposed by the reporters is a relatively simple one, but because it involves agencies with new names it may initially be easier to understand by reference to the following chart:

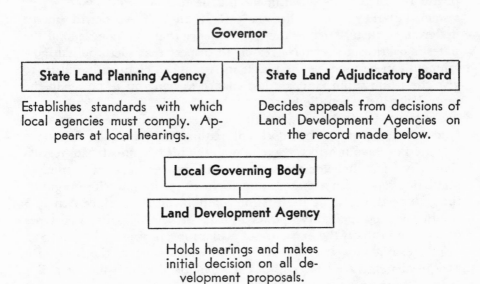

The reporters do not deny the importance of the planning function at the state level. Indeed, it has an essential and independent role in the regulatory process.

In general, the functions of the State Land Planning Agency include the establishment of rules and standards governing development having state or regional impact. However, anyone seeking permission to undertake such development applies to the municipal Land Development Agency where the hearing is held and the initial decision made. The State Land Planning Agency may participate in the hearing and, if the decision is unfavorable, may appeal it to the State Land Adjucatory Board, an independent state board created to hear such appeals. The developer or any other party to the local hearing also has a similar right of appeal.

The benefits of community control are retained because the local agency has the right to make the initial decision in each case. It allows the State Land Planning Agency to concentrate on policy-making functions, but it will participate in individual cases only to the extent it feels such participation is necessary to defend its policies. Allowing the state board to review local decisions on the record made below avoids the necessity of creating an expensive and time-consuming procedure for new hearings at the state level.

The principle that the state would become involved only in the "big cases" is a key element of the Code's philosophy. As I said, probably 90 per cent of the local land development decisions have no real state or regional impact. It is important to keep the state out of those 90 per cent, not only to preserve community control, but to prevent the state agency from being bogged down in paperwork over a multitude of unimportant decisions.

Defining cases that will have state or regional impact thus becomes crucial to the entire system. The ALI Model starts with three basic principles:

(1) Some development has state or regional impact because of its *location*.

(2) Some development has state or regional impact because of its *type*.

(3) Some development has state or regional impact because of its *magnitude*.

Working from these three principles, the reporters have set up three categories of development that are subject to state review.

The first category is development in districts of critical state concern. Section 7-201 authorizes the State Land Planning Agency to define the boundaries of such districts, which may include

. . . an area significantly affected by, or having a significant effect upon, an existing or proposed major public facility or other area of major public investment.[4]

That section defines the term "major public facility" to include highway interchanges, airports, and other facilities servicing a state or region. Districts of critical state concern may also include

. . . an area containing or having a significant impact upon historical, natural, or environmental resources of regional or statewide importance.[5]

Finally, districts of critical state concern may also be designated for the sites of new communities shown on the State Land Development Plan.

The second category of case that is appealable to the state agency under proposed Tentative Draft No. 3 is "development of state or re-

---

4. MLDC § 7-201.
5. *Id.*

gional benefit." This includes development which serves important state or regional needs but may have some adverse impact on the immediate area. Section 7-301 provides:

(1) development by a governmental agency other than the local government that created the Land Development Agency or another agency created solely by that local government;

(2) development which will be used for charitable purposes, including religious or educational purposes, and which serves or is intended to serve a substantial number of persons who do not reside within the boundaries of the local government creating the Land Development Agency;

(3) development by a public utility which is or will be employed to a substantial degree to provide services in an area beyond the territorial jurisdiction of the local government creating the Land Development Agency; and

(4) development by any person receiving state or federal aid designed to facilitate a type of development specified by the State Land Planning Agency by rule.[6]

In each of these cases the developer is given the right of appeal to the state board if the local decision is unfavorable. The Massachusetts zoning appeals law offers perhaps the closest analogy under existing law.[7]

The third category is development which has a statewide impact because of its size. Part 4 of Article 7 of the proposed Code authorizes the State Land Planning Agency to establish for each broad category of development limits of magnitude which, if exceeded, allow the local decision to be appealed to the state board, either by the developer, by intervenors, or by the State Land Planning Agency. For example, the Agency might provide that residential developments of 100 or more units or commercial developments of more than 50,000 square feet of floor area might constitute "large scale development." These limits would undoubtedly be higher within incorporated municipalities than in unsettled areas.

If the Code insists that state or regional interests be weighed in decisions involving "large scale development" and "development of state or regional benefit," what statutory criteria are available to guide the decision-makers first at the local and then the state level? The test that is common to both types of development is that permission shall be granted if the probable net benefit to the state or region ex-

---

6. *Id.* § 7-301.

7. MASS. GEN. LAWS ANN. ch. 40B, §§ 20-23 (Supp. 1971).

ceeds the net detriment to the local community. Section 7-502 tells the administrators what the drafters had in mind when speaking in terms of cost-benefit, and it would be difficult to summarize that section:

In reaching its decision the Agency shall not restrict its consideration to benefit and detriment within the local jurisdiction, but shall consider all relevant and material evidence offered to show the impact of the development on surrounding areas. Detriments or benefits shall not be denied consideration on the ground that they are indirect, intangible, or not readily quantifiable. In evaluating detriments and benefits under § 7-501 the Agency may consider, with other relevant factors, whether or not

(1) development at the proposed location is or is not essential or especially appropriate in view of the available alternatives within or without the jurisdiction;

(2) development in the manner proposed will have a favorable or unfavorable impact on the environment in comparison to alternative methods;

(3) the development will favorably or adversely affect other persons or property and, if so, whether because of circumstances peculiar to the location the effect is likely to be greater than is ordinarily associated with the development of the type proposed;

(4) if development of the type proposed imposes immediate cost burdens on the local government, whether the amount of development of that type which has taken place in the territory of the local government is more or less than an equitable share of the development of that type needed in the general area or region;

(5) the development will favorably or adversely affect the ability of people to find adequate housing reasonably accessible to their place of employment;

(6) the development will favorably or adversely affect the provision of municipal services and the burden of taxpayers in making provisions therefor;

(7) the development will efficiently use or unduly burden public-aided transportation or other facilities which have been developed or are to be developed within the next [5] years;

(8) the development will further, or will adversely affect, the objectives of development built or aided by governmental agencies within the past [5] years or to be developed in the next [5] years;

(9) the development will aid or interfere with the ability of the local government to achieve the objectives set forth in any Land Development Plan and current short-term program; and

(10) the development is in furtherance of or contradictory to objectives and policies set forth in a State Land Development Plan for the area.[8]

---

8. MLDC § 7-502.

Section 7-405 of the Model Code should be of special interest to those who are concerned with the imbalance between the increasing suburban job opportunities and the lack of low and moderate income housing in the suburbs. This section provides that a Local Development Agency shall not grant a permit for "large scale development" that will create more than "[100]"[9] opportunities for full-time employment not previously existing within the municipality unless the Land Development Agency also finds that

(1) adequate and reasonably accessible housing for prospective employees is available within or without the jurisdiction of the local government; or

(2) the local government has adopted a Land Development Plan designed to make available adequate and reasonably accessible housing within a reasonable time; or

(3) a State Land Development Plan shows that the proposed location is a desirable location for the proposed employment source.[10]

That concludes my description of the ALI draft as it relates to the role of the state in land use policy. I do not believe I am guilty of overstatement when I state that this Model Code will be the first legislative model for land use policy of national scope since Secretary of Commerce Herbert Hoover submitted to the nation a Model Zoning Act in 1923. It does not disparage that remarkable effort to say that it is past time that we change policies of land use that were adequate for a quieter, less crowded era.

Let me conclude on a sensitive point that is too frequently overlooked in this age when "Cry Environment" is on thousands of lips. There is a serious risk in the current agitation over the state of ecology. That risk is that a total preoccupation with dirty air, foul streams, and poisoned estuaries may blind us to the dismal fact that for too many millions of our citizens the threshold test of a decent environment is adequate housing reasonably accessible to jobs. Too many proposals for state participation in land use regulation, with their emphasis on what "environment" connotes to the white middle class, may operate to exclude even more persons from adequate housing. Tentative Draft No. 3, particularly in its reference to state responsibility in the areas of "large scale development" and in "development of regional or state benefit," recognizes that the states must act

---

9. The brackets indicate that the precise number is a matter of choice.
10. MLDC § 7-405.

not only to protect our *natural* resources from improper growth but also to encourage growth necessary to benefit our *human* resources and to rectify long-standing abuses of land use regulation. One can do nothing but welcome states' attempts to halt the rape of our natural resources. But we should not allow a righteous concern for the moose and goose to blind us to more critical environmental issues. Adequate housing for humans in an area reasonably accessible to jobs must surely be as legitimate an endeavor in an ethical society as resting places for terns. I see in Tentative Draft No. 3 a remarkable degree of sensitivity to the difficult choices between housing and salt marshs.

21

William Reilly

NEW DIRECTIONS IN FEDERAL LAND USE LEGISLATION

In the days when the environment was coming into its own as a
major area of public concern in the United States, Dennis O'Harrow
attempted to draw the implications of the environmental movement
for an area of long-standing interest to planners. He wrote:

> I see a great national program mounted against water pollu-
> tion. I hear a hue and cry against air pollution. . . . But I see no
> comparable concern over our pollution of the land—which is
> really the scarcest of the three basic resources of human life.
>
> The solution is simply stated, but not easily carried out. We
> need a national land use policy for all land, urban and non-
> urban, a policy with teeth in it, a policy laid down by Congress
> and administered by the White House, using all the tools and
> every governmental power in the Federal arsenal. Similarly, State
> and local governments will need to use all their powers—the
> police power, the power of eminent domain, and the taxing
> power. The time for half measures is past.[1]

O'Harrow's observation was perceptive for, at the time he wrote,
urban planners rarely identified a convergence of interest with environmental objectives. The 1960's, a decade that began with enthusiasm and ended in dashed hopes for many social planners, encom-

---

* Executive Director, Task Force on Land Use and Urban Growth, sponsored
by the President's Citizens' Advisory Committee on Environmental Quality;
Senior Staff Member, Council on Environmental Quality (on leave of absence
since July, 1972). A.B., Yale University, 1962; LL.B., Harvard University, 1965;
M.S., Urban Planning, Columbia University, 1970.

1. U.S. DEP'T OF AGRICULTURE & U.S. DEP'T OF HOUSING AND URBAN DE-
VELOPMENT, REPORT OF THE PROCEEDINGS OF THE CONFERENCE ON SOIL, WATER
AND SUBURBIA 106 (1968).

passed rising environmental expectations that did not fade with the decade, but grew stronger and contributed to several notable legislative breakthroughs. The new laws which the environmental awareness brought about were not only pollution control measures but extended to such issues as coastal zone protection, power plant siting, scenic area preservation and highway planning. The concern with protecting environmental values in land underlay the enactment of several state laws which have been referred to as a "quiet revolution in land use control,"[2] a revolution that has returned land use regulatory power to the several states. Now this revolution has reached Washington where the Senate has passed legislation which would fundamentally alter governmental relationships regarding land use planning and regulation in the United States.[3] Objectives which writers on urban and social problems have long advocated, but which the constituency for planning and housing has never been able to effectuate, stand a fair chance of achievement under the environmental aegis, as O'Harrow apparently anticipated.

This paper will examine the rationale and the historical antecedents behind current efforts to enact national land use policy legislation. It will analyze the land use policy measure under consideration. It will draw some conclusions about what we may reasonably expect from such legislation, recognizing that many important land use objectives will still remain to be achieved after national land use policy legislation is enacted.

I. THE STATES AS AGENTS OF REVOLUTION?

Perhaps one reason the land use revolution has been quiet is that its objective is modest: the transfer of power to regulate the use of privately owned land from local to state control when regional or state interests are affected by the use to which land is put. Local authority over land use, most commonly exercised through zoning and subdivision regulations under police powers delegated by states to municipalities, townships, and in a few states to counties, has become so well entrenched that proposals to transfer any portion of such authority are viewed as an intrusion of the unfamiliar into a field

---

2. F. BOSSELMAN & D. CALLIES, THE QUIET REVOLUTION IN LAND USE CONTROL (Council on Environmental Quality 1971).

3. S. 632, 92d Cong., 1st Sess. (1971). The version of the Bill that passed the Senate can be found in 118 CONG. REC. 15,278-84 (daily ed. Sept. 19, 1972).

where the key players are known and the interests understood. The prospect for different kinds of decisions where the perspective, incentives and responsibilities are supra-local is quite real and is thought to justify significant expectations. This, at least, is the theory behind the movement to enact a federal program which would provide financial assistance to states which undertake to affect land use decisions of regional impact. The Land Use Policy and Planning Assistance Act passed by the Senate, and the analogous Bill reported favorably by the House Committee on Interior and Insular Affairs,[4] but which failed to pass the House of Representatives in the 92nd Congress, would have authorized a new federal grant-in-aid program to states which assert control, directly or concurrently, with their local governments, over "areas of critical environmental concern," "areas impacted by key facilities" (major projects which induce urban growth and development with supra-local impact), and all large-scale development however defined. Although the provision is confusing in the Senate Bill, the states also would apparently be required to provide a method for assuring that "development of regional benefit" (i.e., for which there is a regional need) is not excluded or unduly restricted by local governments. A state which develops a land use program, approved after annual federal reviews, would be entitled to continued financial support under the new federal program, and would be assured that federal agencies would not act inconsistently with the state land use program except under extraordinary circumstances. It seems useful to place the new Bill, with which citizen environmental groups, Governors and many other organizations and observers are in substantial accord, in context, for the Bill's objectives and relationship to existing federal planning programs have not been sufficiently understood.

II. Federal Efforts to Encourage Sound Land Use

In one sense, it is not surprising that federal policy makers should evidence uncertainty when confronted by a proposal to reform governmental power relationships with respect to privately owned land. The federal government itself has remained largely aloof from this field which, unlike air and water pollution, does not cross state boundaries.

---

4. H.R. 7211, 92d Cong., 1st Sess. (1971); H.R. Rep. No. 1306, 92d Cong., 2d Sess. (1972).

However, since its establishment the federal government has been in the land business. Debates continued throughout much of the 19th century over the terms at which public lands were to be made available to westward moving settlers, and whether the proper objective in land disposal should be the encouragement of early settlement (as Jefferson held) or the generation of federal revenue (as Hamilton believed).

A. The Zoning Act: Federal Influence by Example

In this century federal attempts to affect the use of privately owned land have taken three forms. The first and perhaps most successful federal initiative was taken when the United States Department of Commerce commissioned and then published the Standard State Zoning Enabling Act.[5] The Zoning Act, first released in 1922, was the work of an Advisory Committee on Zoning to the Secretary of Commerce, Herbert Hoover. Secretary Hoover conceived of the project as responding to "the greatest social need of the country—more and better housing."[6]

The Act established the framework whereby states would grant their local governments the police powers to regulate the use of privately owned land. The model to which the drafters gave statutory expression, and a federal imprimatur, was one of local authority to allocate land into districts where certain kinds of development were prohibited as undesirable. The governmental relationship envisioned by the Act was one of virtually autonomous local governments going their own way with the full blessing of state government, the state having legislated its own neutrality in the Zoning Act.[7]

This made considerable sense in 1922. Good government forces, which saw the city as the natural focus of most of their progressive reforms, sought building codes to protect health and safety, and tended to identify state intervention in city affairs as officious. The battles against anti-city "special legislation" enacted by rural dominated state legislatures, and the movement for city self-government via "home rule" influenced the urban reformers, who responded by

---

5. U.S. DEP'T OF COMMERCE, A STANDARD STATE ZONING ENABLING ACT (1926).

6. S. TOLL, ZONED AMERICAN 201 (1969).

7. For a more detailed analysis of the Standard Zoning Enabling Act see AMERICAN LAW INSTITUTE, A MODEL LAND DEVELOPMENT CODE xi-xiv (Tent. Draft No. 2, 1970).

inventing zoning and convincing the Commerce Department that it should support a land use control process in which the city was dominant and the state removed.

A key assumption of the zoning process was fixity. The city was seen as a forum in which certain land uses were *per se* incompatible and, hence, were to be confined to discrete physical districts. These districts were to be subject to uniform regulations with respect to, *inter alia*, height, bulk and setback, according to the familiar principle of uniform treatment for essentially similar uses. An assumption implicit in a zoning process administered by the city (or town, township or other local government to which the state delegated police powers to regulate land use) was the adequacy of the city's territorial jurisdiction to influence change. For change is what gave rise to the need for zoning—change toward ever higher buildings and the change of shopping and residential areas into industrial quarters.[8] However, the system was designed according to a model of incremental, lot-by-lot, building-by-building change. Although it was suggested that states might wish to allow cities to anticipate expansion by controlling growth in unincorporated areas which would eventually be annexed, no mechanism for either reconciling the divergent land use plans of neighboring municipalities or for giving expression to regional interests was provided. This, then, was the system which nearly all states, in a remarkably short period of time, enacted into law.

As early as 1937, a critique of the municipal planning and zoning process was offered by a committee reporting to the President. The National Resources Committee observed that "[n]ew methods of transportation have made unprecedented urban decentralization possible. The scale of the interior planning of our cities, however, has not been changed to conform with the new mobility."[9]

B. *The Federal Carrot for Planning: The 701 Program*

In 1954, Congress authorized a program of "Urban Planning Assistance"[10] in accordance with a finding by the President's Advisory Committee on Government Housing Policies and Programs that local

---

8. *See* S. Toll, *supra* note 6, at chs. 2-3.

9. National Resources Comm., Report on Our Cities—Their Role in the National Economy 47 (1937).

10. Housing Act of 1954 §§ 701-03, 40 U.S.C. §§ 460-62 (1964), *as amended*, 40 U.S.C. §§ 460-62 (1970).

planning was not being performed adequately, particularly in smaller jurisdictions.[11] The House Report on the new measure emphasized its relationship to slum clearance:

> Your committee believes that the problem of eliminating urban slums and blight, while national in scope, is essentially a local problem. . . . Federal assistance is justified only if the community is willing to face up to the problem of neighborhood decay and to undertake programs directed to its prevention. . . . The local program must provide for utilizing appropriate private and public resources and must include an official plan of action for effectively dealing with the problem of urban slums and blight within the community and for the establishment and preservation of a well-planned community with well-organized residential neighborhoods. . . .[12]

The 701 program,[13] as it has come to be known, was originally intended to help smaller urban communities develop "plans to correct poor environmental urban conditions . . . ."[14] and to aid "official State, metropolitan or regional planning agencies to perform planning work in metropolitan and regional areas."[15] The type of planning to be supported was to include "surveys, land-use studies, urban renewal plans, technical services, and other planning work. Grants would not be made for planning specific public works."[16]

The 701 program has served as the principal source of federal financial support for comprehensive planning, evolving over the years in response to new priorities and changing planning theory. Areas impacted by approved new communities, areas disrupted by the closing or expansion of federal installations, interstate regional commissions and economic development districts all have been added as eligible grantees. Councils of government, whose functions are perhaps most comprehensive, have been heavily supported by the program. From an initial funding level of one million dollars in matching grants in 1955, the program had expanded by Fiscal Year 1972 to

---

11. H.R. REP. No. 1429, 83d Cong., 2d Sess. 1, 26 (1954).

12. *Id.* at 24-26.

13. Housing Act of 1954 §§ 701-03, 40 U.S.C. §§ 460-62 (1970), *amending* 40 U.S.C. §§ 460-62 (1964).

14. *Hearings on H.R. 5240 Before the Subcomm. of the House Comm. on Appropriations*, 84th Cong., 1st Sess., pt. 2, at 1376 (1955).

15. S. REP. No. 1472, 83d Cong., 2d Sess. 91 (1954).

16. *Id.*

$50 million with a two-thirds federal contribution formula. The earlier emphasis on public developmental planning and land use planning, particularly to avert blight in small communities, has broadened to include planning for human resources, fiscal planning and the preparation of regulatory and administrative measures.[17]

After 1968, comprehensive plans prepared with 701 program assistance were required to contain a "housing element" taking into account

> all available evidence of the assumptions and statistical bases upon which the projection of zoning, community facilities, and population growth is based, so that the housing needs of both the region and the local communities . . . will be adequately covered in terms of existing and prospective in-migrant population growth.[18]

In 1971, the President proposed a further broadening of the program to support state and local government efforts to upgrade their overall management capabilities to handle the new responsibilities to be delegated with federal revenue sharing.[19] The Administration proposed to double the amount of money available under the program.

Both the planning agency grantees and the federal funding agency have moved away from the earlier land use orientation (as the planning profession itself has) and have increasingly emphasized budgetary planning, information systems management and data collection and analysis. Although the program began simply without detailed constraints, in recent years some grant recipients have conveyed the impression that federal scrutiny has been intrusive, and that the housing element requirement has come to prevail over all others in the minds of officials of the Department of Housing and Urban Development when reviewing applications for funding.

Nevertheless, the 701 program, more than any other federal activity, has contributed to the training and development of the urban planning profession. And it has supported comprehensive planning, serving to lessen somewhat the imbalance that has had the designers

---

17. For an account of the evolution of federal planning aids and requirements see McGrath, *Planning for Growth*, in HOUSE COMM. ON BANKING AND CURRENCY, PAPERS SUBMITTED TO SUBCOMM. ON HOUSING PANELS ON HOUSING PRODUCTION, HOUSING DEMAND, AND DEVELOPING A SUITABLE LIVING ENVIRONMENT, 92d Cong., 1st Sess., pt. 2 (Comm. Print 1971).

18. Housing and Urban Development Act of 1954 § 701, 40 U.S.C. § 461 (1970), *amending* 40 U.S.C. § 461 (1964).

19. S. 1618, 92d Cong., 1st Sess. §§ 201-13 (1971).

of roads, sewers and airports determining the shape of our cities, too often leaving the comprehensive planners to smooth out the resulting rough spots.

C. *Federal Planning Requirements*: *The Sticks in the Planners' Arsenal*

The potential of federal programs and activities to disrupt local plans was recognized at least as early as 1949 when federally supported urban redevelopment plans, typically prepared by semi-autonomous urban renewal authorities, were required to be consistent with general plans prepared by local planning agencies.[20] During the following two decades, the conditions of eligibility for federal financial assistance under several programs were altered to exact a greater planning effort on the part of recipient governments. With the Housing Act of 1961,[21] the federal government broadened its concern to areawide planning, making eligibility for federal grants for the acquisition of open space dependent upon a determination that the funds are "needed . . . as part of the comprehensively planned development of the urban area."[22]

Subsequently, nearly every major housing and transportation bill has added planning requirements. During the 1960's, the federal government became more directive, edging steadily towards encouragement of interlocal cooperation, regional coordination and metropolitan government as responses to the realization that neither housing markets nor labor supply could any longer be regarded as purely local problems. Among the objectives sought in the federal planning legislation of the 1960's were the establishment of coordination among local governments, the avoidance of waste and duplication in federal investments through better communication to federal agencies about the nature of regional or metropolitan needs and the subordination of functional or public works planning activities to comprehensive areawide planning objectives. It is difficult to find observers of the planning process who believe that these objectives have been achieved. For, despite repeated Congressional declarations of support for plan-

---

20. Housing Act of 1954 §§ 701-03, 40 U.S.C. §§ 460-62 (1964), *as amended*, 40 U.S.C. §§ 460-62 (1970).

21. Housing Act of 1961, § 703, 42 U.S.C. § 1500(b) (1964), *as amended*, 42 U.S.C. § 1500(b) (1970).

22. *Id.*

ning, the regional planning institutions brought into being largely by federal initiative were without legal authority to work their will, without power to approve or disapprove local or state agency proposals, and without authority to regulate the use of land even where decisions of regional impact were involved. That they were free to make comments directly to federal granting agencies regarding the merits of local applications for funding was partially vitiated by the predominance of local executives among the boards of regional planning agencies. As a result of the impotence of advisory regional planning agencies, the regional interest has remained without an effective advocate, and authentic supra-local planning has been frustrated.

Beginning in 1962, federal highway legislation established the "Triple C" requirement[23] that expenditure of highway construction funds in urban areas in excess of 50,000 population be approved only upon a finding that proposed projects "are based on a continuing comprehensive transportation planning process carried on cooperatively by States and local communities. . . ."[24] This provision put the Bureau of Public Roads (now the Federal Highway Administration [FHWA]) into the planning business and occasioned a substantial increase in funding support for planning, with funds from FHWA for comprehensive transportation planning approximately equalling section 701 funding levels. The metropolitan transportation planning agency was not always the same as the general planning entity, although FHWA grantees were encouraged to cooperate with the planning activities of areawide and local comprehensive planning agencies—an arrangement that at least in its early days led to the graduation of countless metropolitan highway plans into regional plans as the more savvy and experienced highway planners overwhelmed the regional planners.

A particularly significant federal planning encouragement was contained in section 204 of the Demonstration Cities and Metropolitan Development Act of 1966,[25] which required review by a metropolitan planning agency of applications for federal funding for hospitals, airports, libraries, water supply and distribution facilities, sewerage

23. Federal Aid Highway Act of 1962 § 9(a), 23 U.S.C. § 134 (1964), *as amended*, 23 U.S.C. § 134 (1970).

24. *Id.*

25. Demonstration Cities and Metropolitan Development Act of 1966 § 204, 42 U.S.C. § 3334 (Supp. V, 1969), *as amended*, 42 U.S.C. § 3334 (1970).

facilities, waste treatment works, highways, transportation facilities, and water development and land conservation projects. Pursuant to this requirement, and to a later parallel requirement of the Intergovernmental Cooperation Act of 1968,[26] the Bureau of the Budget (now the Office of Management and Budget) issued Circular A-95.[27] Circular A-95 implements the laws by defining the federal programs subject to the review and comment of planning agencies, the procedures for designating state, regional and metropolitan "clearinghouses," and the methods for obtaining review and comment by the areawide agency or clearinghouse of applications for federal assistance.

The procedure grew out of a recommendation of the Advisory Commission on Intergovernmental Relations in 1961.[28] The Commission had

> noted repeated instances where an official of a political subdivision in a metropolitan area learn[ed] through the newspapers of a Federal grant for a hospital, sewage treatment plant or other large physical facility in a neighboring subdivision. Quite often recriminations follow[ed] regarding the need for improved interchange of information and improved coordination in planning for governmental facilities in the metropolitan area. The Commission believe[ed] that considerations of economy alone . . . demand[ed] a firm requirement for full exchange of information within metropolitan areas prior to sizable Federal contributions for physical facilities in the area.[29]

Although federal support for planning had increased through the years, Congress concurred in the conclusion that the planning effort being supported was directed too heavily toward meeting specific functional planning requirements, and had not resulted in effective overall planned development. Moreover, only a few metropolitan areas were found to have "developed arrangements to effectively coordinate actions to implement local planning."[30]

---

26. Intergovernmental Cooperation Act of 1968 § 401, 42 U.S.C. § 4231 (Supp. V, 1969), as amended, 42 U.S.C. § 4231 (1970).

27. Bureau of the Budget Circular No. A-95 (July 24, 1969), revised in Office of Management and Budget Circular No. A-95 Revised (Feb. 9, 1971).

28. ADVISORY COMM. ON INTERGOVERNMENTAL RELATIONS, REPORT ON GOVERNMENTAL STRUCTURE, ORGANIZATION AND PLANNING IN METROPOLITAN AREAS (1961).

29. Id. at 49.

30. S. REP. No. 1439, 89th Cong., 2d Sess. 17 (1966).

Nevertheless, in neither the Demonstration Cities Act nor the Intergovernmental Cooperation Act did the Congress confront directly the facts that not only is the local perspective typically limited by the size of the jurisdiction, but the economic and political incentives under which most American cities operate are counter-regional. Whether the immediate interest is the attraction of revenue-generating industry, or "preserving the character of the neighborhood," the wisest course for the municipality is "beggar thy neighbor."

A statement of minority views took exception to the committee report's claim that the new procedure would help bring together the "many divergent public bodies in metropolitan areas":

> It is suggested that one of the reasons for this legislation is the complexity of metropolitan government and the multiplicity of political jurisdictions and agencies involved. We do not find anything in the bill that would lessen the complexity or reduce the number of jurisdictions.[31]

The signatories to the minority statement perhaps had overheard talk about regional "institution-building" through the new procedure, for they went on to add that if the proposal was really designed to encourage a dilution of local authority, the Bill would be even more objectionable.

The question of whether to give planning agencies (albeit not regional ones) real power to veto projects found inconsistent with comprehensive plans was later raised in the Senate in a provision of the Intergovernmental Cooperation Act—the other legislative parent of Circular A-95—which would have conditioned federal support for most public works activities upon certification, not merely comment, by the governing body of the general local government that the project was consistent with its planning objectives.[32] The measure, however, was dropped at the request of the Johnson Administration.[33]

According to the Report of the Senate Committee on Government Operations, section 401 (b) of the Intergovernmental Cooperation Act[34] was to require

---

31. *Id.* at 35.

32. S. 561, 89th Cong., 2d Sess. § 503 (1966).

33. See the statement by Harold Seidman, Ass't Director, Bureau of the Budget, in *Hearings on S. 561, H.R. 6118, H.R. 10212, H.R. 11863, H.R. 12896, H.R. 17955 Before a Subcomm. of the House Comm. on Gov't Operations*, 89th Cong., 2d Sess. 311 (1966) [hereinafter cited as *Hearings on S. 561*].

34. 42 U.S.C. § 4231(b) (1970).

that all viewpoints—national, regional, State, and local—shall, to the extent possible, be fully considered and taken into account in planning Federal or federally assisted development programs and projects. Regional, State, and local government objectives shall be considered and evaluated within a framework of national public objectives, and available projections of future national conditions and needs of regions, States, and localities shall be considered in plan formulation, evaluation, and review.[35]

In his statement in support of the reported Bill, Senator Muskie, who had introduced the legislation, declared:

It [the Bill] recognizes that the economic and social development of our Nation, our strength in world affairs, and the success of many recently enacted domestic programs depend in large degree on the sound and orderly development of our urban communities. It builds on the theory that such development can best be accomplished first by maximizing the benefits of Federal programs to meet urban needs, and second, by encouraging the States and localities to develop comprehensive planning and programming to take full advantage of these benefits.[36]

This was a heavy load of hopes and expectations that the new process was to bear. How, in fact, has it borne up?

Circular A-95 provides what little muscle there is in metropolitan and regional planning. It permits planners to be heard, not just by the functional program agencies at the state or local level, but also at the federal agency level with regard to funding specific projects. It represents a significant elevation of the comprehensive planning function, and it may one day be regarded in retrospect as a transitional mechanism leading toward effective regional coordination or even to metropolitan government.

As in the case of the 701 program, the A-95 process has enjoyed steady accretions as year by year more A-95 agencies have been designated and more federal programs have been added to those which are subject to the requirement of obtaining review and comment "for the purpose of assuring maximum consistency . . . with State, regional and local comprehensive plans."[37]

---

35. S. REP. No. 1456, 90th Cong., 2d Sess. 18 (1968).

36. See the statement by the Hon. Edmund S. Muskie, Senator from Maine, in *Hearings on S. 561* at 499.

37. Office of Management and Budget Circular No. A-95 Revised 5 (Feb. 9, 1971).

Originally excluded from coverage under A-95, federal housing assistance programs were added in 1971. In 1969, direct federal construction activity, such as that conducted by the Corps of Engineers and the General Services Administration, was also added. A recent notable addition to A-95 is a requirement that civil rights aspects of applications for federal assistance be considered and made subject to review and comment.[38] This provision was a partial response to concerns of center city minority leaders that suburban dominance in councils of government might lead to exclusionary abuse of the procedure in some areas.

Two annual reviews, by the Office of Management and Budget, of the procedures established to implement the parallel planning requirements of the Demonstration Cities Act and the Intergovernmental Cooperation Act have noted "improved interlocal communication, cooperation, and coordination."[39] The agency also reported that the percentage of all reported reviews recommending project changes, *i.e.*, criticizing an application by a local government, special district or functional agency, went from five per cent in 1968 to 18 per cent in 1969.[40] This is an indication that such agencies may have displayed more courage than one might have expected considering the predominance of local political barons on the executive board of the typical areawide planning agency.

Undoubtedly, the cumulative effect of federal incentives for state, regional and metropolitan planning has been significant. As of the summer of 1971, the results of two decades of federal planning legislation included an increase of active planning professionals from 248 to more than 6,200, the growth in recognized graduate planning schools from 12 to 42, the formation of more than 200 metropolitan planning agencies and regional councils, and the preparation of 4,000 local comprehensive development plans.[41] To the extent that the quality of plans is high, federal planning assistance and requirements can be given credit.

However, there is a widespread belief among students of the planning process that planning has received less than a fair shake in the

---

38. Office of Management and Budget Circular No. A-95 Revised (Transmittal Memo. No. 2, Mar. 8, 1972).

39. BUREAU OF THE BUDGET, SECTION 204—THE FIRST YEAR 6 (1968).

40. BUREAU OF THE BUDGET, SECTION 204 OF THE DEMONSTRATION CITIES AND METROPOLITAN DEVELOPMENT ACT OF 1966: TWO YEARS EXPERIENCE 9 (1970).

41. McGrath, *supra* note 17, at 959.

United States. Even defenders of the 701 program and the A-95 process concede the ineffectual nature of much advisory planning, review and comment, and take refuge in the "institution-building" potential of these programs. One authority has written:

> Planning theory and techniques have been evolving at a far faster rate during the past twenty years than the political institutions that might benefit most from planning, and neither the general public nor the vast majority of local political leaders have been able to assimilate the content of planning as an evolving field or to accommodate its offerings. As a general consequence of this generation-lag of public understanding behind the evolution of urban planning, the nation is being deprived of major resources in planning techniques and information which could be used to improve its ability to conduct essential public business and provide a basis for anticipating future problems and opportunities inherent in national growth. . . .
> . . . [Planning] might offer substantial benefits to the nation in the growth years ahead if it were actually tried. . . .[42]

Something, clearly, has not worked. Comments are made, papers generated, and circulars and regulations complied with, yet close observers of the process do not believe that planning in most areas is particularly comprehensive. They do not see local development activity as being well distributed from a regional or metropolitan point of view; nor do they see federal agency activities as coordinated. One could cite examples of local actions, many with federal financial support, taken in disregard of local comprehensive plans and without any concern for regional impact. Two recently documented case histories, discussed below, suffice to make the point.

In 1969, the Board of Supervisors of Fairfax County, a fast-growing Washington, D.C. suburban area, adopted a master plan developed by the county planning staff. The plan was developed with the financial assistance of the Department of Housing and Urban Development under the 701 program.[43] The adopted master plan anticipated a low-density holding zone for a sub-watershed where development was to be deferred for at least five years.[44] The holding zone was

---

42. *Id.* at 948.

43. M. CLAWSON, SUBURBAN LAND CONVERSION IN THE UNITED STATES 250 (1971).

44. This case history has been reported in POPULATION REFERENCE BUREAU, SUBURBAN GROWTH—A CASE STUDY (Population Bull. Vol. 28, No. 1, 1972).

proposed in order to avert continuation of patterns of sprawling development that had characterized much of the county for two decades. It was feared that an immediate go-ahead to development in the particular outlying corner of the county would impose heavy public service costs upon the county and would inevitably lead to scattering, precluding later implementation of plans for satellite clusters.

While the planners were proceeding with the development of the comprehensive plans, a sanitary district, which had been organized by a group of developers and owners of undeveloped property, devised a sewer plan which was based on a far higher population projection for the area than the planning agency accepted, and which would serve many more than the planned number of residents in the holding zone. The sewer plan was actually approved by the Board of Supervisors at the same meeting as the holding zone. The sewer, of course, induced heavy development of the area—development accommodated by frequent rezonings which one supervisor was later quoted as having justified on the ground that, after all, "the sewer is there."[45] Waste treatment facilities and interceptor sewers to which the new sewer was connected were financed in part by grants from the Federal Water Quality Office.[46]

The selection of a site for a new Los Angeles airport, projected to be the largest in the country in passenger volume by 1980, offers a second illustration of planning in actual operation.[47] In this instance, a site proposal developed by the Los Angeles Department of Airports was approved after a 23-day review by the city planning agency. The county regional planning commission took six months before finding the project consistent with regional planning for the county. The commission then found it necessary to study the likely impact of the decision, acknowledging in its subsequent application for federal planning help that airport impacts upon vegetation, hydrology, climate, wildlife, air quality, noise levels and water quality of the region were undetermined. The commission apparently did not consider it necessary to explain its earlier acquiescence in the airport site selec-

45. *Id.* at 16-17.

46. Environmental Protection Agency, Project Register 122 (Dec. 31, 1971).

47. This illustration is based upon an analysis contained in Center for Study of Responsive Law, Power and Land in California I-V-17 to 40, II-VII-71 to 116 (Prelim. Draft of the Rep. on Land Use in the State of Cal. 1971).

tion as not inconsistent with regional planning, given the very significant, basic questions which had not yet been studied.

The Southern California Association of Governments (SCAG), the A-95 agency, was consulted about the consistency of the Airport Department's site decision four months after the decision had been announced. The occasion for consulting SCAG was the A-95 review requirement applicable to the Airport Department's request for federal funds for advance land acquisition. SCAG did not except to the proposal, but did recommend further planning studies. Reportedly, SCAG had never made a recommendation against funding of an application for federal aid under A-95.[48] One reporter concluded: "To take on the Department of Airports, SCAG would have had to step way out of its league."[49]

There is no reason to believe that these two examples are atypical of the way major, development-inducing public works decisions are made. The continued predominance of the public works planners over the comprehensive planners, the local boosters over the regional planners, the immediate and local economic advantage over the long-run and metropolitan interest, taken together with the repeated federal investments and declarations of faith in planning, have contributed to a belief that we have tried regional planning and it has failed.[50] In fact, the federal government, properly declining to impose metropolitan government from the top down, has seemed to be flirting with it, nurturing inclinations toward it and lending its moral support to regionalization. But, in most areas, neither center city minority leaders nor suburban mayors see advantages in metropolitan government. Perhaps concepts such as efficiency, coordination, avoidance of duplication and waste, and better intergovernmental communication are without widespread compelling appeal. Or perhaps yet another governmental device—an unfamiliar one at that—is simply not welcome where it promises no tangible, desired benefit.

In any event, the constituency for federal planning programs has always had a large contingent of mayors and local planning and renewal officials to whom local autonomy and home rule were hard-won victories against rural-oriented states. The very groups that were

---

48. *Id.* at I-V-38.

49. *Id.*

50. For a critique of regional planning see Address by R. Babcock, *Let's Stop Romancing Regional Planning*, University of Notre Dame, Feb. 16, 1972.

fighting for a direct federal-local relationship, a means of bypassing states considered insensitive to the urban crisis in the 1960's, could hardly have been expected to want to surrender certain of their powers over land use to governmental entities further removed than they from their problems.

III. THE ENVIRONMENTAL MOVEMENT AND PLANNING

An ally of extraordinary power recently has entered the battle for more effective planning. The environmental movement, born of solid American ancestry in 19th century naturalism, revived after a long sleep by the idealism of the 1960's and tempered by a string of battles against the public works agencies, has matured during the past few years. The concern for the environment has achieved significant legislative reforms at all levels of government in a very short period of time. The ecological perspective holds that unless we can view proposals as they affect the whole, we will be unable to develop and use resources wisely—an outlook that makes environmentalism a natural ally of comprehensive planning. The infusion of substance, of tangible environmental advantages that are pursued through planning, elevates planning and gives it meaning and purpose in the eyes of those to whom it may once have been abstract and neutral. Saving the bay, the beaches or the mountains from impairment by inappropriate development can rally support for regional planning of a sort that citizens believe will demonstrate the wisdom of resource conservation.

Undoubtedly, the convergence of planning objectives and environmental objectives is not complete. Planners typically are trained to accommodate and shape development and redevelopment. Environmental groups in many parts of the country are taking a skeptical view of urbanization and are attempting to restrict and even halt urban growth.[51] In the process of resisting new development, however, environmentalists are asking the kind of questions that planning agencies ought to have been raising in the course of reviewing project proposals submitted pursuant to Circular A-95. The National Environmental Policy Act (NEPA),[52] has profoundly altered the planning process by permitting citizen groups, public interest lawyers and public environmental agencies to have access to the thinking behind

---

51. For accounts of current attitudes toward urban growth in the United States see *The Land Use Battle That Business Faces*, BUSINESS WEEK, Aug. 26, 1972, at 44; *Banning the Boom*, NEWSWEEK, Aug. 21, 1972, at 40; *The Great Wild Californiated West*, TIME, Aug. 21, 1972, at 15.

developmental proposals and to compel proponent agencies to deal publicly with real planning issues. Section 102 (2) (C) of NEPA[53] requires proponents of major federal actions significantly affecting the quality of the human environment to set forth in a "detailed statement" by a "responsible official" an account of the anticipated impact on the environment, adverse impacts, alternatives that have been considered and forseeable long-term effects asssociated with the proposed action. The questions posed by NEPA, of course, are similar to those posed by the planning process. Any plan rests upon an implicit resolution of choices involving long and short-term considerations, resource conservation and exploitation, and upon an analysis and rejection of alternatives. However, NEPA requires that these formerly implicit considerations be made explicit and public. Moreover, the Act has the effect of placing the proponent agency in the position vis-a-vis the public of advocate for its proposal, justifying it and taking responsibility for it. The questions posed by NEPA must be asked in reference to an imminent decision, often in the glare of public scrutiny and controversy.

NEPA has changed the ground rules for major public works planning and for the planning of other large urban developments in which there is any federal involvement. The guidelines affecting federal agency implementation of NEPA give a broad reading, supported by several court decisions,[54] to federal actions deemed to require impact statements.[55] Since actions potentially subject to the statement requirement include federal insurance, licenses, permits and grants, NEPA reaches many of the important state and local decisions, such as federally assisted highway and airport projects, bridges over navigable interstate waters, insured housing projects and new communities, oil refineries, power plants and other industrial projects sited on waterways subject to federal jurisdiction.[56]

---

52. National Environmental Policy Act, 42 U.S.C. §§ 4321 et seq. (1970).

53. Id. § 4332(2)(C). See also 36 Fed. Reg. 7724-29 (1971).

54. See, e.g., Calvert Cliffs Coordinating Comm. v. Atomic Energy Comm'n, 449 F.2d 1109 (D.C. Cir. 1971); Natural Resources Defense Council v. Morton, 337 F. Supp. 165 (D.D.C. 1971); Environmental Defense Fund v. Corps of Eng'rs, 325 F. Supp. 728 (E.D. Ark. 1971).

55. For a discussion of the breadth of activities that have been reached under § 102(2)(C) of NEPA, including programs in which federal involvement may be minimal or under authority of laws passed long before environmental policies were enunciated, see COUNCIL ON ENVIRONMENTAL QUALITY, THE THIRD ANNUAL REPORT OF THE COUNCIL ON ENVIRONMENTAL QUALITY 224-30 (1972).

56. 36 Fed. Reg. 7724-29 (1971).

NEPA focuses attention on issues involved in major developmental decisions that formerly had often been disposed of without effective public involvement. On the one hand, pre-NEPA critics of proposals could be stilled by referring them to a plan approved some time previously and clearly indicating heavy industry, a highway interchange or an airport in the area—at least if the planners had the foresight to anticipate it. On the other hand, a hasty rezoning intended to accommodate a use altogether unanticipated in a plan was entitled to the same legislative presumption of validity and protection from scrutiny as a long-standing classification. In either event, the plan was a formality and the officially sanctioned use was accorded considerable advantages. As a result, official choices affecting major developmental proposals frequently were inexpert, loosely justified and offered without a need to persuade that alternative means of dealing with developmental needs and resource protection had been exhaustively explored.

In some ways NEPA is similar to federal legislation on regional planning. Section 102 (2) (C) of NEPA does not prohibit substantive choices any more than does section 204 of the Demonstration Cities Act. It merely asks that proposals and alternatives be illuminated through a process of review and comment that elicits views of responsible expert agencies. Yet environmentalists have been merciless in forcing strict compliance by federal agencies with the NEPA process, appealing and winning judicial vindication of their demands that, regardless of the agencies' positions, they employ interdisciplinary planning,[57] fairly assess alternatives[58] and give appropriate agencies sufficient opportunity for review of proposed actions.[59] As of August, 1972, over 200 legal actions to enforce federal agency compliance with the provisions of NEPA had been recorded.[60]

The success of the new procedure is due largely to the environ-

---

57. Environmental Defense Fund v. Corps of Eng'rs, 325 F. Supp. 728 (E.D. Ark. 1971).

58. Natural Resources Defense Council v. Morton, 337 F. Supp. 165 (D.D.C. 1971); Environmental Defense Fund v. Corps of Eng'rs, 325 F. Supp. 728 (E.D. Ark. 1971).

59. Upon the advice of General Counsel, the Secretary of Transportation reconsidered his decision to approve the proposed site location for the new Los Angeles International Airport discussed in the text at 43. What the regional planning agencies could not themselves assume by way of comprehensive analysis, NEPA, as interpreted by the Department of Transportation, thus equipped them to undertake.

60. COUNCIL ON ENVIRONMENTAL QUALITY, supra note 55, at 249.

mental lawyers. They took NEPA seriously and invested their energies in making it an effective law—the far-reaching effects of which even its legislative authors probably did not anticipate. As a result, for practical purposes, the burden of public persuasion is now placed on the proponents of developmental projects with the implicit suggestion: "You're the one who wants to alter the status quo; you justify your action to us now and don't refer us back to a plan that nobody understood or took seriously when it was prepared five years ago or revised yesterday."

Although this new attitude may offend by its acceptance of "ad hockery," the simple fact is that the procedure reflects a more realistic understanding of the way major development is sited. No one any longer expects comprehensive plans to detail precisely the nature and location of new development. The vast majority of large-scale projects are, and always have been, accommodated by rezoning. In fact, progressive elements in the planning profession have moved away from the preoccupation with colored maps showing various use districts because that approach failed to reflect the more sophisticated social dynamics, the mixed uses and variegated possibilities that give distinctiveness and life to a community. The tradition embodied in the A-95 procedure of requiring planning agencies to take the initiative to explain whether a proposed public works project is consistent with regional planning in practice meant that the planning agency really was obligated only if it found the project inconsistent. Then the burden of detailing its critique was imposed, a burden made heavier by the absence in many areas of a comprehensive regional or metropolitan plan to rely on for clear support. The era of positive planning, of active governmental intervention aimed at getting the best in new development and not just in preventing the worst through minimum standards and negative constraints, is brought nearer by the NEPA process with its implicit question: "What is in this proposed project for the public?" NEPA has given planners a new tool and set an important precedent for federal intervention and detailed review of federally supported state, local and private decisions.

IV. PLANNING AND NATIONAL LAND USE POLICY LEGISLATION

Many significant land use bills owe their existence to a crisis. The Land Use Policy and Planning Assistance Act of 1972,[61] which passed

---

61. S. 632, 92d Cong., 1st Sess. (1971). *See* note 3 *supra*.

the Senate by a vote of 60 to 18 on September 19, 1972, and then died in the 92nd Congress, drew strength from the experience of officials in the Executive Branch and in Congress of resisting a local proposal to site an airport adjacent to the Big Cypress swamp in Florida. The federal efforts to deter the Dade County Port Authority from going ahead with a project that would have stimulated considerable urbanization in the swamp, with foreseeable damage not only to the swamp itself but also to the nearby Everglades National Park, which required a steady flow of water from the swamp to sustain its ecology, required a sorting out at the federal level of values and opinions regarding the land use decisions of lower level governments. The aggressive intervention on the part of two federal agencies and the White House to relocate the airport accomplished its purpose but left an impression that something was wrong. Procedures for relating the planning decisions of the local airport authority to the plans of other state and local agencies in Florida were defective. Methods for coordinating the activities of federal agencies supporting public works in the area were inadequate. The power of the airport sponsor to take an action potentially damaging to regional interests in preserving a unique environmental asset was practically unchecked.

Senator Jackson, author of section 102 (2) (C) of NEPA, introduced a bill in 1970,[62] designed to respond to the deficiencies he perceived as a result of the Miami Jetport affair, and several months later the President proposed a National Land Use Policy Act[63] as part of his 1971 legislative program for the environment. The original Jackson Bill would have provided federal funds to states for planning and classifying land use according to several uses including residential, commerical, industrial, agricultural, transportation and recreational.[64] The Bill was simple and, over several months, stimulated a growing familiarity with land use issues, particularly among national environmental groups.

---

62. The bill to provide for a national land use policy was a proposed amendment to the Water Resources Planning Act, 79 Stat. 244 (1965), *as amended*, 82 Stat. 935 (1968) in S. 3354, 91st Cong., 2d Sess. (1970); this was later reintroduced as S. 632, 92d Cong., 1st Sess. (1971).

63. The bill proposed by the President in his 1971 Message to Congress on the Environment was S. 992, 92d Cong., 1st Sess. (1971); H.R. 7211, 92d Cong., 1st Sess. (1971).

64. S. 3354, 91st Cong., 2d Sess. §§ 402-03 (1970).

An initial venture, the legislation did not explicitly attempt to alter the complex institutional relationships that stood in the way of land use reform, relationships between state and local governments and between various state public works agencies. Lands located within an "incorporated city which has exercised land use planning and authority," including some growing urban areas where land use problems are most acute, were excluded from coverage under the Jackson Bill.[65] The notion of classification of areas according to a single, dominant use was unsophisticated in an era when zoning had had its requiem, and mixed uses had come to be highly regarded by planners. Finally, the Bill lacked a social dimension, and failed to prescribe a method to assure that, in addition to protecting some areas against inappropriate development, other areas would be required to accept regionally needed development.

During the summer of 1970, the Council on Environmental Quality (CEQ) published its first annual report on the quality of the environment, as required by NEPA, and included a substantial chapter on land use.[66] Essentially, the chapter acknowledged the complicity of federal programs in exacerbating effective local planning, and distinguished three principal deficiencies in existing local land use control arrangements. First, according to the CEQ analysis, environmental values are often sacrificed because local governments either: (1) fail to appreciate the effects of their decisions upon an ecological system only part of which lies within their boundaries, or (2) realizing an area's environmental significance, nevertheless prefer the tax rateables new development would bring over preservation. Second, social and fiscal pressures felt at the local level make it as difficult to site certain kinds of development as to prevent development in environmentally critical areas, even though a clear regional need for the development may be indisputable. Third, large public works projects, often federally assisted airports and highways, have a disruptive effect upon local planning by inducing overwhelming and ill-considered secondary development in their surrounding areas. The National Land Use Policy Bill proposed by the Administration in early 1971 was designed to deal with these principal issues.

Relying upon the analysis in the CEQ Report, and borrowing heavily from concepts contained in the Tentative Draft of the American

---

65. *Id.* § 406.

66. COUNCIL ON ENVIRONMENTAL QUALITY, *supra* note 55, at 165-97.

Law Institute's Model Land Development Code,[67] the Administration Bill provided for a grant-in-aid to states in order to assist them in reforming land use regulatory procedures. Specifically, states were to be required, as a condition of federal financing, to identify and regulate the use of their "areas of critical environmental concern," defined to include the coastal and Great Lakes zone, shorelands of major rivers and lakes, floodplains, scenic and historic districts, other rare or valuable ecosystems, and areas rendered hazardous to development (*e.g.*, by seismic activity or subsidence) .[68] States were to have a method for assuring that "development of regional benefit," which affects the constituents of more than one local government, is not unduly restricted or excluded by local governments.[69] And states were to identify and control their "areas impacted by key facilities," defined to include major airports, highway interchanges and recreational developments.[70] The legislation also would have required states to control large-scale development.[71]

Three methods of acceptable state "control" were prescribed: (1) direct and exclusive state land use regulation, (2) concurrent state-local regulation as is provided for in most state coastal wetland protection laws, and (3) state prescription of land use criteria and standards subject to local implementation and judicial enforcement.[72]

In early 1971, the Administration submitted amendments intended to assure that the location and design of major airports, highways, highway interchanges and parks were subject to the state land use programs, and that state land use agencies share authority with public works agencies over these decisions.[73]

As passed by the Senate, the Land Use Policy and Planning Assistance Act is a compromise between the planning emphases of the Jackson Bill and the regulatory orientation of the Administration Bill. It requires states to develop first a comprehensive planning proc-

---

67. AMERICAN LAW INSTITUTE, A MODEL LAND DEVELOPMENT CODE, *supra* note 7.

68. S. 632, 92d Cong., 1st Sess. § 501(e) (1971).

69. *Id.* § 303. *See* note 3 *supra*.

70. *Id.*

71. *Id.*

72. *Id*

73. Letter from Rogers B. Morton (Secretary of the Interior) to Wayne N. Aspinall (Chairman, House Comm. on Interior and Insular Affairs), Feb. 8, 1972.

ess involving data collection, information analysis, demographic projections, etc.,[74] and then a selective regulatory program for critical areas and issues.[75]

Unfortunately, the Senate Bill fails to include development of regional benefit in its operative requirements. However, the measure does refer to development of regional benefit in its definitional section and in provisions relating to federal agency review of state programs, suggesting the possibility of an oversight in the more important operative language. The Senate Bill also fails to specifically mention airports, highways and parks as key facilities, although power plants are included. In other important respects (with the exception of sanctions originally proposed as phased reductions of up to 21 per cent of a state's entitlement to highway, airport, and land and water conservation funds in the event of a failure by a state to comply with the new land use program within five years of enactment), the Senate Bill is substantially similar to the earlier Administration measure.

The Bill is premised upon a distinction between land use decisions of regional or state impact which are to be elevated to state agency control, and decisions of purely local impact which are not intended to be affected by the legislation. Far from an effort to scrap our existing land use control system and start anew, the Bill represents an attempt to conserve the best features of local control by disencumbering local governments of decisions which threaten to overwhelm and discredit them. The implicit judgment of the legislation is that the local perspective is often limited, and that local development-dependent revenue collection systems are counter-regional, necessitating that a broader population be represented in decision-making affecting land use allocations of regional significance. Although local planning and implementation may remain intact, major development decisions are to be subject to state veto.

The word "regional" is used here loosely. In fact, the reliance upon the state to make land use decisions of supra-local impact is more a lawyer's than a regional planner's choice. Nothing about the states assures that they will embrace regional ecological systems or distinct areas of housing and labor supply. Rather, it is the fact that states have effective powers to regulate, to tax and, if necessary, to condemn that distinguish them from more rationally organized, if practically

---

74. S. 632, 92d Cong., 1st Sess. § 302 (1971).
75. *Id.* § 303. *See* note 3 *supra.*

impotent, planning entities. Thus, the Bill represents a decision finally to break with the long federal tradition of support for purely advisory planning. For better or worse, the entity with the power is now to be asked to make the key planning decisions.

Like NEPA, the land use Bill is process-oriented legislation. It does not prescribe substantive directives on the use and abuse of land. The Bill would not say to the state "Thou shalt not develop thy wetlands," but rather that states shall have a method of control over land use in areas of critical environmental concern "where uncontrolled development could result in irreversible damage to important historic, cultural, or aesthetic values. . . ."[76] The Bill does not instruct states not to develop within so many feet of the coastline (as Norway prescribes), but merely requests states to identify and control land use in the shorelands of rivers, lakes and streams, beaches and dunes, coastal wetlands and other lands inundated by the tides.[77] The legislation puts faith in a better decision-making procedure to get a better result. The issue is worthy of some analysis, for it was the subject of considerable Senate controversy in debate on the Bill.[78]

There is always danger that any mere procedure may be exploited once the old players become comfortable with the new rules. Environmentally unpopular decisions have been held up for more extended review required by environmental legislation, only to eventually go forward with their deleterious effects unchanged once these effects had been disclosed and alternatives considered on the record. Undoubtedly, the temptation is strong, particularly among those who participated in the battles for better pollution control laws, to try to repeat their achievements in the field of land use. In fact, Senator Muskie, author of air quality and water quality legislation, led the fight in the Senate to insert substantive directives in the land use Bill.

There are three reasons why federal land use legislation should reject substantive directives or standards. First, the essential objective in the field of land use is institutional reform. Decisions are being made by local governments not because they have not been told that wetlands are ecologically significant and should be protected, but because localities have other, more compelling (financial), reasons for developing such areas. Second, political realities of the sort that have

---

76. S. 632, 92d Cong., 1st Sess. § 501 (1971).

77. *Id.*

78. 118 CONG. REC. 15,162-64 (daily ed. Sept. 18, 1972).

delayed land use reforms for several years will be more difficult to overcome if substantive objectives are more detailed and federal intrusion into the review of specific developmental decisions of lower-level governments is made necessary. Third, there is a fundamental difference between air and water quality planning, on the one hand, and land use planning, on the other. It is possible to set ambient air quality or emission standards with precision (so many parts of x pollutant per million) but the analogy to that approach in the land use field would probably be unsuccessful (*e.g.*, compaction allowable in x type of area to y tons per square foot). There is a relative simplicity about our expectations regarding air and water that allows us to measure degradation in terms of disruption of straightforward processes.

What certitudes we can muster about the proper functioning of natural processes in land fail as we enter the built environment where the object is precisely to intrude development (which the less thoughtful environmentalist sometimes analogizes to pollution) sensitively into nature, reorganizing natural characteristics in harmonious and humanly satisfying ways. As a result of the complexity of this exercise, land use standards are invariably expressed not as simple injunctions but as principles for use: "houses shall be sited in such a way as to be substantially indistinguishable from the river," or "waterfront development permits shall be limited to those uses which require or depend upon a waterfront site," or "buildings constructed within the historic district shall be of a style, bulk and height similar to or compatible with the historic buildings." Such principles of use become more vague and less helpful as they are applied more generally without regard for the specific characteristics of an area. The vagueness of such principles, and the differences of interpretation to which they would be subject, should suggest the inappropriateness of making them standards for a federal reviewing agency to apply in determining the adequacy of a state's land use program.

Nevertheless, it is true that where specific values or characteristics can be isolated, general directives could be provided: "biologically productive wetlands shall not be destroyed," "earthquake faults and floodplains shall not be developed." Note that it is easier to prescribe universal principles where development of any sort is undesirable. In fact, in those areas subject to the federal government's own direct authority, such as tidal wetlands, beaches and public lands, and where there are local or regional district offices to administer them, such stringent policies could at least be tried. But it would be a bold act of uncertain consequence for federal law to specifically prescribe in the first major federally inspired land use reform in 50 years, what one level of government shall permit another level of government to allow private landowners to do. Once states have established land use planning and regulatory processes along the lines likely to be required by the federal law, it may be more appropriate to consider specific, substantive directives aimed at preventing irresistible destruction of environmental values.

The fact remains, however, that national land use policy legislation will not assure variety in suburbs, predictability in urbanizing areas, better design of shopping centers, etc. It will not provide states with conservation and development plans. Nor will it resolve the question of how far the public authority may constitutionally go in curtailing the use of privately owned land without running afoul of the Constitution's requirement that governmental takings be compensated.

But the enactment of the Bill, reintroduced in the 93rd Congress, would focus unprecedented attention on these questions, and force a resolution of some of them in each state. By inserting the state into the regionally significant land use decisions, the narrow perspective and the counter-regional incentives which constrain local governments would be reduced. Local control would by no means be undone (indeed, the decentralization that characterizes American land use controls is the envy of some European, particularly French, officials whose system has suffered the opposite emphasis). The clear aim of the legislation is to ask no more of states than that they assert themselves where regional considerations are involved. But that is precisely the Gordian knot that has long needed cutting.

Perhaps most important, a realistic framework for reconciling social and environmental interests is offered in the process which the land use policy legislation would require states to establish. Although the needs of poor people for housing, and the concerns of environmentalists about ecological integrity and aesthetic quality need not conflict, they occasionally do. Superficially this may look like a quality-quantity tension, with those who have the quantity problem pretty well under control turning to quality questions. In fact, the environmental awareness is likely to make possible the enactment of legislation which contains a process for striking down exclusionary land use controls.[79]

79. In a keynote address to the American Society of Planning Officials, Leonard

V. The New Mood in American Attitudes Toward
Urban Development

In recent years, a new attitude toward urban growth has become evident in the United States. This attitude does not accept traditional processes of relatively unconstrained, piecemeal urbanization as entirely desirable or inevitable. Increasingly, new development proposals are measured according to their satisfaction of environmental criteria —what proposed development will generate in terms of additional traffic on the highways, pollution of air and water, erosion and scenic disturbance. To some extent, this attitude reflects sophistication on the part of citizens about the overall, long-term economic impact of development. Immediate economic gains due to job creation and increased purchasing by builders and consumers are being set off against higher public facilities costs for schools, roads, water treatment plants, sewers and human services that new residents will require.

Basically, however, the new attitude toward growth in America is not economically motivated. The new mood appears to be part of a rising emphasis on human values, on the preservation of natural and cultural characteristics that give distinctiveness, charm and desirability to a place as a humanly satisfying environment. The new mood may not be willing to sacrifice an achieved economic status by throwing out existing industry, but in many areas it seems ready to forego a measure of future economic advantage by keeping out new industry, maintaining a stable population, and preserving existing low density and scale.

This new mood can be seen in many parts of the United States, particularly in the most environmentally popular areas. Vermont, Maine, Massachusetts, Delaware, Colorado, Florida, California, Ore-

---

Garment, Special Consultant to the President, referred to publicly assisted housing as one possible example of development of regional benefit. Garment, *The Nixon Revolution*, in PLANNING 1971, at 19 (1971). The environmental parentage of the land use policy bill gave the provision a better chance of enactment than a measure aimed at similar objectives. The latter measure was offered by letter as an amendment to S. 3699, the Housing and Urban Development Act of 1970, from Secretary Romney to Senator Sparkman, Chairman of the Senate Comm. on Housing, Banking and Urban Affairs, dated May 27, 1970. The proposed amendment to S. 3699 would have authorized the Attorney General, after consultation with the HUD Secretary, to bring a civil action against any local government which acted to prevent "the reasonable provision" in undeveloped areas "of low and moderate income housing eligible for Federal assistance in a manner inconsistent with any State or local comprehensive or master plans for such areas." The measure was allowed to die.

gon and Hawaii have experienced broad, state-wide movements concerned with preserving scenic areas, preventing "over-growth," and halting developmental processes that threaten to degrade the environment.[80] In Colorado, Hawaii and Oregon, state officials have begun to consider what the state's optimum population might be, and to reflect on means of assuring that population does not increase beyond a level which land and water resources of the state can support at existing levels of amenity.

The implications of this new attitude cannot be fully appreciated. In some areas the new mood undoubtedly contains an element of exclusionary bias, a hostility to change and to governments which accommodate it. It is clear that actions taken to limit growth in Florida may affect the choices of the citizen of New York or Chicago who intends to retire there, that decisions taken by Delaware to exclude oil refineries could conceivably affect the cost and perhaps even the availability of fuel and energy to the citizens of Philadelphia, that a decision by the people of Boulder to limit population size could possibly raise the cost of housing (by limiting supply), thereby pricing out the poor.

Conversely, the failure of state and local governments to act to preserve their environmental assets can also diminish the choices open to citizens. The subdivision of scenic farmland in California and Pennsylvania, the destruction of coastal wetlands in Louisiana and New Jersey for development, and the loss of historic properties in many areas reduce the environmental satisfactions not only of people in those areas but also of people elsewhere who might settle in or travel to such areas. The unlimited indulgence of everyone's locational and developmental expectations entails the destruction of some of the very values which create the desire to develop in the first place. And the bypassing of places where rehabilitation and redevelopment are badly needed—for example, parts of the central city—entails substantial costs in terms of under-utilized public facilities, duplication of facilities elsewhere and abandonment of properties and people to a depressing future.

The new mood in America carries with it a belief that public

---

80. For an analysis of the way in which citizens at the local level have succeeded in making the limitation of new development a significant public issue see E. FINKLEN, NONGROWTH AS A PLANNING ALTERNATIVE: A PRELIMINARY EXAMINATION OF AN EMERGING ISSUE (ASPO Planning Advisory Service Rep. No. 283, 1972).

authority should deal with these problems, organize and control growth, subsidize redevelopment and prohibit destruction of environmental values, even by private parties on privately owned land. The new outlook sees a connection between the activities of people and the protection of healthy natural systems, between economics and politics on the one hand, and ecology and human welfare on the other. This is what is distinctively new about this historic moment; it is what removes the concerns of urban growth policy from the realm of planners' formulations to basic issues of broad human consequence that affect where and how well people live. The moment is ripe for attempting to give constructive direction to broad popular attitudes that have only recently appeared. It is hoped that a National Land Use Policy law will be enacted which will give constructive focus to the dynamic new energies that have emerged.

22

Library of Congress, Environmental Policy Division

COMPARATIVE ANALYSES OF STATE LAND USE LAWS, LEGISLATIVE PROPOSALS AND MODEL CODES

Throughout the debate surrounding the proposals for a national land use policy act there has been a recurring concern that enactment of a national land use policy would be an infringement on States' powers to regulate land use. In general, the States have divested themselves of their police powers to regulate land use by delegating their authority to local governments. Several of the States, however, have taken the initiative to recoup a portion of their powers over land use from the local governments in order to establish a modicum of statewide planning and regulate development. These recent innovations in State land use law have been discussed extensively in several publications and articles.[1] In addition to the statewide land use programs either adopted or proposed, a number of coastal States have enacted coastal zone management legislation to regulate development along their wetlands. Coastal management laws must be considered in concert with statewide planning programs to get a complete picture of planning law in States with extensive shorelines.

A chart-analysis of a representative sample of statewide planning laws and the A.L.I. Model Code is included in this section. Each law or proposal is compared with a composite list of requirements taken from the legislative proposals pending in the 93rd Congress. The requirements used for comparison are probably more stringent in total than any single land use bill introduced thus far; for instance, S. 792 and the Nelson amendment to S. 268 require the issuance of a permit for land use developments, and S. 268 contains extensive guidelines and criteria for structuring a land use planning process and data system, so the provisions of both bills are merged for the purpose of analysis.

---

[1] See: R. Rubino and W. Wagner, *The State's Role in Land Resources Management*, Council of State Governments (1972). Note: *State Land Use Regulation—A Survey of Recent Legislative Approaches*, 56 Minn. Law Rev. 869 (1972). *Proposals for State-wide Land Planning in North Carolina*, 8 Wake Forest L. Rev. 407 (1972); Babcock, *Comments on the Model Land Development Code*, 1972 Urban L. Ann. 59 (1972); *Comprehensive Planning: Only So Certain As Your Survival*, 8 Hawaii B.J. 115 (1972); Waite, *Problems of National Land Use Planning*, 20 Catholic U.L. Rev. 702 (1971); Krasnowiecki, *Model Land Use and Development Code*, 1971 Urban L. Ann. 101 (1971); F. Bosselman and D. Callies, *The Quiet Revolution in Land Use Control*, Council on Environmental Quality (1971); Walter, *Development Legislation in Maine and Vermont*, 23 Maine L. Rev. 315 (1971); E. Haskell, *Managing the Environment: Nine States Look for New Answers*, Woodrow Wilson International Center for Scholars (1971).

Most of the States which have adopted statewide planning still emphasize the local role in land use regulation. Only Maine and Vermont have opted wholly for State control; the other States place the major responsibility on county and local units, but retain a veto power or other enforcement mechanism to assure that local jurisdictions comply with statewide criteria. The A.L.I. Model Land Use Code has not yet been fully adopted by the American Law Institute, yet elements of the Model Code have been incorporated into legislative proposals now pending before several State legislatures. A bill now being considered by the State of Washington closely parallels the framework of the A.L.I. Model Code.

This comparative analysis of State legislation shows one salient feature: many of the States are prepared to adopt land use laws which will conform in essence to the proposed national land use policy acts. Where deficiencies in the State laws exist with respect to the substantive requirements of the pending bills, the deficiencies are primarily in the land use data components, mechanisms for intergovernmental coordination, and availability of information to the public.

COMPARATIVE ANALYSIS OF STATE LAWS

[Symbols: ● =complies; ♦ =probably complies; ★ =may comply]

LAND USE PLANNING PROCESSES

	Hawaii	Maine	Florida	Vermont	A.L.I.	Proposed	
						Washington	Oregon
INFORMATIONAL COMPONENTS							
Inventory of land and natural resources		★	●[8]	●	●	●	
Compilation of socio-economic data			♦		●	●	
Forecast of future needs			★		●	●	
Inventory of physical conditions which affect land use.		★	●	●	●	●	
Inventory of public lands and needs and priorities for use of Federal lands.			●		●	♦	
Inventory of financial resources for land use planning.					♦	♦	
Inventory of State and local activities which have land use impact.			●		●	♦[17]	
Method for identifying large-scale development and projects of regional benefit.		●	●	●	●	●	●
Inventory and designation of areas of critical environmental concern or impacted by key facilities.		●	●[9]		♦	●	●
Technical assistance and training programs			●		●		
Exchange of land use planning information and data among govermental units.	♦		●		♦	●	
COORDINATING FUNCTIONS							
Method for coordinating State and local agency programs.		●		●	●	●	
Coordination of interstate aspects of land use issues.					●	♦	
PUBLIC PARTICIPATION							
Public hearings on statewide planning process.	●	●			●	●	●
Participation by public in formulating statewide planning process.					●	●	●
STATE LAND USE PLANNING AGENCY							
Primary authority for development and administration of State land use program.	●	●[5]	●	●	●	●	●
Coordination of planning agency with State agencies responsible for environmental matters.		●[6]		●[12]		●	♦
Authority to hold public hearings and permit public participation in developing State land use program.		●				●	
Advisory council of elected or appointed officials			●		●	★[16]	●

STATE LAND USE PROGRAMS

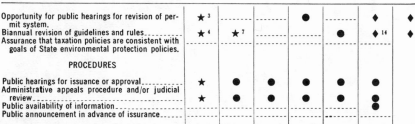

	Hawaii	Maine	Florida	Ver-mont	A.L.I.	Proposed	
						Wash-ington	Oregon
METHODS OF IMPLEMENTATION							
Direct State land use planning		●		●			
Implementation by local governments according to State criteria and guidelines with State veto power.					●		
Implementation by local governments according to State criteria and guidelines with judicial enforcement.	●[1]		●[10]			●[13]	●[16]
EXERCISE OF STATE POLICE POWERS							
Prohibit land use within areas of critical environmental concern impacted by:							
1. Key facilities	●[2]	●	◆[11]	◆[12]	●	●[15]	●
2. Potential and use for regional benefits	●	●	◆	◆	●	●	●
3. Large-scale developments or subdivisions	●	●	◆	◆	●	●	●
PROCEDURE							
Administrative appeals procedure		●	●	●	●	●	●
Judicial review for determining compensation for taking							
PERMIT OR APPROVAL SYSTEM—OVERVIEW							
Opportunity for public hearings for revision of permit system.	★[3]			●		◆	◆
Biannual revision of guidelines and rules	★[4]	★[7]			●	◆[14]	◆
Assurance that taxation policies are consistent with goals of State environmental protection policies.							
PROCEDURES							
Public hearings for issuance or approval	★	●	●	●	●	●	
Administrative appeals procedure and/or judicial review	★	●	●	●	●	●	
Public availability of information						●	
Public announcement in advance of issurance						●	

[1] In the case of special permits issued by local governments under 3 HRS 205–5 (supp. 1970), the State Commission exercises a direct veto power over the issuance of the permit. Enforcement of the statewide land use plan is left to the local government in all other cases.

[2] Provision is made in 3 HRS 183–41 (supp. 1971) for creation of forest and water reserve zones; coupled with restrictions on development of coastal areas contained in sec. 205–31 et seq., a degree of protection is afforded critical areas within these sensitive regions. 3 HRS 205–2 et seq. further provides protection by establishing conservation districts for protecting watersheds and amenities.

[3] Local governments are delegated the authority to grant special permits for other uses within the agricultural and rural districts (3 HRS 205–6 (supp. 1970)). This permit system is not exactly as envisioned by the proposed national land use legislation, but is a variant of the same theme.

[4] Review required every 5 years.

[5] Maine land use law is incorporated into 2 titles of the code: Use Regulation, MSA 681 et seq., and Site Location of Development, 38 MSA 481 et seq. Authority to plan and regulate is shared by the Maine Land Use Regulation Commission and the Environmental Improvement Commission.

[6] Both State agencies are administered by the Department of Environmental Protection.

[7] Revision required every 5 years, but may be revised periodically at will.

[8] The Florida Environmental Inventory Council (14 FSA 370–0212) is given a broad mandate to collect pertinent physical and environmental data.

[9] An upper limit of 500,000 acres or 5 percent of land area is presently placed on acreage which may be designated as critical.

[10] If a development is proposed within the jurisdiction of a local government which has a zoning ordinance, the local government is delegated the authority for approving land use according to State guidelines.

[11] The Land Conservation Act of 1972 (14 FSA 259.0) provides for State acquisition of endangered lands under eminent domain.

[12] The Vermont land use agency, State Environmental Board, is an independent regulatory body within the Agency of Environmental Conservation, an umbrella agency for all departments dealing with natural resources.

[13] If local governments fail to perform satisfactorily, the State may intercede and cure defaults (secs. 3–603; 3–705).

[14] Provision is made for revision of guidelines and criteria, but no specific time period is provided.

[15] The area designated as of "statewide significance" is limited to no more than 1 percent of the land area of the State (sec. 4–502).

[16] Sec. 5–206 leaves the appointment of advisory bodies to the discretion of the director of the State land use planning agency. Sec. 7–302 provides for the appointment of a Users Advisory Committee to guide the performance of the State land information service.

[17] Washington has enacted an environmental impact statement procedure similar to that required by the National Environmental Policy Act of 1969, which requires State agencies to evaluate the environmental impact of their actions.

[18] The State may assume the functions delegated to the counties with respect to administering comprehensive plans, zoning and other land use regulations if a local government fails to comply with the statewide planning requirements (sec. 45). The State may also enjoin any nonconforming land use if counties fail to enforce the requirements (sec. 47).

23

Charles Haar

WANTED: TWO FEDERAL LEVERS FOR URBAN LAND USE — LAND BANKS AND URBANK (excerpts)

I. INTRODUCTION

"National urban growth policy," as a panacea for the national urban crisis of the seventies, is a phrase with most resonant undertones. There is something grand about its reach, and a stirring that catches an important national aspiration.

For these reasons it is too important a phrase to be lost to those who utilize it in order to avoid action. On its theoretical and conceptual plane much intellectual blood can be shed—with little practical consequences. Like the will-o-the-wisp it attracts many earnest workers in the urban field towards a further realm of paradise-to-be, with inevitable losses in energies and in alleviating the miseries of our cities. Even a stop-look-and-listen policy applied to this phrase makes one throw up one's hands—simply because of the breadth of the issue; urban growth entails all the activities, private and public, of society. So in a sense a national policy for it would mean a policy for everything from population control to monetary policy to consumer rights—and cutting through the jurisdictional lines of Executive departments and Congressional committees. Where no exclusionary principle evolves, such an amorphous all-encompassing program does not stand further probing.

By wishing to retain some of the emotive power and the kernel of truth that is contained by the phrase I would like, first, to narrow it to a *national urban land-use policy* and, second, to the *proper federal role* in such activities. This narrowing of focus (still leaving, I submit, a great range for action and concept) means that the focus is on how can the federal government formulate policies for a desirable distribution and location of population activities in metropolitan areas. To rephrase the question, it becomes: on what metropolitan land uses can the federal limited and delegated powers act most effectively, be it by way of incentive, sanction, cash, education, moral leadership, or other traditional tools of government? Couched in terms of the pressing needs of the metropolitan growth problems today and in terms of what the federal government can best do, two programs emerge as of potentially great significance: aids to metropolitan land banks; and a federal urban development bank.

The purpose of this paper, then, is to provide recommendations for two crucial institutions, not now *in esse*, to help solve urban problems and metropolitan growth problems—metropolitan land banks and a Federal Urban Development Bank.

A coherent national policy for urban development has at least three aspects: improving the quality of existing cities; increasing the quantitative capacities of existing cities; and, third, creating new communities. For these ambitious goals many resources and innovating managerial and governmental techniques will have to be employed. Many of these are not visible at this point of time since our knowledge is short, and the state of conditions is uncertainty. Nevertheless, we are beginning to hammer out such a national strategy. Internal organization of the federal departments to make some kind of coordinated federal program dealing with urban land uses a national policy is slowly emerging. Model cities, urban renewal and subsidized housing programs are dealing with the center cities. Title IV of the Housing Urban Development Act of 1968 and Title VII of the Housing and Urban Development Act of 1970 have gone far toward new fusion of public and private energies for new communities. Institutions, like an Urbank and metropolitan land bank, which can implement metropolitan plans and can set a framework for overall metropolitan land-use policies that save money and increase the institutional capacity to respond to social needs, especially those of low-income groups within the metropolitan area, are surely creations that have to be brought forth within this decade.

II. THE FEDERAL INTEREST AND THE FEDERAL MEANS OF INTERVENTION

A. The Federal Interest

Money is a good starting point for any philosophic discussion. As a target for funds from the hard-pressed cities, Washington necessarily has an interest in the wise use of monies for which, after all, it is a fiduciary to the general taxpayer. It has to assure an efficient and managerial use of federal money. Once states and localities turn to Washington for grants-in-aid for sewer and water, for roads, for mass transportation, for open spaces it becomes necessary for Washington in turn to make sure

that the land use plans and programs of these localities and states provide the most efficient, economical and coordinated expenditures on the urban infrastructure. The price paid for land and for capital, if federal aids are to be drawn down, is a matter of concern.

Again the federal government is interested, in terms of eliminating overlapping expenditures and unnecessary duplications, in making sure that area-wide problems are dealt with on an efficient basis. To the Congress, as reflected in successive enactments, this has meant comprehensive planning. Thus from the very outset, from its 701 urban planning grant programs through the grant-in-aid requirements attached to its 702 programs, all the way up to its 204 and 205 conditions attached in the 1966 statute (including the form in which such aid is given, such as the condition of elected representatives under Section 701g of the act), the federal government has tried to avoid the greatest wastes of fragmented and balkanized local units. This is to be achieved by planning and by forethought. For effective planning, capital budgetry is a prerequisite. And ownership of the critical aspects of the land resource calls for more extensive aspects of planning.

From this aspect of the federal interest in national land-use policy has emerged another tactic. With this whole philosophy of metropolitan government emerges a federal concept that man does not live by planning alone but by the results of such planning. And nothing has proven more troubling to the Congress and to the executive branch than the innumerable volumes whose ultimate destination is a library shelf. The federal government is taking the lead in tying implementation, and programming, expenditures, and impact to the realm of plans and ideas. But to make these plans effective there has to be institutional engineering, such as under the 204 and 205 programs. With a metropolitan land bank, and an urban development bank to provide an easier way of borrowing funds for public facilities, there come two potent levers for the emergence of a strong and effective carrying out of metropolitan plans.

These two new institutions can also be perceived as crucial in terms of the federal interest in the survival of its major concentrations of population and investment known as the cities. And the intervention is justified here primarily because local land-use mechanisms can help or hinder national policies. Thus, the policy adopted by the Congress in 1968 of producing 26 million units of housing over the next ten years (including 6 million units of low-cost housing) are running afoul of local zoning provisions and exclusionary building codes. Furthermore the national environmental policy ("repaying our debt to nature.") is frustrated by localities which refuse to prevent industries within their borders from polluting interstate rivers or from casting their smoke into other interstate air sheds. The poverty and social isolation of minority groups in the central city cannot be coped with except by effective metropolitan planning and a metropolitan land-use policy which has some possibilities of not only exhortation but of actually carrying out the program of providing decent housing and suitable living environments for all income groups. Excepting the reality of ethnic neighborhoods based on free choice, nevertheless there is a need for active intervention to include integrated living as a normal option for the American citizenry.

There is a clear and present federal interest in the forms of metropolitan governance. The relative ineffectiveness of the efforts of urban government to respond to urban problems in part flows from the fragmented and obsolescent structure of urban government itself. Federal programs generally do not, like Minerva, spring straight from Jupiter's brow; even when they do, their evolution and follow-through takes place in the sets of human concerns and realities. There is a federal need therefore, to encourage and promote incentives for the reorganization of local government so that it can deal more effectively with these urban problems.

One role all would accord the federal government is that of aider to the private market. The housing and real estate industry is characterized by small scale risk takers with imperfect information as to conditions within the metropoolitan area. As has happened in the urban renewal programs and in the metropolitan planning programs, the federal government can pay for and provide a great deal of data about population, market, and employment trends. In a sense the provision and manufacture of this kind of knowledge eliminates clashes and conflicts between public and private policies, makes possible more rational decisions by private developers and entrepreneurs, and removes frictions in the imperfect land-use market.

These kinds of functions, the federal government has rationalized, underly both institutions that are presented in this paper, and by providing the greater information and eliminating legal and technical impediments to the free and easy use of land within the metropolitan area make possible the solution to some of the more urgent problems.

Finally, the key leadership role of the national government requires its acting in these fields. Under our present system of government we have moved away from what may have been a possibility in the earlier period of federalism when the great spokesman for creative change in that time, Mr. Justice Brandies, spoke of the "laboratory of states." Partly because of the way career lines have opened up and the attractiveness of federal employment for the amateur and for the recent graduate of the professional schools, as well as because of the expense of experimentation and the nonjustifiability of one innovation (such as a new kind of public transportation vehicle, like the dual mode vehicle recommended in *Tomorrow's Transportation*) that the expediting of change to meet new conditions and problems has befallen the federal government. So it is a federal government's role as innovator, experimenter, clearing house of information about successful and unsuccessful experimentation, catalyst of new combinations of public and private energies that these two programs today justify a federal intervention.

B. THE MEANS OF INTERVENTION

The American constitution, with its firmly entrenched federal structure, reserves to the states (and to their local subdivisions) the power to make decisions over the use, abuse, misuse and reuse of urban land. Even under a system where land uses are determined through the market mechanism and by private agreement and disposition, disputes are bound to arise; these conflicts, such as common-law nuisance cases and those arising under doctrines like the rule against perpetuities or restraints on alienation, are primarily settled in the state courts. Even what classes of contracts and leases relating to real property will be specifically enforced by a court of equity are decisions for each state to decide for itself. With the increase in direct planning guidance and in control of the land use, these matters are similarly funneled through state administrative, legislative and judical branches. State constitutions (true, subject always to the restraint of the fourteenth amendment to the federal constitution) determine the extent of permissible regultions; state and urban legislation sets the boundaries for controls over land and over housing; building codes, zoning, subdivision regulation, official map and street controls—to isolate a few prominent examples—are all state creations. The taking of land for housing and other public purposes is a state determination. Again, property taxation, a vast influence on development and on the location and siting of industry throughout our metropolitan areas, is in the main exclusively a local prerogative.

There is, in the strict sense, no Federal police power. Although the Federal government, in dealing with a subject within its enumerated powers, may enact police regulations in connection with that matter, this would prove of limited applicability to land, housing, and other related elements of metropolitan growth. There does exist an independent Federal eminent domain power, but it is narrowly confined to the status of handmaiden to other powers. The Federal Constitution contains no express grant of eminent domain, and as a government of delegated powers, it was not really settled until 1875 that the United States could condemn in its own name in its own courts. Before that date, the state would condemn the property and turn it over to the Federal government. Thereafter, the courts found eminent domain to be an implied power, "necessary and appropriate" for the execution of powers expressly conferred.

In the past, also, legislation relating to the flow of capital and investment was dominantly a matter of state concern. Regulation of savings banks and insurance companies—the repositories of the people's savings—is still controlled by the state legislature, and the minute controls with respect to mortgages, such as permitted area for investment and the loan-to-value ratio, are supervised by state administrative agencies. Even the very methods of proof of titles and rules of foreclosure, so crucial to determining the relative merits of mortgage investments, are jealously guarded provinces of the state. It is a fact of vital importance in the shaping of a national land-use policy that in the control of credit institutions dealing with housing, as in land control, the role of the states is constitutionally dominant.

With the onset of the great depression, however, the weakness of the real estate market seemed beyond the ability of the states to correct. In the home-building field, eyes turned quickly toward the only source, at that time, of funds and initiative, the Federal government; and the Federal government exploited this invitation to launch its own policy for housing and land, mainly through the use of credit. The new Federal agencies dealing with housing credit encountered no special difficulties with the courts. "The preservation of homeowners and the promotion of a sound system for home mortgage," stated the court in *First Federal Savings and Loan Assn.* v. *Loomis*, "is none the less national in scope than the provisions for the unemployed and the aged." When considering, in connection with Federal insurance of mortgage loans, the extent of the fiscal powers granted the Federal Government under the Constitution, the Attorney General stated:

"It is one of the latest in a series of enactments, extending over more than a century, through which the Federal government has recognized and fulfilled its obligation to provide a national system of financial institutions for handling the credit and exchange requirements of industry, commerce and agriculture, supplying a national currency and promoting the fiscal affairs of the government . . . It further seems to me incontrovertible that the purposes of the National Housing Act are for the welfare of the nation as a whole. Not only does the Act provide protection for our national financial structure, but it will also result in encouragement of better housing conditions throughout the country, in the provision of cheap and safe credit for the homeowners of the United States, and in the stimulation of the building industry, and indirectly of the durable goods industry, with consequent improvement in general conditions, including the furnishing of employment to many of the nation's unemployed."

The die was cast. Grants-in-aid and credit policy were to provide the main instrument for forging a national land-use program.

III. A FEDERAL PROGRAM FOR METROPOLITAN LAND BANKS

The decade of the seventies will undoubtedly emerge as the period when the nation adopted a policy to encourage an orderly urban growth for the better development of our cities and metropolitan areas. Signs of this trend abound. There is, first of all, the spate of bills introduced into both houses of the Congress calling for actions which would help establish patterns of urbanization and economic development. There has been crystallization of actions, furthermore; for example, the National Environmental Policy Act of 1969, among whose purposes is a declaration of a national policy to encourage productive and enjoyable harmony between man and his environment; and Title VII of the Housing and Urban Development Act of 1970, which goes far toward giving the Federal government a key role in helping metropolitan areas establish sound land policies for orderly growth and development through encouraging the development of new communities.

Yet another aspect is the national policy, more or less consciously developed, to encourage area-wide planning in order to achieve efficiencies, economies, and to reach solutions to urban problems that cut across fictional boundary lines. And, there has been in the varying amendments and proposals that have been introduced since the initiation of this policy in 1954, a steady insistence by the Federal government that metropolitan planning alone is not enough, that transcendental chatter cannot be the final outcome of man's efforts, but that the Federal government needs to encourage the implementation and carrying out of metropolitan policies and plans. Thus Title II of the Demonstration Cities Act of 1966, through its two important sections, Section 204 and 205, has stressed the need to carry out programs, to the expenditure of funds that will turn planning into reality. In the words of the Presidential message that accompanied the 1966 act, a metropolitan plan is not something to be chucked in the drawer but something to be checked out and to affect activities in the real world.

It is against this background that the proposal for Federal legislation to establish a metropolitan land bank needs to be understood and evaluated.

The Proposal for a Metropolitan Land Bank

It is proposed, in order to improve the management of urban land, that a metropolitan land bank act be passed; it would provide Federal assistance to metropolitan authorities to acquire, manage, and dispose of land according to the conditions of a metropolitan plan.

The key elements in this stronger affirmative role for government are:
The power of eminent domain for site assembly;
The power to spend public monies on the facilities required to achieve a desired form of structure; and
The power to dispose of land to private and public developers in accordance with a metropolitan development plan.

It is also part of the proposal (in conjunction with the Brandeis admonition of the laboratory of the states in a federal system) that metropolitan corporations be established at the outset which have affirmative powers to initiate demonstration projects and major developments at key locations in the suburbs, such as at the sites of important highway interchanges.

A. THE PURPOSES OF A METROPOLITAN LAND BANK

1. General:

The 1970 census indicates that we are no longer an urban, but a suburban nation. We will be building as many homes, roads, sewers, libraries, schools and hospitals in the next 30 years as were built in the hundreds of years since the founding of the nation in Jamestown. This means that existing cities are going to spread out into the surrounding areas and that the trend toward suburban sprawl will be accentuated. Rapid growth of our urban population rapidly increases the demand for urban space in which to live, work, move about, shop, be entertained, and enjoy all other facilities of a metropolitan environment.

Pressure on urban land, all the more severe because of the increase in population, will be exacerbated because the amount of land per capita needed for newcomers will exceed the per capita allotment for today's city dwellers, This must be the case on at least two grounds: the density of population in our cities is to be reduced and the per capita demand for urban space is expected to rise with growing income. Besides, municipal services will probably use more land per city dweller than in the past. The quantity of land available determines the capacity of our cities to meet this demand, and adequate increase on the supply side is a function of the land bank.

The other factor pushing for a land bank as an answer to the urban capacity issue is the growing recognition that current planning is simply inefficient and inadequate not only to satisfy the aspirations and the hopes that a Great Society should produce but even its most minimal requirements. And this is not surprising when one begins to probe the nature of the police power and eminent domain tools available under our constitutional system. The law of nuisance, although coming to life with the recent spate of litigations in the environmental field, is essentially a private ad hoc instrument, administered by courts on a part time and sporadic basis, with no coherent, rational policy underlying it. Zoning, the great tool developed during 1913–1926, when the law of nuisances became increasingly inadequate in coping with interrelated land uses, has served many useful purposes; but not only on its more abused sides, such as parochial zoning, zoning by favoritism and fiscal zoning, but also in its general approach it has been a tool of negativism. It is a nascent instrument, which can veto the excesses of private enterprise but cannot bring into being the purposes or the objectives of a plan, since it does not itself induce or build. Urban renewal, not only because of the political difficulties involved in relocation, but because it operates within the territorial boundaries of a city is also increasingly inadequate to cope with urban problems of the twentieth century.

These two factors conjoin on our growth points, especially the suburban areas, where zoning and building controls are not used so much to ratify the market— as is the case of central city, and where they can do a fairly good job. Where the society is trying to set the patterns for the future and the most desirable use of land, both in terms of the needs of the people and the kinds of environments which encourage and stimulate certain values that we think appropriate for a democratic society, we require more supple public controls over land. We need to achieve certain economies as we face the bills for expenditures on public capital facilities, the extensions of roads, sewers, and other facilities which are necessary to turn raw land into livable space.

This problem becomes all the more exacerbating to a technologist, since land, in an absolute sense, is not scarce. In purely physical terms there is enough space in the United States to accommodate many more urban centers than could possibly be needed in the foreseeable future. Underlying the need for more urban land we are stressing not a physical difficulty but, rather, a management problem. Poor management, not the lack of space, leads to congestion in urban centers; it makes land scarcer than it need be. Uneven rates of development (leapfrogging, sprawl, and the rest of the ribbon development that is scarring the environment), and the consequent mismatch of places to live and places to work cause congestion and inefficient use of land.

2. Special Purposes:

i. Advance acquisition of land for public purposes.—Many government services, roads, schools, hospitals, recreation to name but a few, require substantial amounts of land. Land assembly, as we are continuing to find out, is complicated, legally vexatious, costly, uncertain and time-consuming. And this is a continuing process, so long as government endures. Therefore, for purposes of convenience, so that the necessary land would be available in an appropriate amount when the time came to provide the government service, and also for considerations of cost, advance acquisition would be an important function of a land bank.

ii. Avoiding the expenses of urban sprawl.—The ragged process of subdivision development, including leapfrogging, is often dictated by the price of land as well as by its availability. Consequently, urban infrastructure, paid for by government, has to follow—however reluctantly and expensively—this path of growth.

The pace and pattern of urban growth in practice is determined by what the New York Court of Appeals has, in a memorable phrase, called "the sweet will" of the developer. It means that land relatively close to developed centers often remains idle or unoccupied, while land further from the center is being freshly developed and occupied. Vacant lots and empty buildings are not only a waste of resources in themselves but they contribute to a further waste of resources in transportation; they cause more roads and rails and cars and fuel to be used than would be needed were development more compact, and they oblige travelers to spend more time in transit through these dead spaces that increase the distance from center to periphery. (And while not significant for the purpose of this paper, the interdependency of central city and suburb should always be kept in mind: for example, overexpansion at the center leads the private sector to allow houses in the older residential locations to run down in favor of artificially cheap land at the periphery, which is hastily urbanized at a high cost to the entire community.)

A feasible way to eliminate sprawl and leapfrogging, and the consequent distortions in land values and in the taxpayers' costs of producing public services, is through some mechanism of land reserve. The bank could prevent the development of land whose value as urban land is negative to the community as a whole.

iii. An instrument for perfecting the land market.—Land banks are well adapted to correct the errors and scars of the past. Scattered throughout many of our older suburbs are pockets of underdevelopment, dotted with small lots of odd sizes or occupied by vacant buildings. This collection of sites frequently adds up to an impressive total of developable land, but its present form is uninviting to developers. These odd bits and remnants can and should be assembled into parcels suitable for building. Furthermore, there are often pockets of legal blight, where the land has been rendered undevelopable because of problems over the estate or title. A public agency could assemble these odd pieces of land into economic plots and make them available by sale or lease to developers.

This function emphasizes a most appropriate role for government activity and support at the Federal level—perfecting the market for urban land. This land market is one of the more lagard sectors of the economy. It performs its jobs—setting prices and allocating resources—poorly. Many reasons have been given for this condition, most notably the nature of the land commodity, which is nonhomogeneous: in the terms of the lawyer, every piece of land is unique and therefore appropriate for specific performance. It is also "lumpy" or discontinuous and costly relative to the financial capacities of the participants in the market. There is also a poor flow of information, aggravated by political boundaries and fragmentations of the market. Holdouts have monopoly power. Indeed, it can be said that in the urban land market relative prices do not correspond to real economic scarcities, and resources are therefore not allocated to their most efficient uses. By acquiring such land, and making it available in a planned pattern that imparted more order to the whole process of urban growth, the bank would reduce uncertainty and confusion in the land market. This would mean a stabilization of the market for land—much in the same way as a central bank, such as the Federal Reserve Bank, stabilizes the money market.

Last, not only in its dealing with the knowledge and supply side of the equation, but in its other activities, the land bank, guided by considerations of urban development, and having a clearly discernible basis for its decisions on price and the rate of release of land from its inventories, would be acting to moderate fluctuations in the price of land. In a way, many of the complaints about speculators in metropolitan lands could be alleviated. The functioning of the private land market could be improved, while development decisions could still be left to private persons acting, as always, subject to the controls over land use. In other words, the land bank would perform the holding function and the supply function on precisely the same basis as private holders, by selling or leasing to the highest bidder, but it need not interfere with or encroach on the development function.

iv. A key tool for orderly urban development.—The overwhelming difficulty with metropolitan plans is that few tools exist to realize affirmatively the goals and objectives enunciated in them. Through the techniques of the land bank it should be possible to control the pace at which demand for government services will increase by controlling the speed and direction of urban growth itself. The bank can own undeveloped land on the outskirts, into which the metropolitan area is likely to expand, to insure that this land will come into development in an orderly way. Otherwise the area is at the mercy of developers, who in effect determine through their individual decisions what level of services the area should provide and who should pay for them.

v. Recapturing land values created by government activities.—Land values are enhanced when new government services are provided. These increments, reflecting the activities of society, nonetheless inure to particular individuals who held the land before that progress took place and who, though they may have anticipated such increments and even invested for that very reason, have done little to bring them about. It is fitting that such increments return · to the public purse, thereby permitting lower property taxes than otherwise prevail. Moreover, since public expenditures and regulations have such a profound effect on land values, there are constant pressures toward graft, dishonesty, and subornation of public officials; with a bank, increments in land values should automatically revert to it, and pressures to extend government services to outlying areas would be moderated.

What does emerge as the overall rationale of the program is the relation of metropolitan land reserve policies to comprehensive metropolitan planning and land-use control. It is a flexible and powerful tool for guiding the future growth of the community.

This is crucial as one example of the existing tools that are currently available to local governments in guiding their destinies. Not only are land-use controls unflexible, but they have failed because they did not take into account the forces operating in urban land markets. Under traditional zoning, since districts must be established in advance of development, planners have had to forecast every possible use of land and guard against every possible device for avoiding the ordinance. When it comes to suburban growth, where the land is largely undeveloped, zones have had to be created without any knowledge of how an unregulated market would allocate the land or what the proper allocation of land should be in the future.

By contrast, land reserve policies have a number of advantages. They are the only means by which a public agency can obtain virtually completely control over property, and, therefore, can exercise the necessary discretion. Furthermore there is an important check as we examine our market system of land-use controls and development. Ownership of land gives a city an economic stake in its future use and it has to weigh, with the same canny eye as the entrepreneur, the values sacrificed by imposing restrictions as against the benefits yielded by those same restrictions.

Thus the land reserve policies can heighten flexibility and discretion not only by conditions imposed on sale of land from the reserve but also by choice of the parcel to be brought in to the market. It would allow more sensitive regulation of land use, regulation more adaptable over time, and more discriminating as between sites than is possible with present common law controls which operate by the general rules that are difficult to change, that must be applied evenhandedly, and are always subject to judicial review for interference with vested property rights. And by this meshing with traditional land-use controls, the land banks can provide an affirmative way for inducing the metropolitan development and programs which are the aims of the metropolitan plan.

B. CONSTITUTIONAL AND LEGAL FEASIBILITY OF METROPOLITAN LAND BANKS

A preliminary research into existing constitutional and statute law in the United States indicates that no fundamental legal difficulty stands in the way of establishing metropolitan land banks, or endowing them with the powers needed for carrying out their principal tasks. Particular aspects of existing law in some states would have to be changed, but in relatively superficial ways. The more substantial revision would have to be in terms of state enabling laws and, since it seems appropriate that the banks operate on a metropolitan area rather than on local city bases, new model laws need to be drafted with federal government assistance to provide for the establishment of such bodies. Such provision are necessary in the light of some of the charter and limited rule applications of municipal corporations; there is also the special difficulty in areas that straddle state lines where the land bank would need powers that could only be granted if the two or more states concerned were prepared to act in concert.

1. Legal Powers To Operate a Land Reserve Policy.—Municipal corporations as political subdivisions of the state generally enjoy only the powers conferred on them by the parent state. But while a municipal corporation possesses only those powers which its charter, the laws or the constitution of the state bestow, it is not confined to powers granted explicitly. It also has implied powers, which arise from powers expressly granted or by necessary inference from its essential purposes or functions. As to be expected two rules of construction have evolved: the conservative rule is that the municipality has no power beyond those expressly granted, except as much as may be necessary to effectuate the power expressly granted; as a counterpoint, a more liberal view has developed which is that essential powers not expressly conferred are nevertheless implied, with some jurisdictions even extending the liberal rule to the point that a municipal power may be implied, even if not indispensable, when it is necessary or convenient in carrying out the express power. Most charters or statutes contain general welfare clauses intended to extend the powers of the municipality beyond those specifically enumerated to encompass others which are necessary to accomplish the purposes of government.

There seems at present to be no explicit provision about land reserve policy, either for or against; everything would depend therefore on interpretation. The interpretation in each state would revolve about implied powers, in the main derived from a general welfare clause, and about the distinction between proprietary and governmental functions. Finally in order to determine whether specifically authorized corporate purposes already exist which would justify the operation of the land reserve, compare the possible purposes of a land reserve policy with powers which municipalities already have.

Some purposes of a land reserve policy, such as better planning, more adequate control over urban development and redevelopment, and the adequate and economic provision of public facilities do forward authority of most municipalities. Some purposes of a land reserve policy do not appear to be expressly authorized by existing statute or charter: capture of capital gains for the public and the control of speculation. Yet, although these purposes are not specifically authorized, that a land reserve policy might serve these purposes along with others would probably not invalidate it.

But rather than a field day for lawyers, and difficulties and hesitations in getting things done, a model enabling act should be drafted.

The need for model legislation is also borne out by analogy to other important urban programs initiated by the federal government. Thus prima facie it might be thought that the power to plan, taken together with the power of eminent domain, is sufficient to authorize urban renewal projects. But only one state (Ohio) has held that enabling legislation was unnecessary on the ground that slum clearance and urban development were implicitly authorized by the home rule amendment to the constitution. In most states, enabling legislation was passed for urban renewal and where doubt arose whether the purpose of the taking was public, specific authorization was passed in order to obviate questions concerning the propriety under the state or federal constitution.

This conclusion as to the the necessity for a new legislation is further reinforced by questions of extraterritorial jurisdiction. The general rule is that a municipality may purchase real estate outside its corporate limits, especially where broad statutory provision confers power to purchase and hold real estate sufficient for public use and convenience. In some states specific authorities are conferred to acquire property outside the corporate limits for water supply, and airport, and other similar facilities.

In summary, new model legislation for the creation of metropolitan land bank agencies seems essential. There is no direct precedent to determine whether the operations of a land reserve agency—as a means of exercising planning, urban renewal, and public works powers—come within the general powers of a municipality or within the specific state grants of planning and urban renewal powers. This conclusion is reinforced by our experience with both city planning and urban renewal—where it was thought in the beginning that such powers were dubious enough that special enabling legislation should be sought.

Further, this action is helpful to still doubts as to constitutionality insofar as it affects individual property rights, by obtaining legislative declarations that the land reserve policies are intended to serve a public purpose. With the policy needs dictating extraterritorial jurisdiction on a larger scale than heretofore exercised, new grants of power become still more desirable. Finally it should be noted that the various statutes conferring the power of eminent domain on our municipalities differ in wording, and often in the procedural and substantive requirements; and the desirability for certain methods, such as quick taking and adequate provisions for public hearings and participation, could be written into the special enabling legislation.

2. *Constitutionality of Land Bank Policies.*—Even were the legislation passed so that the purposes of a particular land reserve policy were deemed to be valid municipal ends, any law establishing the operation would have to pass the test of reasonableness of the means to achieve these ends. And although considerable weight is attached to the legislature's declaration of necessity and choice of appropriate means, and although there has been a great deal of judicial liberalization, nevertheless the reasonableness of the means chosen remains subject to judicial review. This curb is a heavy one, particularly so whenever the state court believes that individual rights are being invaded, or, and this may be an even more important unconscious motivation of some court's review, that the bounds of normal and valid public activity are being overreached. There has been a general objection for some time against government interference with the private market, especially on the local level where representation of

minority interests in political decisions is determined by majority votes; here local power should be far more limited, as Chief Justice Stone pointed out in the *Barnette Case*. Absence of technical expertise, too often the rule rather than the exception, leads courts to a more stringent standard of review. But even in the tender area of constitutional determinations, it should be noted, participation of state or federal government gives a color of validity to local actions that they might otherwise lack.

(*a*) *Acquisition.*—The most pertinent rule governing a power to acquire land for a land bank is that a municipal corporation may not become a dealer in real estate nor purchase land for profit alone. This is a corollary from the even more general rule that municipal corporations may not engage in commercial enterprise. Commentators generally agree that this court-made rule was intended to exclude purchase for mere speculative profit in competition with private enterprise, but that courts usually presume that a municipality's purchase of property is for an authorized purpose until proven otherwise. It is also generally the rule that a municipality may purchase land in excess of immediate need so as to make a reasonable provision for future needs.

Although objections based on the prohibition against dealing in real estate may be raised against the municipal land bank, several arguments can be advanced that the bank falls without the scope of the prohibition. For one thing, the prohibition exists to prevent mere speculation in land by the municipality, not to prevent acquisition for valid municipal purposes. And the proper allocation of land among users and the control of city growth have been recognized as vaild municipal purposes. The public ownership is necessary in order to insure that the land is not developed until called for by the metropolitan development plan and to insure coordinated provision of public facilities as the private development takes place.

This argument, it would seem, is further reinforced by a recognition of the nature of eminent domain. If a municipality is allowed under the police power to regulate land use by non-compensatory controls, it should be allowed to do so by means which will be both more effective and more fair to those whose land is regulated, since they are now being compensated.

Thus, the need to move quickly on the establishment of metropolitan land banks is underlined by the probability of future litigation and by the need in many states to redefine public use. In the light of the public housing and urban renewal cases, however, with the expanded interpretation of public use away from meaning "public occupancy" of the property and that "public benefit" is sufficient for validating the taking, there should be little trouble in deciding that it is an appropriate public purpose. The trend, ever since the Supreme Court's sweeping decision in *Berman* v. *Parker*, is to expand the concept to permit broader undertaking in accordance with needs resulting from increased urbanization and pressing metropolitan land development questions. As in the case of urban renewal, the holding of land and its purchase and resale by public land banks is obviously for a public purpose, when the end in view is to improve the physical organization of urban life, A land bank, like a slum clearance project, is subject to be attacked on the ground that publicly owned land has been sold to a private developer for private purposes but it should be defended successfully, as slum clearance has been.

It should be pointed out, however, that it would undoubtedly be argued that the public benefit is merely speculative and that the municipal government is taking land from one private party and giving it to another according to its own whims. This emotional argument could be reinforced by a somewhat more pertinent one that property is being taken for an unknown future use, contrary to strong precedent which disallows this. A question of reasonableness hovers about how distant a future the municipality is providing for. A line of judicial precedents, such as the famous *Arverne Bay Case,* limit the amount of future speculation that a municipality can indulge in when it imposes restraints upon a private property owner. These cases have been decided under the police power. But even in eminent domain, courts have denied the power to acquire land for quite specific public improvement, when the city had taken no specific steps to assure its construction. However, more recent exercise of eminent domain to preserve open space (often in connection with the federal programs) and conservation easements would seem to imply an expansion of municipal powers to hold empty land, at least with contemplated future uses of public open space.

A somewhat different problem arises when it is planned that the condemned land will eventually be developed but it is desired to keep it open to prevent the development occurring until a future time. The law that has been built up on advance acquisition is not really addressed to this problem. Advance acquisition has traditionally been considered only a means for obtaining land for direct public use, as for a school to be built ten years hence or for a public highway for a few years in the future. And there does exist strong predecent against purchase where no immediately foreseeable public uses are contemplated.

Acquisition by a land bank, therefore, would have to be justified on a broader principle or purpose looking to the entire operation. Much as in the case of urban renewal, the courts, attention will have to be directed to the entire context in order to avoid the stigma of simply taking land from one private individual *in invitum* and then giving it to another private individual. Here the case would have to be made on the basis of public advantages obtained from the land bank operation as a whole: mcre economic provision of capital infia-structure, more effective planning, aid in slum clearance, curbing of speculation. Thus a land ban would have to be upheld on the strength of its overall purpose being public and not on the basis of the propriety of each of its purchases. Each taking would still be subject to review; however once the plan itself were approved as aiming at a public purpose, courts would allow the metropolitan agency a great deal of discretion about what property is taken.

(b) *Use and disposal.*—The general rule is that control and management of property is a discretionary function of the municipal governing body, as is the power to dispose of it. Any use may be made of the property which is compatible with the municipal corporate purpose, and there is a great deal of discretion in the sale of or leasing of property. A word of warning is necessary, however, with respect to disposal: the precedents are chiefly concerned with property which has been used for specified municipal purpose, such as a park; there is little law from which to estimate how much discretion will be allowed a municipality disposing of land in order to achieve such purposes as affecting the price of land, giving incentive to certain desired land uses, and otherwise implementing overall development plans.

* * * *

V. Conclusion

So long as the United States continues to be politically open, and, as important, economically open, so that its citizens not only may but effectively do move in large numbers from one place to another, the problem of urban capacity cannot be regarded as a sum of local problems of each city treated separately, but must be treated as a general national problem faced by the whole country.

Most of the current expansion of the nation's urban capacity is taking place by geographic extension of existing metropolitan areas. This is witnessed to objectively by the figures on average density, and subjectively by people's reactions to suburban sprawl and desolation of the countryside. To provide some order and guidance to metropolitan development, as well as to make possible increased national urban capacity, there is urgent need for new legal and financial institutions. They can enable public authorities to provide positive incentives and can operate in a way that the basic energies of private enterprise will continue to be the main focus of land-use development, but in a way that is both more rational and, in the long run, within the self-interest of the developers. In order to carry out public ends of providing a capacity that is available to various groups in the society, and to carry out the strategies of metropolitan area plans, Federal leadership is essential. Land programs are where the greatest needs currently arise. They can best be met by metropolitan land banks, which operate directly to regulate the supply, and by a Federal Urban Development Bank, which can increase the available quantity of urban land by easing the financial strains of supplying the requisite capital infrastructure. These instrumentalities are contemporary manifestations of traditional means of Federal aid in carrying out national policies and those enumerated by State and local governments.

VII

Private Market Alternative
to Land Use Control

24

Bernard Siegan

NON-ZONING IN HOUSTON (excerpts)

V. THE EFFECTS OF NON-ZONING: THE WORKING OF THE SYSTEM

Contrast in Philosophy

Over the years, the contrast between the Houston system of non-zoning and zoning has become greater. What the city in the past and at present exercises, despite some added with the passage of time, is a low level of controls. With zoning the direction has clearly been the other way: greater and more minute control over property use. The drafters of the early zoning ordinances would hardly recognize the ordinances of today. What was once largely an effort to separate uses, and in particular to keep the single-family district pure, has tended to become a detailed account of what can and cannot be done on any parcel of ground. The ordinances proposed for Houston in both 1948 and 1962 were characteristic of the early ordinances. Given the history of zoning, it is likely that, had Houston adopted zoning, there would have been rapid strides to the now-fashionable detailed regulation.

Even the introduction of the newer devices in zoning has served to make the contrast with Houston greater. There has been much praise for such new concepts as "special (or conditional) use," "planned unit development," and "floating zones" and they are being used throughout the country.[105] They have at least one common feature: they give the municipality greater authority over what is erected within its borders. If the city fathers are unhappy with what is proposed under any of these provisions, it is unlikely that it will be done unless so ordered by a court. The courts are not as a practical matter readily usable by many property owners.

In short, the contrast between the two systems can be understood from the following explanation of the zoning power candidly (and quite accurately) made by a New York court:

[105] For readers unfamiliar with these concepts, they may be simply defined as follows: *Special use* is a designated use which will be permitted in a specified district or districts at the approval of the local legislature or an appointed board with such power. A *planned unit development* allows the developer to arrange his buildings and streets with flexibility and without being bound by the specifics of the zoning ordinance—subject to the approval of the council. A *floating zone* is a use described in the text of the ordinance which can be authorized by the local legislature in all or part of the municipality.

I consider that it was the intent of the zoning statute to throw around each community an arm of protection in the form of a local zoning ordinance, which would insure its inhabitants against radical zoning changes (not necessitated by public demand and by changing condition of the neighborhood) which would be detrimental to their established living conditions, their property values, and the most desirable use of their land.[106]

Thus, as some planners would put it, zoning is the control of land use to achieve community objectives. Where the same objectives are generally shared by the residents of the community, as in the "bedroom suburbs," zoning can be used to perpetuate the existing pattern of land use, and to keep out any person or thing that would disrupt it. Zoning in Houston or in any other major city containing many different life styles could not have achieved such uniformity of purpose. In fact its powers over large areas outside its borders have probably served to preclude the incorporation of some such single purpose communities.

The incorporated cities and villages within and adjoining the boundaries of Houston might well exemplify such communities. In passing through some of these municipalities, one can almost see the "invisible wall" which it is sometimes claimed the suburbs around Chicago have erected. But, then, it is contended, this is why so many moved there; to raise their families and live their lives in what they believe to be the better environment. Does this require that they be protected in their way of life to the limits of the town's boundaries which may, of course, be many miles from their homes? In striking contrast are some very expensive subdivisions of Houston, such as River Oaks and Tanglewood, covering much smaller areas, but judging from the price level of the homes, as much or more in demand. This would suggest that the wants and desires of the more affluent members of the population may be reasonably satisfied without the need for their controlling large areas of land. Even more certain is that the many more in number who cannot qualify financially for such a style of living will not be injured by the absence of such powers.

It is also possible that values of suburban homeowners would be more secure if they did not have zoning and had to rely instead on restrictive covenants. (Some or many single-family subdivisions, of course, are subject to both.) Restrictive covenants are more likely to preclude any use of property which might be harmful to values. Thus, under zoning, the local zoning board may grant variations on the size of the required site (from, say, 50 feet of frontage to 25 or 30), churches and home occupations are often permitted uses, and there is generally minimal control over the nonconformist (allowing for, "eccentric" architecture and the use of a "lesser"

[106] Flower Hill Bldg. Corp. v. Flower Hill, 199 Misc. 344, 100 N.Y.S.2d 903 (1950).

quality of materials). More control over the character of one's own neighborhood may enhance values to a greater extent than control over someone else's neighborhood.

A major problem in an academic discussion of zoning is that the writer is bound by the traditional tools of the trade, the words and phrases that make up the ordinances, legal decisions, books, commentaries, and somewhat formal interviews. Necessarily missing are the highly informal insights and observations of attorneys, planners, and aldermen involved in zoning decisions which cannot always be documented but which can be most informative. These experiences should be taken account of, for in some or many instances they may be more revealing of zoning practices than the words of the ordinance. This may be especially true in smaller towns which are unable to employ personnel capable of administering and enforcing a technical legal document, and as a result, where procedures may be on a more or less informal basis.

Nor can it be concluded that even in the larger villages and cities, the zoning ordinance is necessarily revealing of what actually takes place. As an illustration, there are many suburbs that will often defend their zoning ordinance against amendment by resorting to all legal routes, including appeal to the state's highest court if necessary, regardless of the merits of the case. Such a policy will tend to preclude changes as required by the law, and may deny many their rights under the law. Any would-be-plaintiff against such a municipality must have the funds and be in a position to speculate on what business, market and mortgage conditions will be many years later when the final decision is made by the higher court, and, of course, the outcome is uncertain in any litigation. On the other hand, there are cities where land owners have been given very favorable treatment for various reasons, ranging from the philosophical to the avaricious. Knowing or having access to the right people and the help and favors they are prepared to dispense defines the meaning of the zoning ordinance for many more accurately than its words.

How many municipalities fall into these categories is, of course, impossible to ascertain. Yet, such determinations may be essential to understanding and evaluating zoning practices in the country. If there is preponderance of such practices, zoning may actually be more the rule of men than of law.

On occasion, there have been studies of past zoning practices in a city. One of the more recent of these was concluded in 1969 by the Committee on Zoning Practices and Procedures of Los Angeles. A county grand jury investigation into a zoning case involving alleged improprieties prompted its formation and a report was issued after more than a year of hearings and investigation. These are some of its conclusions:

The term "zoning" has lost much of its significance in the City of Los Angeles, for it has come to mean promiscuous changes in the zoning pattern rather than adherence to consistent, comprehensive zoning. Procedures in actual practice have frequently become so loose that even the limited requirements of the City Charter have not been met in numerous variance cases. . . .[107]
Zoning practices in Los Angeles do not now sufficiently reflect sound planning objectives. Piecemeal or spot zoning is resorted to in place of zoning on an area-wide basis. Individual rights are sometimes restricted or privileges granted on the basis of personal circumstances and pressure, rather than on the basis of serving the public interest.[108]
The Zoning Code lags, rather than leads, City development. There has been no comprehensive, over-all review of the Code since 1946. Since then there have been over 300 amendments to the text of the code and several thousand changes in the Zoning map, mainly as a result of individual requests and specific problems.[109]

The writer has no way of knowing whether these conclusions are warranted by the facts, but it is apparent that they could have occurred in most zoned cities. The comments quoted appear to be more descriptive than critical. The practices described are inherent in big city zoning. Los Angeles has had a tremendous growth since 1946, and no one could possibly have envisioned the demands for land use that would result in the subsequent 20 years. Would it have made much difference if the city had comprehensively amended its ordinance in the interim? Dallas comprehensively amended its zoning ordinance in 1965 (more than two years after its city council adopted a resolution for such purposes). Yet, by early 1969, so many changes had been made that zoning became an important issue in the city election of that year.

Any proposals for adopting or comprehensively amending a zoning ordinance must, of course, go through a process of formal public hearings and much informal discussion prior to a decision of the local legislature. In a large city, various individuals and groups will want to have their say, ranging from the local delicatessen owner, whose livelihood may be at stake, to the League of Women Voters, who are concerned with more general matters. A compromise document will emerge that may be entirely satisfactory and appropriate to the legislative processes of a representative society, but may be highly unsatisfactory and inappropriate to the control of land uses. Thereafter, the zoning ordinance will have to be enforced, and this will be subject to (1) officials appointed for this purpose; (2) an administrative appeal

[107] Los Angeles, Calif., Citizen's Committee on Zoning Practices and Procedures, A Program to Improve Planning and Zoning in Los Angeles, First Report to the Mayor and City Council, Summary Report 3, (July 1968).
[108] Id. at 5.
[109] Id. at 6.

body that can grant variations within prescribed limits upon the text of the ordinance; and (3) the local legislature which can pass new amendments. There have, of course, been problems with respect to all three.[110]

A research report prepared in 1968 for the Douglas Commission contains some statistics as to what occurs subsequent to the adoption of zoning procedures. Information was requested from a stratified sample of local governments with populations in excess of 5,000 as to (a) how many rezoning petitions were approved in whole or in part during the preceding 12 months, and (b) how many zoning variances were approved for the same period. Rezoning petitions acted upon averaged 11 per reporting government, and about 73 per cent of those petitions were approved wholly or in part. Requests for zoning variances averaged about 24 per reporting government, and about 78 per cent of these were approved. For the 47 largest cities that reported, each with a population in 1960 of 250,000 or more, the survey indicated an average of 1,030 rezoning petitions acted upon per city with 72 per cent of these approved wholly or in part; and 2,713 requests for zoning variances handled per city with a 76 per cent rate of approval.[111]

Professor Haar reports the following statistics with respect to variances:[112]

City	Period	Applications or Requests	Number Granted	Approximate Percentage Granted
Cincinnati	1926-1937	1,940	1,493	77
Philadelphia	1933-1937	4,800	4,000	83
Cambridge				
(Use Variances)	1952	57	48	84
(Bulk Variances)		59	51	86

[110] Jesse Dukeminier, Jr. & Clyde L. Stapleton, The Zoning Board of Adjustment: A Case Study in Misrule, 50 Ky. L.J. 273 (1962); Note, Zoning Variances and Exceptions: The Philadelphia Experience, *supra* note 36; Curtis J. Berger, *supra* note 62 at 758-784. ". . . a seldom recognized evil in the use variance is that the man who buys property in a residential zone, for example, in reliance on the zoning map where undeveloped land is involved may well discover to his dismay that he bought next to property that is in fact business or industrial property, even though the zoning had never been changed from the pre-existing residential classification. A use variance had been granted and there was no known record except among the few who knew what was happening when it happened." Sheldon J. Plager, The XYZ's of Zoning, Planning (1967), 271, 276, cited in Los Angeles, Calif., Citizen's Committee on Zoning Practices and Procedures, A Program to Improve Planning and Zoning in Los Angeles, First Report to the Mayor and City Council 4 (1968).

[111] Allen D. Manvel, Local Land and Building Regulation (Research Report No. 6, Nat'l Comm'n on Urban Problems) 11, 17, 32-33.

[112] Charles M. Haar, Land Use Planning, A Casebook on the Use, Misuse and Re-Use of Urban Land 296 (1959).

Another study of Philadelphia's Zoning Board of Adjustment shows that during September and October of 1956, it granted 143 applications unconditionally and 49 conditionally, or a total of 75 per cent in 256 cases.[113] For the year spanning 1960 to 1961, the Board of Adjustment of Fort Worth, Texas, granted 95 out of 153 applications for variance or about 62 per cent.[114] The City Council of Austin, Texas, granted 80 per cent of 378 applications for rezoning submitted in 1956 to 1958, inclusive.[115] Lexington-Fayette County Board of Adjustment (Kentucky) granted in the period from January 1960 to May 1961, 79 per cent of 165 petitions.[116]

In Chicago, the record of the Zoning Board of Appeals, as revealed by a number of different studies, has been as follows:[117]

Period	Applications	Number Granted	Approximate Percentage Granted
(a) 1923-1937	4,124	2,379	57.7
(b) 1951			70.0
(c) 1957-1961 (subsequent to passage of comprehensive amendment)	489	466	95.0
(d) 8-month period 1965	269	253	94.0
(e) Hearings for Jan. 24, Feb. 14 and 21, 1967.	33	32	98.0

It is difficult to evaluate the precise meaning of these figures. Thus, where the local legislature has made it clear that it will not approve petitions for apartment or trailer park zoning, few petitions are filed for these purposes and then largely by those prepared to institute litigation. On the other hand, a known policy favorable toward certain uses or exceptions may encourage

[113] Zoning Administration in Philadelphia, App. B, at A-8 (1957). An analysis of the operation of the Zoning Board from July 13, 1954 to September 10, 1954 in which over 569 cases came before the Board is contained in Note, Zoning Variances and Exceptions: The Philadelphia Experience, *supra* note 36.

[114] Fort Worth, Tex., City Planning Department, Planning Fort Worth 46 (1962).

[115] Sidney Wilhelm, Urban Zoning and Land Use Theory 66 (1962). In over 24% of the applications submitted, the author states that the existing land use would not be affected by the change in zoning.

[116] Jesse Dukeminier Jr. & Clyde L. Stapleton, *supra* note 110, at 321.

[117] Richard L. Wexler, A Zoning Ordinance is No Better Than Its Administration— A Platitude Proved, 1 John Marshall J. Prac. & Proc. 74 (1967), contains data and references for (a), (c), (d) and (e), at 74, 75, 77, 78, n.19 (1967); information in (b) is from Comment, Zoning Amendments and Variations, and Neighborhood Decline in Illinois, 48 Nw. U.L. Rev. 470, 480 (1953).

the filing of petitions. Nor do the figures show how many "major" and "minor" matters were involved.

Two conclusions are warranted on the basis of the foregoing evidence and discussion: (1) So many zoning changes in so many communities would not occur if there were general adherence to some form of master planning, and (2) control of property through zoning may be more chaotic than orderly.

Changes in Use

In making a decision to rezone property, the city council or other governing board may be motivated by one or any number of considerations. It may vote from what may be considered the highest motive, the health, safety and welfare of the "people" as conceived by its members, or it may vote for the basest of reasons, the payment of graft. And there certainly are many other possibilities in between. The public also participates in these decisions to the extent that a public hearing is required on all petitions for rezonings. A developer in Houston is never confronted with the problems inherent in these legislative judgments. The Greenway Plaza development is illustrative of this difference. This development was originally a 55-acre existing and proposed complex of high rise and other commercial buildings contiguous on one side to a street which adjoined an expressway, on two sides to commercial uses, and on the remaining side to single-family subdivisions. The developer, in 1968, offered to purchase on an all or nothing basis each of the 97 homes in the subdivision which bordered him on the west for cash and with permission for the owners to stay in their homes for five years, rent free. The offer was accepted, and the developer made a similar offer the following year to each of the 140 homeowners in the subdivision adjoining to the west the one he had already acquired. This latter subdivision also adjoined on its west a smaller subdivision. This offer was accepted by all but a few of the homeowners, and the developer proceeded to consummate the purchase of all the other homes. The properties are to be used to enlarge the original development to a total of 115 acres for a major commercial complex to include high-rise office and apartment buildings, a luxury hotel, and shopping facilities.

Except for one 88-unit apartment building, the only uses in both subdivisions were single-family homes, and had Houston adopted zoning in 1962, both would have been zoned single-family. A rezoning to a business district would have been required for these properties to be used as proposed. There would have been public hearings, and probably opposition would have come from the neighboring homeowners. Many suggestions (and demands) for improvement and modification would have been offered, and some would have charged that only "greed" motivated the developer to the "detriment" of the "people." Questions of traffic, engineering, and virtually all items of development would have been discussed and commented on by laymen, politicians, professionals, the press, etc., and much free advice would have been offered. It is an interesting speculation as to how it would have come out, how long the proceedings would have taken, and what changes would have been required to accommodate and appease the opposition and others, and at what cost. Would it have been possible for the two subdivisions to be purchased separately, or would the opposition within the second (and largest) subdivision have required both to be purchased at one time? If so, would this have been economically feasible? Equally important is whether all of the owners of either or both subdivisions would have been willing to commit their properties to binding option for the entire time required to obtain a decision from the zoning commission and the city council.

Had 20 per cent of the property owners across the street from the property sought to be rezoned, advised the council in writing of their opposition, Texas law would have required a three-quarter vote of the council,[118] or seven affirmative votes out of a total council membership of nine, to pass the zoning amendment. Even so, it is likely that any large city would have allowed for the development of a major commercial complex of the magnitude contemplated. Approval would probably have come if the politically necessary compromises had been made. However, these would have increased the cost of the development and possibly even affected its feasibility.[119] (These compromises presumably would not remove the dissatisfaction felt by local owners who wished to continue living in the midst of residential property.) Given all of the problems presented by zoning requirements, it is quite possible that the developer never would have undertaken this project were zoning in effect in Houston.

The problems involved in rezoning property are suggested by the experiences of three of the zoned (bedroom) communities within the boundaries of Houston, which if not necessarily representative are still highly informative. These examples should dispel any beliefs, based on the poor performance of zoning in popular elections, that homeowners in this area of the country differ from those elsewhere when it comes to zoning. Two blocks of the south side of Bissonet (a major thoroughfare), between Buf-

---

[118] Tex. Rev. Civ. Stat. Ann., *supra* note 30.

[119] Under zoning, a developer's techniques for seeking approval for a proposed project may have to be quite devious. By petitioning for more than he wants or needs, the developer will allow the council to "severely" curtail what is proposed, yet authorize fully the development he actually desires. The council in turn may receive much approbation for protecting the public interest.

falo Speedway and Wakeforest, are within the corporate limits of the City of West University Place. Both blocks were vacant and originally zoned single-family. West of this property, across Buffalo Speedway, is a church, and east, across Wakeforest, a gas station. Backing up to the property are middle-income, single-family homes which front on Wroxton Street. The property directly across on the north side of Bissonet is in Houston and is, and has been, used for many years for commercial purposes, including a gas station and a five story office building. Beginning in 1947, more than a dozen requests to rezone the two vacant blocks on the West University side of Bissonet, for either apartments, commercial or duplexes were denied or not acted on because of local opposition. Finally, in 1966, it was rezoned to a newly-created district for townhouses. The restrictions of the district were such as to assure the erection of expensive townhouses, notwithstanding the commercial characteristics of Bissonet and the properties on this street. But even this did not terminate the fight against any rezoning by the home-owners on Wroxton Street. They caused a city-wide referendum to be held in January of 1967. However, the rezoning ordinance was upheld by a vote of 1,032 to 845.

In the City of Spring Valley, in May of 1969, a petition was denied to rezone from single-family to commercial for a specified use, two contiguous tracts on Old Katy Road containing six acres of vacant property. One tract was of ordinary depth, and the other many times deeper. The smaller tract adjoined on one side commercial buildings which were part of a strip development fronting on Old Katy Road; the balance of the properties bordering both parcels were zoned single-family and were vacant except for one home and two churches, one of which was also on Katy. There were no residential uses on Katy for more than a block on either side of both tracts, and all of such property was zoned commercial except for the site containing the church. At this location, Old Katy Road parallels Interstate Highway 10, and between it and the highway are railroad tracks and a frontage road. The owner of an adjoining 5-acre tract (not on Katy) supported the rezoning, alleging that he was unable to sell his property for the development of homes. A subsequent request to rezone only that portion of the two tracts no deeper than the adjoining strip areas was also denied. Similar efforts apparently had been made for some years prior. Newspaper accounts said that close to 700 people signed a petition opposing the original request, and an overflow crowd was present during the council vote.

When the city council of Bellaire, despite considerable opposition, approved with certain qualifications a rezoning of about four acres for a high-rise motel-office complex at a major intersection, a suit was filed by some residents of the city contesting council action on this and three other zoning actions approved at the same time. These objectors, upon losing in the lower courts, appealed to the Texas Supreme Court which refused their application for review. The first public hearing on the proposal was held in January of 1968 and the Supreme Court's denial of the petition occurred in April of 1969. One of the limitations to which the rezoning was made subject was that if the contemplated construction was not commenced within two years after the council's action, the zoning would revert to the original category of single-family.

When Greenway acquired the subdivision of 140 homes, a smaller subdivision lying to the west became contiguous to what would in time become a commercial development and it would, therefore, no longer be buffered by a section of homes. Although there may be personal hardships of moving for some, in this instance at least, there appear to be substantial financial rewards in adjoining a major commercial development, and probably none of the homeowners will suffer financial loss. (Obviously, this has been proven with respect to the 140-home subdivision.) Such considerations apparently have not been persuasive for many homeowners in zoned areas. As in the examples cited, many attempts to change zoning will bring out adjoining or nearby owners, as often as not out of fear that any change might be adverse to them. Their presence alone may very well serve as a veto over any change regardless of the merits of the case; the question of the proposed rezoning becomes subordinate to a contest between many local people and one or a few non-resident landowners. This may give comparatively small groups the power to influence property uses affecting much larger areas.[120]

To solve this problem in a manner seemingly fair to both an adjoining property owner and the community, it has been suggested that compensation be paid him for the loss he sustains as a result of rezoning.[121] Another proposal is that the landowner be compensated for the loss he sustains when rezoning is denied on the basis of its adverse effect upon adjoining properties.[122] The problems involved in (a) setting up the mechanism to provide for such compensation, and (b) establishing tests to determine the amount thereof, will probably put such proposals to rest.

It can be assumed that the petitioner for reclassification has made efforts to settle his differences with the objectors by offering compensation in some form but has failed. He may have offered cash or property, or modification of the proposed development to make it more acceptable. Faced with opposition in the council, a developer may have to give some form of consideration

---

[120] Richard F. Babcock, *supra* note 13, at 33-38, 140-141, well describes the attitudes and powers of homeowners.

[121] T. Nicholaus Tideman, *supra* note 36, at 48.

[122] Richard F. Babcock, *supra* note 13, at 169-173.

to the city itself (if not to the council members) to obtain the requested rezoning. Contributions to a school or park district, acceptance of height or density limitations less than allowed by ordinance, or setting aside land for a buffer zone are not uncommon. But there are difficulties in consummating such an arrangement. This kind of agreement has been referred to as "contract zoning" and its legality is questionable; many courts will nullify it if litigation arises.[123] When done in the form of a planned unit development, or floating zone, both of which ordinarily involve a "deal" between the developer and the municipality, however, it may be valid because these concepts imply some form of agreement between the parties.

Costs of Zoning and Non-Zoning

One of the problems of being a non-zoned city is that it is more difficult to forecast requirements in various areas for different facilities. Thus, it would appear that in April 1969, permits for some 8,000 to 10,000 apartments were being temporarily withheld in certain areas of Houston pending installation of adequate sewer facilities to serve the areas.[124] Had zoning limited the area to single-family lots, most of the sewers would have been adequate and there would have been no such problem. Confronted with this situation, the city began to install, at substantial cost, the necessary sewer facilities. Builders and developers of the apartments were not required to pay for or to contribute to the cost involved. At most, they might have to bear the cost of installing a main solely intended for their developments, connecting to a trunk line installed by the city.

Houston was doing no more nor less than what is generally expected of a municipality, that it service all properties within its borders on a reasonably equitable basis. It was providing sewer service for sections of the city (and not specific properties) on the basis of need. Interestingly enough, the city attorney has suggested that in part the city's program of enforcing deed restrictions is predicated on the desire of the city to maintain single-family use for the areas involved. It hopes thereby to avoid the cost of increasing the size of utilities required to serve the greater concentration of people which might result from the termination of such restrictions.[125]

If there had been zoning in Houston, the nature of the problem would

[123] Cases and discussion of this point are presented in George Lefcoe, Land Development Law, Cases and Materials 1335-1345 (1966). Requiring contributions by a developer for a school or park is illegal in some jurisdictions, Pioneer Trust and Savings Bank v. Village of Mt. Prospect, 22 Ill.2d 375, 176 N.E.2d 799 (1961), but may not be in others, Jenad, Inc. v. Village of Scarsdale, 18 N.Y.2d 78, 218 N.E.2d 673 (1966).

[124] Cf. Has the Housing Industry Become Whipping Boy? Houston Post, April 20, 1969.

[125] William A. Olson, City Participation in the Enforcement of Private Deed Restrictions, Planning 1967, at 266.

have been far different. Much of the property in the areas in question would have been zoned for single-family. Probably it would not have been rezoned for apartments unless there was some certainty that the existing facilities were adequate to serve the development, or that the developer would pay most or all of the costs to make them adequate. Regardless of the merits of the case and the likelihood for ultimate recovery of cost, the possibility of added cost to the community (and "unearned enrichment" for the developer) would probably be sufficient to result in a denial of the petition— almost as a matter of political self-preservation on the part of the council members.

Such an approach would invariably exclude, for one, trailer camps, which are often not subject to real estate taxes. On the other hand, a proposal for industrial or commercial zoning for an area removed from many local objectors would be most welcome as a source of additional revenue. For many years, many suburbs kept industry out as a threat to their "garden cities"; now there is some tendency to "overzone" for it at the expense of residential uses. Not infrequently, a village board will be reminded as to how unwise its predecessors were in denying zoning to a certain industry which thereafter located elsewhere. Given the sentiment prevailing when the original decision was made, these critics would probably have supported it. As taxes continue upward, some suburbs may even, for tax reasons, someday change their attitude about apartments, but by then it may also be late.

Have Houston's policies relative to land use and development adversely affected its taxpayers? This is difficult to answer: I know of no way to compare real estate taxes in one community with those of another, because of unusual situations that may exist and of differing approaches to valuation and rates. However, it does appear that at the least the many debits and credits of the various uses that are allowed under non-zoning may cancel each other out. Thus, although the initial cost may be substantial, in the long run the citizens of Houston will profit in tax dollars from the installation of the sewers to the areas, as above described. According to city officials, most of the apartment units proposed for the areas will contain no more than one bedroom. Apartment buildings consisting largely of efficiency and one-bedroom units generally contain few children. Since cost of schools is the major item of real estate taxes, such developments will cost the community less per tax dollar received than if the same property were developed for average, middle-income homes, (or for middle income two or three bedroom apartments or townhouses).[126] The cost of the additional services

[126] George Sternlieb, Garden Apartment Development: A Municipal Cost-Revenue Analysis (1964); Wesley F. Gibbs, Development of A System for Predicting School Enrollment Using Selected Housing Factors (1966); Prince George's Cy. Md., Economic Development Committee, A Study of Income and Expenditures by Family Dwelling, Apartment and Business Units and Individual School Children For the Fiscal Year

required for multiple-family occupancy are generally not sufficient to overcome this tax advantage. High density development will also bring into the area many more business establishments for additional tax benefits.

The "profits" and "losses" of various uses are often difficult to evaluate. Perhaps because zoning practice involves public participation, zoning may be more receptive to the fears of "losses" than the possibility of "profits." By providing living quarters for employees, trailers may be contributing to the development of industry. The usual pariahs of zoning, gas stations and motels, provide useful facilities; and strip commercial allows for many commercial opportunities, some of which would obviously be denied by restrictions.

Considered on an overall basis, there is substantial cost to a community in maintaining a zoning ordinance. First, there is, of course, the expense of administration and enforcement of the ordinance. Second, and perhaps the major cost in a city where restrictive covenants have been reasonably effective, is the misallocation of resources that results. Zoning or restrictive covenants in general do maximize values of homes, at least for a time, within the areas covered. Zoning does not serve a similar purpose for the balance of real estate uses within a community. Rather, it serves to hinder the allocation of resources to such purposes. Even if it is argued that with zoning the gain in values for single-family dwellings offsets the reduction in the value contributed by other uses, such an argument is inapplicable in a community where restrictive covenants are generally in force and are effective. Thus, were Houston to adopt zoning at the present time, it would have little effect on the amount and value of single-family construction, but probably would affect much more other forms of construction. The importance of examining the effect on such other construction is made clear from Houston building statistics. The total value shown on permits for single-family construction in 1968 was $68,632,780.00, while the value shown for new construction for all other non-governmental uses was $220,272,827.00. The ratio in the five prior years averaged about two to one.[127]

VI. LESSONS OF HOUSTON

These in brief are the conclusions drawn from this examination of Houston's system of non-zoning, with appropriate comparisons with, and conclusions about zoning.

1963-1964 (1963); Frank S. Kristof, The New Zoning Ordinance and Privately Financed New Residential Construction in Manhattan, Rep't to Dep't of City Planning, City of New York 9 (1968); Charles B. Hetrick, Ass't City Manage, Residential Land Use and Schools: A Study of Current Relationships for Park Ridge, Illinois (1964); Richard F. Babcock & Fred P. Bosselman, *supra* note 50, at 1062-1065; American Society of Planning Officials, School Enrollment by Housing Type (ASPO Report No. 210, 1966).

[127] Based on annual records of Houston's Building Department.

1. Economic forces tend to make for a separation of uses even without zoning. Business uses will tend to locate in certain areas, residential in others, and industrial in still others. Apartments, however, may be built in almost any area except within an industrial one. There is also a tendency for further separation within a category; light industrial uses do not want to adjoin heavy industrial uses, and vice versa. Different kinds of business uses require different locations. Expensive homes will separate from less expensive ones, townhouses, duplexes, etc. It is difficult to assess the effectiveness of zoning in furthering this process. It is highly successful in this respect in the "bedroom" suburbs, but much less so in the larger cities.

2. When these economic forces do not guarantee that there will be a separation, and separation is vital to maximize profits (or promote one's tastes and desires), property owners will enter into agreements to provide such protection. The restrictive covenants covering home and industrial subdivisions are the most prominent example of this. Adjoining property owners (such as those on a strip location) can also make agreements not to sell for a use that will be injurious to one or both.

3. Because many of the early restrictive covenants in Houston were (a) limited in duration, or (b) legally insufficient, or (c) not enforced by owners, zoning would have kept more areas as strictly single-family. The covenants created subsequent to 1950 were more durable and as a practical matter will remain in force for long periods. They may be as effective as zoning in maintaining single-family homogeneity.

4. When covenants expire, land and properties will be used as economic pressures dictate. Most business uses will not locate on interior streets because they require favorable traffic conditions available only on major thoroughfares. Within recent years, the most important factor influencing diversity in non-restricted interior areas is the strong demand for multiple-family accommodations. But this demand does not extend to all sections of the city. Accordingly, some areas fronting on interior streets will remain relatively free of diverse uses after their covenants expire.

5. A non-zoned city is a cosmopolitan collection of property uses. The standard is supply and demand, and if there is economic justification for the use, it is likely to be forthcoming. Zoning restricts the supply of some uses, and thereby prevents some demands from being satisfied. It may likewise impede innovation. However, in general, zoning in the major cities, which contain diverse life styles, has responded and accommodated to most consumer demands. This has not occurred usually in the more homogeneous suburbs.

6. Zoning is a legislative function. As such, political, economic and social pressures of many, or even a relatively few, often influence or control zoning

decisions. These pressures may even be more important than the provisions of the zoning ordinance. Such forces play no part in a non-zoned city.

7. The most measurable influence of zoning is its effect on multiple-family dwellings. If Houston had adopted zoning in 1962, this would probably have resulted in higher rents and a lesser number and variety of apartments and, in consequence, some tenants would have been priced out of the new apartment market. Most adversely affected would be tenants of average incomes.

8. The experience of the FHA suggests that the appreciation over the years in values of new and existing single-family homes has not differed in Houston from those of zoned cities.

9. The role of planning under zoning is a curious one. The original zoning ordinance will largely freeze the existing pattern of land use. All subsequent decisions on the ordinance will be made through the legislative process, which would seem inherently more responsive to political and economic opinion and pressures than the recommendations of the planners. As one result, changes in zoning in the major cities seem to follow a more chaotic than orderly pattern.

10. In Houston, the level of control over land use and development has not increased appreciably over the years. The most significant policy adopted in recent years has been the city's enforcement since 1965 of the restrictive covenants in residential subdivisions. By contrast, zoning has tended to give the municipality greater and more minute control. One reason is that the failure of existing controls has usually led to more severe controls, not lesser ones.

Conclusion

Much criticism has been levelled at zoning within recent years. It might almost seem from reading the commentaries, that no matter how bad the Houston system, it could hardly be worse than what is described as having occurred under zoning.[128] Yet it is clear that the critics are not moved to study the Houston system. Instead, they advocate additional government controls over the use and development of property. The dogma persists that if zoning does not work, it is desirable to try more of it. Given the history of zoning, the new efforts will lead in their turn to even more controls.

The experience of Houston should not be ignored by those seeking to solve problems stemming from property use and development by the use of zoning techniques. Instead of newer and stronger controls, the reverse approach may

[128] American Society of Planning Officials, *supra* note 1; Richard F. Babcock, *supra* notes 13 and 50; John W. Reps, *supra* note 73; Douglas Commission Report, *supra* note 15; Sheldon J. Plager, *supra* note 110.

be in order. About 40 years have elapsed since the Commerce Department persuaded state legislatures to enact legislation authorizing zoning ordinances. The changes that have occurred since then have often not been for the better; the opposite is nearer the truth. Government has acquired more powers when less were warranted. Zoning in this respect has not differed from the usual pattern of government regulation. The example of Houston is sufficiently clear, however, to warrant at least an exception to the rule in the area of zoning.